THE
HANDY
DINOSAUR
ANSWER
BOOK

AUDREY SAUER

A U D R E Y
S A U E R

To Dave Bilcik, for his friendship and humor—and for years of

jawless fishes. . . .

THE
HANDY
DINOSAUR
ANSWER
BOOK™

Thomas E. Svarney • Patricia Barnes-Svarney

VISIBLE
INK
PRESS

The Handy Dinosaur Answer Book™

Published by Visible Ink Press®
a division of Gale Research
27500 Drake Rd.
Farmington Hills, MI 48331-3535

Visible Ink Press and *The Handy Dinosaur Answer Book* are trademarks of Gale Research.

Most Visible Ink Press books are available at special quantity discounts when purchased in bulk by corporations, organizations, or groups. Customized printings, special imprints, messages, and excerpts can be produced to meet your needs. For more information, contact Special Markets Manager, Visible Ink Press, 27500 Drake Rd., Farmington Hills, MI 48331-3535. Or call 1-800-776-6265.

Front cover photo of skeletal mount of dinosaur courtesy of University of Michigan Exhibit Musuem of Natural History.

Front cover photo of clawed hand of an *Allosaurus* and back cover photo of *Tyrannosaurus* teeth courtesy of Michael S. Yamashita/Corbis.

Front cover photo of toy dinosaur courtesy of Corbis.

Background back cover photo of *Archaeopteryx* courtesy of James L. Amos/Corbis.

Art Director: Eric Johnson
Typesetting: The Graphix Group

ISBN 1-57859-069-8

Contents

INTRODUCTION *xi*
ACKNOWLEDGMENTS *xiii*

IN THE BEGINNING. . .1

Birth of the Solar System. . .The Early
Earth. . .Beginnings of Life

FORMING FOSSILS. . .39

Geologic Time. . .First Fossils. . .More Recent
Fossils. . .Dinosaur Fossils

EVOLUTION OF THE DINOSAURS. . .73

Dinosaur Ancestors. . .Dinosaurs Appear. . .
Dinosaurs in the Mesozoic

TRIASSIC PERIOD. . .93

The Continents During the Triassic Period. . . Major Triassic Dinosaurs. . .Other Life in the Triassic Period

JURASSIC PERIOD. . .117

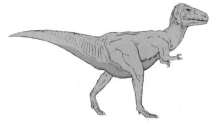

The Continents During the Jurassic Period . . . Major Jurassic Dinosaurs. . .Other Life in the Jurassic Period. . .

CRETACEOUS PERIOD. . .137

The Continents During the Cretaceous Period. . . Major Cretaceous Dinosaurs. . .Other Life in the Cretaceous Period

DINOSAUR BONES. . .159

Growing Bones. . .Building Dinosaur Skeletons . . .Abnormal Dinosaur Bones. . .Specific Dinosaurs and Their Bones

DINOSAUR ANATOMY. . .179

Dinosaur Skin. . .Teeth and Claws. . .Dinosaur Metabolism. . .Size of Dinosaurs

DINOSAUR BEHAVIOR. . .203

Dinosaur Delicacies. . .Dinosaurs in Motion. . .
Dinosaur Young. . .Older Dinosaurs

WHAT HAPPENED?. . .231

The Cretaceous Extinction. . .Theories on
Extinction. . .The Latest Theories on Dinosaur
Extinction

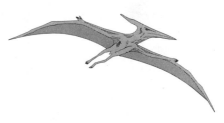

AFTER THE DINOSAURS. . .253

Modern Birds. . .The Link Between Birds and
Dinosaurs. . .Dinosaurs Around Us?. . .The
Search for the Missing Link

U.S. DINOSAUR DISCOVERIES. . .277

Early Dinosaur History in the United States. . .
Recent Dinosaur Finds

INTERNATIONAL DINOSAUR DISCOVERIES. . .291

Early Dinosaur History Outside the United
States. . .Recent Finds

DIGGING FOR DINOSAURS. . .307

Finding Dinosaur Fossils. . .Putting Dinosaurs Together. . .Getting Educated

LEARNING MORE . . .331

Dinosaur-Mania. . .Media Sources. . .Dinosaurs on the Internet

DINOSAUR RESOURCES. . .351

Books. . .Museums. . .Organizations. . .Publications. . .Dinosaurs on Video. . .Websites

BIBLIOGRAPHY *393*

INDEX *395*

Introduction

In today's world, we are surrounded on land by animals no larger than the African bush elephant and, in the seas, no greater (that scientists know of) than the blue whale. Our backyard wildlife consists of small squirrels, songbirds, and the occasional opossum or deer. In fact, when we see a hawk, condor, or owl, we are mesmerized by its size—a flying creature larger than the usual cardinal or blue jay that visits the birdfeeder.

That is what fascinates the general public when it comes to dinosaurs: It's almost impossible to believe that something larger than a house once stomped on the grounds of our school or workplace—or in our own backyards. Admittedly, the land has changed over 65 million years—but just to think that a *Tyrannosaurus rex* may have looked for dinner on a distant hill, or a *Parasaurolophus* may have waded in a stream that once flowed nearby, is almost beyond our ken.

Everyone loves to hear and read about dinosaurs for other reasons as well—and their interest has been provoked by discoveries made in the past decade. We know now that dinosaurs had diverse behaviors. Some were strictly herbivores, while others were omnivores or carnivores. None were found in the oceans or in the sky, but rather made their home over most of the known landmasses. Their defenses varied, as did their body shape and height. Some of them may have been warm-blooded. Many wandered in herds and had social groups. And one of the most perplexing questions in science has to do with dinosaurs: How and why did such a wide range of reptiles die out at such a seemingly rapid rate?

Still other questions intrigue: From what animals did the dinosaurs evolve? Who found the first dinosaur remains? What other plants and animals lived at the same time as the dinosaurs? How many dinosaurs lived on the planet? How do scientists classify these creatures? What were the continents like during the time of the dinosaurs? Did dinosaurs have muscles? What is the largest dinosaur claw ever found? What is the largest dinosaur bone ever found? How accurate was the movie *Jurassic Park?*

The Handy Dinosaur Answer Book attempts to answer these questions, taking you through the highlights of three main periods of geologic history: the Triassic, Jurassic, and Cretaceous—the age of the dinosaurs. As with all sciences, it is good to remember that the field of dinosaur study is in a constant state of flux. One reason is that scientists—amateur and professional—are continually discovering new dinosaur bones. They are digging deeper into the layers of rock, using new instruments and tools to analyze the bones—and discovering new connections between dinosaurs and other species. We've made every effort to ensure the accuracy and reliability of this book's contents; but even as we wrote the text, new discoveries were being made. It seemed as if every week we were adding to the text—covering the latest, greatest findings, along with the accompanying shifts in dinosaur theory.

Even after we thought we finished this introduction, for example, we learned of the discovery in October 1998 of dozens of fossilized reptile nests in Arizona's Petrified Forest—which may be the oldest fossils of their kind in the world. They are believed to be 220 million years old—twice as old as the next-oldest reptile nest fossils. Scientists are attributing the origin of such nests either to phytosaurs (crocodile-like animals), aetosaurs (armored reptiles), or ancient turtles.

Because of these recent discoveries, the study of dinosaurs prompts some great debates. Are birds really dinosaurs? Were any of the dinosaurs warm-blooded? What was the cause of the dinosaurs' demise? All these questions and more are constantly being examined and discussed—and will continue to be for decades to come.

The Handy Dinosaur Answer Book is meant to take you deep into the world of dinosaurs—a great ride through what we currently know (and are debating) about these creatures and their surroundings. It will pique your interest and expand your knowledge of the field. It may even convince you to study dinosaurs, or to go out to seek fossils in your own backyard—not only of dinosaurs, but also of other ancient life.

And who knows? You may be the one to find the next major dinosaur discovery!

Acknowledgments

This book would not have been possible if not for the hard work and dedication of the editors at Visible Ink Press. Many thanks go out to Michelle Banks for her efforts in overseeing this project and crossing many bridges that arose; Julia Furtaw and Christa Brelin for their guidance and insight on this project; and Eric Johnson for his unique cover design.

Additional thanks must be extended to Rebecca Nelson-Ferguson for advice and the creation of a detailed resource section; Robert Huffman for providing photos; Barbara E. Cohen for indexing the book; Edna Hedblad for her photo acquisition work; Pam Reed and Randy Bassett for photo scanning and cropping; Judy Galens and Carol Schwartz for last-minute proofing; and Marco Di Vita from The Graphix Group for his speedy and commendable typesetting.

THE
HANDY
DINOSAUR
ANSWER
BOOK

IN THE BEGINNING

BIRTH OF THE SOLAR SYSTEM

What do we mean by the **solar system**?

Our solar system—and presumably others—consists of a star, planets, satellites, comets, asteroids, meteoroids, and interplanetary dust and gas. Our solar system includes the following:

Sun—The Sun is at the center of our solar system, and is an average star when compared with other stars in the universe. It is classed as a typical G2-class star, represents about 99.86 percent of the mass of the solar system, and is about 864,000 miles (1,390,180 kilometers) in diameter, or about 109 Earth diameters across. It is thought that the Sun arrived at its present brightness about 800 million years ago, and will probably burn for another seven billion years.

Nine known planets—From the Sun outward, the planets are Mercury, Venus, Earth, Mars (the inner, or terrestrial, planets); Jupiter, Saturn, Uranus, Neptune (the outer, or gaseous, planets, or gas giants); and Pluto (which is more similar in characteristics to the terrestrial planets).

Moons—More than 64 moons (satellites) circle the various planets. In addition, a moon has also been found around the small minor planet (asteroid) Ida, and some scientists believe such tiny moons around asteroids may be common. Saturn has the most known moons (more

3

than 22); Earth and Pluto have one each; and Mercury and Venus have none.

Comets—Numerous short- and long-term comets swing through our solar system. Short-term comets pass by the Sun in an elliptical orbit, taking up to 200 years to complete an orbit. For example, comet Halley is a short-term comet, swinging by the Earth once every 76 years. Long-term comets take thousands of years to complete an orbit. Many long-term comets probably just pass once through our solar system, then disappear altogether.

Asteroid—More than 6,500 asteroids have been found and catalogued, most in a rocky belt between the orbits of Mars and Jupiter; others are found in stray orbits around the solar system. Scientists believe there are more than 10,000 asteroids in our solar system, ranging in size from more than 100 feet to 600 miles (1,000 kilometers) across. They are thought to be very old, and the best representatives of objects that existed in the early solar system.

Dust and gas—Traces of interplanetary (and probably interstellar) dust and gases are found in our solar system. Most of these micro-sized particles are from the collision between other space bodies, such as meteor and early asteroid collisions; the release of dust and gases from comets; and interstellar particles as the solar system moves through space (though such rare particles are often more difficult to detect and distinguish from other interplanetary dust and debris).

What are some of the **physical characteristics** of the **planets**?

The nine planets of the solar system all have unique characteristics depending on a multitude of reasons—known and unknown. For instance, Mercury has no atmosphere mainly because of its closeness to the Sun; Saturn has the most extensive ring system, although Jupiter, Uranus, and Neptune also have rings, albeit much smaller, but no one truly knows why.

What were the **early ideas** on the formation of the **solar system**?

There were several early theories on the formation of the solar system. In 1796, Marquis Pierre Simon de Laplace (1749–1827), a French math-

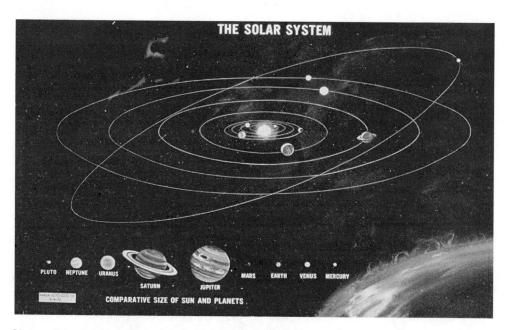

Diagram of the solar system. (Photo courtesy of U.S. National Aeronautics and Space Administration.)

ematician, astronomer, and physicist (and who is also called the "French Newton"), proposed the nebular hypothesis. He believed that the solar system developed from a rapidly rotating disk of hot gas, with the outer part of the disk experiencing a centrifugal force that caused a ring of material to form and eventually condense into the planets. Independently, German philosopher Immanuel Kant (1724–1804) also proposed that the solar system started as a dust cloud. He even extended the idea, suggesting that systems similar to our own formed in the same way elsewhere in the universe.

In the eighteenth century, French naturalist Comte de Georges Louis Leclerc Buffon (1707–1788) suggested that the solar system formed from a more or less tangential collision between the Sun and another star. The strike knocked enough material off the Sun to form the planets. Still another theory that involves another star was developed around the turn of the eighteenth century. The tidal, or Chamberlin-Moulton, theory was proposed by American astronomer Forest Ray Moulton (1872–1952) and American geologist Thomas Chrowder Chamberlin (1843–1928). In 1905, they suggested that a star passed by, pulling off a ribbon of material from the forming Sun, with the debris eventually forming the planets.

What is the **big bang theory** of the universe?

The big bang theory consists of the following: Fifteen to twenty billion years ago, a big bang, or explosion, occurred, creating the universe. The universe began as an infinitely dense, hot fireball, a scrambling of space and time. Within the first second after the bang, gravity came into being. The universe expanded rapidly and became flooded with sub-atomic particles that slammed into one another, forming protons and neutrons. Three minutes later, when the temperature was a mere 500 billion degrees Fahrenheit (280 billion degrees Celsius), protons and neutrons formed the nuclei of hydrogen, helium, and lithium (the simplest elements).

It took another 500 thousand years for atoms to form and 300 million more years for stars and galaxies to begin to appear. Countless stars, condensed from swirling nebulae (masses of gas and dust), evolved and died before our own sun and its planets came into being in a galaxy named the Milky Way. And it was only four and one-half billion years ago that our solar system was formed from a cloud of dust and gas.

What is the **inflationary theory**?

The inflationary theory is a recent addition to the big bang theory. It attempts to answer questions such as why matter is so evenly distributed throughout the universe. It was developed in 1980 by American astronomer Alan Guth and says, in short, that at its earliest stages, the universe expanded at a rate much faster than it is expanding today.

What is the **steady-state theory** of the universe?

The steady-state theory claims that the universe has always been essentially the same as it is today, and that it will continue that way forever. The theory stems from the cosmological principle, which states that the universe is the same everywhere. It proposes, in other words, that the same objects and gases fill the universe from end to end and that the view from one galaxy is not much different than the view from any other galaxy. The originator of the steady-state theory applied this concept of sameness to time as well as space to come up with the steady-state theory, claiming that the universe should look the same, not only in all places, but at all times—past, present, and future. The steady-state theory was offered in response to the other major theory of how the universe began, the big bang theory.

What is the **plasma theory** of the origin of the universe?

Originated by Swedish astrophysicist Hannes Olof Göost Alfvéen, the plasma theory argues that 99 percent of the matter in the universe is composed of plasma. His theory states that electrical currents in plasma interact with each other to produce swirling strands, which initiate a chain reaction. The strands cause matter to clump together, which produces greater swirling, followed by more matter, and so on. According to the theory, stars, planets, and other celestial objects were formed by this process.

What is the **most widely accepted modern theory** of how the **solar system formed**?

Today, the most widely accepted theory of solar system formation is a variation of Laplace's and Kant's nebular hypothesis—that the system formed from a solar nebula. But there are also two variations of this theory, as the processes that occurred after the formation of the solar nebula are not well understood. (What is known is that nuclei, or cores of material, formed and eventually grew—a process called accretion—into the planets we know today.)

One idea is called the planetesimal theory. In 1944, German physicist Baron Carl Friedrich von Weizsäcker (1912–   ) made the nebular hypothesis more acceptable by suggesting that small bodies called planetesimals were attracted to each other to form the planets. In this scenario, the solar nebula starts with grains of dust from which larger aggregations of material developed as the cloud cooled. The material condensed into small, rocky bodies; then more collisions formed large bodies. Some collections of the bodies smashed into one another, forming even larger planetesimals. Eventually, some of the collisions produced planetary-sized bodies, with the Earth and other planets formed by this accretion.

What is the age of the solar system?

The nebula that formed the solar system is believed to have developed about five billion years ago. The planets and satellites we see today are thought to have formed about 4.6 billion years ago. To compare, the universe is thought to be about 15 to 20 billion years old. These dates are highly debated, as recent satellite data continue to puzzle astronomers—some interpretations suggesting that the universe may be as young as 8 to 12 billion years old.

The other major variation is the protoplanet hypothesis, which also states that the system started as an immense cloud of dust and gas. But in this case, it was a hot, heterogeneous accretion, with the collapsing dust and debris forming large and massive protoplanets due to gravitational instabilities in the nebula.

The planetesimal theory seems to best support the formation of the inner planets, their gaseous atmospheres probably blown away or greatly reduced when the Sun went through a time of intense early activity. The huge gaseous planets of the outer solar system seem to be best supported by the protoplanet hypothesis. These planets kept much of their original gases; in addition, the Sun's early activities did not affect the outer planets as much, allowing the gas giants to maintain their thick atmospheres.

Are there **other solar systems** in the universe?

Astronomers have long suggested that there are extrasolar planets (planets existing outside our solar system) in other solar systems, but the majority of claims have been refuted. It took new techniques and advances in technology before the existence of extrasolar planets was verified. In 1991, Polish astronomer Alexander Wolszczan and American astronomer Dan Frail found the first evidence of extrasolar planets

Stellar view of Mars, a planet scientists have been studying for years to determine if other life forms exist there. (Photo courtesy of National Aeronautics and Space Administration.)

orbiting pulsar PSR B1257+12, discovered by picking out the minute variations in the pulses sent from the spinning, dying neutron star. The planets had masses of 2.8 and 3.4 times that of Earth; in 1993, Wolszczan found evidence of another planet around the same pulsar. By 1995, Swiss astronomers Michael Mayor and Didier Queloz found a planetary companion around star 51 Pegasi b. Currently, close to a dozen such planets have been discovered.

These planets are extremely distant from Earth. To reach the nearest stellar system at Alpha Centari 4.4 light years away (26 trillion miles, or a billion trips around the Earth) traveling at the same speed as the *Voyager 1* spacecraft, it would take 40,000 years. For a planetary system similar to one found recently, the trip would be much longer, as the planet is about 35 light years away.

Is there **life** on planets in **other solar systems**?

Because of the great distances, it has been impossible for scientists to determine whether or not planets in other solar systems contain life. If we were able to gather certain data about the extrasolar planets, we may be able to tell if there is life on a planet other than our own. In particular, the presence of carbon dioxide could tell us that the planets have an atmosphere; water vapor (which is unique to the Earth's atmosphere in our solar system) would tell us that a planet has an ocean; and finally, ozone, the layer of gas that protects life on Earth from the ultraviolet radiation from the Sun, may tell us if a planet has life. In many ways, it would be exciting to know that the Earth was not unique in the universe. It would also be interesting to find out if there is any life out there similar to humans—or to dinosaurs.

What is **Mercury**?

Mercury is a small, bleak planet, and the closest object to our sun. Mercury is the second smallest planet in the solar system; only Pluto is smaller. Mercury's diameter is a little over one-third the Earth's, yet it has just 5.5 percent of Earth's mass. On average, Mercury is 36 million miles (58 million kilometers) from the sun. One effect of the Sun's intense gravitational field is to tilt Mercury's orbit and to stretch it into a long ellipse (oval). Mercury is named for the Roman messenger god with winged sandals. The planet was given its name because it orbits the Sun so quickly, in just 88 days. In contrast to its short year, Mercury has an extremely long day. It takes the planet the equivalent of 59 Earth days to complete one rotation.

How **visible is Mercury** from Earth?

Because of the Sun's intense glare, it is difficult to observe Mercury from Earth. Mercury is visible only periodically, just above the horizon, for about one hour before sunrise and one hour after sunset. For these reasons, many people have never seen Mercury.

What forms **Mercury's core**?

The space probe *Mariner 10* gathered information about Mercury's core, which is nearly solid metal and is composed primarily of iron and nickel. This core, the densest of any in the solar system, accounts for about four-fifths of Mercury's diameter. It may also be responsible for

Surface view of Mercury.
(Photo courtesy of National Aeronautics
and Space Administration.)

creating the magnetic field that protects Mercury from the Sun's harsh particle wind.

What is **Venus**?

Venus is the second planet out from our Sun and the closest planet to Earth. Beginning in 1961, the United States and former Soviet Union have deployed a long string of space probes that have examined the Venusian atmosphere and peered beneath its dense cloud cover. The probes have revealed that Venus is an extremely hot, dry planet, with no

11

signs of life. Its atmosphere is made primarily of carbon dioxide with some nitrogen and trace amounts of water vapor, acids, and heavy metals. Its clouds are laced with sulfur dioxide.

What is the **cause** of the **tremendous heat on Venus**?

Venus provides a perfect example of the greenhouse effect. Heat from the Sun penetrates the planet's atmosphere and reaches the surface. Atmospheric carbon dioxide prevents the heat from escaping back into space. The result is that Venus's surface temperature is a fierce 900 degrees Fahrenheit (482 degrees Celsius), even hotter than that of Mercury, its neighbor closer to the Sun.

What are the **surface features** of **Venus** like?

U.S. and Soviet space probes studying Venus uncovered a rocky surface covered with volcanoes (some still active), volcanic features (such as lava plains), channels (which look like dry riverbeds), mountains, and medium and large craters. No small craters exist, apparently because small meteorites cannot penetrate the planet's atmosphere. Another set of features found on the surface are arachnoids. These features are circular formations ranging anywhere from 30 to 137 miles (48 to 220 kilometers) in diameter, filled with concentric circles, which extend spokes outward.

What is **Mars**?

Mars, the fourth planet out from the Sun in Earth's solar system, is about half the size of Earth and has a rotation period just slightly longer than one Earth day. Since it takes Mars 687 Earth days to orbit the Sun, its seasons are about twice as long as ours. Mars has two polar caps. The northern one is larger and colder than the southern. Two small moons, Phobos and Deimos, orbit the planet.

What are the so-called **canals seen on Mars**?

Mars is marked by what appear to be dry riverbeds and flash-flood channels. These features could mean that ice below the surface melts and is brought above ground by occasional volcanic activity. The water may temporarily flood the landscape before boiling away in the low atmospheric pressure. Another theory is that these eroded areas could be left over from a warmer, wetter period in Martian history.

What are **conditions like on Mars**?

Spacecraft sent to Mars revealed a barren, desolate, crater-covered world prone to frequent, violent dust storms. They found little oxygen, no liquid water, and ultraviolet radiation at levels that would kill any known life form. The high temperature on Mars was measured at -20 degrees Fahrenheit (-29 degrees Celsius) in the afternoon, and the low was -120 degrees Fahrenheit (-84 degrees Celsius) at night.

THE EARLY EARTH

How **old** is the **Earth**?

The Earth is currently believed to be about 4.6 billion years old, but that number came after centuries of debate. In 1779, French naturalist Comte de Georges Louis Leclerc Buffon (1707–1788) caused a stir when he announced 75,000 years had gone by since Creation: it was the first time anyone had suggested that the planet was older than the Biblical reference of 6,000 years. By 1830, Scottish geologist Charles Lyell (1797–1875) proposed that the Earth must be several hundred million years old based on erosional rates; in 1844, British physicist William Thomson (1824–1907), later first baron of Largs (Lord) Kelvin, determined that the Earth was 100 million years old, based on his studies of the planet's temperature. In 1907, American chemist and physicist Bertram Boltwood (1870–1927) used a radioactive dating technique to determine that a specific mineral was 4.1 billion years old (although later on, with a better knowledge of radioactivity, the mineral was found to be only 265 million years old). Using different adaptations of Boltwood's methods, scientists now estimate that the Earth is about 4.6 billion years old.

A view of the Earth from space. (Photo courtesy of U.S. National Aeronautics and Space Administration.)

Granite patterns in the Wallowa Mountains of Oregon. (Photo courtesy of Gary Braasch/Corbis.)

How did the discoverer of Halley's comet try to determine the **age of the Earth**?

English astronomer Edmond Halley (1656–1742) attempted to estimate the age of the Earth by calculating the amount of salt the rivers had dumped into the seas over the years. Astronomers currently believe the Earth was formed with the rest of the solar system, about four and a half billion years ago.

What does the **Earth's atmosphere** consist of?

The Earth's atmosphere is made of 78 percent nitrogen, 21 percent oxygen, and 1 percent argon, with minute quantities of water vapor, carbon dioxide, and other gases.

How old is the **oldest rock and mineral** so far found on **Earth**?

The oldest rock is a 3.96 billion-year-old granite, found in the tundra of northwestern Canada near the Great Slave Lake. The oldest mineral is 4.3

Surface of the Moon. (Photo courtesy of U.S. National Aeronautics and Space Administration.)

billion years old, found in 1983 in Australia. The mineral was zircon in the form of crystals, which had eroded from their original rock.

How **far away and how big is the Earth's moon**?

On average, the Earth's moon is 238,900 miles (384,390 kilometers) from Earth. It measures about 2,160 miles (3,475 kilometers) across, a little over one-quarter of the Earth's diameter. The Earth and its moon are the closest in size of any known planet and satellite, with the possible exception of Pluto and its moon, Charon.

How strong is **gravity on the Moon**?

Gravity on the lunar surface is about one-sixth that of Earth.

What is the **Moon made of**?

The Moon is covered with rocks, boulder, craters, and a layer of charcoal-colored soil from 5 to 20 feet (1.5 to 6 meters) deep. The soil consists of rock fragments, pulverized rock, and tiny pieces of glass. Two types of rocks are found on the Moon: basalt, which is hardened lava; and breccia, which is soil and rock fragments that have melded together. Elements found in moon rocks include aluminum, calcium, iron, magnesium, titanium, potassium, and phosphorus. In contrast with the Earth, which has a core rich in iron and other metals, the Moon appears to contain very little metal.

How old is the **oldest rock** so far found on the **Moon**?

The oldest rock carried back from the Apollo Moon missions is called the "Genesis rock," and is 4 billion years old. Scientists know there are probably older rocks on the lunar surface, as the Earth's satellite no doubt formed at the same time as our planet.

What are the **layers** of the Earth?

As the Earth cooled, it settled into several layers like a giant onion, with each layer having its own particular characteristics. In general, from the inside out, the layers include the inner and outer core, mantle, and crust.

There is little direct evidence of what lies beneath our feet. The deepest mines extend to just over two miles (3.3 kilometers), and the deepest boreholes are only about nine miles (15 kilometers) below the surface—mere scratches on a planet that has an average radius of 4,000 miles (6,400 kilometers). Most of what we know about the Earth's interior is based on the study of seismic waves generated by earthquakes, as the waves pass through—or don't pass through—certain layers of the interior.

When did the Earth's **crust** become **solid**?

The Earth's crust solidified at the same time as the rest of the inner planets—and even the Moon—about 4.6 billion years ago. The early crust was not as stable as today, as the heat from the planet's formation continually created cracks, spectacular volcanic activity, and huge mountain chains. Today, the crust has cooled more and settled down considerably, although it is still extremely active with volcanoes, earthquakes, and continental movements. The crust is not the same thickness everywhere either: It is typically only about four miles (six kilometers) thick under the oceans, and about 20 miles (32 kilometers) under the continents.

Which elements are contained in the **Earth's crust**?

The most abundant elements in the Earth's crust are listed in the table below. In addition, nickel, copper, lead, zinc, tin, and silver account for less than 0.02 percent with all other elements comprising 0.48 percent.

Element	Percentage
Oxygen	47.0
Silicon	28.0
Aluminum	8.0
Iron	4.5
Calcium	3.5
Magnesium	2.5
Sodium	2.5
Potassium	2.5
Titanium	0.4
Hydrogen	0.2
Carbon	0.2
Phosphorous	0.1
Sulfur	0.1

How many **kinds of volcanoes** are there?

Volcanoes are usually cone-shaped hills or mountains built around a vent connecting to reservoirs of molten rock, or magma, below the surface of the Earth. At times the molten rock is forced upward by gas pressure until it breaks through weak spots in the Earth's crust. The magma erupts forth as lava flows or shoots into the air as clouds of lava fragments, ash, and dust. The accumulation of debris from eruptions causes the volcano to grow in size. There are four kinds of volcanoes:

What is the Late Heavy Bombardment, also called the Great Bombardment?

While the Earth's crust was in its infancy, the solar system was still in the process of formation. The area was cluttered with chunks of debris orbiting the Sun. From about 4.0 to 3.8 billion years ago, large rocks and debris were attracted to, and thus constantly bombarded, the largest planets and satellites—including our Earth and Moon. This Great Bombardment is most evident on our own Moon, seen as the hundreds of large and small craters on the lunar surface. Because the Moon has no atmosphere, these large craters and basins are essentially "fossils," showing the massive bombardment phase that took place. Today, there are fewer space objects striking the Earth and Moon. But every year, the Earth attracts more than a million tons of new material from outer space. Luckily, the majority of the debris and dust is small enough to burn up in our atmosphere.

Cinder cones are built of lava fragments. They have slopes of 30 degrees to 40 degrees and seldom exceed 1,640 feet (500 meters) in height. Sunset Crater in Arizona and Paricutin in Mexico are examples of cinder cones.

Composite cones are made of alternating layers of lava and ash. They are characterized by slopes of up to 30 degrees at the summit, tapering off to 5 degrees at the base. Mount Fuji in Japan and Mount St. Helens in Washington are composite cone volcanoes.

Shield volcanoes are built primarily of lava flows. Their slopes are seldom more than ten degrees at the summit and two degrees at the base. The Hawaiian Islands are clusters of shield volcanoes. Mauna Loa is the world's largest active volcano, rising 13,653 feet (4,161 meters) above sea level.

What caused the early Earth's **water** and **atmosphere** to form?

No one really knows how the oceans filled with water. One theory is that volcanoes released enough water vapor to condense and fill the oceans. Another theory states that comets bombarded the Earth just after the formation of the solar system, bringing enough water to eventually fill the oceans.

The origin of the Earth's atmosphere is also debated, but not as intensely. In this case, it is more likely that some of the atmosphere originated from the gases that were part of the solar nebula; other gases were produced from volcanic activity. The Earth probably would have had a thicker atmosphere, too, but the young active Sun's heat boiled away the lighter materials—elements that are still found today around the "gas giant" planets (Jupiter, Saturn, Uranus, and Neptune).

How **deep** are our present oceans?

The average depth of the ocean floor is 13,124 feet (4,000 meters). The average depth of the four major oceans is given below.

	Average depth	
Ocean	**Feet**	**Meters**
Pacific	13,740	4,188
Atlantic	12,254	3,735
Indian	12,740	3,872
Arctic	3,407	1.038
average	13,124	4,000

What does the atmosphere of **Venus** have in common with the **Earth's early atmosphere**?

Scientists believe that the Earth's early atmosphere—before plants developed photosynthesis and started producing oxygen—was somewhat similar to the atmosphere of Venus. The early atmosphere had a great deal of carbon dioxide, mostly in the form of gases spewed out by volcanic activity. Venus continued to build up carbon dioxide, the gas

How did oxygen form on early Earth?

The early atmosphere was composed mainly of water vapor, carbon dioxide and monoxide, nitrogen, hydrogen, and other gases released by volcanoes. By about 4.3 billion years ago, the atmosphere contained no oxygen and about 54 percent carbon dioxide. Just over two billion years ago, plants in the oceans began to produce oxygen by photosynthesis, which involved taking in carbon dioxide. By two billion years ago, there was 1 percent oxygen in the atmosphere and only 4 percent carbon dioxide—reduced from the intake by plants and taken up by carbonate rocks. By about 600 million years ago, atmospheric oxygen continued to increase as volcanoes and climate changes buried a great deal of plant material—plants that would have absorbed oxygen from the atmosphere if they had decomposed in the open. Today, the Earth's atmosphere levels measure 21 percent oxygen, 78 percent nitrogen, and only 0.036 percent carbon dioxide.

produced by the intense solar heat scorching carbonate rocks. This created a condition now called the greenhouse effect—the global temperatures rise when certain gases, including carbon dioxide, trap the Sun's energy and keep it within the global atmosphere. But things changed for the Earth: The carbon dioxide in the atmosphere gradually dwindled over millions of years. Life on Earth eventually produced oxygen, using carbon dioxide for photosynthesis; and even more carbon dioxide was absorbed by carbonate rocks.

How do the **atmospheres of Venus, Earth, and Mars** compare today?

The atmospheres of these three inner planets (Mercury is the other inner planet but has no true atmosphere) vary considerably. Overall, Venus's and Earth's atmospheres are the thickest; Venus's atmospheric composition (carbon dioxide) and closeness to the Sun cause it to have one of the hottest surface temperatures in the solar system.

How is **energy produced in the Sun**?

Energy in the form of heat and light is produced by a reaction called nuclear fusion in the Sun's core. The pressure at the core (312,000 miles, or 500,000 kilometers, below the Sun's surface) is great enough to squeeze gas molecules into a material ten times as dense as gold. And the temperature is 27 million degrees Fahrenheit (15 million degrees Celsius). In that intensely hot, pressurized environment, four hydrogen nuclei combine into one helium nucleus, releasing a tremendous amount of energy in the process.

What is the **greenhouse effect**?

The greenhouse effect, as its name implies, describes a warming phenomenon. In a greenhouse, closed glass windows cause heat to become trapped inside. The greenhouse effect functions in a similar manner on the scale of an entire planet. It occurs when a planet's atmosphere allows heat from the Sun to enter but refuses to let it leave.

Which **planets experience** the **greenhouse effect**?

A prime example of the greenhouse effect can be found on Venus. There solar radiation penetrates the atmosphere, reaches the surface, and is reflected back up. The re-radiated heat is trapped by carbon dioxide, the primary constituent of Venus's atmosphere. The result is that Venus has a scorching surface temperature of 900 degrees Fahrenheit (480 degrees Celsius). The greenhouse effect can also be found on Earth and in the upper atmospheres of the giant planets: Jupiter, Saturn, Uranus, and Neptune.

How does the **greenhouse effect work on Earth**?

On Earth, solar radiation passes through the atmosphere and strikes the surface. As it is reflected back up, some solar radiation is trapped by atmospheric gases (such as carbon dioxide, methane, chlorofluorocarbons, and water vapor), resulting in the gradual increase of the Earth's temperature. The rest of the radiation escapes back into space.

What **causes the Earth's greenhouse effect**?

Human activity is largely responsible for the buildup of greenhouse gases in the Earth's atmosphere, and hence the Earth's gradual warming. For instance, the burning of fossil fuels (such as coal, oil, and natural gas) and forest fires add carbon dioxide to the atmosphere. Methane buildup comes from the use of pesticides and fertilizers in agriculture. Large amounts of water vapor are emitted as an industrial by-product. And chlorofluorocarbons (CFCs) are produced by some aerosol spraycans and coolants in refrigerators and air conditioners.

How **serious** is the **greenhouse gas buildup** in Earth's atmosphere?

Between the start of this century and 1970, the atmospheric carbon dioxide level rose 7 percent and that rate is on the rise. The resulting temperature increase has caused more water to evaporate from the oceans (as well as some ice to melt in the Arctic), which, in turn, increases the clouds in the atmosphere. While the greater cloud cover blocks some solar heat from entering our atmosphere, it also worsens the greenhouse effect by trapping more of the heat that does make it down to the surface. With a slow but steady increase in the world's temperature, the Earth could, far in the future, become like the scorching Venus.

What is **ozone** and how does it benefit the **Earth**?

Ozone, or three molecules of oxygen (O_3, as compared with the O_2 we breath), usually refers to a blanket of gas found between 9 and 25 miles (15 and 40 kilometers) up in the Earth's atmosphere (in the layer called the stratosphere). The so-called "ozone layer" is produced by the interaction of the Sun's radiation with certain air molecules. The blue-tinged ozone gas is also found in the lower atmosphere. While beneficial in the stratosphere, ozone forms what is called photochemical smog at ground level. This smog is a secondary pollutant produced by the photochemical reactions of certain air pollutants, usually from industrial activities and cars.

The stratosphere's ozone layer is important to all life on the planet because it protects organisms from the Sun's damaging ultraviolet radiation. Scientists believe that about two billion years ago, oxygen was being

23

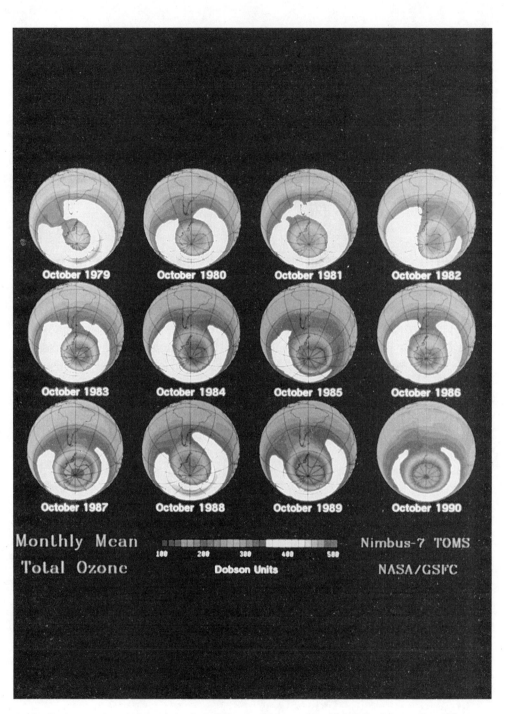

A chart showing ozone layer depletion during the last 20 years. (Photo courtesy of U.S. National Aeronautics and Space Administration.)

produced by shallow-water marine plants undergoing photosynthesis. This sudden, geologically speaking, outpouring of oxygen helped to build up the ozone layer. As the oxygen levels increased, ocean animals also arose. Once the protective ozone layer was in place in the atmosphere, it allowed the marine plants and animals to safely spread onto land.

Why are we **concerned** about the **ozone layer today**?

The stratosphere's ozone layer blankets the entire Earth. During certain times of the year, the ozone layer over the Southern Hemisphere's Antarctic continent diminishes, creating an "ozone hole." Over the years, scientists have been measuring the ozone hole using Earth-orbiting satellites, and have noticed an increase in the size of the hole. There is also concern that an ozone hole detected recently over the Arctic in the Northern Hemisphere is also increasing. The reason for concern about the ozone holes is understandable: The loss of ozone means some sensitive organisms—and those vital to the Earth's food chain—may be killed by exposure to intense ultraviolet radiation from the Sun.

No one knows the actual reason for the increase in the ozone holes, but many scientists have pointed to chlorofluorocarbons, organic compounds containing chlorine and fluorine (CFCs) as the culprit. Although the United States banned the use of fluorocarbon aerosols in 1978, and other measures have been taken to reduce the use of CFCs around the world, scientists have not yet noticed a dramatic shrinkage of the ozone hole. Some researchers believe that it will take time for the Earth's ozone to "adjust" to the lower levels of CFCs—but no one knows how long. Other scientists believe that CFCs are not the culprit, and that the ozone hole expansion may be a natural change.

BEGINNINGS OF LIFE

When did **life first** begin on **Earth**?

No one knows the precise time that life began on Earth. One reason is that early life consisted of single-cell organisms. Because the soft parts of an organism are the first to decay and disappear after death, it is almost impossible to find the remains of such organisms. In addition, because the organisms were so small, they are difficult to detect in ancient rocks. Some modern viruses are only about 18 nanometers (18 billionths of a meter) across; and modern bacteria typically measure 1,000 nanometers across—much larger than the early organisms. Despite such obstacles, scientists estimate that the first life began about four billion years ago. These organisms did not survive on oxygen, but on carbon dioxide.

What did the **earliest life on Earth** look like?

Because scientists have found so little fossil evidence, it is difficult to know all the true shapes of the earliest life. Scientists believe that early life was composed of primitive single-cells and started in the oceans. The reason is simple: Life needed a filter to protect it from the incoming ultraviolet energy from the Sun—and the ocean waters gave life that protection.

Is there **life** on any of the **planets or satellites** in our solar system?

So far, scientists have found no verifiable evidence of life on any planet in the solar system except Earth. Recent images taken by spacecraft at various moons around the planets have caused scientists to speculate about other life in the solar system. For example, Europa, one of the largest moons around Jupiter, may have a huge ocean underneath its thick cover of surface ice. Some scientists believe that such an ocean may harbor some type of life. The largest moon around Saturn, called Titan, has the thickest atmosphere of any satellite in the solar system—and includes hydrocarbons necessary for life to form. All this is pure speculation until scientists can gather better data.

The closest scientists have come to finding life within the solar system is based on a meteorite that allegedly came from Mars: In 1996, meteorite ALH84001, found in Antarctica years before, reportedly showed fossil evidence of minuscule bacteria, biogenerated materials, and organic compounds suggestive of life. Whether or not the rock contains the traces of life is highly debated. Some scientists say that the carbonates found were deposited at temperatures far above the boiling point of water, and would thus destroy the life; others say that the tiny worm-

Meteorite ALH84001, which is 4.5 billion years old. (Photo courtesy of U.S. National Aeronautics and Space Administration.)

shapes and ovid features are artifacts of the techniques used to analyze the rock. The jury is still out on this finding—at least until more Martian rocks can be examined. But if true, it would be one of most significant scientific discoveries of all time.

Who found **ALH84001,** the celebrated **"life on Mars"** meteorite?

In 1984 Roberta Score, a member of the Antarctic Search for Meteorites (ANSMET) team, found the famed meteorite that may contain indication of ancient life on Mars. More than 60 research groups are now studying pieces of ALH84001.

Why did **life** develop on Earth and not on the **other planets**?

Scientists recognize something called the "life zone," a region around a star in which life can develop if the conditions, especially temperatures, are right. The Earth had the right temperature to allow water to circulate in all three states—solid, liquid, and water vapor—conditions that eventually helped to produce life as we know it.

27

What **conditions on the early Earth** could have **led to life**?

Two major theories explain how life could have grown on the early Earth. The first theory states that life grew from a primordial "soup," a thick stew of biomolecules and water. Chemical reactions were then triggered—either by the Sun's ultraviolet rays, lightning, or even the shock waves from a violent meteor strike. These reactions produced various carbon compounds—including amino acids, which make up the proteins found in all living organisms. This theory was first postulated after a famous experiment performed at the University of Chicago in 1954, by then-graduate student Stanley Miller, and his advisor, chemist Harold Urey. They showed that the amino acids could be formed from chemicals thought to exist in the early Earth atmosphere, when these were combined with water and zapped by lightning.

The second theory of life conditions centers around a more recent discovery: hydrothermal vents, which are cracks caused by volcanic magma seeping through the deep ocean floor. There were probably many more hydrothermal vents on the early Earth, as the crust was newer, and thus thinner, than today's cooled, thicker crust. The organisms around these vents did not need to rely on photosynthesis for energy. Today's volcanic vent organisms live off the bacteria around the vents, which in turn extract energy from the hot, hydrogen sulfide-rich water found around the sunless cracks in the ocean floor. Early organisms could have survived in much the same way.

In actuality, the conditions described by both theories could have existed simultaneously to produce the planet's early life.

Who originated the idea called **panspermia**?

Panspermia is the idea that microorganisms, spores, or bacteria attached to tiny particles of matter have traveled through space, eventually landing on a suitable planet and initiating the rise of life there. The word panspermia means "all-seeding." The British scientist Lord Kelvin (1825–1907) suggested in the nineteenth century that life may have arrived here from outer space, perhaps carried by meteorites. In 1903, the Swedish chemist Svante Arrhenius (1859–1927) put forward the more complex panspermia idea that life on Earth was "seeded" by means

Did life arrive from space?

There is another theory (known as *panspermia*) of how the precursors of life were brought to Earth: By the early bombarding of comets and asteroids that contained complex organic materials. In the late 1960s, radio astronomers discovered organic molecules in dark nebulae. Since that time, other sources have been discovered, including organic molecules in space bodies such as asteroids, comets, and meteorites. In 1969, analysis of a meteorite showed at least 74 amino acids within the chunk of rock. Scientists began to speculate that the organic molecules could have traveled to the Earth via meteorites, cometary dust—or, during the early years of the Earth, by way of comets and asteroids. Although many scientists argue that the heat from the impact of a giant asteroid or comet would fry the organics, many other scientists disagree. They propose that only the outer layers of a large body would have been affected; or that the fine, unheated dust of comets could have brought the necessary amino acids to the early Earth. If this theory is true, as many scientists say, we are apparently all—from dinosaurs to humans—made of "starstuff." Also, if there is more scientific evidence to support such a theory, it would simplify the search for the origin of life on Earth.

of extraterrestrial spores, bacteria, and microorganisms coming here on tiny bits of cosmic matter.

How did **life** begin to **replicate itself** on Earth?

The early Earth no doubt had organic compounds, most likely held in a watery soup many have termed the "primordial soup." But in order for early life to form and self-replicate, there had to be some mechanism to encourage the early biomolecules to "stick" together. There are plenty of theories; the following lists the rock surfaces and/or conditions that could have allowed small organic molecules to assemble into self-replicating biomolecules:

pyrite— Pyrite, or iron sulfate, may have been a catalyst, the surface of the rock allowing the molecules to adhere and begin an energy-producing reaction—perhaps something similar to an early form of photosynthesis.

zeolites—Zeolites, a silica-rich mineral, is hydrophilic (waterloving), tending to absorb water from its surroundings. Among the zeolites is a recently discovered type called mutinaite, a naturally-occurring organophilic zeolite that prefers to absorb organic materials out of water. It is possible that mutinaite, which has aluminum in place of silica, loses aluminum at its surface as it weathers. If such zeolites were at the right place at the right time, the remaining aluminum within the rock would have provided centers for organic molecules—especially amino acids—to assemble and thus, eventually produce life.

clay—Surfaces of clay, a sedimentary rock, may have been perfect places to produce self-replicating biomolecules. One reason is that clay can store energy, change it, and then release it in the form of chemical energy. This release of energy may have been harnessed by the early biomolecules, advancing the growth of life.

bubbles—One of the more interesting ways of growing biomolecules is through bubbles—similar to those you see at the foamy edge of the water on a beach. The bubbles could have "gathered" the biomolecules, encouraging the growth of life.

spontaneous reaction—One of the most simple theories (but harder to explain) is that organic molecules eventually and spontaneously produced self-replicating biomolecules.

How do **rocks** differ?

Rocks can be conveniently placed into one of three groups—igneous, sedimentary, and metamorphic.

Igneous rocks, such as granite, pegmatite, rhyolite, obsidian, gabbro, and basalt, are formed by the solidification of molten magma

The chemical composition of pyrite (pictured here) may have sparked cells into self-replicating. (Photo courtesy of Field Mark Publications.)

that emerges through the Earth's crust via volcanic activity. The nature and properties of the crystals vary greatly, depending in part on the composition of the original magma and partly on the conditions under which the magma solidified. There are thousands of different igneous rock types. For example, granite is formed by the slow cooling of molten material (within the Earth). It has large crystals of quartz, feldspars, and mica.

Sedimentary rocks, such as brecchia, sandstone, shale, limestone, chert, and coals, are produced by the accumulation of sediments. These are fine rock particles or fragments, skeletons of microscopic

31

What were the first primitive plants to appear on land?

The first primitive plants appeared on land about 470 million years ago, according to recent findings. But these plants did not look like the lush greenery we see around us today. Rather, they were rootless patches of thin, leaf-like plants called liverworts, so named because some species resemble green livers; they used a specialized filament, called a rhizoid, to absorb water and adhere to rocks.

After the Cambrian Explosion of life, about 544 million years ago, the oceans teemed with multicellular plants and animals. But the land remained empty of life, except for an occasional microbe—probably in shallow pools. Animals in the oceans had no incentive to colonize the land, because there was nothing for them to eat. So it was up to the plants, specifically the liverwort, to make the great leap from the oceans and become the first multicellular organisms to live on dry land.

We still have liverworts in the world today, such as the common and braided liverworts in the United States. They, too, lead moss-like lives, and are often shaped like a flat, green liver. But so far, scientists do not know how the familial relationship among the more than 8,000 species present on Earth fits in with the lineage of the ancient liverworts.

organisms, or minerals leached from rocks that have accumulated from weathering. These sediments are then redeposited under water and later compressed in layers over time. The most common sedimentary rock is sandstone, which is predominantly quartz crystals.

Metamorphic rocks, such as marble, slate, schist, gneiss, quartzite, and hormsfel, are formed by the alteration of igneous and sedimentary rocks through heat and/or pressure. One example of these physical and chemical changes is the formation of marble from thermal changes in limestone.

Did **life** develop **many times** over?

Many scientists believe that life may have started over and over on the Earth. They speculate that once life began—either around ocean vents and/or in the shallow seas—comets and asteroids would strike the planet, killing off all the beginning stages of life. This may have happened many times over millions of years—until life became stable enough to sustain and diversify itself.

What are the **oldest-known fossils** found in rock on Earth?

The oldest-known fossils in rock have been found in Australia. One set of fossils found in western Australia are dated between 3.45 and 3.55 billion years old. They show evidence of layered mounds of limestone sediment called stromatolites, formed by primitive microorganisms similar to blue-green algae called cyanobacteria. Scientists know that stromatolites exist today: The fossils look amazingly like the stromatolites from the shallow waters off the coast of modern Australia.

There are other contenders for the oldest-known fossils: Tiny simple cells have also been found in ancient cherts (rocks) from Australia, and similar ones from Africa. These cells are preserved by the silica from the chert, and appear to show a cell wall of some kind.

What is the **oldest-known land life** found in rock on Earth?

In 1994, the earliest-known land life was allegedly found in Arizona—fossil tubular microorganisms dating from 1.2 billion years ago. With better detection techniques, more such ancient fossils will be found—confirming this find, and determining what type of life existed so long ago.

When did the **first plants** appear in the **oceans**?

The first fossil evidence of plants—and the earliest recorded evidence for life on Earth—was found in Australian rock dated between 3.45 and 3.55 billion years old. But scientists believe that life actually started long before that, about four billion years ago. There are two reasons that scientists have not found fossils that are old enough to substantiate this belief. First, it is difficult to find rock that has not been changed by heat, pressure, or erosion over the past four billion years. Second, because the single cells are so small, they are difficult to find; and because they were made of soft parts only, they probably decayed after death—leaving no evidence of their existence.

When did the **first true plants** appear on **land**?

Fossils reveal that the first true plants to colonize land appeared about 420 million years ago, and included flowerless mosses, horsetails, and ferns. They reproduced by throwing out spores, or minute organisms that carried the genetic blueprint for the plant. The ferns eventually bore seeds, but it took until about 345 million years ago. Vascular plants—those with roots, stems, and leaves—evolved about 408 million years ago.

How do scientists know that **liverworts** were probably the **first plants** to colonize the land?

Because of recent research into plant genetics, scientists know that liverworts were the first plants to colonize dry land. For a long time, scientists believed that plants made the transition to land just once, as opposed to the apparent repeated transitions of animals. Their conclu-

Jellyfish, one of the first soft-bodied creatures to appear in the oceans. (Photo courtesy of Jeffrey L. Rotman/Corbis Corporation.)

sion, then, was that the first land plant was the ancestor of all living plants.

The problem was to determine which plant was truly the first. The two contenders for this title were the most simple, primitive plants known—the mosses and liverworts, both of which are related to the ocean's green algae. Unfortunately, the fossil record is incomplete—with no good indications of which plant was the original colonist.

Recently researchers turned to genetic research, focusing on extraneous pieces of genes known as introns, which are found in more than three hundred modern plants. Over the course of evolution, introns have "pushed" their way into the genes of plants; they get "cut out" of the gene before it makes a protein. Scientists narrowed their research to three ancient introns, none of which are present in green algae. They found that trees, flowers, and other common modern plants have at least two of the three ancient introns present, as does moss. The liverworts, on the other hand, lacked all three ancient introns, making them the closest relatives to the water-loving green algae. And because of this relationship—and knowing that green algae was one of the oldest types of organisms—many scientists now believe liverworts were the first plants to colonize the land.

Before dinosaurs dominated the Earth, insects and spiders had already appeared on land. (Photo courtesy of Field Mark Publications.)

When did the **first soft-bodied animals** appear in the oceans?

Fossils reveal that the first soft-bodied animals appeared about 600 million years ago in the oceans, and included a form of jellyfish and segmented worms.

When did the **first primitive dinosaurs** appear?

The first primitive dinosaurs appeared about 230 million years ago. They were much smaller, and less fierce, than the *Tyrannosaurus rex* we often think of when someone mentions the word "dinosaur."

When did the **first humans appear**?

The first appearance of anatomically modern humans known as *Homo sapiens* occurred approximately 130,000 to 100,000 years ago—meaning we have been around in our current form for an extremely short period, geologically speaking. Our subspecies of humans, *Homo sapiens*

sapiens, have only been around for less than 100,000 years. But our humanoid ancestors have been around for four to six million years—a blink of time when one considers that the Earth is about 4.6 billion years old.

FORMING FOSSILS

What is the **geologic time scale**?

The geologic time scale is a way of putting the Earth's vast history into an orderly fashion, giving a better perspective of events. At the turn of the 19th century, William Smith (1769–1839), an English canal engineer, observed that certain types of rocks, along with certain groups of fossils, always occurred in a predictable order in relation to each other. In 1815, he published a map of England and Wales geology, establishing a practical system of stratigraphy, or the study of geological history layer by layer. Simply put, Smith proposed that the lowest rocks in a cliff or quarry are the oldest, while the highest are the youngest. By observing fossils and rock type in the various layers, it was possible to correlate the rocks at one location with those at other locations. Smith's work, combined with the first discoveries of dinosaur fossils in the early 1800s, led to a framework (the geologic time scale, with its various, arbitrary divisions of time including eras, periods, and epochs) that scientists still use today in order to divide the Earth's long history. Established between 1820 and 1870, the time divisions are a relative means of dating; that is, rocks and fossils are dated relative to each other as to which are older and younger. It was not until radiometric dating was invented in the 1920s that absolute dates were applied to rocks and fossils—and thus, also the geologic time scale.

What does the **geologic time scale** look like?

The geologic time scale divisions have changed significantly over time, mainly because of new fossil discoveries and better dating techniques—and it will no doubt continue to change, too. The following is a general listing of the geologic time table, based on current interpretations of rocks and fossils, indicating how long ago each era ended.

Geologic Time Scale

Era	Period	Millions of years ago	Life form(s) at that time
Cenozoic	Quaternary	2	Modern life, including man, evolves; man takes the place of dinosaurs and becomes the dominant creature of the land.
	Tertiary	65	Flowers begin to flourish and mammals diversify into myriad shapes and sizes.
Mesozoic	Cretaceous	144	As many dinosaurs become extinct, flowering plant-life appears.
	Jurassic	136	Huge dinosaurs (divided into herbivores and carnivores) roam the Earth, toothed-birds appear along with the first primitive marine life and reptiles.
	Triassic	245	Dinosaurs evolve from thecodont (socket-tooth) reptiles; Dicynodonts (two-dog tooth), or primitive mammals such as Kannemeyeria, and early placental mammals such as Zalambdalestes, appear.
Paleozoic (Time of Early Life)	Permian	250	Seed plants (gymnosperms) begin to grow; insects, snails, and other invertebrates face mass extinction.
	Carboniferous	290	Forests flourish with fern trees; huge insects, amphibians, and evolving reptiles take advantage of the growing foliage.

Geologic Time Scale

Era	Period	Millions of years ago	Life form(s) at that time
	Devonian	350	Cartilaginous fishes (sharks and eels) abundant; first amphibians, invertebrates, and land plants appear.
	Silurian	400	Invertebrates dominate the land and wide coral reefs cover the Earth; agnathans (fish without jaws) and armored fish flourish.
	Ordovician	510	First vertebrates (agnathans) appear, along with marine invertebrates of all shapes and sizes.
	Cambrian	550	Only marine invertebrates exist, along with few land creatures.
Pre-Cambrian		600 million to 4.6 billion years ago	Origin of the solar system and Earth, only one-celled, soft-bodied marine organisms exist.

How are the divisions on the **geologic time scale named**?

Most of the major divisions on the geologic time scale are based on Latin names, or areas in which the rocks were first found. For example, the Carboniferous period gets its name from the Latin words for "carbon-bearing," in reference to the coal-rich rocks found in England, and after which the period is named. The Jurassic period is named after the Jura Mountains along the border of France and Switzerland, where rocks from the period were found. The names of the stages or ages most often depend on city and regions where the rocks were found; this is why division names frequently vary on geologic time scale charts from different countries.

Why do some **dates differ** on the various **geologic time scale** charts?

Determining the true age divisions of the past 4.6 billion years for the geologic time scale is not a perfect science. Determining the date of a rock layer is not as precise as knowing your own age: A human usually knows when they were born—and they only have to keep track of decades, not

What is the Pre-Cambrian era?

The Pre-Cambrian era represents the time of the Earth's beginning to just before the big explosion of life in the oceans—from about 4.6 billion to about 600 million years ago. During this time, the Earth was cooling, developing its oceans, and building the continental crust; in addition, scientists believe that during the early part of the Pre-Cambrian, life began. The following lists the three Pre-Cambrian periods, the approximate dates, and major evolutionary events during these times:

Archaeon—4.6 to 2.5 billion years ago, a time in which blue-green algae and bacteria (some photosynthetic; some anaerobic) evolved.

Proterozoic—2.5 billion years to 610 million years ago, a time in which protoctista, fungi, and photosynthetic plants evolved.

Vendian—610 to 600 million years ago, a time in which multi-celled eukaryotes (cells with a definitive nucleus) evolved. These organisms were the beginning of animal life.

eons. In addition, there is often disagreement about how long certain periods lasted, since rocks and fossils found on different continents vary. Even radiometric dating does not reveal the true age of a rock or mineral—there is always a certain amount of estimation involved.

What was the "Cambrian Explosion"?

Just after the end of the Pre-Cambrian era, about 600 million years ago (during the Cambrian period), a great burst of evolutionary activity began in the world's oceans. For some reason, new animals appeared at breakneck speed, geologically speaking, filling the oceans with life. No one really knows why the animals started to appear, and scientists have suggested theories ranging from a change in climate to the idea that a natural threshold had been reached. For example, some scientists

A recreation of the Cambrian period showing the vast marine life that existed. (Photo courtesy of University of Michigan Exhibit Museum of Natural History.)

believe temperature or oxygen levels reached a point that allowed the proliferation of organisms.

Recently researchers have begun looking at the genes common to modern animals to try to determine a possible cause for the proliferation of life. One study found that an ancient common ancestor—a worm-like animal from which most of the world's animals subsequently evolved—had special genetic machinery that was so successful that it survives to this day. These genes, used to grow appendages (arms, legs, claws, fins, and antennas), were operational at least 600 million years ago. With appendages, animals swam faster, grabbed tighter, and fought with greater efficiency, and thus, could eventually dominate the Earth.

What was the **rate of growth** during the **Cambrian Explosion**?

Based on the fossil record of the Cambrian period, scientists estimate that the number of orders of animals doubled roughly every 12 million years. At this time, too, most of the modern phyla (broad caregories) of animals began to appear in the fossil record.

45

What are some possible **geological causes** for the **Cambrian Explosion**?

Scientists have suggested various explanations for the Cambrian Explosion. One theory includes the gradual breakup of a supercontinent into the continents as we know them today, which may have led to just the right distribution of oceans and continental masses. This breakup would have allowed currents to stir the ocean waters, distributing oxygen and other nutrients around the world. Another suggestion is that there was a change in sea water chemistry, as water ran around and through volcanically active mid-ocean ridges. In addition, rock sediment and fragments eroded from mountains and were dumped in the oceans, also changing the chemistry of the sea water.

What **recent theory** attempts to explain why the **Cambrian Explosion** occurred?

A recent study places the blame, or credit, for this evolutionary explosion on our planet itself—and although not everyone agrees, it is an interesting theory.

Some scientists theorize that more than 500 million years ago shifting masses within the Earth essentially unbalanced the planet, or "tipped" it, causing the entire surface to re-orient itself in an effort to become balanced again. In a process called true polar wander, the ancestral North America moved from near the South Pole up to the region of the equator; the large continent of Gondwanaland (made up of present-day South America, Antarctica, Australia, India, and Africa) traveled all the way across the Southern Hemisphere. This movement all happened at more than twice the rate of continental drift found in the present-day shifting of the Earth's crust.

Evidence for this new theory comes from the Earth itself. During the formation of rocks, the minerals inside naturally align themselves with the existing magnetic field of the planet. By studying the orientation of grains in the minerals, scientists can determine the position of ancient continents relative to the magnetic north pole, which almost always lies close to the Earth's axis of rotation. When the positions of the continents were plotted using this data, scientists found that there was a major movement of the continents within a relatively short period of time around the Cambrian era. The data showed that ancestral North America moved to the equator between 540 and 515 million years ago; while Gondwanaland shifted between 535 and 500 million years ago.

How could **"tipping"** of the Earth have led to the **Cambrian Explosion**?

If the Earth did "tip" during the Cambrian period, with the accompanying rapid movement of the continents, there would have been dramatic changes in the worldwide climate and oceans. Many ecological systems could have been disrupted; but at the same time, many new ecological niches would have been created. This would have opened up many new opportunities for life, leading to rapid evolution and expansion of new species—which is just what occurred during this time frame.

Some scientists feel that the rapid diversification of life had already begun 10 million years before this "tipping" event, and was caused by different factors. However, this continental movement could have reinforced and even strengthened an explosion of life that might already have been under way.

Could there be a **biological explanation** for the **Cambrian Explosion**?

Yes, there may have been biological factors—or factors dealing with organisms—that helped spur the Cambrian Explosion. Many scientists believe that the complex webs of living organisms would have been extremely vulnerable to changes in the environment such as the rapid movement of the continents—and thus, such changes would have decreased, not increased, the number of animals.

Instead, many scientists point to the decline in the growth of stromatolites (algal mats) at the end of the Pre-Cambrian era as an indication that there was competition between animals. And when animals compete for territory, they often increase in diversity and numbers. Plus, early animals were developing skeletons at this time. If the skeletons evolved as a form of armor against predators, and competition was

47

What are the Paleozoic, Mesozoic, and Cenozoic eras?

The divisions between the eras on the geologic time scale represent major changes on the Earth. The division between the Pre-Cambrian and Paleozoic, about 600 million years ago, represents an increase of life on Earth. The division between the Paleozoic and Mesozoic represents a major decrease in plant and animals species (called an extinction) about 250 million years ago. It is also called the "Permian Extinction" or the "Great Dying," in which up to 90 percent of all species died out. The division between the Mesozoic and Cenozoic, about 65 million years ago, also represents a major extinction of plant and animal species—including the dinosaurs. This extinction was not as extensive as that of the Great Dying; only about 50 percent of all species died out at this time.

intense, a great diversity of animals with hard parts would emerge in a relatively short time—in a kind of biological "arms race."

What are the **divisions** of the **Mesozoic era**?

The Mesozoic era, often referred to as the "age of the reptiles" or the "age of the dinosaurs" (even though dinosaurs did not evolve until well into the Mesozoic), lasted from approximately 250 to 65 million years ago. It is divided into three periods: the Triassic, Jurassic, and Cretaceous.

What are the **more recent time divisions** on the **geologic time scale**?

The Cenozoic era is divided into the Tertiary and Quaternary (or Anthropogene) periods. The Quaternary is further divided into the Pleistocene epoch, a period of advances and retreats of huge ice sheets; and the Holocene epoch, or recent times, which began about 10,000 years ago.

Fossil of the prehistoric fish Lepidotes Maximus from the Mesozoic era. (Photo courtesy of Jonathan Blair/Corbis Corporation.)

FIRST FOSSILS

What is **paleontology**?

Paleontology is the study of ancient life, which usually entails studying the remains of plants and animals in the form of fossils. Since paleontology includes the study of past plants and animals, the field has been divided into two subdisciplines: paleozoology is the study of ancient animal life; and paleobotany is the study of plant life of the geologic past.

What is **micropaleontology**?

Micropaleontology is the study of very tiny fossils—those so small as to require a microscope for examination.

What is a **fossil**?

The remains of plants and animals that have been preserved in the Earth, close to their original shape, are called fossils. This word comes from the

49

Latin *fossilis,* meaning "something dug up." The different types of fossils depend on the remains and conditions present at the time the organism died. Fossils may be formed from the hard parts of an organism, such as teeth, shells, bones, or wood; they may also be unchanged from their original features, the entire organism replaced by minerals such as calcite or pyrite. Animals and plants have also been preserved in other materials besides stone, including ice, tar, peat, and the resin of ancient trees. Fossils of single-celled organisms have been recovered from rocks as old as 3.5 billion years. Animal fossils first appear in rocks dating back about one billion years. The occurrence of fossils in unusual places, such as dinosaur fossils in Antarctica and fish fossils on the Siberian steppes, is due to the shifting of the plates that make up Earth's crust and environmental changes (such as ice ages) over time. The best explanation for dinosaurs in Antarctica is not that they evolved there, but that Antarctica was once part of a much larger landmass with which it shared many life-forms.

How does a **fossil form**?

There are a number of ways a fossil forms, based on the type of remains and the environment. In general, the process for most fossils is much the same: The hard parts of animals, such as bones, teeth, and shells, as well as the seeds or woody parts of plants, are covered by sediment, such as sand or mud. Over millions of years, more and more layers of sediment accumulate, burying these remains deep within the Earth. The sediment eventually turns to stone, and often the remains are chemically altered by mineralization, becoming a form of stone themselves (these are the type of fossils often viewed as the recreated dinosaur skeletons seen in many museums). The same process also produces petrified wood, coprolites (petrified excrement), molds, casts, imprints, and trace fossils.

Most fossils are found in sedimentary rocks, those rocks produced by the accumulation of sediment such as sand or mud. Wind and other weathering conditions wash away sediment on land, depositing it in bodies of water. For this reason, fossils of sea creatures are more common than those of land creatures. Land animals and plants that have been preserved are found mostly in sediments in clam lakes, rivers, and estuaries.

A fossil may also consist of unaltered original material. Bones and teeth are not uncommonly preserved this way. However, far more often the pores of bones and teeth are filled in with minerals, in a process called permineralization (what many have called petrifying). Circulating ground water carries silica or calcium carbonate that fill the pores.

How is **petrified wood** formed?

Petrified wood is formed when water containing dissolved minerals such as calcium carbonate ($CaCO_3$) and silicate infiltrates wood or other structures. The process takes thousands of years. The foreign material either replaces or encloses the organic matter and often retains all the structural details of the original plant material. Botanists find these types of fossils to be very important since they allow for the study of the internal structure of extinct plants. After a time, wood seems to have turned to stone because the original form and structure of the wood have been retained.

What are **carbon films**?

Under the temperatures and pressures of burial, the flesh of many soft-bodied animals will completely decay, leaving behind only a carbon film. However, sometimes this film will preserve the outlines of the animal's body. Much of the fauna of the Burgess Shale in British Columbia has been preserved this way. And a well-known specimen of an ichthyosaur (an extinct marine reptile of the Mesozoic) was preserved with a carbon film outlining the body shape. From this, paleontologists learned that the ichthyosaur had a fleshy dorsal fin that did not possess skeletal elements. Also, the group of organisms known as graptolites appear as carbon films in fine black shales. These animals lived in colonies in small tubular chambers strung along a thread-like axis. They were very tiny and decayed quickly, but the chambers were slightly more durable; upon burial these became flattened into distinctive films that look a little like a band-saw blade. It is not uncommon for the leaves of some plants to be preserved as carbon layers. The outline of a leaf and a hint of the pattern of veins may be all that can be recognized, but this is often sufficient to identify the plant from which the leaf came.

How hard is it for an **organism** to become a **fossil**?

Not all organisms survive to become fossils and the chances of a living organism becoming a fossil is generally very low. Many organisms completely decay or are chewed apart by other animals. Because of this, some scientists estimate that although billions of flora and fauna have lived on the Earth, very few survived into fossil form. Thus, the fossils we do find on Earth represent only a small fraction of the animals and plants that have ever lived on our planet.

An organism has the best chance to become a fossil if it is quickly covered by moist sediment after death, protecting the decaying organism from predators, scavengers, and bacteria. The soft parts of the organism (such as skin, membranes, tissues, and organs) will quickly decay, leaving behind teeth and bones. The majority of found fossils are from almost 500 million years ago, when organisms first began to develop skeletons and other hard parts.

The following are the steps in the fossilization process, using a dinosaur as an example. This outline also shows how difficult it is for a dinosaur to become a fossil:

Scavenging and decay—When a dinosaur died, it didn't take long for scavengers to remove the soft, fleshy parts of its body. Those parts that were not eaten decayed at a fast or slow rate, depending on the prevailing climate. In any case, within a short time, only a skeleton would remain. But even the remaining hard body parts were not impervious to change. They were often weathered by wind, water, sunlight, and chemicals in the environment, rounding the bones or reducing them to small pieces.

Location—If the dinosaur's skeleton was in an area in which rapid burial did not take place, then the chances of fossilization were slim. The bones would break and scatter, often moved by the action of changing river courses or flash floods. But occasionally, this transport increased the chance of fossilization, moving the bones to a better area for preservation, such as a sandbank in a river.

Burial—The most crucial step in the fossilization process is burial: The sooner the burial of the dinosaur bones, the better the chance a good fossil was created. If the bones were covered by mud or sand, whether before or after transport, then the amount of further damage would have been lessened; in addition, oxygen is lessened, thus reducing additional decay of the dinosaur bones. Some damage still might have occurred, however, primarily from the pressure created

Fossil bones of a Hypacrosaurus. (Photo courtesy of Tom Bean/Corbis Corporation.)

by the increasing amount of sediment on top of the bones, or even from acidic chemicals that can dissolve into the sediment.

Fossilization—The fourth step was the actual process of fossilization itself. Here, the sediments surrounding the fossil slowly turned to stone by the action of pressure from the overlying sediment layers and loss of water. Eventually the grains became cemented together into the hard structure we call rock. The dinosaur bones fossilized, as the spaces in the bone structures filled with minerals, such as calcite (calcium carbonate) or other iron-containing minerals; or the actual mineral component of the bone itself, apatite (calcium phosphate), may have recrystallized.

53

Fossil of a prehistoric reptile. (Photo courtesy of Kevin Schafer/Corbis Corporation).

Exposure—Lastly, deeply-buried dinosaur bones must be exposed on the surface where they can be discovered. This process involves the uplift of the bone-containing sedimentary rock to the surface, where erosion by wind and water expose the fossilized skeleton. If the bones are not found in time, the action of the wind and water can destroy the precious record of the ancient species.

How do scientists determine the **age** of **fossils**?

A number of methods are used today to date fossils. Most of the methods are indirect—meaning that the age of the soil or rock in which the fossils are found are dated, not the fossils themselves. The most common way to ascertain the age of a fossil is by determining where it is found in rock layers. In many cases, the age of the rock can be determined by other fossils within that rock. If this is not possible, certain analytical techniques are often used to determine the date of the rock layer.

One of the basic ways to determine the age of rock is through the use of radioactivity. For example, radioactivity within the Earth continuously

Do humans become fossils?

Yes, the bones, teeth, and other hard parts of ancient humans have fossilized when conditions were right. The fossilized skeleton of the earliest known human ancestor was found in 1974 in Ethiopia, by anthropologist Donald Johanson (1943–). Nicknamed "Lucy," the fossil was of a 3.5-foot (1-meter) high, approximately 20-year-old female. The fossils were about three to 3.5 million years old–making Lucy's species, *Australopethicus afarensis,* one of the oldest links to our past.

bombards the atoms in minerals, exciting electrons that become trapped in the crystals' structures. Using this knowledge, scientists employ certain radiometric techniques, including electron spin resonance and thermoluminescence, to determine the age of the minerals. By determining the number of excited electrons present in the minerals—and comparing that number with known data that represents the actual rate of increase of similar excited electrons—the time it took for the amount of excited electrons to accumulate can be calculated. In turn, this data can be used to determine the age of the rock—and the fossils within the rock.

There are other methods for determining fossil age. For example, uranium-series dating measures the amount of thorium-230 present in limestone deposits. Limestone deposits form with uranium present, and almost no thorium. Because scientists know the decay rate of uranium into thorium-230, the age of the limestone rocks, and the fossils found in them, can be calculated from the amount of thorium-230 evident within a particular limestone rock.

Why are there **gaps** in the **fossil records**?

Gaps in the fossil records—eras or evolutionary stages that are "missing" from the known collection of fossils—are most often the result of erosion. This geologic process erodes away layers of rock and embedded

Anthropologist Donald Johanson with his famous fossil find, Lucy. (Photo courtesy of Morton Beebe-S.F./Corbis Corporation.)

fossils, usually by the action of wind, water, and ice. Gaps in fossil records can also be caused by mountain uplift, which destroys fossils, and volcanic activity, which can bury fossil evidence with hot magma rock that physically changes the rock, and thus fossils.

What are **molds** and **casts**?

Molds and casts are types of fossils. After burial, a plant or animal often decays, leaving only an impression of its hard parts (and less often, soft parts) as a hollow mold in the rock. If the mold is filled with sediment, it can often harden, forming a corresponding cast.

What are **trace fossils**?

Not all fossils are hardened bones and teeth, or molds and casts. There are also fossils that are merely evidence that creatures once crawled, walked, hopped, burrowed, or ran across the land. Trace fossils are just that: The traces a creature left behind, usually in soft sediment like sand or mud. For example, small animals bored branching tunnels in the

Two ammonite fossils. (Photo courtesy of Maurice Nimmo, Frank Lane Picture Agency/Corbis Corporation.)

mud of a lake bed in search of food; and dinosaurs hunted for meals along a river bank, leaving their footprints in the soft sand. Similar to the fossil formation of hard parts, the footprints and tunnels were filled in by sediment, then buried by layers of more sediment over millions of years, eventually solidifying. Today we see the results of this long-ago activity as trace fossils. Many originators of trace fossils are unidentifiable—in other words, there are no hard fossils of the creatures left in the area, just their tracks. Some of the most famous trace fossils are those of dinosaurs tracks (for example, in Culpepper, Virginia, and near Golden, Colorado) and of human-like footprints (such as those found in east Africa)—all found in hardened sediment.

What can some **trace fossils** of **dinosaur tracks** tell us about the animal's speed?

There are numerous fossilized dinosaur footprints, called a trackway, located north of Flagstaff, Arizona, on the Navajo Reservation. This site was first discovered by Barnum Brown of the American Museum of Natural History in the 1930s, but had been lost until recently. It includes an example of a running dinosaur that left tracks with an eight-foot (2.4-meter) space between the right and left prints; from these prints, scientists calculated that the dinosaur ran at a speed of 14.5 miles (23.3 kilometers) per hour—one of the faster dinosaurs known. The speed record, however, is presently held by a Jurassic carnivore that left a 16-foot (5-meter) gap between the right and left tracks, in a Glen Rose, Texas, trackway. The calculated speed of this dinosaur was about 26.5 miles (42.8 kilometers) per hour, faster than the speediest human.

What is the difference between **tracks and trails**?

Tracks are generally the traces of distinct footprints, whereas trails may have been produced by an animal dragging its feet or some other appendage as it moved. Tracks, therefore, are more distinctive, and different animals can be distinguished by their own peculiar footprints. Trails can seldom be associated with a particular animal.

MORE RECENT FOSSILS

What and when were the **Ice Ages**?

In 1795, Scottish naturalist James Hutton (1726–1797) was the first to publish the idea that, in the past, Alpine glaciers had been much more extensive than they are today. He based his observations on strangely-shaped glacial boulders called erratics near Geneva. (Ironically, although he recognized the evidence of glaciation in Switzerland, he never realized the abundant evidence in his Scottish homeland.) It took several more decades before J. Esmark, in 1824, proposed that glaciation on a continental scale occurred in the past. By 1840, prominent Swiss biologist Louis Agassiz (1807–1873) became the leading champion of continental glaciation, proposing that ice once covered nearly all of northern Europe, including Britain. Later, he also found evidence of this phenomenon in New England.

Today, we describe an ice age as any part of geologic time when huge glacial ice sheets covered more of the Earth's surface than during modern times. The most recent ice age—often referred to as the "Ice Ages" or the "Great Ice Age"—began about two million years ago (at the beginning of the Quaternary period) and ended about 10,000 years ago.

It is thought that the plains of North America cooled in the latter half of the Cenozoic era (and the beginning of the Quaternary era, Pleistocene epoch), about two million years ago. Ice sheets soon spread south from Canada's Hudson Bay area, and eastward from the Rocky Mountains. Toward the end of the Pleistocene epoch, the ice sheets advanced and retreated numerous times—each event lasting from about 10,000 to 100,000 years. The last retreat occurred about 10,000 years ago. In the United States, the last ice age advance and retreat is called the Wisconsinan stage; in Europe, it is called the Wöyrmian stage. Erosional and depositional glacial features from this latter stage are still evident in many of the regions once covered by the huge ice sheets.

At their maximum extent, the Pleistocene ice sheets reached into the upper part of the northern United States, Greenland, northern Europe and Asia (although Siberia was little glaciated because it was too dry), Antarctica, southern South America, and high spots throughout Asia including the Himalayas. All together, geologist believe that up to 10 percent of our Earth was once buried in ice (though not simultaneously) during the Ice Age periods, the ice often miles thick.

How **many ice ages** occurred over geologic time?

Geologic records show that there have been relatively few times that ice ages have occurred—perhaps only less than 1 percent of the time in the last 600 million years. The first known large-scale ice age occurred about 2.3 billion years ago, during the Pre-Cambrian era.

A great deal of what scientists know about the ice ages they have learned from the study of mountain glaciers. For example, when a glacier moves downward out of its mountain source, it carves out a distinctive shape on the surrounding land. The "footprints" left by continental glaciers formed during the ice ages are comparable to those formed by mountain glaciers.

The transport of materials from one part of the Earth's surface to another part is also evidence of continental glaciation. Rocks and fossils normally found only in one region of the earth may be picked up and moved by ice sheets and deposited elsewhere. The "tracks" left by the moving glacier provide evidence of the ice sheet's movement. In many cases, the moving ice may actually have left scratches on the rock over which it moved, providing further evidence of changes that took place during an ice age.

What **changes** the **Great Ice Age** cause?

There is no doubt that the Great Ice Age caused major changes in the Earth's overall climate over the past millions of years. Global mean (average) temperatures fluctuated radically up and down. For example, during the most recent Ice Age, the temperatures were about 10° F cooler than today; and during the interglacial times, when the ice sheets retreated, the temperatures averaged 5° F warmer than today.

The Great Ice Age was also responsible for the migration and movement of animals over the past two million years. Because sea levels fell as the ice sheets advanced, narrow land bridges were often exposed and used by many living things to search for new territory and better food supplies. For example, a narrow land bridge (at Bering Strait) between Asia and North America is believed to have allowed North American native animals, such as camels, horses, and cheetahs, to migrate to Asia during the Ice Age; while mammoths, mastodons, bison, and muskox crossed from Asia to North America. In fact, this land bridge was probably also used by our own species—*Homo sapiens*.

Did the **Great Ice Age** really **end**?

Some scientists believe that the Great Ice Age never truly ended, and that we are merely in the middle of a warming trend during this ice age; others believe that we are living during an interglacial period, and thus, the temperatures will continue to rise. But since no one knows how an ice age actually "begins" or "ends," it is difficult to tell if we are in the advance or retreat of an ice age cycle.

The following chart outlines current areas of glaciation around the world.

Place	Square miles
Antarctica	5,250,00
North Polar Regions (Greenland, Northern Canada, Arctic Ocean islands)	799,000
Asia	44,000
Alaska & Rocky Mountains	29,700
South America	10,200
Iceland	4,699
Alpine Europe	3,580
New England	391
Africa	5

How much of the Earth's surface is **permanently frozen**?

About one-fifth of the Earth's land is permafrost, or ground that is permanently frozen. This classification is based entirely on temperature and disregards the composition of the land. It can include bedrock, sod, ice, sand, gravel, or any other type of material in which the temperature has been below freezing for over two years. Nearly all permafrost is thousands of years old.

What is the **difference** between a **mammoth** and a **mastodon**?

Contrary to what most people think, mammoths and mastodons were two different animals. The mastodon seems to have appeared first. It appeared in the Oligocene epoch (about 25 to 38 million years ago) and survived until less than one million years ago. The mastodon lived in Africa, Asia, Europe, and North and South America, and grew to a maximum of 10 feet (3 meters) tall. Mastodons were covered with dense, woolly hair, and had tusks straight forward and nearly parallel to each other.

The mammoth may have been a side branch of the mastodon, and lived in North America, Europe, and Asia. Mammoths evolved less than two million years ago, and died out about 10,000 years ago, at the end of the Ice Age. They grew to about 9 to 15 feet (2.7 to 4.5 meters) tall, and had long tusks that curled upward and out. They also had dense woolly hair,

61

What are the La Brea Tar Pits?

The La Brea Tar Pits of Los Angeles, as the name implies, are huge pits filled with thick, gooey tar. The importance of the pits is the animals they trapped—animals of the Ice Ages, including mammoths, mastodons, giant ground sloths, dire wolves, and saber-toothed cats. The animals were trapped as they entered the area and accidentally walked into the tar pits. As they struggled to get free, other predatory animals would often attack, and they, too, would become ensnared in the tar. Soon, the tar would encase the animals, preserving them by cutting off oxygen that would otherwise decay the bones, and protecting their bodies from being chewed by other animals. The fossils in La Brea are well-preserved—so much so that DNA from the bones of a 14,000-year-old saber-toothed cat found at the pit have been analyzed. The data showed that this cat was closely related to modern cats, such as lions and tigers.

with an additional coarse layer of outer hair that protected them from the cold.

No one really knows why the mastodons and mammoths died out. Scientists theorize that the mastodon died out because of climate changes, and the resulting changes in the environment. Mammoths may also have died out because of climate changes, as ice sheets retreated about 10,000 years ago. Early humans may have also hastened the extinction process by hunting the mammoths.

Are there any **"living fossils"** on Earth?

There are some modern animal and plant species that are almost identical to those living millions of years ago. Many of these "living fossils" were discovered as actual fossils before they were found as modern living organisms. Plants such as the horsetail existed during the Devonian period almost 380 million years ago; one species of modern ginko survives from the Triassic period about 220 million

These mammoth tusks were found underground. (Photo courtesy of The National Archives/Corbis Corporation.)

years ago; and the magnolia, one of the earliest true flowering plants, existed during the Cretaceous period, about 125 million years ago. Living fossils of animals include the tuatara, the only living survivor from a reptile group that was abundant during the Triassic period; didelphids are marsupials, including the modern opossum, that lived at the end of the Cretaceous period; and the modern brachiopod *Lingula* is scarcely distinguishable from its ancestor that lived during the Devonian period. Ancient insects include cockroaches and dragonflies, which evolved during the early Carboniferous period about 350 million years ago.

One explanation for the longevity of a certain species may be its ability to adapt and live in stable ecological niches. For example, the *Lingula* live in the intertidal zone, a specialized niche along coastal areas. Even if the sea levels changed, these brachiopods could adapt by changing location with the water levels.

One of the most famous of all "living fossils" is the coelacanth, a fish that has a three-lobed tail and fins with arm-like bases. The first such fish was found as a fossil in Devonian period rock; it was thought to have become extinct about 60 million years ago, at the beginning of

Mammoths, like this one, came after mastadons. (Photo courtesy of Jonathan Blair/Corbis Corporation.)

the Cenozoic era. But in 1938, fisherman Captain Hendrik Goosen caught a living coelacanth in the Indian Ocean off the coast of South Africa. The ichthyologist who identified the fish, Professor J. L. B. Smith of South Africa, offered a reward of £100 (about $50 in current American currency) to anyone who found a second one. It took until 1952 for someone to catch another modern specimen; and since that time, many have been photographed alive in water 200 to 1,310 feet (60 to 400 meters) deep off the coast of the Cormoro Islands near Madagascar.

Will **animals** and **plants** that die **today** become fossils?

In many cases, yes, if the conditions are right. Many organisms will quickly decay, as sunlight, water, or air interacts with them, especially if the organisms do not have resistant hard parts. If the organisms do have hard parts, those that are quickly buried have the best chance of becoming fossils, as sediment stops much of the decay. Most of the future fossils will be from oceans, lakes, and rivers—areas in which quick burial, and thus fossilization is more likely to occur.

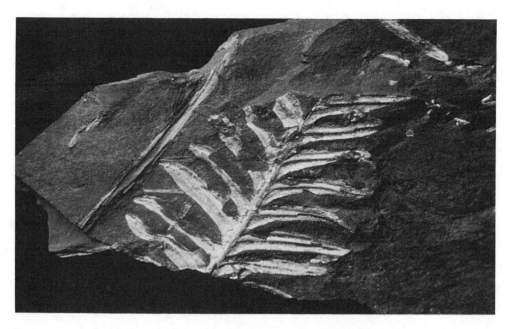

Fossil of a white fern leaf that is 320 million years old. (Photo courtesy of Field Mark Publications.)

What is the **oldest-known living organism** on the Earth today?

In northern Michigan, a huge *Armillaria bulbosa* fungus spawned from a single spore 1,500 or more years ago; it covers about 30 acres and weighs about 100 tons. The fungus is actually known as the button or honey mushroom, and feeds on decaying matter, such as dead wood.

What is the **largest-known living organism** on the Earth today?

Contrary to popular belief, blue whales and giant sequoia trees are not the largest-known organisms in the world. The prize goes to a grove of aspen trees in the Wasatch Mountains, south of Salt Lake City, Utah. The 106-acre aspen system contains about 50,000 aspen stems and is estimated to weigh about 6,000 tons. The grove may look like separate trees, but in reality, they are different parts of the same plant, all growing from one root system. Scientists have determined that the aspen grove is one unit—the leaves all have identical sizes and shapes, and turn the same colors at the same time each fall.

Aspen trees of Utah grow from one root system, making it just one tree. (Photo courtesy of Galen Rowell/Corbis Corporation.)

DINOSAUR FOSSILS

What does the term **dinosaur mean**?

Dinosaur comes from the term *dinosauria,* which is a combination of the Greek words *deinos* and *sauros*. *Deinos* means "terrible" and *sauros* means "lizard" or "reptile." Thus, dinosaur means "terrible lizard."

Who **invented** the term "dinosaur"?

The term dinosaur was invented by the well-known British anatomist Sir Richard Owen (1804–1892). He coined the term in 1842 to describe the 175-million-year-old fossil remains of two groups of giant reptiles that corresponded to no known living creatures. In 1854, Owen prepared one of the first dinosaur exhibitions for display at Crystal Palace, the famous museum in London, England.

How do paleontologists **identify species of dinosaurs** from other fossils?

One of the best ways to identify dinosaur fossil bones is by size, as many of the bones are huge. For example, the upper leg bone, or femur, of an adult *Apatosaurus* often measures over 6 feet (1.8 meters) long.

But size is not everything, as many dinosaurs were the same size as a chicken or cat. The way scientists detect the differences between dinosaurs and other animals species is by the construction and orientation of their bones—including heads, tails, and hip bones. In addition, dinosaur fossils are often found in association with other dinosaurs at a site. Many times these fossils represent dinosaurs—from meat-eaters to plant-eaters—that gathered together along the shore of a lake or ocean. The dinosaurs were all in search of food along the banks of the water, a place that would attract many animals and plants.

Of course, not all dinosaur fossils are found in the conventional way. In 1998, an amateur fossil collector saw the movie *Jurassic Park* and recognized that a fossil he had—which he had thought was a bird—was actually a dinosaur. The specimen, only 9.5 inches (24 centimeters) long, is a young dinosaur that had just hatched before it died. In this case, the dinosaur remains probably washed into oxygen-starved waters where it was quickly buried. This may be one of the most important dinosaur fossils ever found, as many of its soft body parts were preserved, including the intestines, muscle fibers, and maybe even the liver.

When was the first **dinosaur bone** collected and described?

The fossilized bones of dinosaurs have probably been found throughout human history, but no records or descriptions were kept until fairly recently. References to fossilized sharks' teeth and shells are recorded from the European Medieval period, but because Medieval Europeans believed that no animal or plant made by God could become extinct, they explained the findings in other ways. For example, many of the fossils were interpreted as the remains of modern species as opposed to ancient, extinct species; others were thought of as merely pebbles that resembled the remains of animals and plant species.

67

Sir Richard Owen coined the word dinosaur. (Photo courtesy of Harold S. Chapman/ Corbis-Bettman.)

The first recorded description of a dinosaur bone was made in 1676 by Robert Plot, a professor of chemistry at the University of Oxford, England, in his book *The Natural History of Oxfordshire.* Although he correctly determined that it was a broken piece of a giant bone, Plot did not know the bone came from a dinosaur. Instead, he felt it belonged to a giant man or woman, citing mythical, historical, and biblical sources. In 1763, the same bone fragment was named *Scrotum humanum,* by R. Brookes, to describe its appearance, but the name never gained wide or serious acceptance. Based on Plot's illustration, modern scientists believe the bone fragment is actually the lower end of a thigh bone from a *Megalosaurus,* a meat-eating dinosaur from the

What connection did dinosaurs fossils in Italy have to literature?

Prior to the discovery of dinosaur tracks in the Alps near Trento, Italy, in the early 1990s, there was virtually no evidence of dinosaurs in Italy. The dinosaur tracks were found around the area of an eighth century landslide, a geological feature that served as the model for the stairway to the pits of hell in Dante's *Inferno*.

middle Jurassic period that roamed the area now known as Oxford-shire, England.

In 1787, Caspar Wistar and Timothy Matlack discovered a large fossil bone in the state of New Jersey. Although they reported their finding, it was ignored and unverified—but may have been the first dinosaur bone ever collected in North America.

What did the **Chinese** think **dinosaur fossils** were?

The Chinese have been collecting dinosaur fossils for over 2,000 years, but they never identified the pieces as being from ancient creatures. The Chinese thought the fossils were the remains of dragons—a prominent symbol in Chinese culture. Even today, ground-up "dragon's" teeth are thought to have medicinal healing properties.

With much scientific evidence to dismiss the Chinese association of huge bones with the existence of dragons, concerted efforts have been made to investigate the lands of China, where many great archeological and paleontological finds have been made.

In the early 1900s, the bones of a stegosaur and of a hadrosaur were found in desert regions of China. In a southwest region of Beijing, the famed Peking Man (the fossilized skeleton found in a Pleistocene cave) was discovered in 1926.

Throughout the latter half of the twentieth century, joint ventures by Chinese and Canadian anthropologists and paleontologists and other field workers have excavated over 60 tons of important fossils that have helped professionals around the world better study the life-forms and conditions of life millions of years ago.

What was the possible connection between the **mythical griffin** and **dinosaurs**?

The griffin, a mythical creature often depicted by the Greeks and Romans until about 3 A.D., was more than likely based on skeletons of the dinosaur *Protoceratops*. This dinosaur existed during the Cretaceous period about 65 to 141 million years ago; its skeletons are found in profusion in Mongolia's Gobi Desert, south of the Altai Mountains. If nomads crossing the desert were to see the skeletons of the large creatures embedded in the rock—especially fossils of its sharp beak, elongated shoulder blade, and neck shield—they might have interpreted the fossils as the remains of the mythical creature, spreading the stories as they traveled and traded with western cultures.

What did the **American Indians** think **dinosaur fossils** were?

Several American Indian tribes found large old bones, but did not identify them as dinosaur fossils. Because of their great size, the dinosaur bones were called the grandfathers of the buffalo, one of the largest animals the Indians knew.

What did early **English** think **dinosaur fossils** were?

Before discovering the bones' true nature in the nineteenth century, some English, including chemist Robert Plot, believed that dinosaur fossils were actually the remains of elephants that had been brought to England by the Romans. Later, some believed the bones to be those of a giant human. Another early English theory, and one closer to the truth, suggested that the bones came from giant lizards.

What are some of the **oldest dinosaur fossils** found to date?

There are several dinosaur fossils that scientists claim to be the oldest ever found—and most of them have been discovered in South America. The oldest dinosaur skull was found in Argentina—a Herrerasaurus, a meat-eating dinosaur that lived some 230 million years old. The Eoraptor, a 228 million-year-old dinosaur, was also found in Argentina, and is currently thought of as the most primitive dinosaur known. More recently, paleontologists also discovered the fossilized bones of three prosauropods, plant-eating dinosaurs that lived approximately 220 million years ago, in Santa Maria, an area of southern Brazil.

EVOLUTION OF THE DINOSAURS

DINOSAUR ANCESTORS

What is **evolution**?

The term evolution actually represents two basic ideas: First, it is the theory that living organisms change over time, adapting to environmental conditions to which they are exposed over that time. Small animals have evolved into large creatures and vice versa, as moderate-sized reptiles evolved into some gigantic dinosaurs. Second, it is the theory that life on Earth developed gradually, geologically speaking, from one or several simple organisms to more complex organisms. This is called organic evolution.

What was **Charles Darwin's theory of evolution**?

English naturalist Charles Darwin (1809–1882) developed the theory of evolution, publishing his famous thesis in 1859, *On the Origin of Species*. Darwin participated in the around-the-world voyage of the HMS *Beagle* during the years 1831 to 1836. During this trip, he studied the plants and animals found in remote parts of the planet, especially the flora and fauna from areas that had been isolated for long periods of time, such as the Galapagos Islands. From the data he accumulated he was able to develop his theory of evolution.

His idea stated that there have been, and continue to be, continual, gradual changes in living organisms over the millions of years of Earth history. The changes themselves are caused by random genetic mutations in species during the reproductive process. Those organisms that survive have adaptations that are favorable to the prevailing environment; while those with inappropriate mutations die off. Darwin called this process natural selection. The actual process occurs over long time spans; because it happens slowly, this theory is also known as gradualism.

Charles Darwin's explanation of natural evolution changed the ideas that biologists and paleontologists had about the natural world. No longer were humans thought of as the pinnacle of creation—and no longer was the world thought of as unchanging and as simply created by God for human enjoyment.

How did **Darwin's theory of evolution** affect the early interpretations of **dinosaur fossils**?

Darwin's theory of evolution filled in the missing blanks when it came to interpreting the first dinosaur remains found in England in the latter 1800s. Thanks to the theory of evolution—in which it was realized that species could evolve and split into different groups, or even disappear altogether—scientists finally were able to account for the origin and disappearance of the dinosaurs. They could also finally visualize the vast potential for variations in dinosaur species over time, including an increase or decrease in body size, a change from walking on four feet to two feet, and changes in diet and/or habitat.

How did **life evolve** after the early single-celled organisms?

Over hundreds of millions of years after the evolution of single-celled organisms, the oceans abounded with a huge variety of life. The first soft-bodied animals, such as worms and jellyfish, evolved toward the close of the Pre-Cambrian era; the first animals with hard parts, such as shelled mollusks, evolved during the Cambrian period of the Paleozoic era.

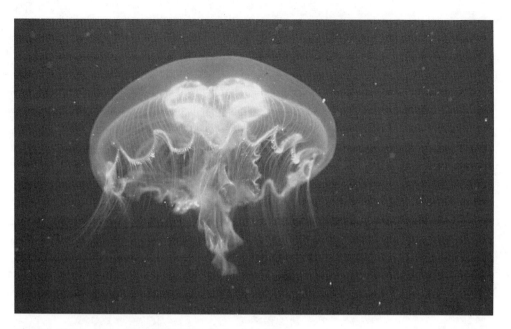

A jellyfish. (Photo courtesy of Amos Nachoum/Corbis Corporation.)

What are **vertebrates**?

The first vertebrates, or animals with backbones, evolved during the late Cambrian to early Ordovician periods as jawless, freshwater fish. By the Devonian period (the "age of fishes"), jawed and armored fishes dominated the oceans. But during the same time period, a line of fish with a bony skeleton developed air-breathing lungs and "limbs" strong enough to support them. These were the precursors to the amphibians, creatures that made their first move toward land probably in response to the spread of plants to land around the early Silurian period.

From what animals did the **amphibians evolve**?

The fossil records of amphibians are scarce, so the precise ancestry of amphibians may never be known. However, scientists do agree that amphibians first evolved from a group of animals known as the lobe-finned fishes during the Devonian period. In fact, these four-legged land vertebrates, called tetrapods, had fishlike heads and tails, and their limbs were no more than jointed, lobed fins. But these animals could do something that no fish could do: breathe air, with the change over from gills to lungs coming dur-

77

What are amphibians and when did they first live?

Amphibians were the first air-breathing land vertebrates; the first fossil record of their existence supports that they appeared approximately 360 million years ago, during the late Devonian period. These early amphibians were direct descendants from the early fish, and represent a transition stage from complete water dwellers to land dwellers. Amphibian comes from the Greek *amphi* meaning "both," and *bios* meaning "life," signifying that these animals could live both in and out of the water. The Carboniferous period of the Paleozoic age, from approximately 360 to 290 million years ago, was known as the "age of amphibians." During that time, the climate was warm and humid, and there were many swamps, marshes, and lakes—perfect for the water needs of the amphibians.

ing the early larval stage of the amphibian. Amphibians were also the first vertebrates to eventually have true legs, tongues, ears, and voice boxes.

What is the **earliest known amphibian**?

Fossils of the earliest known amphibian, the *Ichthyostega,* have been uncovered in Greenland. This early amphibian lived in the swamps of the late Devonian period, in mild, warm climates. By this time, too, insects had evolved on land, providing food for the slow-moving amphibian. The *Ichthyostega* was a 3-foot (1-meter) long animal with four limbs and a fin on its tail—a combination of amphibian and fish features that allowed it to climb on land and swim. This was the earliest known common ancestor of today's modern amphibians.

What were some of the **problems** as amphibians moved from **water to land**?

The early amphibian's main problem was support. In the water, a body is virtually "weightless," supported by the buoyancy of water. But on land,

Amphibians, such as this Asian tree frog, are able to live both on land and in water. (Photo courtesy of Field Mark Publications.)

the amphibian's body had to be held up from the ground, and the internal organs protected from being crushed—thus, a strong ribcage was needed. The backbone, ligaments, and muscles also had to strengthen, supporting not only the weight of the body between the front and hind legs, but also the head. The limbs and limb muscles also had to change to allow walking; hind limbs turned on the strengthened pelvis, and the skeleton as a whole was made stronger.

Another problem was adapting to breathing on land. The amphibians had to modify their respiratory system (changing from gills to lungs), as lungs took over more and more of the breathing. The reproductive system, water balance, and senses also had to adapt to the new life in and out of the water. For example, the first amphibians probably spent much of their time in the water, giving birth to totally aquatic young (tadpoles) that would eventually be able to live both in and out of water. An amphibian's water balance adapted by allowing the creature to live out of water as long as they at least stayed damp. Their senses also had to adapt—their sight, smell, and hearing taking on more important roles as they started living more on land. For instance, amphibian eardrums developed to enable the semi-land dwelling animals to hear sounds in the air. Their eyes had to be modified to see in air instead of water; protective eyelids developed; and tear ducts evolved, allowing their eyes to be continually moistened with tears.

Even after all these changes, amphibians still were tied to ponds, lakes, or the edges of the oceans, especially since the eggs still had to be laid and hatched in water. Evolution did not change the amphibians too much—modern amphibians are still tied to water.

What **amphibians** are living **today**?

Names of modern amphibians are familiar to us: frogs, toads, salamanders, and newts. They represent the descendants of groups that did not become extinct at the end of the Mesozoic era (when dinosaurs died out). Of the modern amphibians, the newts and salamanders are probably the most similar to the early amphibians, although they are much smaller.

The vertebrate class Amphibia today includes about 3,500 species in three orders: frogs and toads (order Anura), salamanders and newts (order Caudata), and caecilians (order Gymnophiona). There is, however, a much larger number of extinct species of amphibians, because this ancient group of animals were the first vertebrates to begin to exploit terrestrial environments, where they fall prey to other species.

When did **reptiles** first **evolve** from amphibians?

It is thought that during the Carboniferous period, a group of amphibians gave rise to the reptiles. The first reptiles were small, lizard-sized animals, but they had many differences from their

A salamander is one of the species of amphibians living today. (Photo courtesy of Field Mark Publications.)

amphibian ancestors—including waterproof skins and thick-shelled eggs. This made it unnecessary for the reptiles to stay near water, to keep moist, or to lay their eggs in water. In fact, the evolution of the reptiles, geologically speaking, occurred very rapidly—and within about 40 million years, the reptiles had produced thousands of different species.

What is the **difference** between a **reptile and an amphibian**?

Reptiles are clad in scales, shields, or plates, and their toes have claws; amphibians have moist, glandular skins, and their toes lack claws. Reptile eggs have a thick, hard or parchment-like shell that protects the developing embryo from moisture loss, even on dry land. The eggs of amphibians lack this protective outer covering and are always laid in water or in damp places. Young reptiles are miniature replicas of their parents in general appearance if not always in coloration and pattern. Juvenile amphibians pass through a larval, usually aquatic, stage before they metamorphose (change in form and structure) into the adult form.

81

The ability for reptiles to reproduce with an amniote egg allowed for these creatures to evolve into exclusively land animals. (Photo courtesy of Field Mark Publications.)

What was one of the **most important changes** that enabled **reptiles** to become true land-dwelling animals?

The development of the amniote egg freed the reptiles completely from life in the water by allowing them to fully reproduce on land. Unlike the young of amphibians, who had to go through a larval stage in the water before metamorphosing into an adult, the amniote egg acted as a sort of "private pond" for the young reptiles.

The egg itself had a hard shell, which contained numerous small pores. These pores allowed air to enter, but the shell prevented the inside from drying up as long as the surroundings were humid. The eggs were fertilized inside the mother's body before being laid. There were three very thin bags inside the shell itself, each of which had a specific function: The first bag held the developing young and a liquid (which took the place of the pond or stream); this area was called the amnion, from which the egg gets its name. The next bag contained the yolk, the source of food for the developing embryo. The third bag was in contact with the air diffusing in through the shell. Thus, the young reptiles had food, air, protection from predators, and an aquatic envi-

What were some of the earliest known reptiles?

Two of the earliest known reptiles, the *Hylonomus* and *Palaeo-thyris,* both descended from amphibians during the mid–Carboniferous period of the Paleozoic era. The best evidence of the change from amphibian to reptile were the early reptiles' high skulls, evidence of additional jaw muscles, and thicker egg shells. The *Hylonomus* lived about 310 million years ago, and the *Palaeothyris* evolved about 300 million years old. The fossils of the reptiles are found near Nova Scotia, Canada, in ancient tree stumps. Apparently the animals fell into the stumps in pursuit of insects and worms; they were trapped inside and eventually died.

ronment in which to grow. The young would eventually hatch into a miniature version of its parents, able to fend for itself. Because of the egg, the reptiles no longer had to have a source of water to reproduce, and could spread out—populating the land as well as hunting for its prey well away from water.

What is a **pelycosaur**?

The pelycosaurs are a group of mostly medium to small carnivorous and insectivorous reptiles. However, included in the group are two relatively well-known genera—*Dimetrodon* and *Edaphosaurus.* These were among the largest of the pelycosaurs, reaching up to almost ten feet in length (about three meters) and having great extensions of the vertebrae extending up from their spines. The most probable purpose of these "sails" would be for regulating body temperature. Both of these animals had a rather sprawling gait and were probably not very agile. *Dimetrodon* probably benefited as a carnivore by turning broad-side to the morning sun, raising its body temperature and therefore becoming more active before its intended prey. *Edaphosaurus* may represent the defensive response to this threat, for it was a herbivore and might well have been the target of *Dimetrodon*'s hunger. So, it too developed a "sail" to absorb heat quickly, which would speed up the animal's response time. Of course, this is a speculative answer—the evidence is not conclusive by any means.

Why did the **reptiles dominate** during the Mesozoic?

Besides the ability to not depend on water as much as amphibians, there are probably two main reasons why reptiles became dominant in the Mesozoic. First, reptiles developed adaptations in their skeletal and bone structure, allowing them to move much quicker than amphibians. Second, during the Permian period, the climate became hotter and drier, and many water sources disappeared. The reptiles' new adaptations—from the development of scales to hold in water, to eggs that could survive without staying in water—allowed them to thrive at the expense of the amphibians.

Did some **reptiles return to the oceans**?

Yes, as the reptiles spread out over the land, some of them returned to the water. Over a period of time, they evolved and adapted to the water again: Their legs gradually evolved into fins and flippers; eyes adapted to seeing in the water; and bodies became streamlined for better speed in the water. In addition, they could no longer lay their eggs on land. Thus, they evolved a way of producing living young within their bodies, a process called ovoviviparous. The ichthyosaurs, or "fish lizards," were the most fish-like true reptiles.

How are **reptiles grouped**?

During the next 100 million years after the first reptiles appeared, various reptile lines continued to evolve. Today, 16 orders of reptiles are recognized, but only four have survived to present day (crocodiles, lizards and snakes, *Sphenodon*, and turtles and tortoises). The others died out over time.

The 16 orders are divided into four distinct groupings (or subclasses), called the anapsids, synapsids, diapsids, and euryapsids—all recognized by the pattern of openings in the skull. The anapsids had no openings in

An *Edaphosaurus,* a reptile during the Early Permian era. (Photo courtesy of University of Michigan Exhibit Museum of Natural History.)

the skull and eventually evolved into today's turtles and tortoises. The synapsids, or "same hole," had a low skull opening, and were the ancestors of modern mammals. It was the animals of the diapsid line, or "two skull openings," that eventually gave rise to the dinosaurs. One of the more debatable lines is the euryapsids, characterized by a single opening on the side of the skull. They evolved into the placodonts ("plate tooth") ichthyosaurs and plesiosaurs—none of which were dinosaurs—and into all marine reptiles that quickly went extinct.

DINOSAURS APPEAR

How did the **reptiles** give rise to the **dinosaurs**?

It was the diapsid group of the reptiles that eventually produced the dinosaurs. The jaw muscles in these reptiles were attached to the two openings on each side of the skull, giving their jaws better leverage and

85

What are some of the earliest known primitive dinosaurs?

Two of the earliest known primitive dinosaurs were both fast-running carnivores: The *Eoraptor,* or "dawn hunter," a small, three-foot (one-meter) long dinosaur; and the *Herrerasaurus,* measuring from nine to 18 feet (three to six meters) long. Both lived approximately 230 million years ago, in the area known today as Argentina. Still another earlier dinosaur was the *Staurikosaurus,* a carnivore with a fully upright gait that allowed for speed. After the evolution of these early specimens, other dinosaurs evolved quickly, becoming more and more diverse, and reaching out into all the ecological niches.

strength. Sometime in the Permian period, the diapsid line branched into two groups, called the lepidosaurs and archosaurs. The lepidosaur group evolved into today's lizards and snakes; while the archosaurs, or "ancient lizards," gave rise to the thecodonts, which then gave rise to the dinosaurs, pterosaurs ("flying reptiles"), and crocodiles.

What were **early archosaurs** like?

One of the first archosaurs—and probably typical of many archosaurs—was the big-headed *Shansisuchus,* an early Triassic period creature that lived in the area now known as China. It was about 12 feet (4 meters) long, and had long back legs and short front legs.

What steps did **evolution** take to go from the **archosaurs to the dinosaur**?

The archosaurs eventually gave rise to the thecodonts, or socket-toothed reptiles, which then gave rise to the pterosaurs, crocodiles, and dinosaurs. In other words, the thecodonts are the direct ancestors of the dinosaurs. Some, like the *Gracilisuchus,* could run on their hind legs over short distances; others, like the *Chasmatosaurus,* were heavy carnivores that walked on all fours.

What was the **next stage** in the **evolution** toward true dinosaurs?

As time went on, another phase of dinosaur evolution took place: The animals' skeletal structure changed—especially the hips, which gave many of the dinosaurs the ability to run on two legs. *Euparkeria* was a small lizard-like reptile that lived on land and walked on all fours, but could run on two legs when in a hurry. Further along in time was *Ornithosuchus,* or "bird crocodile," which was a two-legged predator. Its front limbs were too small to use for walking on all fours, and its thighs were nearly vertical. From this evidence, it appears that *Ornithosuchus* walked only on its hind legs.

How were the dinosaurs **unique** among the **reptiles**?

Dinosaurs, unlike other reptiles, had their legs tucked in underneath their bodies. This gave them the ability to run and walk very efficiently, eventually leading to some species becoming totally bipedal (two-footed). They also had a keener sense of smell, sight, and hearing, unlike the amphibians and primitive reptiles.

What were **early carnivorous** and **herbivorous dinosaurs** like?

The earliest carnivorous dinosaurs, or meat-eaters, came in many different shapes and sizes. It is thought that the *Dilophosaurus* was a typical carnivore: The dinosaur had strong hind legs, but short, weak forelimbs. It also had thin parallel ridges on its forehead, which could have acted as radiators to control temperature, or as decoration, possibly for territorial or mating displays. The earliest herbivorous dinosaurs, or plant-eaters, also came in many different shapes and sizes. One typical herbivore was the *Heterodontosaurus,* a small, turkey-sized dinosaur that had sharp incisors, canine-like tusks, and grinding teeth for chewing plants.

How are **dinosaurs classified**?

Dinosaurs are in the Reptilia class of animals—thus, they are called reptiles. They are from the subclass of diapsids, and in their own infraclass of dinosauria. They are divided into two main groups, based historically on their hip-bone structure. Those with hips that had the two lower bones pointing in opposite directions, with the pubis bone pointing forward, were called saurischian, or lizard-hipped, dinosaurs. Those with hips that had the two lower bones lying together behind the back legs, and the pubis bone pointing backward, were called ornithischian, or bird-hipped, dinosaurs. The *Tyrannosaurus rex* is an example of a lizard-hipped dinosaur, while the *Iguanodon* is an example of a bird-hipped dinosaur.

How are **dinosaurs named**?

Dinosaur names come from a number of places, but in general, they are named after a characteristic body feature (for example, the *Hypsilophodon,* or high-crowned tooth); after the place in which the first bones were found (for example, the *Muttaburrasaurus*); or after the person(s) involved in the discovery (for example, the *Leaellynasaura*).

In many cases, the names include two Greek or Latin words, or even combinations of the words. For example, *Tyrannosaurus rex* is a combination of Greek and Latin, which translates as, "king of the tyrant lizards." Overall, the two names, known as the genus and species names, are used by biologists to describe all organisms on Earth, such as humans (*Homo sapiens*), domestic dogs (*Canis familiaris*), or rattlesnakes (*Crotalus horridus*).

How many **species of dinosaurs** are currently known?

Currently, approximately 700 species of dinosaurs have been named. But there is a major caveat: Only about half of these specimens are complete skeletons—and usually only complete (or nearly-complete) skeletons allow scientists to confidently say the bones represent unique and separate species. All of the species are listed in the approximately 300 verified dinosaur genera—which are groups (such as *Tyrannosaurus* or "tyrant lizard") of species (such as *Tyrannosaurus rex*, or "king of the tyrant lizards") linked by common characteristics. Amazingly, many scientists speculate there may be 700 to 900 more dinosaur genera that have yet to be discovered!

What kinds of dinosaurs were in the saurischian group?

The saurischians were a diverse group of dinosaurs, which included both carnivores and herbivores. They exhibited two-legged and four-legged means of propulsion.

The carnivores included the large, two-legged *Allosaurus*, *Ceratosaurus*, *Tarbosaurus*, and the *Tyrannosaurus*. There were smaller, two-legged carnivores, such as *Ornithomimus*, and the *Dromaeosaurus*, which had specialized feet and their unique, slashing, raptorial claws.

The herbivorous saurischians that are best known are the large, four-legged sauropods, the largest dinosaurs to have walked the Earth. These dinosaurs had long necks and tails, with relatively tiny heads. Included in this group are *Brachiosaurus*, *Camarasaurus*, *Diplodocus*, *Mamenchisaurus*, and *Seismosaurus*.

How do the number of known **dinosaur species compare** to some modern species?

Even if there are truly 700 valid dinosaur species, the number is still less than one-tenth the number of currently known bird species; less than one-fifth the number of known mammal species; and less than one-third the number of known spider species.

What **kinds of dinosaurs** were in the **ornithischian** group?

The ornithischians were all herbivores and had two and four-legged types. There were the four-legged armored dinosaurs such as *Ankylosaurus* and *Stegosaurus*. There were large, horned dinosaurs such as *Eucentrosaurus* and *Triceratops*. Two-legged types included *Iguanodon*, and many of the duck-billed dinosaurs (hadrosaurs), such as *Cory-thosaurus, Lambeosaurus,* and *Maiasaura.*

How did **dinosaurs evolve**?

The following chart offers a simplified vision of dinosaur evolution. Ideas expressed on this chart will no doubt modify over time, as more dinosaur fossils are discovered.

Evolutionary Tree of the Dinosaur

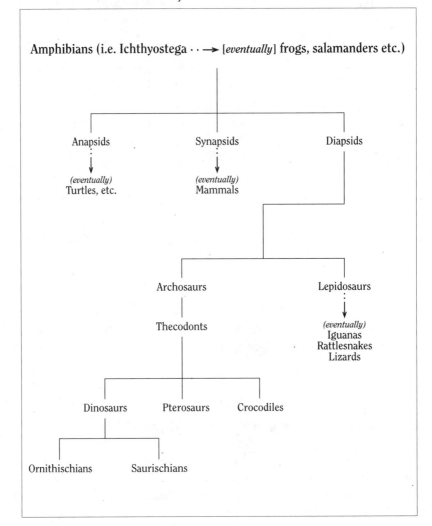

DINOSAURS IN THE MESOZOIC

What **events** led to the **dominance** of dinosaurs in the **Mesozoic** era?

Approximately 250 million years ago, at the end of the Permian period, or the beginning of the Triassic period (and thus, the end of the Paleozoic era and the beginning of the Mesozoic era), there was a mass extinction. This extinction eliminated close to 90 percent of all the species present on our planet—coming extraordinarily close to total extinction on Earth. The extinction was not selective; it eliminated organisms in the oceans and on land, including many invertebrates, armored fish, and reptiles.

The true reasons for the extinction are unknown, although there are several theories. One is that a collision of the Earth with an asteroid or comet caused dust and debris to fly into the upper atmosphere, cutting off sunlight and radically changing the global climate. Another idea is that the moving continents changed the climate, sea levels, and thus, habitats, causing some species to change and adapt, while others died out. Still another theory focuses on Siberian flood basalts, in which tons of volcanic material erupted over a huge area in Asia toward the end of the Permian, changing the climate and certain habitats.

Whatever the scenario, species that survived did so by adapting to the ecological niches that became vacant, allowing them to further evolve. After the Permian extinction, and throughout the Mesozoic era, it was the reptiles in general, and the dinosaurs specifically, who diversified the most and became the dominant species on Earth.

How **long** were dinosaurs **dominant** on Earth?

The dinosaurs were the dominant species on Earth for approximately 140 to 150 million years. The Mesozoic era, often referred to as the "age of the reptiles," lasted from approximately 250 to 65 million years ago. It includes the Triassic, Jurassic, and Cretaceous periods.

It is interesting to note that at the beginning of the Mesozoic, there were no dinosaurs; other reptiles were dominant. But, by the end of the Triassic period, the dinosaurs became dominant—and stayed that way for about 140 to 150 million years. Dinosaurs were not the only form of life that existed during this time. For example, there were smaller, lizard-like reptiles, small early mammals, insects, amphibians, invertebrates, and a wide variety of plants. In fact, these organisms helped the dinosaurs to stay dominant—as many of the dinosaurs used this abundance of life for their sustenance and growth.

When did the **age of dinosaurs end**?

The age of the dinosaurs came to an end approximately 65 million years ago. From this point onward, there are currently no known dinosaur fossils. The time of the great dinosaur (and other species) extinction is used by scientists to delineate the end of the Cretaceous period as well as the end of the Mesozoic era. After this point, the Cenozoic era begins, starting with the Tertiary period.

TRIASSIC PERIOD

What is the **Triassic period** and how did it get its **name**?

The Triassic period follows the Permian period on the geological time scale. During this time, dinosaurs first began to evolve from the thecodont reptiles, the first primitive mammals appeared, and the armored amphibians and mammal-like reptiles died out. The Triassic was one of the first labeled divisions on the geologic time scale. It is named after three (or "tri-") layers of sedimentary rocks representative of the time period—from bottom to top, a sandstone, limestone, and copper-bearing shale—first found and analyzed in Germany. The Triassic is the first of three periods (the others are Jurassic and Cretaceous) making up the Mesozoic era.

How long did the **Triassic period last**?

The geologic time scale is not exact, and depending on the country or scientist, the dates of the Triassic period can vary by about five to ten million years. On the average, the Triassic period is said to have lasted from about 250 to 205 million years ago, for a total of about 45 million years in length.

What are the **divisions** of the **Triassic period**?

In general, the informal way to define parts of the Triassic period is to use the terms lower, middle, and upper Triassic. More formally, they are capitalized (Lower, Middle, and Upper) and include subdivisions within

A plateosaurus roams the land during the Triassic period. (Photo courtesy of University of Michigan Exhibit Museum of Natural History.)

those groupings. The following table lists a general interpretation of the Triassic epochs (although note that many researchers use slightly different notations; for example, many do not list the Rhaetian Age).

Triassic Period

Epoch	Age	Millions of Years Ago (approximate)
Late	Rhaetian	210 to 205
	Norian	221 to 210
	Carnian	227 to 221
Middle	Ladinian	234 to 227
	Anisian	242 to 234
Early	Olenekian	245 to 242
	Induan	250 to 245

What did the **Triassic period signify**?

The Triassic period represented the time after the great Permian period extinctions. It also was important as a time of transition—when the old life of the Paleozoic era gave way to a more highly developed and varied form of life of the Mesozoic era. The Permian period extinctions wiped out most of the animals and plants on the Earth (about 90 percent of all species), making the very early Triassic an eerie place, almost completely devoid of the abundant life that existed for perhaps hundreds or thousands of years before. Certain flora and fauna still dotted the land, and eventually, after about 10 million years or more, life began to emerge in full force again. But it still took even longer for larger animals, coral reefs, and other specialized animals to recover or evolve after the extinction at the end of the Permian period.

THE CONTINENTS DURING THE TRIASSIC PERIOD

Do the Earth's **continents change positions**?

Yes, the continents continually change positions, but it takes them millions of years to shift and move great distances. The Earth's continents are actually part of the thick plates that make up the planet's crust, all of various sizes and shapes. These plates fit together like a jigsaw puzzle. They don't move fast—only fractions of an inch to inches per year.

What are **continental drift** and **plate tectonics**?

The reason (or reasons) for the Earth's crustal movement is still somewhat of a mystery. The most accepted theory of plate movement is called continental drift, and the theory of its mechanism is called plate tectonics. These theories suggest that the continental plates move laterally across the face of the planet, driven by the lower, more fluid mantle of the Earth. At certain plate boundaries, molten rock from the mantle rises at a mid-ocean ridge (such as the Mid-Atlantic Ridge, a long chain of volcanic mountains that lie under the Atlantic Ocean) or at its equivalent on land, the rift valley (such as the one in eastern Africa), the magma solidifying and moving away to either side of the ridge. At other

97

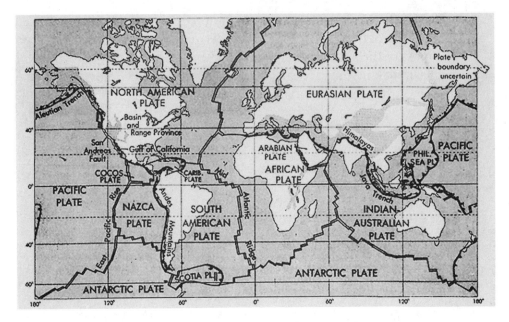

Plate tectonics.

plate boundaries, plates are pushed under an adjacent plate, forming a subduction zone, in which the crust sinks into the mantle again. And at other boundaries, plates just slip by, which is what happens at the San Andreas Fault in California, where a part of the North American plate slides by the Pacific plate.

But not everyone agrees on these theories. One reason is because, although the idea of moving plates seems logical, the mechanisms for developing plate tectonics are not fully understood. Therefore, some scientists believe in continental drift, but not plate tectonics. Most of these scientists believe that the reason that the continents shift is that the Earth is actually expanding, causing a false illusion of movement (although no one can explain why or how the Earth is expanding). Another hypothesis is called surge tectonics, in which the features of the Earth's surface are explained by the sudden surge of plate movement, as opposed to a constant flow created by the steady movement of the mantle. And still others suggest that the continents have always been in the same positions.

Overall, no one really can explain the reason for the continual movement of the plates. One thing is certain: The plates do move. Since the advent of Earth-orbiting observation satellites, scientists have been able

German meteorologist and geophysicist Alfred Wegener. (Photo courtesy of UPI/Corbis-Bettman.)

to track the plates using sophisticated laser-ranging instruments that measure the minute movements.

When did scientists **determine** the jigsaw puzzle **fit of the continents**?

The actual connection between the continental fit was first proposed in 1858, by Antonio Snider. Other scientists mentioned this idea for years afterward, but it was not until 1912 that German meteorologist and geophysicist Alfred Wegener (1880–1930) expanded the theory, suggesting that the continents at one time formed a supercontinent he called

99

What did the Earth look like at the start of the Triassic period?

Similar to today, most of the Earth during the Triassic period was ocean, but the distribution of the landmasses was not the same. Scientists believe there was essentially one large expanse of water called the Panthalassa Ocean. It surrounded the one very large landmass, or supercontinent, called Pangea, meaning "All Earth." This giant landmass straddled the planet's equator roughly in the form of a "C"; the smaller body of water enclosed by the "C" on the east was known as the Tethys Sea (or Ocean). Only a few scattered bits of continental crust were not attached to Pangea, and lay to the east of the larger continent. They included pieces of what we now call Manchuria (northern China), eastern China, Indochina, and bits of central Asia. In addition, the sea level was low, and there was no ice at the polar regions.

Pangea (or Pangaea). Wegener's theory was not taken seriously until about the 1960s, when scientists believed they had finally worked out a mechanism (plate tectonics) for the movement of the continental plates.

What is **biogeography**?

Biogeography examines the distribution of plants and animals in terms of climate; barriers to the spread of the organisms (such as where the organisms are in relationship to barriers such as the oceans, mountains, and deserts); geographical distribution of resources and rock types; and the evolutionary history of the organisms.

Why is **biogeography** important to the study of **ancient life**?

Biogeography is important to the study of ancient life for many reasons. In particular, it helps scientists discover information about the past dis-

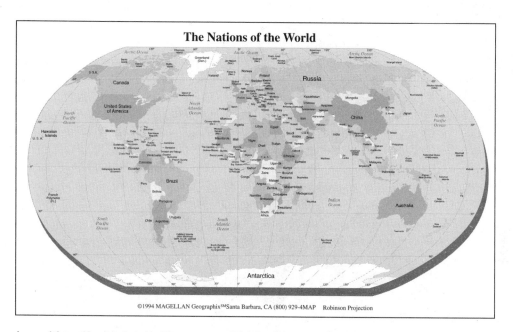

The Nations of the World

©1994 MAGELLAN Geographix℠Santa Barbara, CA (800) 929-4MAP   Robinson Projection

A map of the world as it looks today. (Photo courtesy of Magellan Geopraphix/Corbis Corporation.)

tributions of plants and animals; the position and movement of the continents, oceans, and islands over time; and it reveals information about past climates. Overall, the field is called paleobiogeography.

Paleobiogeography is also one of the reasons scientists discovered that the continental plates actually moved across the Earth's surface. Initially, scientists found that the *Dryosaurus* from the late Jurassic of North America's Rocky Mountains seemed to be closely related to the *Dysalotosaurus* of the Late Jurassic of southern Tanzania, Africa. The researchers speculated that the creatures must have somehow lived close to each other, even though today, the continents are far apart. Now they know, based on paleobiogeography, sea-floor spreading, and other evidence, that Africa was adjacent to South America and not far from North America during the late Jurassic. Thus, the two species were put into a single genus, *Dryosaurus,* based on geographical grounds.

Paleobiogeography has since been used to discover additional information about the Earth's early fauna (animals) and flora (plants). For example, it showed that the position and movement of the continents had a profound effect on the distribution of the early ancestors of the dinosaurs—and eventually, on the dinosaurs themselves.

101

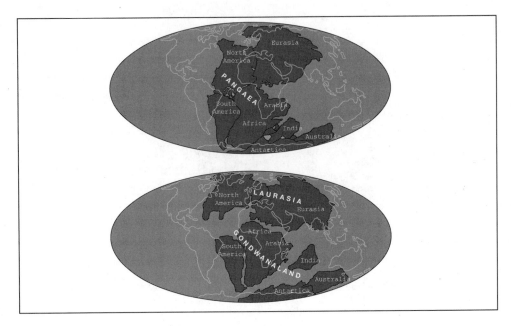

The supercontinent Pangea broke apart to form Laurasia and Gondwanaland. (Photo courtesy of AP/Wide World.)

What led to the original **formation of the supercontinent Pangea**?

Scientists believe the same process that would eventually break apart Pangea led to its formation—the continents seemingly moving around the planet like icebergs on an ocean. There were two large landmasses on Earth during the Paleozoic era—Laurasia (made up of present-day North America and Eurasia) to the north of the equator, and Gondwanaland (or Gondwana; including South America, Africa, India, Antarctica, and Australia) to the south of the equator. These two continents slowly collided during the late Paleozoic era, forming the supercontinent of Pangea. By the beginning of the Mesozoic era, Pangea was still the only true continent on the planet.

How did **the supercontinent Pangea** change during the **Triassic period**?

In the early Triassic period, Pangea gradually began to break apart into two major continents again, the result of a seafloor-spreading rift. (This rift was similar to today's mid-ocean ridge in the Atlantic Ocean, a volcanic seam that continues to spread, and along which the volcanic island of Iceland was born.) The Triassic rift extended westward from the Tethys Sea across what is today the Mediterranean Sea. The action of this rift separated northern Laurasia from southern Gondwanaland, which would eventually lead to the opening of the proto-Atlantic (or early Atlantic) Ocean. As northern Africa split from southern Europe, there was a gradual rise in sea level that flooded south and central Europe.

Toward the middle and late Triassic period, the spreading rift between northern Africa and Europe grew westward, and began to separate Africa from the eastern part of North America. The resulting rift valley was the first true stage in the formation of the proto-Atlantic Ocean.

Where are **Triassic period rocks** found?

Layers of Triassic period rocks are found in many countries around the world. They occur in certain localities in eastern and western North America, South America, the British Isles, western Europe, Asia, Africa, and Australia. The thickest Triassic period rock layer so far discovered lies in the Alps and it measures about 25,000 feet (7,500 meters) thick.

How did the **Newark Supergroup** form and why does it contain so many Triassic fossils?

The movement of the continental plates was mainly responsible for a westward-spreading tear in the Earth's crust between North America and northern Africa. This area of thinning and stretching became a rift valley, similar to the one found today in northeast Africa. The valley, with its shallow lakes, streams, and swamps, became one of the prime habitats for many flora and fauna of the Triassic period. As death occurred, the organisms' remains were apparently quickly buried by the large amounts of sediments eroding from the Appalachia Mountains to the west. Over millions of years, the pressures changed the sediments to rock and preserved the remains as fossils.

What is the **Newark Supergroup** and why is it **significant**?

The Newark Supergroup is a layer of Triassic period rocks located in the eastern United States; it is famous for its rocks and fossils from this period. The rock layers represent the remnants of several thousands of feet of sedimentary and volcanic rocks deposited in a chain of basins over a span of 45 million years. This layer is found in many locations, including New Jersey, Virginia, and North Carolina. The sedimentary strata (layers) contain a good cross-section of fossils from the late Triassic period, including insects, fish, turtles, archosaurian reptiles (including dinosaurs, lizards, and snakes), lissamphibians (frogs, salamanders, and caecilians), and numerous plant fossils. Paleontologists hope to find additional vertebrate fossils in the Newark Supergroup layers that will shed more light on the stages that lead to the evolution of groups of many organisms—especially the dinosaurs— during the Triassic period.

What were the **major oceans** during the **Triassic period**?

There was only one large ocean during the Triassic period, the Panthalassa Ocean. A smaller body of water was called the Tethys Sea (or Ocean), which was actually a huge bay to the east of the supercontinent Pangea. Eventually, late in the Triassic period, Pangea's separation into northern Laurasia and southern Gonwanaland led to the opening that became the early Atlantic Ocean.

What were the major **ocean currents** during the **Triassic period**?

Because there was one major continent during the Triassic period, the ocean currents were much different than they are today. There were warm currents generated around the equator, slipping up the east coast of the supercontinent Pangea in a general northward direction. Cooler currents ran by the western coast of the continent, one from the north and one from the south—with both converging at the equator. The Tethys Ocean (also called the Tethys Sea) also contained several cooler currents, all of which flowed southward past the west coasts of the larger islands and toward the equator.

What was the **climate** like during the **Triassic period**?

Because the landmass Pangea straddled the Earth's equator, the temperature on land during the Triassic period was constantly warm and dry.

What were these first true dinosaurs like?

Based on current fossil finds, the first true dinosaurs emerged in the Late Triassic period, between about 230 to 225 million years ago. They were small, agile, carnivorous reptiles whose unique characteristics, such as two-legged motion, enabled them to quickly dominate the available ecological niches.

Apparently, by the time dinosaurs evolved, they had already split, even at this early stage, into two major groups: the ornithischians and the saurischians. These two main groups of dinosaurs are based historically on their hip bone structure.

There were no polar ice caps or large inland seas to truly change the conditions or affect the climate. Because of this, too, there was little seasonal variation in temperatures, and the climate around the equator stayed relatively stable all year long. The only differences in climate came toward the end of the Triassic period, when the land became hotter and drier. The fossil record does show one puzzling finding: The plant life between northern and southern Pangea seem to be extremely diverse and distinct, indicating a difference in climate. But so far, scientists have no explanation for the difference in plant life.

What was the **landscape** like during the **Triassic period**?

There were many changes in the landscape during the Triassic period—but there were too many to explain them all here! In summary, during the early Triassic period (and the late Permian period), the area we now know as Siberia released huge fields of volcanic material, called the Siberian Traps. Volcanic activity was also occurring in the areas we know today as Europe, North and South America, and northwestern Africa. This activity created the opening that became the Atlantic Ocean. Pangea also began to break up slowly into two large continents; and as the planet's crust stretched in response, huge areas collapsed (or subsided), creating many large basins that filled with water.

During the middle and late Triassic period, several mountains were being pushed up by the movement of the continental plates, including a swath of land extending from present-day Alaska to Chile—a process that is similar to the current rising of the Andes Mountains of South America—created as the Pacific Ocean crust wedged (subducted) beneath the Americas.

MAJOR TRIASSIC DINOSAURS

Were there many **dinosaurs during the Triassic period**?

Based on the current findings in fossil records, there were not many dinosaurs living during the Triassic period. Dinosaurs began to evolve from the reptiles toward the end of the Triassic period, but great numbers of the creatures did not flourish until the Jurassic period.

Why did the **dinosaurs** begin to **thrive** in the **late Triassic period**?

Scientists theorize that there were a number of reasons for the emergence of dinosaurs in the late Triassic period. One reason was that dinosaurs evolved to become biologically superior. For example, they developed an erect posture with bipedal motion. This development gave them a longer stride and quickness, enabling them to catch and devour semi-erect reptiles. Another adaptation might have been warm-bloodedness—although this idea is highly controversial. If it is true that the reptiles developed a form of warm-bloodedness, it would have allowed them to be more active than their cold-blooded cousins.

Still other scientists feel that these adaptations were not the reason for the dominance of dinosaurs. Instead, they believe a major extinction of the therapsids (reptilian ancestors of mammals), rhynchosaurs (lizard-like reptiles), and early archosaurs (reptiles comprising dinosaurs, pterosaurs, and crocodilians) in the middle of the Triassic period opened up ecological niches that the dinosaurs then filled.

What were some of the **early dinosaurs**?

This partial list describes some early dinosaurs of the Triassic period. It will undoubtedly change in the future as more dinosaur fossils are found and dated.

Selected Triassic Period Dinosaurs

Name	Common Name	Approximate Age (millions of years ago)	Locality	Length (feet/meters)
Anchisaurus	Near Lizard	200-190	USA	up to 6.5/2
Coelophysis	Hollow Form	225-220	USA	up to 10/3
Eoraptor	Dawn Hunter	225	Argentina	up to 3/1
Herrerasaurus	Herrera Lizard	230-225	Argentina	up to 10/3
Plateosaurus	Flat Lizard	about 210	France, Germany & Switzerland	up to 23/7

Which **Triassic period dinosaurs** were **herbivores**?

There were numerous herbivorous dinosaurs that evolved at the end of the Triassic period. The *Thecodontosaurus*, a small herbivore, was one of the first Triassic dinosaurs ever found; it was reported in England in 1836. The *Plateosaurus* was also a plant-eating dinosaur that lived during the Triassic period; the first fossils were found in Germany in 1837. They were considered the first really large dinosaurs, and had peg-like teeth and huge thumb claws that were perhaps used to gather plants from taller trees.

Which **Triassic period dinosaurs** were **carnivores**?

The first carnivorous dinosaurs in the Triassic period were the *Eoraptor* and *Herrerasaurus*. Both dinosaurs were small and bipedal, with powerful hindlimbs and long tails for balance. The later *Coelophysis* was also a

Plateosaurus, the largest member of the prosauropod group, reached lengths of up to 26 feet. This dinosaur fed on ground-level plants and the leaves of tall trees, its long neck enabling it to seek food at various heights. Its fossilized remains have been found in what is now Germany. This model, one-tenth the actual size, represents the body structure common to all prosauropods.

A *Plateosaurus*, a major herbivore during the Triassic period. (Photo courtesy of University of Michigan Exhibit Museum of Natural History.)

meat-eater. Some of the first fossils of this dinosaur were found in the southwestern United States—and were the first to show evidence of a herding behavior.

What were the **smallest dinosaurs** known to have existed during the **Triassic period**?

At present, the smallest Triassic period dinosaurs known to have existed were the early, carnivorous bipeds, *Eoraptor* and *Herrerasaurus*. The *Eoraptor* was about three feet (one meter) long; whereas the *Herrerasaurus* was about nine to 18 feet (three to six meters) in length.

What was the **largest dinosaur** known to have existed during the **Triassic period**?

At present, the largest dinosaur known to have existed during the Triassic was the herbivorous *Plateosaurus,* with a length of up to 23 feet (seven meters).

Did any **Triassic period dinosaurs fly**?

No. As was true throughout the entire Mesozoic era, there were flying and gliding reptiles—but never any flying dinosaurs.

Did any **Triassic period dinosaurs** live in the **oceans**?

No. There were a variety of marine reptiles in the water, but at no time did marine dinosaurs exist. The entire classification of dinosaurs is limited to land-dwelling reptiles with specific characteristics.

OTHER LIFE
IN THE TRIASSIC PERIOD

What were the **major groups of land organisms**?

The true numbers, types, names, and evolutionary events of the Triassic land animals is often highly debated—which is typical when we try to interpret our ancient past. (Fossils are subject to explanations that sometimes vary from scientists to scientist—often making it difficult to arrive at any definite statements about these animals.)

The following are the major Triassic land organisms.

Amphibians
Primitive amphibians: only a few large, primitive amphibians, called labyrinthodonts, survived into the Mesozoic era after the Permian period extinction; they gradually declined in abundance and diversity during the Mesozoic; most of them were aquatic, the majority living in freshwater environments.

Primitive frogs, toads: first links to these modern amphibians (or lissamphibians) evolve during the early Triassic; the oldest member of the frog group was the *Triadobatrachus,* which is the only known link between the true frogs with jumping motion and the primitive ancestors of frogs.

109

Reptiles (anapsids, diapsids, and euryapsids)

First turtles: of the several Paleozoic groups of anapsids, only turtles and procolophonids survived into the Mesozoic; the oldest subgroup, proganochelydians, were moderately large, but the animal could not pull its head inside its shell.

Procolophonids: lizard-like in their overall habits and shape; they probably ate insects and smaller animals, and some plant material; even though they looked like lizards, the true lizards did not appear until the late Jurassic.

Rhynchosaurs: short-lived diapsid reptiles of the group Archosauromorpha; they were herbivorous, walked on all fours, and had huge beaks that helped them bite off vegetation; they were so widespread during the Triassic that their fossils are often used to correlate deposits on different continents.

Tanystropheids: very short-lived diapsid reptiles of the group Archosauromorpha; they lived near (and sometimes in) marine waters; they had an extremely odd shape, with a tiny head on an extremely long neck, and a short, medium-sized body; the reason for such a long neck is unknown, but one theory suggests that it helped the tanystropheid stretch its neck low over the water in order to catch fish.

Archosaurs: part of the diapsid reptile group Archosauromorpha, and the dominant tetrapods on the continents during most of the Mesozoic; the archosaurs ("ruling reptiles") were the precursors to dinosaurs; they are characterized by their better adaptation of legs, feet, and hips, giving them agility on land; others categorize the archosaurs by the openings in their skull; the earliest archosaurs were relatively large and carnivorous, and either lived on land or led a semi-aquatic existence.

aetosaurs: heavily armored, herbivorous archosaurs.

phytosaurs: lived during the late Triassic only, and looked very much like modern crocodiles.

crocodylomorphs: a group that includes crocodiles, alligators, caimans, and gavlals, known to exist from the late Triassic to the present; not all survived to the present, including the fast-running saltoposuchians.

rauischians: the creature's upright front and hind legs were under the trunk of the body, making them the dominant land predator during the Triassic period.

ornithosuchian: relatively large (ten feet [three meters] in length), land predators that may have walked on all fours, but ran fast only on the hind legs; they were the most dinosaur-like of the non-dinosaur archosaurs.

ornithodira: the middle and late Triassic group of archosaurs to which the dinosaurs belong; it also includes the pterosaurs, birds, and some early forms of creatures that appear to be closely related to dinosaurs and pterosaurs.

Aerial Reptiles (diapsids)

Gliding reptiles: the three main late Triassic gliding reptiles used either skin membranes on the wings and legs (such as the *Sharovipteryx*), scales (*Longisquama*), or fan-like wings (*Kuehneosaurus*)—all of which acted as an airfoil, allowing the reptiles to glide through the air; they probably did not flap their "wings" for powered flight.

Flying reptiles: the pterosaurs (also called pterodactyls, which actually refers to only one subgroup of pterosaurs); the front legs (or arms) were modified into true wings by the elongation of the fourth finger, which supported a skin membrane stretching to the body; they probably flapped their wings occasionally for powered flight; they lived from the ocean shores and inland, eating fish, insects, and other small animals; they evolved during the late Triassic period.

Mammals and Their Reptile-like Relatives (synapsids)

Therapsids: more advanced synapsids; varied group of mammal-like reptiles that apparently evolved from the pelycosaurs, the earliest known mammal-like reptiles that evolved in the late Carboniferous period, about 290 million years ago, and went extinct in the late Permian period; the biggest change was their ability to walk more efficiently with their limbs tucked beneath their body, whereas pelycosaurs walked with their limbs in a sprawled position; one group of therapsids gave rise to mammals, known from the late Triassic to today.

anomodonts: the most common subgroup were the dicynodonts, large, herbivorous, mammal-like reptiles; it includes the *Lystrosaurus*, a three-to-six-foot (one-to-two meter) long, pig-like animal that has been found as fossils in Australia, South Africa, India, China, and Antarctica, and hippopotamus-like *Kannemeyeria,* a ten-foot (three-meter) long animal with two big canine-like teeth in the upper jaw that died out during the late Triassic period.

111

Were there any flying animals during the Triassic period?

The first true flying animals were reptiles called pterosaurs. One of the first of these flying creatures was the *Eudimorphodon*. This reptile probably skimmed the surface of the water looking for fish, using the end of its long tail as a "rudder" to steer through the air. With a sufficient wing span and structure, *Eudimorphodon* is considered to have been a heavy flyer, similar to a modern bird. Other reptiles also took to the air, but only glided. For example, the *Kuehneosaurus* used a membrane stretched over its elongated ribs as a kind of parachute. The creature would then close the membranes when resting in a tree, folding both sides like fans close to the sides of its body.

cynodonts: carnivorous, mammal-like therapsid reptiles; they walked more upright, with limbs held more underneath their bodies; some were probably wolf-like animals, and some seem to have had whiskers, pointing to the possibility that they had fur, and thus, may have been warm-blooded; they evolved during the late Permian to the middle Jurassic; at least one group of cynodonts evolved into mammals.

therocephalians: existed from the late Permian to middle Triassic period, these therapsid reptiles had their peak during the late Paleozoic era; they were small to middle sized, walked on all fours, and ate insects or small animals.

True mammals: small, about the size of a rat or mouse, with the largest about the size of a cat; they were probably nocturnal; they probably ate insects or small animals, and at least one group ate plants; they evolved in the latter part of the Triassic, at the same time as the dinosaurs first appeared.

triconodonts: late Triassic to late Cretaceous mammals; among the oldest fossil mammals; three cusps of teeth in a straight row give them their name.

haramyoids: late Triassic to middle Jurassic mammals; among the oldest fossil mammals; their teeth had many cusps in at least two parallel rows.

Other Creatures

Insects: very profuse.

Spiders: very profuse; spiders had been around for millions of years already, showing up in fossils dating back to the Cambrian period.

Earthworms: very profuse; earthworms had been around for millions of years already, showing up in fossils dating back to the Cambrian period.

If the dinosaurs were just evolving, which **land and marine animals dominated** the **Triassic period**?

On land, the true dominant species of the Triassic period, even after the dinosaurs started to evolve during the late Triassic, were the non-dinosaurian predators, the archosaurs; the main herbivores were the dicynodont (synapsids). In the oceans, many types of reptiles and fishes dominated.

What were the **major land plants** living during the **Triassic period**?

The Triassic land plants flourished in the hot climate. The main vegetative types were conifers, which could easily adapt to changing water conditions (dry or damp). Gymnosperms bore seeds, including conifers, cycads, and ginkos. The following table lists some of the major plants.

Major Triassic Land Plants

cycads	leaves are similar to palm fronds, with unbranched, usually bulbous trunks; they had specialized pollen and seed cones for reproduction; ten genera survive today
horsetails	massive plants similar to the horsetails we find in the wild today
conifers	grew as trees and shrubs; the trees would reproduce with seeds found on the projecting scales of the conifer cones; the petrified wood found in the late Triassic layer of the Chinle formation, at Arizona's Petrified Forest, are conifers (they are almost identical to the modern Norfolk Island pines)

113

ginkos	the leaves were fan-shaped, and similar to the one remaining species, the *Gingko biloba*; the sex organs were on stalks, with separate male and female trees
cycadeoids (bennettitales)	leaves are similar to palm fronds, and thus, somewhat similar to cycads; a fruiting stalk contained the pollen and seeds for reproduction; they may be more closely related to flowering plants than cycads, as the fruiting stalks somewhat resembled primitive flowers; none survive today, as the cycadeoids became extinct at the end of the Cretaceous period

What were the **major marine animals** living during the **Triassic period**?

There were many marine animals that swam the oceans of the Triassic, and many of the species still continue to this day. In general, the oceans held the animals listed in the following table, although with new fossil discoveries, this list may eventually change.

Reptiles (euryapsids)	
ichthyosaurs	or "fish reptiles," were predatory sea reptiles that probably preyed mostly on shellfish, fish, and other marine reptiles; they looked similar to, and probably had some of the same habits of, modern dolphins, whales, and sharks; they lived in the oceans from the early Triassic to middle Cretaceous periods, probably outcompeted by the mosasaurs of the middle Cretaceous period
plesiosaurs	medium to large, long- to short-necked reptiles, with bulbous bodies; their four legs were modified into paddles; they probably ate mostly fish; they lived mostly in marine environments, but some also lived in freshwater lakes; they lived from the early Triassic to the end of the Cretaceous period and are often sighted as the model for what the Loch Ness monster is presumed to look like
placodonts	large marine reptiles that had long trunks and tails, with feet that were probably webbed; their teeth were used for crushing, and they probably ate clams and other shelled invertebrates from the ocean floor
nothosaurs	small to moderate-sized marine reptiles with long necks and sharp, conical teeth for spearing fish; their legs were modified flippers, rather than the paddle-shaped legs of the more advanced eurapsids; they lived from the early to late Triassic period

114

Ginkos were one of several plants flourishing in the Triassic period. (Photo courtesy of Field Mark Publications.)

Other Marine Creatures

sea urchins	the few pencil urchins that survived the Permian period extinction are also the ancestors of all modern urchins; the Triassic period was also the time of the first burrowing urchins
corals	first relatives to the modern corals evolved during the Triassic period
crabs and lobsters —crustaceans	first close relatives of modern crabs and lobsters evolved during the Triassic period
ammonoids	ammonoids, or chamber-shelled organisms, rapidly diversified during the Triassic period
bony fishes	found in salt, brackish, and fresh water, and could often move back and forth among the three; they are divided into two groups, based on their structure: the ray-finned (for example, the Triassic period's *Perleidus*) and lobe-finned (for example, the Triassic period's *Diplurus*)
sharks	during the Triassic, the intermediate form between primitive and modern sharks evolved; the earliest sharks evolved during the Paleozoic era, middle Devonian period, about 130 million years before; one of the modern survivors of this group is the Port Jackson shark

What were the **most vicious marine reptiles** in the **Triassic period seas**?

Probably the most notorious marine reptiles were the plesiosaurs, or "near lizards," giant reptiles that evolved during the Triassic period and became extinct at the end of the Cretaceous period. They lived in the water and ate fish to survive; but one group of plesiosaurs, the pliosaurs, became very large, feeding on other, large marine reptiles. The plesiosaurs have been described as "a snake drawn through the body of a turtle," with long necks and bulbous bodies. Most of them lived in the oceans, but there were some species that adapted to freshwater lakes.

What **discovery** was recently made about the **plesiosaur's diet**?

Recently, a partial plesiosaur skeleton was excavated out of an outcrop along a river on the island of Hokkaido, Japan. In the stomach area of the fossilized skeleton, pieces of tiny, beak-like ammonite jaws were found, measuring less than six-tenths of an inch (1.5 centimeters) long. Ammonites were spiral-shelled mollusks that are now extinct. Scientists feel that these jaws did not get there by accident, but were preserved as dietary remains within the digestive tract of the plesiosaur. The size of the jaws also suggests that the mollusks were very small.

The teeth of smaller plesiosaurs have long been regarded as being too slight to crush the hard shells of ammonites, but this latest evidence suggests that these marine predators did indeed make ammonites part of their diet. The way scientists see it, the plesiosaurs simply swallowed the small ammonites whole—a kind of plesiosaur popcorn!

What animals lived near **freshwater rivers, lakes, and ponds** during the **Triassic**?

Animals that lived near freshwater rivers, lakes, and ponds included several types of broad-headed amphibians and phytosaurs, distant relatives of the crocodiles. These animals were in search of the shellfish and fish that lived in the rivers and lakes. Other reptiles would frequent the shorelines of the lakes and ponds, including several of the early dinosaur species, and smaller reptiles.

JURASSIC PERIOD

What is the **Jurassic period** and how did it get its **name**?

The Jurassic period follows the Triassic period on the geological time scale. Though the dinosaurs had their origins and approximately 25 million years of evolution in the Triassic period, it wasn't until the Jurassic period that this group really blossomed. This was the time when the giant, herbivorous sauropods like *Apatosaurus* roamed the land; when plated dinosaurs like *Stegosaurus* first appeared; and when large carnivorous species like *Allosaurus* preyed on the other dinosaurs. It was also when *Archaeopteryx*—a creature that many paleontologists consider to be the first ancestor of the birds—flew through the air.

The name Jurassic comes from the Jura mountain range, a chain of mountains that straddle the border between France and Switzerland. It was here that the first Jurassic period sedimentary rock and accompanying fossils were found. The Jurassic is the second of three periods (the first is the Triassic and the last is the Cretacous) making up the Mesozoic era.

How long did the **Jurassic period last**?

The Jurassic period lasted from approximately 202 (or 205) to 141 million years ago, a time period of approximately 60 million years. The exact dates are debated, of course, and there are some variations of the dates in the literature, but the time frame is close.

What are the **divisions** of the **Jurassic period**?

The Jurassic period has been divided into three main divisions, or epochs: Scientists use the Early, Middle and Late; more informally, the period is labeled with lowercase letters, or the early, middle, and late Jurassic. In turn, each of these main epochs is further broken up into subdivisions. To make things more confusing, these small ages have different names (and often dates) depending on whether you are using European, North American, or Australian and New Zealand nomenclature. The following table gives the general North American divisions of the Jurassic period. These dates are not absolute, and may vary slightly from source to source.

Jurassic Period

Epoch	Age	Millions of Years Ago (approximate)
Late	Morrison	156 to 141
	Sundance	163 to 156
Middle	Twin Creek	170 to 163
	Gypsum Springs	178 to 170
Early	Navajo	195 to 178
	Kayenta	202 to 195

What is the **Morrison formation** and where is it found?

The Morrison formation is a layer of sedimentary rocks that are world famous for the number and diversity of their Jurassic period dinosaur fossils. This formation, named for Morrison, Colorado, is found throughout a large region of western North America.

What **event occurred** at the division between the Triassic and Jurassic periods, and why was this **important to the dinosaurs**?

There was apparently a major extinction between these two periods that led to the almost complete disappearance of many marine groups, such as some of the ammonoids (a type of mollusk with a flat, spiral shell); as

What events led to the development of the Morrison formation?

In the late Jurassic, subduction (crustal plate movement) along the west coast of North America began to uplift land inland; it eventually became the Sierra Nevada mountains. A shallow sea, called the Sundance Sea, flooded the basin created to the east of the uplifting Sierra Nevada mountains, inundating what is now Montana, the Dakotas, Wyoming, Utah, Colorado, and Nebraska. Toward the end of the Jurassic period, this interior seaway began to retreat as the continuing uplift of the Sierra Nevadas caused Nevada, Utah, and Idaho to rise. The climate in this area, along with the numerous flood plains, rivers, and lakes, supported large numbers of dinosaurs. When they died, they were quickly covered with sediment that was flowing down from the eroding Sierra Nevadas. This late Jurassic layer of dinosaur-rich sedimentary rock is the world-famous Morrison formation of western North America.

well as the complete disappearance of some reptiles, including some types of archosaurs, phytosaurs, aetosaurs, and rauisuchians. Though many scientists speculate that this extinction was caused by an asteroid impact, the crater that is leading candidate in support of this theory, Manicouagan in British Columbia, Canada, has been dated at 10 million years too early. There are thus heated debates as to the causes of this extinction event.

Some scientists feel that the end-of-the-Triassic period extinction event opened up more ecological niches into which the dinosaurs dispersed, allowing them to flourish and become dominant. However, others feel that the dinosaurs were already on their way to dominance due to the major extinction event at the end of the Permian period. The real sequence of these events may never be known, but in any case, the dinosaurs did start to become dominant during the early Jurassic period.

THE CONTINENTS
DURING THE JURASSIC PERIOD

Where were the **continents** located during the **Jurassic period**?

In the early Jurassic period, the continents were still clustered around the equator in the shape of a rough "C" that bordered the Tethys Sea. However, unlike the Triassic period, in which the continents were all part of one giant landmass known as Pangea, a split formed during the Jurassic period that divided Pangea into roughly two large land masses. The most accepted theory for the breakup of the supercontinent Pangea is the action of plate tectonics.

What were **Laurasia** and **Gondwanaland**?

Laurasia and Gondwanaland (or Gondwana) were the two major continents of the Jurassic period. As the gap between North America and Africa widened, driven by the spreading rift, so did the gap between North and South America. Water filled this gap, separating Pangea into the northern continent of Laurasia, and the southern continent of Gondwanaland. Despite the separation of the huge continent, scientists have found fossil skeletons of the *Brachiosaurus* and plated *Stegosaurus* in Africa and North America. This indicates that although the continents were separating, there were probably land bridges that popped up from time to time, allowing the species to spread to both continents.

What is the difference between **Gondwanaland** and **Gondwana**?

There really is no difference between the terms Gondwanaland and Gondwana. They are synonymous, and the use of the terms appears to be a personal preference.

What **modern-day continents** were linked together to form **Laurasia**?

Laurasia included the present-day continents of Europe, North America, and Siberia. Also included in this large land mass was Greenland.

How did the northern continent of Laurasia and the southern continent of Gondwanaland change during the Jurassic period?

As the rift grew westward, separating Pangea into Laurasia and Gondwanaland, and millions of years passed, there were numerous changes on each of these large continents. Africa began to separate from Europe, starting the formation of the Mediterranean Sea. Italy, Greece, Turkey, and Iran were attached to the northern African part of Gondwanaland, while Antarctica and Australia detached from Gondwanaland, but were still in contact with each other. And the block of land we now call India drifted northward.

North America separated from Gondwanaland and drifted west, resulting in the formation of the Gulf of Mexico, and the widening of the north Atlantic Ocean. South America and Africa began separating, creating a long, narrow seaway that would eventually become the south Atlantic Ocean. In addition, sea levels rose during this period, resulting in shallow seas flooding parts of North America and Europe in the late Jurassic.

What **modern-day continents** were linked together to form **Gondwanaland**?

Gondwanaland included the present day continents of Africa, South America, India, Antarctica, and Australia.

Where were parts of the present-day **Asia located** during the Jurassic period?

Sections of Asia were essentially found in pieces during the Jurassic, as large "islands" in the Tethys Ocean. The islands that contained modern central Asia and southeast Asia were off the east coast of Gondwanaland,

and the islands that contained today's China and Manchuria were off the east coast of Laurasia.

What were the **major oceans** and how did they **change** during the **Jurassic period**?

The major ocean continued to be the Panthalassa Ocean, which covered most of the planet. But as the gap between North Africa and North America widened, the north Atlantic Ocean began to grow.

What was the **climate** like during the **Jurassic period**?

The evidence to date seems to suggest that for the majority of time during the entire Jurassic, the climate was warm and moist over much of the land-masses, with only small temperature differences from the equator to the poles. Similar to the Triassic period, there were no ice caps at the poles.

What caused the **climate** to **change** from hot and arid during the Triassic period to warm and moist during the Jurassic period?

The previous period, the Triassic, had been hot and arid; during the Jurassic, temperatures fell slightly and rainfall increased, allowing lush tropical vegetation to grow over large areas. The climate during the Jurassic period was probably affected by the break-up of Pangea and creation of the large seas—and no doubt the accompanying changes in sea level and ocean currents.

What were the **most common plants** growing during the **Jurassic period**?

Because the climate had turned moist and tropical, vegetation was lush. Among the most common plants were cycads and lycopods (small tree-like plants); ginkos and tree ferns covered the areas near rivers and lakes—some of which eventually became the coal seams we mine today. There were also extensive numbers of ferns and horsetails covering the

Plants such as ferns flourished during the Jurassic period. (Photo courtesy of Field Mark Publications.)

ground; and forests of tall conifer trees—for example, sequoias and monkey puzzles—dominated the land.

What were the major **ocean currents** during the **Jurassic period**?

Ocean currents during the Jurassic period changed in some ways from the Triassic period, mainly because of the changes in the continents. The warm currents of the equator still swept northward along the east coast of what was once Pangea, and was now Laurasia and Gondwanaland. And along the western coastlines of both continents, colder currents flowed south along Laurasia and north along Gondwanaland, both currents heading toward the equator. Smaller currents also set up in the more open oceans, the cooler currents flowing from the north and south, toward the equator.

Were there any **major geologic events** that occurred during the **Jurassic period**?

During the early Jurassic, the east coast of what was now Laurasia and Gondwanaland was quietly accumulating sediment. As the rifting con- 125 tinued between North and South America, starting the Gulf of Mexico, the sea dropped layers of evaporites. Today, we see evidence of this: The evaporites eventually pushed upward as salt domes through younger sediments, forming petroleum traps—with Texas and Gulf of Mexico oil wells today taking advantage of the deposits.

During the late Jurassic, the westward drift of North America also started a period of mountain-building in the areas of today's Rocky Mountains and the Sierra Nevadas. A huge basin called the Sundance Sea formed across Montana, the Dakotas, Wyoming, Utah, Colorado, and Nebraska during the West Coast mountain building. Much of northern and central Europe flooded; the resulting lagoon, protected by a bank of reefs, produced a fine-grained limestone.

MAJOR JURASSIC DINOSAURS

How did **dinosaurs** become so **prolific** between the **Triassic and Jurassic periods**?

Scientists believe that the end of the Triassic was one of the busiest times in the history of land vertebrates. There were all types of animals (except birds)—crocodiles, turtles, lizard relatives, pterosaurs, therapsids, giant amphibians, the first mammals, and dinosaurs. But during a short period of time—maybe only about five to ten million years—at the beginning of the Jurassic, dinosaurs began to dominate the land, filling almost every available niche.

There are several theories that attempt to explain why. The first one is competition, as the dinosaurs out-competed the other animals for food. The second theory is opportunism, in which the dinosaurs took advantage of their specialized characteristics to take over the territories of other animals. Another suggestion is that the dinosaurs' specialized anatomy allowed them to beat out competitors, with the dinosaurs able to walk upright because of the way their hips were put together. This gave the dinosaurs an edge, allowing them to free their forearms to grasp prey—something no other animals could do.

What are some of the major **dinosaurs** that lived during the **Jurassic period**?

There were two groups of dinosaurs during the Jurassic: the saurischians (reptile or lizard-hipped), divided into the sauropods (herbivores) and theropods (carnivores); and the ornithischians (bird-hipped), such as the stegosaurs, ankylosaurs, ornithopods. This latter group were all herbivores. The following table lists some of the dinosaurs that lived during the Jurassic. New fossil finds are occurring all the time and the list will subsequently grow.

Jurassic Period Dinosaurs

Name	Common Name	Approximate Age (millions of years ago)	Locality	Length (in feet/meters)
Apatosaurus	Deceptive Lizard	154-145	USA	up to 70/21
Allosaurus	Other Lizard	150-135	USA	up to 50/15
Archaeopteryx*	Ancient Wing	147	Germany	up to 1.5/0.5
Barosaurus	Heavy Lizard	155-145	USA	u p to 80/24
Brachiosaurus	Arm Lizard	155-140	USA, Tanzania	up to 75/23
Camarasaurus	Chambered Lizard	155-145	USA	up to 65/20
Camptosaurus	Bent Lizard	155-145	USA	up to 16/5
Coelurus	Hollow Tail	155-145	USA	up to 8/2.4
Compsognathus	Pretty Jaw	147	Germany	26 inches
Dacentrurus	Pointed Tail	157-152	France, England	about 20/6
Diplodocus	Double Beam	155-145	USA	up to 90/27
Dryosaurus	Oak Lizard	155-140	USA, Tanzania	up to 13/4
Kentrosaurus	Spikey Lizard	140	Tanzania	up to 10/3
Mamenchisaurus	Mamenchi Lizard	155-145	China	up to 72/22
Massospondylus	Massive Vertebra	208-204	England, South Africa	up to 13/4
Megalosaurus	Big Lizard	170-155	Tanzania	up to 30/9
Ornitholestes	Bird Robber	155-145	USA	up to 6.5/2
Pelorosaurus	Monstrous Lizard	150	England	unknown
Scelidosaurus	Limb Lizard	203-194	England	up to 13/4
Stegosaurus	Roof Lizard	155-145	USA	up to 30/9
Tuojiangosaurus	Tuojiang Lizard	157-154	China	up to 21/6.4

*Dinosaur origin/nature has been debated since the first fossil was found in 1861.

127

Which major Jurassic period dinosaurs were herbivores?

The largest dinosaurs in the Jurassic period tended to be the plant-eaters (herbivores). The best known examples include the long-necked sauropods like *Brachiosaurus* and *Apatososaurus,* creatures that ate leaves off the tops of high trees. In addition, all of the ornithischians were herbivores, such as the plated *Stegosaurus* and the ankylosaurs. Ornithopods such as *Camptosaurus* competed with the large sauropods for vegetation.

Which major **Jurassic period dinosaurs** were **carnivores**?

The theropods were all carnivores, and evolved into large predators, such as the *Megalosaurus* and the well-known *Allosaurus.*

What were the **smallest dinosaurs** known in the **Jurassic period**?

Currently, the smallest dinosaur on record that lived in the Jurassic was the *Echinodon,* an herbivorous ornithischian that was about the size of a modern chicken.

What were the **largest dinosaurs** known in the **Jurassic period**?

Some of the dinosaurs living during the Jurassic period had evolved into the largest creatures ever to live on land—the majority being plant-eaters. And it seems as if every year brings a new fossil discovery that unearths another, larger dinosaur.

There are many famous, large herbivorous sauropods that lived during the Jurassic period. One is the *Diplodocus,* one of the longest plant eaters, measuring 90 feet (27 meters) in length. At one time, scientists believed that this huge creature had to live in the water to support its

Skull of an *Apatososaurus* (formerly known as the *Brontosaurus*), a herbivore during the Jurassic period. (Photo courtesy of University of Michigan Exhibit Museum of Natural History.)

great bulk; but the latest research suggests that the dinosaur was able to carry its weight on land. (This dinosaur may not end up being the longest Jurassic dinosaur, though: A possible 150-foot [46-meter] dinosaur called a *Seismosaurus* is still being dug out from a chunk of sandstone found in New Mexico.)

Another large sauropod was called the *Apatosaurus,* otherwise known as the *Brontosaurus,* which weighed up to 51 tons. But the true winner for sauropod weight may prove to be the *Brachiosaurus,* a 75-foot (23-meter) animal with unusual longer front legs and shorter back legs. Its weight is disputed, ranging from 32 to 78 tons—but either way, it was a heavyweight. Still another large plant-eating dinosaur was the *Barosaurus*—an animal closely related to the *Diplodocus*—that had an enormously elongated neck, rivaling even the long neck of the *Brachiosaurus*. The neck of the *Brachiosaurus* reached about 43 feet (13 meters), higher than the average three-story building; to compare, a giraffe grows to about 18 feet (5.5 meters).

There may have been even larger herbivorous sauropods, but many of these are still debated, as not many fossils of these dinosaurs have been found. In North America, one such relatively rare set of dinosaur bones includes the huge sauropod *Supersaurus*. This giant dinosaur measured 80 to 100 feet (24 to 30.5 meters) long and 54 feet (16.5 meters) high; other reports say that the dinosaur was closer to 130 feet (40 meters) long, making this sauropod the longest known land animal. Another possibility was also found on the same continent—the *Ultrasaurus,* or *Ultrasauros,* which may have grown to at least 100 feet (30.5 meters) long. The actual existence of this dinosaur is highly debated—but if it is designated as a separate species (some scientists believe it may be a large *Brachiosaurus,* while others believe it is often mistaken for a *Supersaurus*), it will be classed as one of the Jurassic period's largest.

Larger carnivorous dinosaurs included the *Allosaurus,* measuring about 50 feet (15 meters) in length. Scientists believe the attack of the *Allosaurus* was amazing: It would open its mouth to the furthest extent, running headlong into its victim. Its 60 curved, dagger-like teeth would plunge into its prey, driven by two tons of dinosaur.

Did the first **dinosaur fossil to be named** come from the **Jurassic period**?

Yes, the first dinosaur fossil to be named was the *Megalosaurus,* named by geologist William Buckland (1784–1856) in 1824. The fossil came from the middle Jurassic, and was found in Oxfordshire, England.

What happened to the ***Brontosaurus***?

The *Apatosaurus* was formerly known as the *Brontosaurus*. Fossils from the *Apatosaurus* were officially named in 1877, while the *Brontosaurus* fossils were named in 1878. It wasn't until later that it was noticed that the fossils of the two dinosaurs were really the same. Since the *Apatosaurus* had been named first, it was adopted as the official designation for this animal.

What **Jurassic period** dinosaurs were the **longest lived** of the dinosaur lines?

The herbivorous ornithopods were the longest lived of dinosaurs lines, from the early Jurassic to the late Cretaceous period. They include a series of successively larger and more massive dinosaurs that spread throughout most of the continents. One was the *Heterodontosaurus* of the early Jurassic period, a quick, four-foot (1.3-meter) dinosaur, with strong front canine tusks and flexible hands used for digging and grasping vegetation.

OTHER LIFE IN THE JURASSIC PERIOD

What were the **major land plants** living during the **Jurassic**?

The major land plants were similar to those in the Triassic period (see the plant table on page 113 for more information), but were more profuse. Ferns and horsetails covered the ground; ginkos and tree ferns lined rivers and lakes; and cycads, conifers, and sequoias forested thousands of square miles of the drier lands. The biggest difference was the diversification and increase in abundance of the cycads (the Jurassic is often referred to as the "Age of Cycads") and conifers, with most of the modern families evolving, such as cypresses, redwoods, yews, and junipers. The first truly modern ferns also appeared at this time.

What were the **more profuse small marine plants** living during the **Jurassic**?

In the early Jurassic, coccolithophorids (calcareous nanoplankton) first appeared. These were very small, single-cell algae that were covered with calcium carbonate disks.

131

Were there any insects during the Jurassic period?

Because of the mild climate and lush vegetation, flying insects were very profuse during the Jurassic period. In addition, the early ancestors of the bees and flies developed (although some scientists believe that early ancestors of the flies may have evolved even earlier, during the late Triassic).

Besides dinosaurs, what **other land animals** were present during the **Jurassic period**?

Although the dinosaurs were the dominant animals, there were other animals that existed during the Jurassic period. Because of the relative stability of the climate and the lush vegetation, many land animals diversified and increased in numbers. But not all creatures survived through the Jurassic period; many became extinct, probably because competition increased.

What follows is a summary of the many other animals that existed along with dinosaurs in the Jurassic period:

Amphibians
Frogs, salamanders: first modern frogs and salamanders appeared.

Reptiles
Turtles: first modern turtles appeared in the early Jurassic period; they were able to retract their heads into their upper shell.

Lizards: first true lizards appeared in the middle Jurassic period.

Crocodylians: first true crocodylians appear, and were small, three-foot (one-meter) long reptiles that walked on all fours; they had longer hind legs, indicating that their ancestors were bipedal.

Therapsids: few families of therapsids, or mammal-like reptiles, lived into the middle Jurassic period; the anomodonts and therocephalians no longer existed, but the cynodonts did survive into the middle Jurassic .

Mammals

Small mammals: small mammals became more profuse and diverse during the Jurassic period; they were still very small animals, about the size of a mouse or rat, with the largest the size of a cat; they were mostly nocturnal (active at night).

triconodonts: late Triassic to late Cretaceous mammals; one of the oldest fossil mammals; three cusps of teeth in a straight row give them their name.

haramyoids: late Triassic to middle Jurassic mammals; one of the oldest   fossil mammals; their teeth had many cusps in at least two parallel rows.

symmetrodonts: late Jurassic to early Cretaceous mammals; they had upper and lower cheek teeth with many cusps in a triangular pattern.

docodonts: middle to late Jurassic period mammals; they had elaborate cheek teeth, with most of the cusps in a T-shape.

multituberculates: the multituberculates were the largest group of mammals in the Mesozoic, first appearing in the late Jurassic period.

Were there any **animals in the air** during the **Jurassic**?

Similar to the Triassic period, there were many gliding and flying animals—all of them reptiles—during the Jurassic period. They became more diverse, and some much larger than in the Triassic period. The pterosaurs, the flying reptiles, became extremely diverse and abundant, flying over all the continents. They included the *Rhamphorhynchus,* with a six-foot (1.75-meter) wing span, and the *Pterodactylus,* with an eight-foot (2.5-meter) wing span.

The first birds also may have developed during this time, although the actual lineage is still often debated. The most famous fossils of the late Jurassic period, besides those of dinosaurs, are of the *Archaeopteryx.* Only about five fossils of this reptile have been found in late Jurassic period limestone rock in Germany, each retaining many distinctive dinosaur features, pointing to the idea that birds probably evolved from small, meat-eating dinosaurs.

133

Archaeopteryx fossil, with wing impressions. (Photo courtesy of James L. Amos/Corbis Corporation.)

What were the **major marine animals** living during the **Jurassic**?

There were many marine animals that thrived during the Jurassic period, ranging from small seabed dwellers, to large swimming predators. Most of these animals were similar to those found in the Triassic period, although many had diversified and increased in number during the Jurassic period.

Modern shark families developed at this time; bony fishes, the teleosts, with symmetrical tails, diversified (they account for the great majority of modern fishes—over 20,000 species). The first oysters evolved; modern squids and cuttlefishes appeared; and squid-like belemnites diversified. The ammonoids

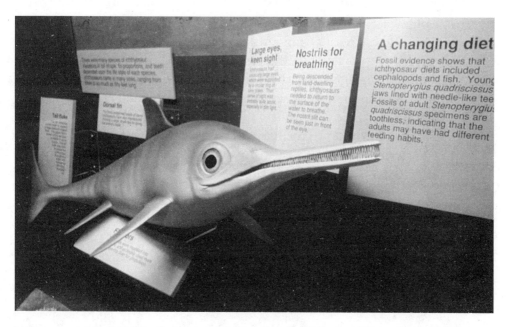

The following text appears on the display cards in the photograph:

Large eyes, keen sight

Nostrils for breathing

A changing diet
Fossil evidence shows that ichthyosaur diets included cephalopods and fish. Young *Stenopterygius quadriscissus* jaws lined with needle-like teeth. Fossils of adult *Stenopterygius quadriscissus* specimens are toothless, indicating that the adults may have had different feeding habits.

Ichthyosaur, a marine animal during the Jurassic period. (Photo courtesy of University of Michigan Exhibit Musuem of Natural History.)

almost disappeared during the late Triassic extinctions; one family survived (out of eight) and quickly diversified during the Jurassic period.

The ichthyosaurs, such as the *Ichthyosaurus* and *Stenopterygius,* flourished in the Jurassic period oceans. Plesiosaurs were also abundant, such as the *Muraenosaurus,* a late Jurassic period reptile with a 36-foot (11-meter) neck (it included 40 vertebrae); and the *Liopleurodon,* a short-necked pliosaur with a huge, elongated neck, was 39-feet (12-meters) long, with a ten-foot (three-meter) head.

What was so **special** about the evolution of the **ichthyosaurs**?

Ichthyosaurs were a group of streamlined, dolphin-shaped reptiles—but their backgrounds differed from many reptiles living around them: These creatures' ancestors went back to the sea from the land. Some scientists believe that ichthyosaurs were the first major group of reptiles to return to the sea. At first, they no doubt stayed close to the shoreline, similar to seals and walruses. But after millions of years, the creatures went into the oceans, spread, and eventually became totally fish-shaped.

The oldest ichthyosaur fossils, and the most primitive so far, are 240-million-year-old fossils found in Japan. The primitive ichthyosaur, measuring about nine feet (2.7 meters) long, probably lived its entire life in the water. Its shape was not yet like a dolphin; and its pelvis bone was still attached to the vertebrae—similar to those of land animals and dissimilar to the later ichthyosaurs. The primitive ichthyosaurs also had fins that were similar to the limbs of land reptiles (with splayed fingers). In other words, this primitive fossil shows the first step the ichthyosaurs took from the land to the oceans.

There was one other strange characteristic of the ichthyosaurs: For unknown reasons (as evident in the fossil record), about 135 million years ago, the animals began to fade away—becoming totally extinct between 90 and 100 million years ago. This was much earlier than the demise of the dinosaurs—animals that became extinct about 65 million years ago.

CRETACEOUS PERIOD

What was the **Cretaceous period** and how did it get its **name**?

The Cretaceous period followed the Jurassic period on the geologic time scale; it was the last period in the Mesozoic era. Most of the Jurassic's large sauropods, stegosaurs, and theropods disappeared in the early part of this period, but were replaced by an incredibly large diversity of new dinosaur groups. These included the horned types, the duckbilled, the armored, and new types of theropod carnivores.

The Cretaceous period got its name from the type of rock deposited along the northern shores of the Tethys Sea at this time, in a band running from what is now Ireland and Britain, to the Middle East. This rock—formed from the metamorphosed deposits of the tiny limestone skeletons of algae known as diatoms—is known as chalk. The Latin for chalk is *creta,* and thus, the name Cretaceous.

What are the major **divisions** of the **Cretaceous**?

Scientists divide the Cretaceous into two divisions, or epochs: The Early Cretaceous (also called the Lower Cretaceous), from approximately 144 to 89 million years ago; and the Late Cretaceous (also called the Upper Cretaceous), from approximately 89 to 65 million years ago. Each of these main epochs is broken up into smaller ages. The following chart gives the European nomenclature for each age.

During the Cretaceous period some dinosaurs slowly died out while armored dinosaurs flourished. (Photo courtesy of University of Michigan Exhibit Museum of Natural History.)

Cretaceous Period

Epoch	Age	Millions of Years Ago (approximate)
Late	Maastrichtian	74 to 65
	Campanian	83 to 74
	Santonian	87 to 83
	Coniacian	89 to 87
Early	Turonian	93 to 89
	Cenomanian	97 to 93
	Albian	112 to 97
	Aptian	125 to 112
	Barremian	132 to 125
	Hauterivian	135 to 132
	Valanginian	141 to 135
	Berriasian	144 to 141

How long did the **Cretaceous period last**?

The Cretaceous period lasted from approximately 144 to 65 million years ago, or approximately 80 million years. The geologic time scale is not exact, and the dates of the Cretaceous period can vary by about five to ten million years.

Why did the dinosaurs **thrive and diversify** during the **Cretaceous**?

Although there is no clear answer to this question, paleontologists know that a revolution in life occurred during this time period. This took place as many types of modern flora and fauna made their first appearances. Some scientists theorize that it was the development, and eventual dominance, of a new group of plants, the angiosperms (flowering plants), in harmony with the development of new groups of insects, that provided fresh sources of food that could be exploited by the dinosaurs. All these new food sources allowed the dinosaurs to continue to dominate throughout the Cretaceous period.

THE CONTINENTS
DURING THE CRETACEOUS PERIOD

What was the **Earth** like during the **Cretaceous period**?

During the Cretaceous period, what we recognize as our modern-day continents were becoming much more distinct. The breakup of Pangea into Laurasia and Gondwanaland continued, and these two large continents themselves began to break apart. Sea levels rose worldwide, inundating many formerly dry areas. Similar to the Jurassic period, it was warm and humid, with no ice caps at the poles. By the end of the Late Cretaceous, the planet closely resembled our modern world. But today, of course, we lack the small and large dinosaurs roaming our continents—although some scientists believe that birds are truly dinosaurs and therefore these creatures never really completely died away.

141

What was the global sea level like during the Cretaceous period?

The global sea level continued to rise through the Cretaceous period; but by the Late Cretaceous, mean sea level reached as high as any time during the past 500 million years—about 600 feet (200 meters) higher than present levels. This led to extensive flooding of many land areas, including most of Europe, North Africa, the Middle East, and western Russia. The fluctuations in sea level also brought about the appearance and disappearance of many land bridges between landmasses.

The reason for this rise in mean sea level is highly debated. Some scientists point to the fact that there were no polar ice caps, so the water that filled the oceans was at its peak. One theory for the dramatic rise in mean sea level was the increase in the volume and height of the sea floor: The increased amount of the oceanic crust—due to the spreading mid-oceanic ridge—displaced the water upward, causing the rise in sea level.

How did **Laurasia** and **Gondwanaland** change during the **Cretaceous period**?

During the Cretaceous period, both Laurasia and Gondwanaland separated from each other and each fragmented into smaller landmasses. The whole motif of the Cretaceous was change—change from the ancient topography to the more familiar forms we see today.

In the early Cretaceous period, Laurasia began to break up due to the action of an extension of the Mid-Atlantic Ridge, with North America and Greenland separating from Eurasia. Rifting occurred in Gondwanaland, with South America and Africa beginning to separate. In the middle of the Cretaceous period, Gondwanaland had separated into four major landmasses: South America, Africa, the combined India and Madagascar, and the combined Antarctica and Australia.

By the late Cretaceous, North America and Greenland began to split, as did Australia and Antarctica, and India and Madagascar. The Atlantic Ocean continued to widen, and India and Australia moved northward. By the end of the Cretaceous, the continents began to assume their modern outlines and headed toward their current destinations on the planet's surface. This also led to the development and widening of the modern oceans and seas.

What is the **Wealden Basin** and why is it **significant**?

The Wealden Basin was an area of northwest Europe that extended over southern England, northern France and Germany, Belgium, and northeast Spain. In the early Cretaceous period, this area was not yet flooded by the rising sea level. It was a low-lying area with broad streams, lakes, and scattered forests—prime habitat for the dinosaurs of the time. Because of this, some of the best Early Cretaceous period dinosaur fossils have been found in the rock of this region, including the second and third dinosaurs to be named: The *Iguanodon* and *Hylaeosaurus* were both named by fossil hunter Gideon Mantell in the early 1800s. (The first dinosaur fossil to be named was the *Megalosaurus* of the Middle Jurassic period.)

What was the **climate** like during the **Cretaceous period**?

Similar to the Jurassic period, the early and middle Cretaceous period climate was warm and humid over most of the continents. By the middle Cretaceous, pronounced summer and winter seasons developed, but the temperatures never dropped below freezing, even in the polar regions. And in the late Cretaceous, the mean global temperatures were as high as any time during the past 500 million years.

What were the **major oceans** during the **Cretaceous period**?

As Laurasia and Gondwanaland continued to separate during the Cretaceous, water began to fill in the gaps. The Panthalassa Ocean continued to be the largest ocean on the planet, slowly taking its modern-day shape as the Pacific Ocean. The Tethys Sea (Ocean) continued to shrink: millions of years after the Cretaceous period ended, it would evolve into today's Mediterranean Sea. The North and South Atlantic oceans continued to widen, a process that continues today.

What were the major **ocean currents** during the **Cretaceous period**?

The Cretaceous period ocean currents differed greatly from the Triassic and Jurassic periods, as the continents of Laurasia and Gondwanaland continued to break apart. A cold current ran up South America's west coast toward the equator; another cold current rushed between the ever-spreading area between Africa and Antarctica, India, and Australia; and two more cold currents continued from the north, past Europe and Siberia, and into the Tethys Sea. Warmer currents still ran to the west along the equator; another flowed north along the east coast of North America; and still another ran south, past the east and west coasts of Africa.

Were there any **major geological events** that occurred during the **Cretaceous period**?

The westward movement of North America led to further mountain uplift along the west coast, which continued throughout this period. Rifting in Gondwanaland, with the movement of South America, led to the start of mountain building along the west coast, and eventually resulted in today's Andes mountains. Mountain-building also caused an increase in erosion, and thus, there were great areas in which sediments were deposited all over the globe. There were several major volcanic eruptions that spewed out huge volumes of volcanic material. One of the most famous is called the Deccan Traps that formed at the end of the Cretaceous period; the highlands of India formed from these ancient lava flows.

Skull of a Triceratops. (Photo courtesy of University of Michigan Exhibit Museum of Natural History.)

MAJOR CRETACEOUS DINOSAURS

What were the **major dinosaurs** during the **Cretaceous period**?

Many of the forms of dinosaurs from the Jurassic had disappeared, replaced by new and more diverse forms. Of the saurischian sauropods (herbivorous dinosaurs with small heads, long necks, long tails, and five toes on each foot), only the titanosaurids (Late Jurassic or Early Cretaceous) remained, and these herbivores were mostly found on the landmasses that made up Gonwanaland until the end of the Cretaceous period (although these creatures present a problem to scholars, as no complete skeleton or skull has ever been found). Many of the saurischian theropods (carnivorous dinosaurs) became extinct during the Cretaceous, whereas others diversified into a wide range of animals, from large carnivores like *Tyrannosaurus,* to speedy, agile predators like *Velociraptor.*

The ornithischian dinosaurs (which had bird-like pelvises) were the most numerous and diverse of all the dinosaurs in the Cretaceous period. They include the ornithopods (which walked erect on their hind legs), such as the *Iguanodon,* and the duck-billed dinosaurs, such as the

145

Edmontosaurus and *Maiasaura;* the armored ankylosaurs, including the *Ankylosaurus,* with its protective plating and tail-club; the thick-headed pachycephalosaurs (thought to engage in head butting), such as the *Stegoceras;* and the ceratopsians, four-legged animals with long, bony frills and horns, like the *Triceratops.*

How did the **distribution** of dinosaur species change during the **Cretaceous period**?

The earlier Triassic and Jurassic periods were characterized by joined landmasses throughout the planet. By the time the Cretaceous began, these landmasses began to separate, isolating some species of dinosaurs, and leading to different areas having different species. For example, the amphibious titanosaur sauropods were mostly present in former Gondwanaland areas, such as South America; while the horned ceratopsians and hadrosaurs (a type of ornithopod) were found mainly in Laurasia. But many interpretations are highly debated: One of the main reasons for the present uncertainty about the overall distribution of dinosaurs is the incompleteness of the known dinosaur fossil record.

What were some of the **dinosaurs** that lived during the **Cretaceous period**?

The number of dinosaurs that lived during the Cretaceous period was immense—and too many to list in this volume. And as more fossils are found, the number continues to grow. What follows is a partial listing of cretaceous dinosaurs.

Cretaceous Period Dinosaurs

Name	Common Name	Age (millions of years ago)	Locality	Length (feet/meters)
Albertosaurus	Alberta Lizard	76-74	Canada	up to 30/9
Avimimus	Bird Mimic	about 75	Mongolia	up to 5/1.5
Baryonyx	Heavy Claw	about 124	England	34/10
Centrosaurus	Horned Lizard	76-74	Canada	up to 16/5
Chasmosaurus	Cleft Lizard	76-74	Canada	up to 16/5
Corythosaurus	Helmet Lizard	76-74	Canada, USA	up to 33/10

Craspedodon	Edge Tooth	86-83	Belgium	unknown
Deinocheirus	Terrible Lizard	70-65	Mongolia	unknown, arms about 10/3
Deinonychus	Terrible Claw	110	USA	up to 11/3
Dromaeosaurus	Running Lizard	76-74	Canada	up to 6/1.8
Dryptosaurus	Wounding Lizard	74-65	USA	about 16/5
Edmontonia	Of Edmonton	76-74	Canada	about 13/4
Edmontosaurus	Edmonton Lizard	76-65	Canada	up to 43/13
Euoplocephalus	Well-armored Head	about 71	Canada	up to 20/6
Gallimimus	Chicken Mimic	74-70	Mongolia	up to 18/5.5
Gilmoreosaurus	Gilmore's Lizard	80-70	China	about 20/6
Hadrosaurus	Big Lizard	83-74	USA	up to 26/8
Hylaeosaurus	Woodland Lizard	150-135	England	up to 13/4
Hypsilophodon	High Ridge Tooth	about 125	England	up to 7.5/2
Iguanodon	Iguana Tooth	130-115	USA, England, Belgium, Spain, Germany	up to 33/10
Kritosaurus	Noble Lizard	80-75	USA	up to 26/8
Lambeosaurus	Lambe's Lizard	76-74	Canada	up to 30/9
Maiasaura	Good Mother Lizard	80-75	USA	up to 30/9
Ornithopsis	Bird-like Structure	about 125	England	unknown, perhaps 65/20
Orodromeus	Mountain Runner	about 74	USA	up to 6.5/2
Ouranosaurus	Brave Monitor Lizard	about 115	Niger	up to 23/7
Oviraptor	Egg Thief	85-75	Mongolia	up to 6/2
Pachycephalosaurus	Thick-headed Lizard	about 67	USA	up to 26/8
Pachyrhinosaurus	Thick-nosed Lizard	76-74	Canada, USA	up to 20/6
Parasaurolophus	Like *Saurolophus*	76-74	Canada, USA	up to 33/10
Parksosaurus	Park's Lizard	76-74	Canada	up to 10/3
Protoceratops	First Horned Face	85-80	Mongolia	up to 6/2
Psittacosaurus	Parrot Lizard	124-97	China, Mongolia, Russia	up to 6/2
Rhabdodon	Rod Tooth	83-70	Austria, France Spain, Romania	up to 10/3
Saurolophus	Ridged Lizard	74-70	Canada, Mongolia	up to 40/12
Saurornithoides	Bird-like Lizard	80-74	Canada, Mongolia	up to 6.5/2
Scartopus	Nimble Foot	about 95	Australia	unknown
Segnosaurus	Slow Lizard	97-88	Mongolia	up to 13/4
Struthiosaurus	Ostrich Lizard	83-75	Austria, Romania	up to 6.5/2
Styracosaurus	Spiked Lizard	85-80	Canada, USA	up to 18/5.5
Tenontosaurus	Sinew Lizard	110	USA	up to 21/6.4
Triceratops	Three-horned Face	67-65	USA	up to 30/9
Troodon	Wounding Tooth	75-70	Canada, USA	up to 8/2.4
Tyrannosaurus	Tyrant Lizard	67-65	USA	up to 40/12
Velociraptor	Quick Plunderer	84-80	China, Mongolia	up to 6/12

147

Which **major dinosaurs** from the **Cretaceous period** were **herbivores**?

All of the remaining sauropods, such as *Saltasaurus, Alamosaurus,* and *Argentinosaurus,* were plant-eaters. The most numerous and diverse herbivores in the Cretaceous, however, were the ornithischians (whose hips resembled those of birds), including the duck-billed ornithopods, the horned ceratopsians, the thick-headed pachycephalosaurs, and the armored ankylosaurs.

What were the **smallest dinosaurs** known in the **Cretaceous period**?

It is difficult to determine the smallest dinosaurs known from the Cretaceous period—there were very few, as most of the "smaller" dinosaurs were about five to six feet (1.5 to 2 meters) in length, such as the *Avimimus.* In general, the smallest herbivorous and carnivorous dinosaurs could be as small as a chicken. Most of the carnivorous ones ate insects as their main supply of food; and of course, the smallest herbivores ate plants.

What were the **largest dinosaurs** known in the **Cretaceous period**?

Scientists probably have yet to uncover the largest dinosaurs of the Cretaceous period, although they will likely come from the *Sauropoda* suborder. The herbivorous sauropods have small heads, long necks, and

Did any dinosaur species survive the extinction at the end of the Cretaceous period?

The general consensus among scientists is that no dinosaur species survived the mass extinction at the end of the Cretaceous period. There are a few paleontologists who don't believe that the dinosaurs died off at the end of the Cretaceous period, but actually lived on, dying out gradually during the Cenozoic era. This theory will continue to be highly debated until dinosaur fossils are proven to exist past the Cretaceous period in rocks. Some scientists claim they have found such evidence, but their findings are still controversial.

In addition, if the definition of dinosaurs includes birds, then, yes, this family of dinosaurs did survive the extinction. After the Cretaceous period, birds greatly diversified into numerous species—and as we all know, these are species that are living everywhere on the planet today.

long tails. One of the largest and most relatively complete skeletons comes from the *Brachiosaurus* of Tanzania, Africa, which measured up to 75 feet (23 meters) in length. But this sauropod didn't make it through the Cretaceous—it evolved around the Upper Jurassic period and died out during the Early Cretaceous.

More recent fossil discoveries may lead to even larger sauropods. One includes a massive herbivorous dinosaur *Argentinosaurus huinculensis,* a South American sauropod of the Titanosauridae family. But this fossil is still difficult to interpret, as it is only known from vertebrae and limb bone fossils.

The largest carnivorous dinosaur from the Cretaceous period seems to be a toss-up between the perennial favorite and two newcomers. The favorite is the theropod *Tyrannosaurus* found in North America and Asia and measuring over 40 feet (12 meters) in length. The two new challengers are the *Giganotosaurus* of South America, and the *Carcharo-*

dontosaurus of North Africa. Both of these huge, meat-eating theropods are thought to have been bigger—and even heavier—than the *Tyrannosaurus.*

What was the **largest ornithomimosaur,** the ostrich-like dinosaur, known from the **Cretaceous period**?

The largest currently known ornithomimosaur was the *Gallimimus,* a late Cretaceous dinosaur that grew up to 20-feet (6-meters) in length. The *Deinocheirus* may have been a large ornithomimosaur, but the only fossil evidence to date is a pair of 10-foot (3-meter) long forelegs and hands.

What was the **top predator** among the Cretaceous dinosaurs?

This question is difficult to answer. The carnivorous dinosaurs were all vicious as they attacked their prey. Some, like *Tyrannosaurus,* used their size to catch their meals; while others, like pack hunters such as the *Velociraptor,* trapped their prey as a unit. Or was it better to be fast or even agile, such as the *Utahraptor* or *Megaraptor*? In other words, which Cretaceous dinosaur was the "top predator" is a matter of opinion.

Where did the **last** dinosaurs **live**?

The last dinosaurs apparently lived in the western regions of North America. Their remains have been found through the late Cretaceous period rocks. In other regions of the world they disappeared well before the end of this period.

What was the **last** dinosaur **species** to arise?

Scientists have determined there were two late-arriving species. The latest known species of dinosaurs to arise in the late Cretaceous period were the *Triceratops,* an herbivore, and *Tyrannosaurus rex,* a carnivore.

OTHER LIFE IN THE CRETACEOUS PERIOD

Were there any **insects** during the **Cretaceous period**?

In addition to some earlier forms, such as dragonflies that had survived into the Cretaceous period, many new groups of insects evolved and diversified. Their success is thought to be due to their joint evolution with the new flowering plants that arose during this time period.

Cretaceous Period Insects

Insect	Description
dragonflies	diversified in Carboniferous and Permian periods; many groups continued to modern times
beetles	continued from Jurassic
flies	continued from Jurassic; some believe fly ancestors may have evolved during the Triassic period
butterflies	fossils known only from early Cretaceous onward
moths	fossils known only from early Cretaceous onward
ants	fossils known only from early Cretaceous onward
bees	true bees developed; fossils known only from early Cretaceous onward
wasps	fossils known only from early Cretaceous onward
termites	fossils known only from early Cretaceous onward
hymenopterans	sawflies evolved from the Triassic

What kind of **plants** made their **first appearance** during the **Cretaceous period**?

The kind of plants that made their first appearance during the Cretaceous period were the angiosperms, or flowering plants. These plants

Dragonflies and other insects survived throughout the Cretaceous period. (Photo courtesy of Field Mark Publications.)

had flowers and a fully enclosed ovule. Their pollen was present on long stamens found around a central area that contained the ovaries. This pollen was transported to the stigma, a sticky surface above the ovule, by the action of the wind or, more importantly, by insects looking for nectar.

The plant's ability to flower and more controlled pollination allowed the angiosperms to become the dominate form of plant life by the end of the Cretaceous period. And as we can see just by looking around us, this has continued up to modern times.

What were the **most common plants** growing during the **Cretaceous period**?

Some species of plants continued to evolve from previous periods, while others are known only from the Cretaceous onward. In the Early Cretaceous, the cycads began their decline, leaving the conifers to dominate. Also in this time period, the angiosperms, or flowering plants, made their first appearance—considered the biggest environmental change during this time. The flowering plants diversified during the middle Cretaceous, taking over many areas that once held only the ferns and horsetails; by the end of the period, angiosperm diversity had surpassed that of the conifers. Of the 500 modern families of flowering plants, 50 appeared during the Cretaceous period, including the sycamore, magnolia, palm, holly, and trees of the willow and birch family.

The reason for the rapid spread of the flowering plants during the Cretaceous period may have been the dinosaurs themselves: As larger dinosaurs of the Early Cretaceous began to trample the low-growing angiosperms, the plants grew back very rapidly—similar to today's flowering plants that respond to cutting by growing even more profuse. In addition, insects, passing dinosaurs, flying or gliding reptiles, and wind probably carried the angiosperm seeds to other areas.

What types of **small marine plants** lived during the **Cretaceous period**?

Tiny plants called diatoms (single-celled forms of algae, or plants with silica shells) came in many forms in the oceans. Their abundance led to great chalk deposits, such as the strip that runs from Great Britain to the Middle East, which were created as the diatom "skeletons" or shells metamorphosed into a chalky limrestone.

Besides dinosaurs, what **other animals** were present during the **Cretaceous period**?

Similar to the Jurassic, there were many other animals that surrounded the dinosaurs, competing for space and food. Most of them are familiar

153

Were there any flying animals during the Cretaceous period?

The flying animals during the Cretaceous period were the pterosaurs, birds, and various winged insects. There were over 50 species of pterosaurs, and they were found everywhere except Antarctica. They all disappeared at the end of the Cretaceous period.

The birds, winged reptiles that began during the Jurassic period, greatly diversified during the Cretaceous period. There were also the forms with reduced wings, such as the flightless, ground-dwelling *Patagopteryx* that looked like a chicken with very short wings; and the aquatic diving bird, *Baptornis,* also with tiny wings, webbed feet, and sharp teeth.

Winged insects also greatly diversified during the Cretaceous period—and quickly, probably in response to the arrival of the flowering plants.

from the Triassic and Jurassic periods; while others diversified and evolved. But not all creatures survived; many became extinct, probably because competition increased.

Here are some non-dinosaurian land animals of the Cretaceous period:

Amphibians
Frogs, salamanders, newts toads, caecilians: all modern amphibians; they continue to evolve and diversify.

Reptiles
Turtles: *Archelon,* a large sea turtle, grows up to four feet in length.

Snakes: earliest known snakes appear.

Crocodiles: many crocodiles become massive, including the *Deinosuchus,* a large terrestrial crocodile that reached 50 feet (15 meters) in length.

Lizards: true lizards continue to evolve and diversify.

Mammals

Triconodonts: Late Triassic to Late Cretaceous mammals; one of the oldest fossil mammals; three cusps of teeth in a straight row give them their name.

Symmetrodonts: Late Jurassic to Early Cretaceous mammals; they had upper and lower cheek teeth with many cusps in a triangular pattern.

Multituberculates: Late Jurassic to Late Eocene mammals; they had cheek teeth with many cusps in more than one row; they probably filled a "rodent" niche that had once been filled by cynodont therasids, and was later filled by true rodents.

Monotremes: first appearance; Early Cretaceous to the present; these animals eventually lead to the true mammals (especially with hair and mammary glands); the only living form lays eggs (like a reptile duck-billed platypus).

Early marsupials: first appearance; middle Cretaceous to the present; these pouched animals had distinct lower and upper cheek teeth.

Early placentals: first appearance; middle Cretaceous to the present; the mother nourished her developing fetus through a placenta; the cheek teeth were even more elaborate; the Late Cretaceous placental mammals include insectivores, or mammals that ate insects

What was the **largest flying animal** of the **Cretaceous period**?

The largest flying animal of all was the *Quetzalcoatlus,* a late Cretaceous period pterosaur found in Texas. This giant of the sky, though not a dinosaur, was comparable in size to our modern small airplanes, with an estimated wingspan of 36 to 50 feet (11 to 15 meters).

How did the **pterosaurs** get around on the **ground**?

Similar to most birds today, the pterosaurs did not constantly fly in the sky. There were times that the animals had to land, either to rest or to feed. But how did these creatures get around on the surface?

155

A pterosaur, one of the few winged-creatures in the Cretaceous period. (Photo courtesy of University of Michigan Exhibit Museum of Natural History.)

In the past few years, paleontologists have found numerous footprints that reveal the possibilities. In the western United States, hundreds of fossilized tracks recently found are attributed to pterosaurs. The fossil impressions appear to be made by forelimbs and hindlimbs of the animals, suggesting that they walked on all fours like a bat. The trace fossils also show distinct toe and finger impressions, indicating that the pterosaurs had a four-toed triangular foot and three short, clawed fingers. A very elongated fourth finger also developed to support the wing, which the pterosaurs would fold backward over their body. Although most of the tracks in the United States showed only the three finger impressions, trace fossils of pterosaurs in France do show the impressions of a fourth finger.

But not all scientists agree: Many believe these reptiles actually walked and ran on two legs (bipedal), similar to birds. Still other scientists don't believe the tracks found in the United States or France are those of pterosaurs—but suggest they were made by crocodiles (or crocodile-like reptiles). The problem is familiar: Even though the impressions look like those a pterosaur would make, there are no other fossils—bones or other hard parts—around the site to confirm the identity.

What were the **major marine animals** living during the **Cretaceous period**?

As with all life in the Cretaceous, there was a mixture of the older groups and the emergence of modern, living groups. The Mesozoic "marine revolution" occurred during the Cretaceous period, and included the appearance of new, modern predators that could feed on the older, hard-shelled forms.

Many modern families of marine animals appeared during the Cretaceous period, including the modern crabs, clams, and snails; sharks also evolved into their modern families by the late Cretaceous. Larger animals included mollusks and lobsters. Amazingly, many bony fishes continued to evolve from much earlier periods than the Mesozoic era.

Marine reptiles still lived in the seas, most of them until the end of the Cretaceous.

Mosasaurs, or marine lizards with paddle-like flippers that grew up to 33 feet (10 meters) in length, were around until the late Cretaceous. Plesiosaurs and ichthyosaurs still swam in most of the oceans, but died out in the late Cretaceous. And there were also a few marine crocodiles left over from the Jurassic period.

DINOSAUR
BONES

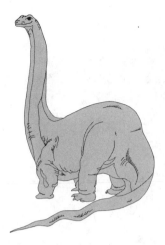

GROWING BONES

What were **dinosaur bones made of**?

Contrary to popular belief, there is not just one type of dinosaur bone; these complex structures formed the skeletons of complex animals. There are volumes of dinosaur bone tissue studies—most based on the various stages of growth and development—and they cannot be completely explained here.

Overall, there were three main types of dinosaur bone tissues: the primary bone, Haversian (or secondary) bone, and growth ring bone tissue. These varied between the different bones in a dinosaur, and sometimes even within individual bones. And they certainly differed from dinosaur to dinosaur.

When did **primary bones** develop during a dinosaur's life?

Scientists believe primary bones, also called fibro-lamellar bones, were formed during the rapid growth phase of a dinosaur's life—or in particular, when the dinosaur was young. These bones were very similar in structure to bones with blood vessels found in birds and mammals; the dinosaur's primary bones also contained blood vessels, which helped them to grow fast. These tissues are especially noticeable in fossil dinosaur leg bones.

161

Bones of a dinosaur's spine. (Photo courtesy of Corbis Corporation.)

When did **Haversian (or secondary) bone tissue** develop during a dinosaur's life?

In some dinosaurs, the primary bone tissue was later replaced by Haversian bone tissue in a process called remodeling. These tissues had many blood vessels with dense, bony rings around them. This type of bone, similar to those of large modern mammals, had more strength and was more resistant to stress.

When did **growth ring bone tissue** develop during a dinosaur's life?

The growth ring bone tissue, found in some dinosaur bones and modern, cold-blooded reptiles, look similar to growth rings found in trees. Tree rings grow each year, responding to changing seasonal conditions—and by counting the rings, it is sometimes possible to tell the approximate age of a tree.

The presence of similar structures in certain dinosaur bones suggests the animals' growth rates slowed later in life; one interpretation is that the animals became more reptile-like. One major problem is interpreting a dinosaur's growth ring bones: Unlike a growth ring on a tree, no one knows the amount of time represented by each growth ring in a dinosaur bone.

What do these **three types of bone tissue** indicate about **dinosaur physiology**?

The presence of these three bone tissue structures suggests dinosaurs had a unique physiology—probably somewhere in between cold-blooded reptiles and warm-blooded birds or mammals. Perhaps this unique physiology made dinosaurs extremely adaptable, and enabled them to dominate the land for about 150 million years.

BUILDING DINOSAUR SKELETONS

How **many bones** made up the **average dinosaur skeleton**?

Although the largest dinosaurs may have had a few more bones in their necks and tails, the number of bones in the average dinosaur was approximately 200.

Can you tell the **difference** between **male and female dinosaurs** from their bones?

No, it is really not possible (at present) to determine the gender of a dinosaur by looking at its fossil bones. There are few clues to determine a dinosaur's gender, although some scientists believe certain species may have had features that distinguished gender. For example, some hadrosaurs (duck-billed dinosaurs) sported certain types of bony head crests. But just which gender *had* the crest is unknown. Currently, scientists are trying to base dinosaur gender ideas on examples from today's animal world—and even then, it's still almost impossible to determine a male from a female dinosaur.

163

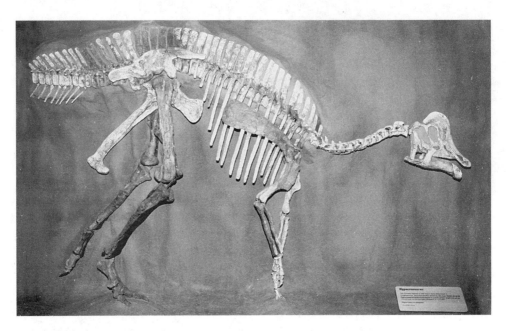

The skeletal structure of a hadrosaur. (Photo courtesy of Kevin Schafer/Corbis Corporation.)

Did **dinosaurs differ** in **bone structure**?

Overall, each dinosaur had a skeleton made up of the same basic structures: the skull, spine, ribs, shoulders, hips, legs, and tail. But individual dinosaur fossil bones do have structural differences. This is apparently dependent on several factors, including where the bones were located in the dinosaur; the bone's purpose or purposes; and the species of dinosaur. In general, dinosaurs that depended on speed needed long, light bones, while larger, slower-moving dinosaurs needed strong, solid bones.

What are some **specific differences** between dinosaur **bone structures**?

Some of the best examples of the differences between dinosaur bone structures are seen in the bipedal and quadrapedal herbivores. The large, heavy sauropods walked on all fours; they needed strong legs to support their enormous weight, so their bones were huge and solid. The smaller, fast-running bipedal herbivores like *Dryosaurus* needed to be fast; thus, they had long, thin-walled bones. These bones were essential-

What do dinosaur bones tell us about a dinosaur's stance?

All dinosaur skeletons show that these creatures had a "fully improved stance." In other words, dinosaur legs were held straight under their bodies at all times. This enabled dinosaurs to grow bigger, cover longer distances, and move faster, compared to their reptile cousins that had their legs spread out on either side of their body. The dinosaur stance also enabled some of the animals to become bipedal (walk on two legs); it also helped all dinosaurs with something called "locomotor stamina"—or the ability to run and breathe at the same time.

ly hollow tubes, and the insides were filled with a light bone marrow. This gave them a strong, flexible, but light-weight, structure, enabling them to move swiftly when circumstances demanded it—such as running from a predator.

What can paleontologists tell about the **lifestyle** of a **large herbivore** from its fossil bones?

The bones of giant dinosaurs like the *Dipoldocus* tell us a great deal about this herbivore. Its legs were thick and widely spaced, acting as pillars to hold up the cross beams of its shoulder bones and hip girdle. The vertebrae across the hip were fused for strength, allowing it to support an almost 11-ton body weight. The legs ended in short, broad feet (similar to an elephant's) with claws on the back foot used as an anti-slip device. The bone structure limited the dinosaur to a normal walking pace of approximately four miles (6.4 kilometers) per hour, although they could have moved modestly faster for short periods of time. Thus, they were thought to be large, slow moving, four-legged walkers. In addition, the large adult herbivores (sauropods) were probably relatively immune from predators because of their large size.

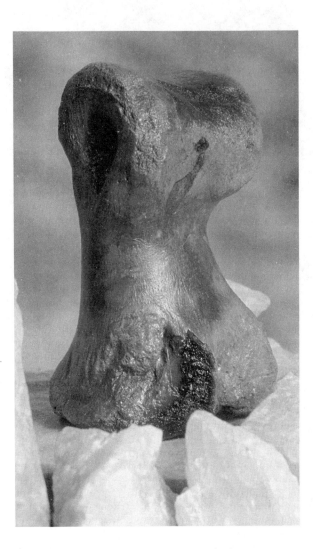

A toe bone from a *Tyrannosaurus*. (Photo courtesy of Corbis Corporation.)

What can paleontologists tell about the **lifestyle** of a **small herbivore** from its fossil bones?

One good example is the *Hypsilophodon*, a small herbivore (ornithischi-an) with a much different skeleton than its larger sauropod cousins. The small dinosaur's entire structure seemed "shrunk down"—giving it strength with minimum weight. Its bones were hollow and thin-walled for lightness, and the thigh bone was very short for rapid stride move-ments. The small dinosaur's feet were long and thin, with long upper foot bones (metatarsals), and it had short, sharp claws for gripping the ground. The long tail bone was stiffened by bony rods, and probably swung from side to side, helping it to quickly change directions. All of these structures paint a picture of a small, two-legged herbivore using its bony features to swiftly run and maneuver as a defense against predators.

What can paleontologists tell about the **lifestyle** of a **midsize herbivore** from its fossil bones?

A good example of a midsize herbivore is the *Iguanodon* (ornithischian), a 33-foot (10-meter) long animal that weighed approximately four tons. The skeleton of the *Iguanodon* was very similar in structure to the smaller *Hypsilophodon,* but the bone proportions were different. The thigh bone was much heavier and longer, and the upper part of the foot bone was shorter. This prevented the *Iguanodon* from running very fast, but did provide support for its heavier weight. The vertebrae along the dinosaur's spine were wide and tall, strengthened along the whole length by numerous bony tendons. Thus, the dinosaur walked on two legs (bipedal), with a nearly horizontal posture; its back legs supported most of its weight. The huge shoulder bones, long arm bones, and fused wrist bones (carpals) gave the *Iguanodon* the ability to drop down on all fours for locomotion when the situation demanded it.

What can paleontologists tell about the **lifestyle** of a **large carnivore** from its fossil bones?

The *Tyrannosaurus* is currently the most recognizable of the large carnivorous dinosaurs (theropods). Its skeleton had heavy, large bones, with massive vertebrae, hip girdle, and thigh bones. The upper foot bones (metatarsals) were locked together for strength, while the toes were powerful and short. The knees show evidence of thick cartilage, similar to modern birds.

There are two scenarios concerning the speed and mobility of the *Tyrannosaurus* based on the animal's skeletal structure—and both sides point to the same evidence to bolster their claims. One group feels that the skeletal structure of a *Tyrannosaurus* caused the animal to move at a slow pace, which limited its main hunting abilities to scavenging or camouflage and ambush. The other group feels that the dinosaur's bone structure, along with the animal's massive musculature, enabled the *Tyrannosaurus* to run and sprint, making it an active, dangerous hunter.

Until more direct evidence is gathered, the most agreed-upon theory is based on a major deduction: The *Tyrannosaurus* would need more meat than was available from scavenging—thus it would have to hunt. And to hunt, it would have to at least match the speed of its prey. In other words, it would have to keep up with such dinosaur prey as the herbivores *Triceratops* and *Edmontosaurus* (ornithischians)—both of which are thought to have reached speeds of 9 to 12 miles (14 to 19 kilometers) per hour for short bursts.

ABNORMAL DINOSAUR BONES

What do **dinosaur bones** indicate to paleontologists about the **health** of these animals?

Dinosaurs, in general, seem to have been relatively healthy animals, if the evidence from—and the interpretation of—the fossil records are to be believed. A few fossilized bones have shown evidence of abnormalities, such as asymmetrical bone growth, healed traumatic and repetitive stress fractures, arthritis, ossification (the development of bonylike material) of spinal ligaments, and the fusion of the animal's spinal bones (or vertebrae).

What caused **asymmetrical bone growth** in dinosaurs?

Asymmetrical bone growth could have occurred, for example, when a tendon was ripped off the bone. This probably happened during some form of exertion, such as running after prey for carnivores, or trying to escape a predator for herbivores. If bone growth continued in this area after the tendon was torn, it would often grow back in an abnormal shape.

What do traumatic fractures in the bones of large theropods (carnivores) tell us about the behavior of these animals?

Some carnivorous dinosaur bones do show signs of traumatic fractures. One example was recently found by scientists using x-rays of the rib bones from a dinosaur known as an *Allosaurus*. Scientists believe the fractures could have been caused by a belly flop onto the hard ground while running. This suggests that these large theropods were not sluggish creatures—but were active hunters, running after prey fast enough to crack ribs if they fell during the pursuit.

What caused **traumatic** and **repetitive stress fractures** in dinosaur bones?

Another feature that has been seen in some dinosaur bones, such as *Tyrannosaurus* and *Iguanodon,* are healed traumatic fractures. Such fractures may have occurred during struggles with other dinosaurs or even during mating activity.

Another type of fracture, called a stress fracture, apparently occurred in dinosaurs as a result of repetitive stresses to the bone. Stress fractures found in ceratopsians, such as the *Triceratops,* have often been blamed on foot stamping, sudden accelerations in response to predators—or even fractures brought about during long migrations.

Do **dinosaur bones** show evidence of **arthritis,** a common affliction in humans?

Yes, certain dinosaur bones show signs of certain types of arthritis—in particular, osteoarthritis and inflammatory arthritis. In humans, osteoarthritis, or degenerative arthritis, is common in the elderly. In general in humans, degenerative arthritis is caused by the increased deterioration of cartilage around the bone due to age, or from a propensity toward this type of arthritis. Inflammatory arthritis, or gout, in humans usually occurs when crystals of uric acid are deposited in a joint. The excess amounts of uric acid are usually unexplainable, but the condition has often been tied to dietary excesses.

In the vast majority of cases, dinosaur bones show almost no sign of osteoarthritis, leading some paleontologists to theorize that these creatures had highly constrained joints, or bone joints with little rotational movement. Two specimens of *Iguanodon,* however, were found to have evidence of osteoarthritis in the ankle bones—weight-bearing parts of the body. Because scientists don't know the lifespans of dinosaurs, they also don't know whether or not the arthritis was caused by old age. In addition, two tyrannosaurid dinosaur remains show evidence of inflammatory arthritis in the hand and toe bones—possibly the result of a rich, red meat diet.

What **bone phenomena** do both **humans** and **dinosaurs** share?

Humans and dinosaurs share a process called "diffuse idiopathic skeletal hyperostosis" (DISH)—or when the ossification (when something becomes bonelike) of the spinal ligaments stiffens the spinal area. Although it sounds bad, it is a normal process—and not recognized as a disease in either humans or dinosaurs.

Creatures such as ceratopsians, hadrosaurs, iguanodonts, pachycephalosaurs, and some sauropods all show DISH—a stiffening of the dinosaurs' tail area that made it easier to hold the tail off the ground. Dinosaurs that used their tails as weapons, such as the stegosaurs, needed them to be flexible like whips—so they do not show evidence of this spinal ligament fusion. The discovery of DISH in dinosaurs dovetails nicely with a newer theory: That many dinosaurs did not drag their tails, but rather held them off the ground as a form of counter-balance.

Another bone-related phenomena humans and certain dinosaurs share is vertebral fusion, where the bones of the spine (the vertebrae) actually become joined and ossified together (as opposed to the spinal ligaments in the DISH process). In the adult ceratopsians, such as the

Triceratops, this fusion was limited to the first three neck (cervical) vertebrae, leading to speculation that this was not a disease, but a developmental adaptation: Stiffening in this area may have evolved to better support the animal's massive skull. More recent fossil findings reveal that smaller, perhaps younger ceratopsians had incomplete fusion in this area, whereas the fusion was complete in larger, presumably older animals.

How were **dinosaurs' bony skeletons** held together?

Dinosaur skeletons, similar to those of humans, were held together by a combination of ligaments, muscles, and tendons. The ligaments and tendons probably served the same function as those in modern humans: To connect the many tissues of the body to the skeleton. Muscles in dinosaurs also served the same function as in human bodies— to give the animals both strength and dexterity. In addition, some specialized muscles and tendons, such as those of the jaw, acted together in certain ways. For example, the model of a *Tyrannosaurus'* jaw is complex, with the muscles and tendons interacting in just the right way to allow the jaw to expand to its enormous size—and quickly snap shut to hold on to its prey.

How do paleontologists tell how **dinosaur muscles** were connected?

Some fossil bones have "muscle scars," or roughened patches, where the muscles were apparently attached. These scars often make it possible to estimate the position and size of some of the main muscles. From a mostly complete skeleton of a dinosaur, scientists can estimate where many of the muscles were located; how they worked with and against each other to move the dinosaur; and the general size and shape of the animal. Over the years, our overall view of how a particular dinosaur behaved had a great influence on how we determined muscle size and brawn. Early ideas of a slow-moving *Tyrannosaurus* led to suggestions of a relatively weak and puny set of muscles; the newer idea of the *Tyrannosaurus* as an active hunter has led scientists to suggest that the animals had large, strong muscles.

SPECIFIC DINOSAURS AND THEIR BONES

What **bone adaptations** did early birds like **Archaeopteryx** have?

The early birds—of which *Archaeopteryx* is the most well known—had hollow, pneumatic (containing air in the bone cavities) bones that provided lightness and strength. Some bones, particularly in the arm and wrist area, eventually became fused. There was not much difference in bones between the earliest birds and the smaller, carnivorous theropods. Only the presence of feathers truly distinguished the early birds from the land-limited small carnivores.

What were the purposes of **bony head projections** on some **dinosaurs**?

Although the true purposes are not known at present, scientists do have some theories as to the function of certain dinosaurs' bone head projections: The researchers believe these odd-shaped head projections would catch the eye, and thus, were used to attract mates or warn an enemy. Some projections could have been used for attack or defense, and others for some sort of sound generation.

Which group of **dinosaurs** had the most **prominent head projections**?

The hadrosaurs (also called duck-billed dinosaurs) had the most prominent head projections. All of their bodies were very similar, and resembled the earlier iguanodontids. One set of the hadrosaurs looked like many other reptiles, but with small crests. The other set of hadrosaurs had the most striking features on their heads—specifically, large, spectacular, and distinctive bony crests adorning their heads.

One fine example of dinosaurs with head projections is the *Corythosaurus,* a hadrosaur with a crest resembling a dinner plate on end. Another, the *Parasaurolophus,* had a long, hollow, horn-shaped crest

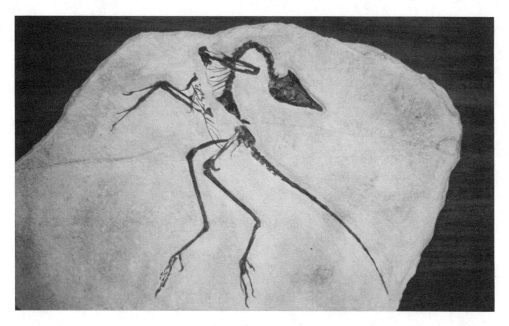

A fossil of an *Archaeopteryx* without its feathers. (Photo courtesy of University of Michigan Exhibit Museum of Natural History.)

rearing backward on top of its skull. The *Saurolophus* had a prominent bony ridge on top of its skull, sweeping back to form a spike; and the *Tsintaosaurus* had a forward-pointing hollow tube on top of its skull.

What **purpose** did the **long, hollow crest** serve on the skull of dinosaurs, such as the *Parasaurolophus*?

No one really knows the true purpose of this dinosaur's (or any other dinosaur's) hollow crest. Several theories have been proposed in the past, such as the hollow crest was used as a snorkel while looking for food near or in water. This is now known to be impossible, as the crest has no opening at the end. Another idea was that the crest served as a foliage deflector, as the animal searched for food or ran from predators. This idea has not been disproved, but it is highly unlikely.

Currently, scientists believe this dinosaur's three-foot (one-meter) long, hollow chamber, with its complex arrangement of tubes and chambers, acted as a resonator. Air from the dinosaur's lungs was blown through the tubes, giving off a distinctive low sound. These sounds could have

Duck-billed dinosaur or hadrosaur. (Photo courtesy of University of Michigan Exhibit Museum of Natural History.)

been used for communication, aggressive displays during mating season, or to sound the alarm when a predator was near.

Has anyone speculated on the **type of sounds** certain dinosaurs made?

Scientists have recently reproduced and released a recording of sounds a *Parasaurolophus* might have made using its skull crest. A full-scale model of this dinosaur's skull crest—reproducing exactly the shape and size of the internal chambers and tubes—was used to duplicate the possible sound. Blowing through the crest produces a low, oboe-like sound—a strange noise like none other made by a living creature in our time.

How big were the **early ceratopsians**?

The *Psittacosaurus* was an early ceratopsian that seemed to bridge the gap between ornithopods and later ceratopsians. It had a curved beak, but no neck frill. The dinosaur was approximately 6.5 feet (two meters) long; when it was on its two hind legs, it would reach up to about the shoulder height of an average human. A more recognizable early cer-

Which dinosaurs had a large skull with an integral bony neck frill?

The group of dinosaurs with large, triangular-shaped skulls (when viewed from above), horns, curved beaks, and large, bony neck frills were the ceratopsians, or "horned faces." They were ornithischians, were herbivorous, and evolved during the late Cretaceous period. These dinosaurs were stocky and walked on four legs, similar to modern rhinoceroses.

The large, bony neck frill, which is the dominant feature of these animals, is used by paleontologists to loosely group these animals into long-frilled and short-frilled types. The reason for the neck frill is unknown, although there are several theories: One suggests that the frills were used to make the animal look much larger in order to scare away potential predators. Another theory states that groups of the animals may have gathered together en masse, not only using their bulk and head armor to scare away predators, but the frills to look more menacing in a massive threat display.

atopsian dinosaur was the *Protoceratops*, with a well-developed neck shield, but no horn. This animal was approximately six feet (1.8 meters) long, and walked on all fours, rising up to mid-thigh height of an average human.

Which **dinosaur** was the most well known of the **ceratopsians**?

The ceratopsian most people recognize is the *Triceratops*—a three-horned, large, herbivorous quadruped with a short neck frill. This animal was one of the largest of the ceratopsians, weighing up to 5.4 tons; it had an average length of 29.5 feet (9 meters). It also had a long horn above each eye, and a shorter one on the front snout. The head alone of the *Triceratops* could be up to 6.5 feet (2 meters) long!

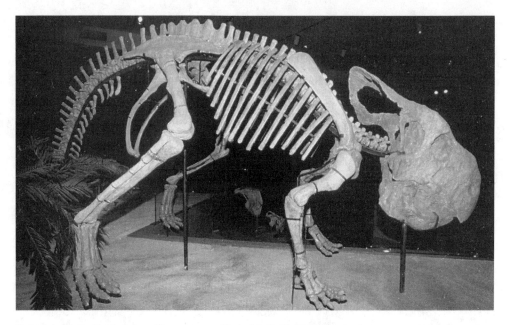

Skeletal mount of a *Protoceratops*. *(*Photo courtesy of Kevin Schafer/Corbis Corporation.)

What does the **skull** of the ***Triceratops*** tell us about the way it lived?

The *Triceratops*, like most of the ceratopsians, had a distinctive skull, with a large, bony frill; horns; and a narrow, but deep, beak-like snout, similar to the beak of a parrot. The teeth grew so that the cutting edges were almost vertical, allowing the *Triceratops* to slice plants like scissors; the continual growth of the teeth provided a self-sharpening edge. This allowed them to eat the low-lying, tough vegetation they found on the ground.

The long horns were probably used for display purposes; shoving matches to establish dominance and territory; and as protection against predators. The bony neck frill acted as a protection for the brain and as an attachment point for the powerful jaw muscles; it was possibly used for territorial or mating displays.

What purpose did the **bony plates** on the back of the ***Stegosaurus*** serve?

Originally, the bony plates of the *Stegosaurus*, an herbivore, were thought to form a single row down the animal's spine; now paleontolo-

Skull of a dinosaur from the ceratopsian family. (Photo courtesy of University of Michigan Exhibit Museum of Natural History.)

gists feel there were two staggered rows of plates, with a row on either side of the spine. Scientists also once thought the bony plates functioned as a defense from predators, or to attract mates. More recent studies in wind tunnels have shown that the staggered arrangement of plates is the most efficient pattern for shedding heat in a light breeze. Thus, the function of these plates is now thought to be one of heat regulation.

Where are **extremely large dinosaur bones** being found and why?

Some of most consistently large dinosaur bone discoveries are being made in South America—especially in northwest Patagonia, in Argentina; this includes such examples as the *Giganotosaurus, Argentinosaurus,* and *Megaraptor.* And although scientists believe they know why these animals evolved differently from their northern counterparts, they truly don't know why the animals became so large.

One theory to explain the large South American animals involves locality. At the beginning of the Mesozoic era, all the land on Earth was merged into the continent of Pangea. During the Jurassic period, the

177

supercontinent broke into the continent of Laurasia (which would eventually become North America and Asia) and Gondwanaland (eventually Africa, Antarctica, Australia, India, and South America). And not long afterward, South America and Africa began to split apart.

Most scientists theorize these splits were the pivotal points in these large dinosaurs' evolution. For a short time, the dinosaurs crossed a land bridge from North to South America; geologic activity eventually destroyed the bridge, cutting off access and allowing creatures like the migrated *Megaraptor* to evolve separately in the south. The North American animals, such as the *Tyrannosaurus rex,* developed specialized skull, forelimbs, and pelvis; the South American dinosaurs, such as the *Giganotosaurus* maintained most of the general features of their ancestors—and became much larger.

Other scientists believe that southern *Megaraptors* and their northern counterparts originally evolved separately from common ancestors. They suggest that the reason the two carnivorous giants such as the *Tyrannosaurus rex* and *Giganotosaurus* resembled each other was possibly due to similar environmental conditions. And when the landmasses began to break up, the animals continued to evolve separately.

Besides finding such large animals from long ago, scientists are also excited about another possibility: There is no doubt that environmental conditions differed greatly on all the continents. If this truly caused distinct differences in the dinosaurs, there are probably many different types of dinosaurs still to be discovered all around the world. But time will tell if scientists can determine the true reasons why the South American dinosaurs were giants of the Cretaceous world.

DINOSAUR ANATOMY

DINOSAUR SKIN

Are there any **fossils** of **dinosaur skin**?

The rarest types of dinosaur fossils are those showing skin texture—but not the actual skin itself. The fossilization process that produced such rare fossils required very specific conditions: The body of the dinosaur needed to be in a dry environment, which would allow some parts to mummify (dry up and shrivel). These mummified parts would then leave impressions on surrounding rock.

What was a **dinosaur's skin** like?

The few fossils of dinosaur skin uncovered to date show that most dinosaur skin was tough and scaly, like that of modern reptiles. For example, there was the tough, wrinkled skin with bony plates of the Cretaceous period hadrosaur *Edmontosaurus*. Similar to the hadrosaurs, ornithopods had thick, wrinkled skin with embedded bony knobs of various sizes. Some small theropods, like the recently discovered *Sinosauropteryx,* may have had feather-like features on its skin for heat regulation.

No one, as yet, has been able to tell anything about the color of a dinosaur's skin. The skin "fades" as it is mummified, and the rocks eventually give their own color to the fossil. But paleontologists theorize that dinosaurs,

181

Two dinosaur skin casts illustrating the scaly and wrinkled skin of a dinosaur. (Photo courtesy of University of Michigan Exhibit Museum of Natural History.)

like some modern animals, used color and patterns to both camouflage and identify themselves. Therefore, the dinosaurs' skin color probably ranged from light and dark browns to greens in various patterns—all earth colors, allowing them to hide or blend in with their environment.

But there may have also been brightly colored, smaller dinosaurs. After all, today's birds—thought by many paleontologists to be directly related to the dinosaurs—are often brightly colored in order to attract a mate, and warn other birds (and even predators) from their territory.

Did all **dinosaurs** have the **same type of skin**?

The amount of fossilized skin uncovered to date is extremely small, and most of our ideas of dinosaur skin come from extrapolation from modern reptiles. The chances of all dinosaurs having the same skin is probably small, since, over millions of years, these animals adapted to their environment and specialized needs. Thus, they probably adapted skin-wise, too.

In fact, today's reptiles do not have the same types of skin. If you don't believe it, just look at the various reptilian skins—from heads to tails—

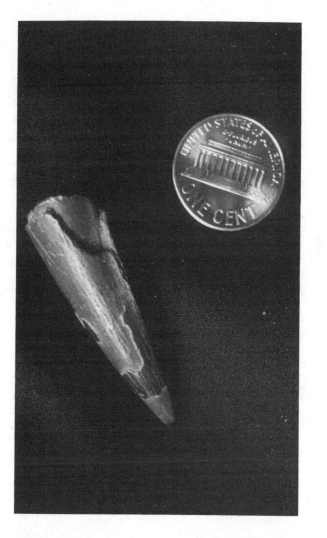

A tooth of a *Spinosaurus*. (Photo courtesy of University of Michigan Exhibit Museum of Natural History.)

of the large and small lizards, turtles, crocodiles, skinks, various snakes, and even the worm lizards. They vary from a lizard's protective covering of scales or plates to the hard bony shell of turtles—all different adaptations to their specific needs and environments.

Have any other **soft parts** of **dinosaurs** been found?

Yes, some impressions of soft parts of dinosaurs have been found in the past, but they are rare. Plus, some fossils display the outlines of internal organs, and some fossilized remains indicate what the animals had just eaten.

183

But an even more exciting finding was recently uncovered: The fossil of a small, baby carnivorous dinosaur, hardly more than a hatchling, was discovered in Italy. The dinosaur was actually found by an amateur collector in the southern part of the country in 1981, but he thought it was just the fossil of a bird. In 1993, the fossil collector saw the movie *Jurassic Park* and realized his fossil looked very similar to the movie's *Velociraptor* (in reality, true *Velociraptors* were smaller than what was depicted in the movie). In 1998, after the fossil was examined by paleontologists, it was determined to be the bones of a young dinosaur—and was also the first dinosaur ever discovered in Italy.

This dinosaur, called *Scipionyx samniticus,* is about 113 million years old; and although it is a distant cousin of both the *Tyrannosaurus rex* and *Velociraptor,* it is considered to be an entirely new family. The fossil also shows something that usually does not survive millions of years of fossilization: Soft parts, including a fossilized digestive tract running down through the skeleton, from the throat to the base of the tail. Even the wrinkles in the dinosaur's intestines were preserved.

TEETH AND CLAWS

What do we know in general about **dinosaur teeth**?

Scientists know that most dinosaurs had more teeth than do humans. In addition, the dinosaurs would shed their teeth throughout their life, much like animals such as sharks do today; for example, the hadrosaurs had hundreds of teeth waiting to replace their worn out teeth. Other dinosaurs, such as the ornithomimids, had no teeth at all, but had a beak similar to that of a bird. Some dinosaurs also had a combination of a beak and teeth.

As to how their teeth were aligned, there were many differences. In humans, most of the teeth are aligned so we can chew plants; the canines represent our carnivorous past. Dinosaurs had all different kinds of teeth alignment: Some were similar to that of today's carnivorous crocodile reptiles; others had teeth perfect for gnashing tough plants. In other words, similar to modern animals, teeth alignment depended on what the dinosaur ate.

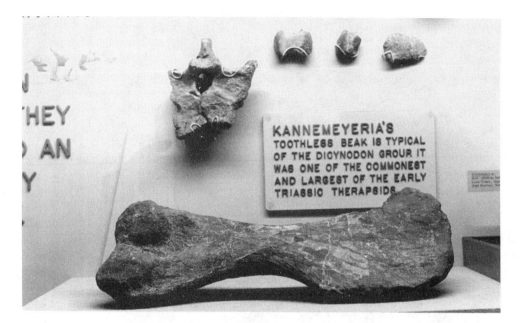

The *Kannemeyeria*, whose beak is shown here, was toothless. (Photo courtesy of University of Michigan Exhibit Museum of Natural History.)

What can scientists tell from the **shape** of **herbivorous dinosaurs' teeth**?

From the shape of the teeth, scientists can often interpret how different dinosaurs processed their food. In general, the teeth of herbivorous dinosaurs were very closely spaced, with either no gaps or a few small gaps between them. A herbivore's teeth were mostly the same size for a simple reason: The herbivores chewed mostly on softer plants—thus, they didn't break their teeth as much as did the carnivores that chewed on hard bones.

Teeth varied between the herbivorous dinosaurs. For example, the teeth of some large sauropods, like *Dipoldocus,* were located in a short row at the front of the mouth. These teeth were about the size and shape of the average pencil. These teeth were inadequate for extensive chewing, and paleontologists theorize the teeth were simply used to rake off the tender leaves from the treetops. This organic material was swallowed whole—leaving the breakdown of the plant material to the digestive tract of these animals.

The *Edmontosaurus,* a hadrosaur, did not have the same type of teeth as *Dipoldocus*: After cutting or pulling the vegetation, its tongue would push the material back toward multiple rows of teeth located in its

185

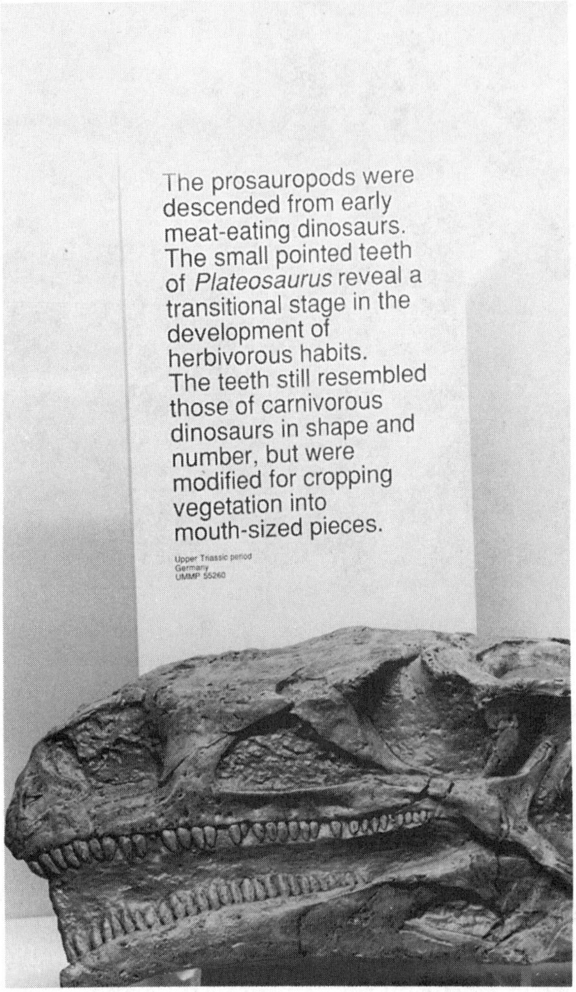

The prosauropods were descended from early meat-eating dinosaurs. The small pointed teeth of *Plateosaurus* reveal a transitional stage in the development of herbivorous habits. The teeth still resembled those of carnivorous dinosaurs in shape and number, but were modified for cropping vegetation into mouth-sized pieces.

Upper Triassic period
Germany
UMMP 55260

Mount of a toothy herbivore, the *Plateosaurus.* (Photo courtesy of University of Michigan Exhibit Museum of Natural History.)

cheeks, called tooth batteries. Here, the upper teeth meshed with the lower teeth, with each tooth having dips and ridges—and numbering close to 1,000 teeth! Combined with the powerful jaw muscles and cheeks, this grinding machine of a dinosaur allowed even the toughest plant material to be ground up before being digested. Because of this, paleontologists feel that the *Edmontosaurus* lived on mostly tough organic material, such as conifer needles, pine cones, and bark—in other words, food that most other herbivorous dinosaurs could not eat.

Yet another dinosaur—and one of the most common animals of its time during the Late Cretaceous—was the *Protoceratops,* a herbivore with a

186

Skeletal mount of an *Allosaurus*. (Photo courtesy of University of Michigan Exhibit Museum of Natural History.)

sharp, narrow beak that easily sliced off vegetation. The scissor-like teeth at the back of its mouth would finely cut and chop the organic material, but not grind it, before it was swallowed. This allowed the *Protoceratops* to subsist on the tough, low-growing plants, such as palms and cycads.

What can scientists tell from the **shape** of **carnivorous dinosaurs' teeth**?

The teeth of carnivorous dinosaurs were much different than those of herbivores. In general, a carnivore's teeth had large gaps between them; the teeth acted as daggers, powered by the force of the jaw muscles and the dinosaur's weight. The teeth in a carnivorous dinosaur were different sizes, since new teeth were continually growing to replace those lost or broken— mostly from biting into bone or even fighting with other carnivores.

A typical large carnivore, like an *Allosaurus,* had backward curving, knife-like teeth; each tooth had serrations on the front and back edges. Paleontologists theorize a large carnivore like the *Allosaurus* would practice what is called macropredation: It would run into its victim,

187

Clawed hands

With eight-foot strides of its long, powerful rear legs, allosaurus could overtake almost any prey, and then grab and hold its victim with the sharp curved claws on its front limbs. In life, the claw seen here was covered by a horny sheath, making it even longer and sharper.

This claw from an *Allosaurus* would definitely be a menace to its prey. (Photo courtesy of University of Michigan Exhibit Museum of Natural History.)

mouth open as wide as it could to drive the teeth in as far as possible. Closing its jaws, it would begin to jerk its powerful neck, ripping off a huge chunk of meat. The animal would then swallow this chunk whole, letting its digestive system take care of the rest. It would continue tearing off pieces of its prey until it was full.

What were the **arms** of some **carnivorous dinosaurs** used for?

The arms of some carnivorous dinosaurs were equipped with ferocious claws. The claws allowed the animal to grasp prey while the animal ripped off large chunks of meat with its mouth, or to hold down prey

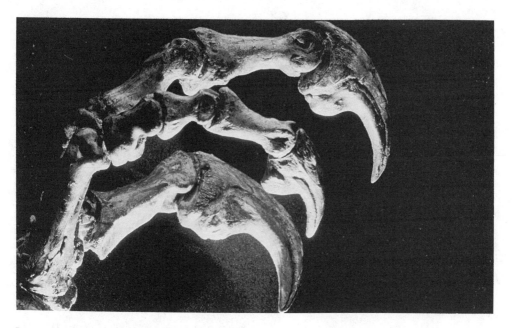

Bone structure of the hand from a carnivorous dinosaur. (Photo courtesy of Michael S. Yamashita/Corbis Corporation.)

while the animal bit and slashed, trying to bring down its victim. Others, such as a *Deinonychus,* would hold down its victim with its long arms, positioning itself to slash the prey with its large, hind claws.

What were the **dromaeosaurids** and what type of **claws** did they have?

The dromaeosaurids take their name from the first dinosaur fossil of their type found: the *Dromaeosaurus,* or "running reptile." This group includes species such as the *Dromaeosaurus, Velociraptor, Deinonychus,* and the more recently discovered *Utahraptor.* These dinosaurs were fast-running meat-eaters, with long legs and light bone structures. They exhibited a blend of features from both the carnosaurs and the coelurosaurs—with some unique characteristics of their own.

Probably the most well-known feature of the dromaeosaurids was their large, sickle-shaped claws on the second toe of their foot. These huge, curved claws were probably used to tear and rip apart their prey. Dinosaurs from this group are known colloquially as "raptors." The best-known raptors are the "velociraptors" from the movies *Jurassic Park* and *The Lost World.* In reality, true *Velociraptors* were smaller than those portrayed in the movies; the movie raptors were closer in size to

189

How did the dromaeosaurid carnivorous dinosaurs capture their prey?

These large dinosaurs probably ran down their victims, grasping them with powerful front-arm claws resembling grappling hooks. They would then bite the prey with their backward-sloping needle-sharp teeth. Then they would slash and disembowel the prey with large, curving toe claws, which could be flexed in a wide arc to better penetrate their victims. When running, this toe claw could be raised up and back—preventing the claw from hitting the ground and becoming rounded.

the *Deinonychus,* a dromaeosaurid that was about twice the size of a *Velociraptor.* Overall, they were all thought to be vicious pack hunters you wouldn't want to meet in a dark alley—or in the tall grass!

What features did **raptors (dromaeosaurids)** share with **birds**?

Dromaeosaurid dinosaurs share many features with birds: They both had hollow bones (some with holes) that made them lighter and stronger. The raptors also evolved in such a way that they eventually lost or fused some bones in the same areas as did birds.

What was the **most savage predatory dinosaur** known to have walked the Earth?

This is a subjective call, and the answer probably depends on who was chasing whom at the time! Whether you feel the larger, but slower carnosaurs, like *Tyrannosaurus* or *Giganotosaurus,* were more savage, or the smaller, but quicker dromaeosaurids, like *Utahraptor* or *Deinonychus* took the prize, in the end, the victim usually ended up eaten. It would be like asking which animal is more savage—a lion or a polar bear.

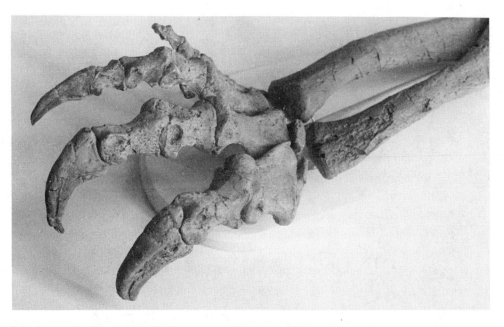

Bone structure of a *Plateosaurus* hand. (Photo courtesy of University of Michigan Exhibit Museum of Natural History.)

In their own way, and in their own habitat, each is a major predator in our modern world.

What is the **largest raptor claw** found to date in **North America**?

The largest raptor claw found to date in North America belongs to a *Utahraptor.* This dinosaur had a length of about 20 feet (six meters) and a height of about seven feet (two meters); the estimated weight of this animal is between 1,000 and 1,700 pounds. It had large, crescent-shaped claws on its forefeet and hind feet, with the two largest claws measuring 12 inches (30.5 centimeters) in length. While the dinosaur was alive, the claws were covered with a sheath of keratin and were somewhat larger (they probably shrunk during fossilization). Fortunately for us, *Utahraptors* only lived during the Cretaceous period.

What is the **largest raptor** found to date in the **world**?

The largest raptor that has been found to date in the world is the *Megaraptor namunhuaiquii.* *Megaraptor* means "giant thief," while *namunhuaiquii*

191

is an Indian word meaning "foot lance." The raptorial claw of this dinosaur, measuring about 15 inches (38 centimeters) long, was discovered in the Patagonia region of Argentina, South America. Paleontologists estimate that the *Megaraptor* was about 25 feet (7.6 meters) long, and lived roughly 100 million years ago during the Cretaceous period. This dinosaur does not seem to be closely related to the dromaeosaurids of North America and Asia—but may be a case of parallel evolution, in which two types of organisms form at the same time in a different regions of the world. Future digs should locate more bones and produce further data.

DINOSAUR METABOLISM

What do the terms **ectothermic** and **endothermic** mean?

Ectothermic and endothermic are terms used to describe the heat source animals use to maintain an activity temperature—or a safe body temperature for that organism. Ectothermic means the animal must depend on an external source of heat, such as sunlight. Endothermic means the animal uses an internal source of heat for this purpose. For example, reptiles, such as snakes, are primarily ectothermic; humans (and all mammals) are primarily endothermic.

What do the terms **poikilothermic** and **homeothermic** mean?

Poikilothermic and homeothermic are terms used to describe if an animal can maintain a steady internal temperature in its normal environment, regardless of changes in daily ambient temperatures. Poikilothermic means the animal cannot maintain a steady internal temperature, while homeothermic means the animal can maintain a steady internal temperature. For example, reptiles are poikilothermic; humans are homeothermic.

What do the terms **tachymetabolic** and **bradymetabolic** mean?

Tachymetabolic and bradymetabolic are terms used to describe the rate at which an animal's metabolism, or body chemistry, runs.

Tachymetabolic animals, such as modern birds, have a high rate of metabolism; bradymetabolic animals, such as reptiles, have slow rates of metabolism.

How were **dinosaurs described in the past**?

Up until about 1970, most scientists felt that the dinosaurs were "cold-blooded," that is, ectothermic and poikilothermic, similar to many modern reptiles. Thus, dinosaurs were viewed as sluggish, stupid creatures. Mammals, on the other hand, were "warm-blooded," or endothermic and homeothermic, and were quick, agile—and thus, intelligent. This notion of cold-bloodedness colored all aspects of the way dinosaurs where viewed, including their behaviors (dull and stupid) and social structures (literally none).

Why did **Robert Bakker** believe **dinosaurs** were **endothermic homeotherms (warm-blooded)**?

Some of the reasons paleontologist Robert Bakker gave for dinosaurs being endothermic homeotherms, or warm-blooded, are: Dinosaurs had complex bone structures (with evidence of constant remodeling), a feature of modern mammals, not reptiles; dinosaurs had an upright structure, similar to birds and modern mammals; dinosaurs (at least the small theropods) had, from the evidence to date, active lifestyles; predator-to-prey ratios were closer to that of modern mammals than reptiles; and dinosaurs were found in polar regions, where cold-blooded creatures could not survive.

What is the **predator-to-prey ratio**?

The predator-to-prey ratio is a mathematical concept used by scientists to estimate the maximum number of predators that can be supported by a given population of prey animals in a specific location. Predatory animals, being carnivorous, depend on other animals for their sustenance; an overabundance of predators in a given area will lead to the rapid depletion of the prey animal population and perhaps the starvation death of some predators. An area that has too few predators will see a

193

Who first proposed that dinosaurs were warm-blooded?

In the late 1960s and early 1970s, paleontologists John H. Ostrom and Robert T. Bakker first suggested that dinosaurs were not sluggish, stupid, "cold-blooded" animals. Their work paved the way for the theory that many of these animals were actually agile, dynamic, and smart.

In 1969, John Ostrom published a description of the *Deinonychus,* a Cretaceous period carnivorous dinosaur. Based on his study of the creature, he theorized that dinosaurs may have been warm-blooded. In 1975, Robert Bakker summarized his ideas about dinosaur endothermy in an article published in *Scientific American.* This set off a new era in dinosaur paleontology that has continued through today—especially in advancing ideas on how dinosaurs truly regulated their bodies' metabolism and heat.

rapid increase in the population of the prey animals, leading to overgrazing and starvation of the prey animals. Over time, an optimum balance between the predators and their prey is reached and can be described by the predator-to-prey ratio.

On the African veldt, where lions prey on animals such as gazelles and wildebeests, the carnivores usually constitute 1 to 6 percent of the total animal population, which is typical of a mammal-type community. The ratio is low because these predators are endothermic, or warm-blooded, and need large amounts of food to sustain their metabolism; a given population of prey can only support a very small number of these predators.

Scientists estimate that an animal community with ectothermic, or cold-blooded, predators would have a ratio approximately ten times larger, since ectotherms do not need as much food to sustain their metabolism. A given population of prey could support a much larger number of this type of predator.

What does the **predator-to-prey ratio** tell paleontologists about **dinosaurs**?

The predator-to-prey ratio tells paleontologists that the predatory dinosaurs (carnivorous theropods) were probably endothermic, or warm-blooded. For example, the different kinds of dinosaurs collected from the Oldman rock formation in Alberta, Canada, show that for every *Tyrannosaurus rex,* there were approximately twenty herbivorous dinosaurs—giving a predator-to-prey ratio of 5 percent. This is comparable to ratios found in modern mammalian (warm-blooded) communities.

Can we really use the **predator-to-prey ratio** when we talk about **dinosaurs**?

There are essentially two reasons to question that the predator-to-prey ratio applies to certain dinosaurs—especially when interpreting whether the dinosaurs were truly warm-blooded. First, the assumption that the number of carnivorous dinosaurs was limited only by the available food supply may be true. But this also may not be true, as the number of carnivorous dinosaurs may have been limited by other, unknown factors.

Second, the predator-dinosaur-to-prey-dinosaur ratio makes the assumption that the current, known numbers of fossils accurately reflect dinosaur populations. Considering the long, hazardous process of fossilization, and the difficulty in collecting and identifying remains, the known fossil record may not really reflect the true dinosaur population. These cautions make the fixing of a ratio—and the extrapolation to warm-bloodedness—a somewhat nebulous process. Further data and research are needed in order for scientists to understand if and how the ratio applied to dinosaurs.

What can **dinosaur bones** tell us about the animals' **internal heat regulation**?

Dinosaur bones, like modern reptile bones, often show signs of not growing—as if these animals went through periods of little or no growth. One of the reasons for a lack of growth could be hibernation during periods of seasonal cold, indicating that the animals used an ectothermic method of heat regulation. Mammals and birds, on the other hand, are endothermic, and show no lines of arrested growth. Thus, the presence or absence of these lines give paleontologists clues about the way dinosaurs regulated their internal temperature.

Were any **dinosaurs** really **warm-blooded**?

No one really knows for sure. Besides the issue of how the dinosaurs died off, the question of whether or not any dinosaurs were warm-blooded is one of the most highly debated issues in paleontology. The debate will continue until more fossil evidence is found to support dinosaur warm-bloodedness.

How did the **largest dinosaurs** possibly regulate their **internal temperature**?

Although there is still a lot of debate on this subject, with new findings almost every day, the general agreement is that the largest dinosaurs were ectothermic homeotherms. In other words, the animals received the majority of their heat externally— most likely from the Sun (similar to modern reptiles). But, because of their very large mass, they were also able to maintain a constant internal temperature. A large mass takes a long time to heat up or cool down, thus maintaining an even core temperature; this property is known as mass homeothermy.

How did the **smaller dinosaurs** possibly regulate their **internal temperature**?

A recent study of small, herbivorous dinosaurs from Australia belonging to the hypsilophodontids seems to indicate that these dinosaurs were indeed endothermic (warm-blooded). They lived in cold southern Australia, south of the Antarctic Circle, approximately 100 million years ago. But their bones show no signs of arrested growth—rather the animals had sustained, rapid growth. This would indicate that these dinosaurs did not hibernate, but were able to maintain an elevated internal temperature even in the cold. It would appear this species of dinosaurs, at least, may have been endothermic.

The fossilized remains of another small dinosaur were recently found northeast of Beijing, China, and may also be a link to endothermic dinosaurs. This animal had a long tail, and was about the size of a large turkey. Estimates place the age of this dinosaur, called *Sinosauropteryx,* between 120 and 140 million years old or even older. What was exciting about this discovery was the appearance of feather-like features along the animal's neck, back, and tail. Scientists think that these feather-like features were not useful for flight—rather *Sinosauropteryx* was warm-blooded and used these feathers to retain heat.

Other dinosaur bones found to date have also been intriguing. For example, those bones showing alternating lines of bone growth, then no bone growth, could indicate that the species' physiologies lie somewhere between modern reptiles and mammals.

SIZE OF DINOSAURS

What was the purpose of the **different sizes** and **shapes** of dinosaurs?

Similar to today's animals, the different sizes and shapes were the result of adaptations to the many dinosaurs' surrounding environments. In particular, the dinosaurs were probably typical of most animals: They needed to adapt to the prevailing conditions and changing food supplies in order to survive. And many times, these adaptations took the form of certain sizes and shapes—and probably even colors.

Was there an **upper limit** to the **size of a dinosaur**?

The answer to this question probably depends on the availability and locality of the dinosaur's food supply. In general, to support a larger weight, the dinosaur's bone size must have also increased, or else the bones would literally break under the animal's own weight. Plus, as the

Skeletal mount of a Brachiosaurus. (Photo courtesy of Gail Mooney/Corbis Corporation.)

bones became thicker to support the increasing weight, the animal would have become more and more cumbersome, limiting its ability to obtain food. Thus, for each dinosaur species, there was probably a definite limit to its size.

What was the **average size** among the **dinosaurs**?

The popular conception of dinosaurs is one of hugeness. But dinosaurs came in all sizes and shapes and types and they were extremely diverse, much like today's birds. They ranged in size from the gigantic sauropods, like *Brachiosaurus,* to small, chicken-sized ones like *Compsognathus,* and every size in between. Because we have only found relatively few fossils, it's hard to say what the average size of dinosaurs was.

What is the **largest dinosaur fossil** found to date?

Because so many different large dinosaur fossils have recently been found, it is difficult to definitively point to the largest dinosaur fossil.

Which carnivorous dinosaur was biggest?

The favorite contender is the theropod *Tyrannosaurus*, the Cretaceous period carnivore found in North America and Asia; it measured over 40 feet (12 meters) in length. The two new challengers are the *Giganotosaurus* of South America, and the *Carcharodontosaurus* of North Africa, two huge meat-eaters.

So far, the *Tyrannosaurus* seems to be in the lead, thanks to a huge fossil of a *Tyrannosaurus'* pubis bone found in 1997 in Fort Peck, Montana. This creature was so massive, scientists have given the fossil its own name: *Tyrannosaurus imperator*. This tyrannosaur's pubis bone measured 52.4 inches (133 centimeters) long; the pubis of *Giganotosaurus* was only 46.5 inches (118 centimeters) in length—which would make the Montana *Tyrannosaurus* about 15 to 20 percent larger than any other known meat-eating dinosaur.

No doubt, this is only the beginning. The hunt for the largest carnivore—and dinosaur—will continue. Paleontologists will find new dinosaur bones, and one of them may one day prove to be the largest dinosaur ever known.

On one end of the scale were the large sauropods, of which the *Brachiosaurus* ("arm lizard") is the most familiar. We believe the *Brachiosaurus* is one of the largest dinosaurs, mainly because we have found so many complete fossil skeletons of these huge species—thus, we know more about them. This large plant-eater measured about 70 feet (22 meters) long, about the length of two large school buses, and 40 feet (12.2 meters) high—or about as tall as an average three-story building. One of the largest whole skeleton specimens of the *Brachiosaurus* is in the Humboldt Museum in Berlin, and it measures 72.75 feet (22.2 meters) long and 46 feet (14 meters) high. The weight of this specimen is estimated to have been about 34.7 tons. The average weight of a typical *Brachiosaurus* is disputed, ranging from 32 to 78 tons—but either way, they were enormous animals.

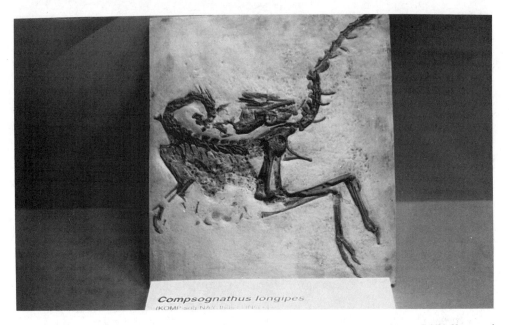

Fossilized remains of a *Compsognathus,* the smallest dinosaur. (Photo courtesy of University of Michigan Exhibit Museum of Natural History.)

Bone fragments have also been found of dinosaur species even larger than the *Brachiosaurus.* For example, the *Supersaurus, Ultrasaurus, Argentinasaurus,* and *Amphicoelias* are all very large-boned animals, most of them carnivores. Since complete skeletons of these dinosaurs have not been found to date, their exact size cannot be determined. But some scientists believe some of these species may have been one-and-a-half to two times larger than the *Brachiosaurus.*

What are the **smallest dinosaur fossils** found to date?

The smallest adult dinosaur fossil found to date is that of the *Compsognathus* ("pretty jaw"). The animal was slightly larger than a turkey, with a total length of approximately three feet (one meter), and weighed approximately 6.5 pounds. This small carnivore, nicknamed "Compy," lived during the Jurassic period, and was a fast-running and agile predator, probably subsisting on insects, frogs, and small lizards.

The smallest dinosaur fossil so far uncovered, regardless of age, is that of the *Mussaurus,* or mouse lizard. Fossils of this animal were found in 1979 in South America. Once thought to be the smallest dinosaur, it is now known the *Mussaurus* fossils were actually hatchlings of *Coloradisaurus,* which, when fully grown, would be larger than a *Compsognathus*. Their eggs were only one inch (2.54 centimeters) long; the fossil hatchlings were only 7.8 to 16 inches (20 to 40 centimeters) long.

Where have **dwarf dinosaur fossils** been found?

Dwarf dinosaur fossils have been found in Hateg, Romania. During the late Cretaceous period, much of the land area of Eastern Europe was inundated by the waters of the Tethys Ocean. Thus, the land existed in the form of islands.

Dinosaurs, along with other animals and plants, were isolated on these islands, cutting off the flora and fauna from other larger landmasses. Over time, the dinosaurs on these islands became smaller in response to the limited ecological environment. For example, the *Telmatosaurus,* a primitive hadrosaur found in Hateg, was about 15 feet (5 meters) long, and weighed approximately 1,103 pounds, or just over a half ton. This is about one-third the length and one-tenth the weight of other *Telmatosaurus* fossils found in other parts of the world. The larger dinosaurs were able to take advantage of greater territories and habitats, growing much more than their smaller, island-bound cousins.

Which **dinosaur** had the **longest neck** of any animal known?

Although the true longest-neck prize is highly debated, it is thought that the *Barosaurus,* or "heavy lizard," had the longest neck of any known dinosaur. The reason for the debate is that fossils of the *Barosaurus* are some of the rarest known. Because there are not many other specimens to back up the longest-neck claim, many scientists do not believe this animal is the winner.

Even though there is still debate, the *Barosaurus,* related to the *Diplodocus,* did have an enormously long neck—thought to be longer than the *Brachiosaurus*. Fossil remains of the *Barosaurus* have been found in the western United States and in Africa. The only mounted skeleton in the world of *Barosaurus* is found in New York City, at the American Museum of Natural History—depicted rearing up on its hind legs, confronting a predator.

Most of the longest necks belonged to the sauropod (herbivore) dinosaurs, creatures who probably needed the longer necks to reach food in the higher tree branches. Other major contenders include the usual favorite, the *Brachiosaurus,* a sauropod that reached a height of 40 feet (12.2 meters)—with much of that height a combination of its long neck and front legs. Still another long-necked dinosaur was the *Mamenchisaurus,* a sauropod dinosaur with a 33-foot (10 meter) long neck.

What **fossil find** may lead scientists to the **longest dinosaur** ever found?

The longest dinosaur ever found may not be known for a while. The fossils of a possible 150-foot (46-meter) Jurassic period dinosaur called a *Seismosaurus* is still being dug out from a chunk of sandstone found in New Mexico. It will take years to carefully dig out the specimen for display: Because of the hard sandstone surrounding the skeleton, scientists can only uncover a few square inches of bone per day.

What was the **longest predatory dinosaur**?

Scientists believe that the carnivore *Spinosaurus aegypticus* may have been up to 56 feet (17 meters) long—one of the largest predators, if not the longest. The animal's long spine evolved during the early Cretaceous period. (In fact, the entire vertebra of a *Spinosaurus* is taller than the average-size human.) The tall spines formed a skin-encased sail-like structure; some scientists suggest that the long spine was needed to hold the sails. No one knows the function of the structure, but there are some theories: One states that, because the animals lived in the tropics close to sea level, the sails may have been used to cool off the animals. Another idea is that the sails were used for attracting potential mates or for scaring off potential rivals—or even other dinosaur predators.

DINOSAUR BEHAVIOR

DINOSAUR DELICACIES

What did **dinosaurs eat**?

Based on the popular representations of dinosaurs in the media, these large, vicious creatures could eat anything they wanted—and some probably did! In reality, there is very little direct evidence of what the dinosaurs ate. But, from rare evidence and other factors, paleontologists have made some assumptions about dinosaur diets.

Since dinosaurs lived on our planet for about 150 million years, they must have slowly adapted to the changing flora and fauna. Overall, there were apparently two major types, and one minor type, of dinosaurs: herbivores, carnivores, and omnivores, respectively. Most of the dinosaurs were herbivores, or animals that ate available plants; the carnivorous dinosaurs, of course, ate other animals, including dinosaurs; and very few dinosaurs were omnivores, or animals that ate meat and plants.

Did **dinosaurs** need **water**?

It is probably safe to assume that dinosaurs, like all living creatures, needed water to live. They probably obtained water much like modern reptiles, either directly from a water source; or from their food, such as the plants they ate (in the case of herbivores), the animals they consumed (carnivores), or both (omnivores).

What **evidence** do paleontologists use to determine the **diets of dinosaurs**?

Because the actual, physical evidence of dinosaur diets is so rare (the soft parts of a dinosaur are rarely fossilized), paleontologists have turned to indirect evidence to form some idea of the feeding habits of dinosaurs. These include coprolites (fossils of excrement), trackways, fossil assemblages, and tooth marks on bones.

What are **coprolites**?

Coprolites, or scat, are the fossilized droppings, or feces, of dinosaurs. Because of the soft nature of this fecal material, soft dinosaur droppings would often disintegrate before they had a chance to fossilize. And if they dropped in the "wrong" place (such as the shore of the ocean where the waves would wash the material away), the chances of the dung becoming fossilized were almost non-existent.

Also, the shapes and sizes of most coprolites are not readily distinguishable between animals. Thus, there are, at present, few coprolites unequivocally traced back to dinosaurs—but the ones that have been traced offer tantalizing clues to dinosaur diets. In particular, such coprolites give us an insight into what the animal was eating, how it ate, and what happened afterward in terms of digestion.

What have paleontologists **learned** from **dinosaur coprolites**?

Paleontologists have found—in coprolites thought to be from herbivorous dinosaurs—quantities of cycad leaf cuticles, conifer stems, or conifer wood tissues, giving some clues as to what these dinosaurs ate. Also, in some cases, the nature of the fragments shows these dinosaurs were well-equipped to chew up and digest the tough, woody food available at the time.

Several coprolites from carnivorous dinosaurs have also been found. One recent find was astounding: In 1998, near the town of Eastend, Saskatchewan, Canada, scientists found a huge coprolite, almost as large as a loaf of bread. The 65-million-year-old coprolite measures 17 inches (43 centimeters) and is thought to be from a *Tyrannosaurus rex;* it is one of the largest coprolites ever found. The analysis of the coprolite also produced an intriguing suggestion: The remains look as if the *Tyrannosaurus* did not swallow the bones of its prey somewhat whole—but actually chewed and pulverized the animal's bones. This is contrary to what paleontologists have believed for a long time—that these carnivores "gulped and swallowed" their prey. But the verdict is still out on the subject until scientists find more such coprolites.

Did **dinosaurs urinate**?

No one knows if dinosaurs urinated, as the soft anatomical parts to indicate such an activity do not readily fossilize. But it is probably safe to assume they did, if modern reptiles and birds are similar to their ancient cousins, the dinosaurs. In fact, they may have excreted a solid form of urea, or guano, similar to modern birds and reptiles.

What are **fossil assemblages,** and what do they tell us about **dinosaur diets**?

Fossil assemblages are groups of fossils from different dinosaurs. For example, one assemblage found in the sandstones of the Gobi Desert (Mongolia) is of a carnivorous *Velociraptor* intertwined with an herbivorous *Protoceratops.* The *Velociraptor's* clawed feet were attached to its prey's throat and belly, while the *Protoceratops'* jaws had trapped the arm of the predator. This assemblage suggests the struggling dinosaurs, predator and prey, died together as a massive sandstorm overcame them.

In fifteen sites in Montana, major fossil assemblages have been found: The teeth of the carnivorous dinosaur *Deinonychus* was found in association with the fossil remains of herbivorous dinosaur *Tenontosaurus.* Dinosaur teeth were continually shed, as new ones grew in, and vigorous biting could have increased tooth loss. Since there is lack of *Deinonychus* teeth found with the remains of other dinosaurs, paleontologists have concluded that the *Tenontosaurus* was the favorite prey of this predator.

207

What are trackways and what do they tell paleontologists about dinosaur diets?

Trackways, the multiple fossilized footprints of dinosaurs, have given paleontologists some idea of the feeding habits of many dinosaurs. For example, an early Cretaceous period site in Texas, as well as a late Cretaceous period site in Bolivia, show footprints of what appears to be a pack of theropods actively stalking a herd of sauropods. In a Cretaceous period site in Australia, fossilized tracks suggest a herd of over one hundred small coelurosaurs and ornithopods stampeded as a large, single therapod stalked the group. In a Utah coal mine, Cretaceous period footprints of herbivorous dinosaurs clustered around fossil tree trunks give some indication of their foraging behavior.

What do **tooth marks** tell us about **dinosaur diets**?

Another piece of evidence used by paleontologists to determine dinosaur diets are tooth marks. Most of the grooves or punctures found associated with fossilized dinosaur bones were the result of attacks by carnivorous dinosaurs. Most of the time, however, this evidence does not reveal whether the victim was actively hunted or scavenged—and except in certain cases, the identity of the predator cannot be determined.

In one instance, the spacing of the scoring found on the bones of an *Apatosaurus,* a herbivore, matched the spacing of teeth from the jaw of an *Allosaurus,* a carnivore. In another case, dental putty was used to make molds of puncture marks found in a *Triceratops'* (a herbivore) pelvis, and an *Edmontosaurus'* (another herbivore) phalanx. The resulting molds nicely matched the fossilized teeth of the suspected predator, a carnivorous *Tyrannosaurus*. In one rare instance, a *Tyrannosaurus* tooth was found stuck in the fibula of a herbivorous hadrosaur, *Hypacrosaurus*. And of course, in the most obvious cases (and the most rare), predators could be identified if the fossil bones—and teeth—of the two animals were locked in mortal combat.

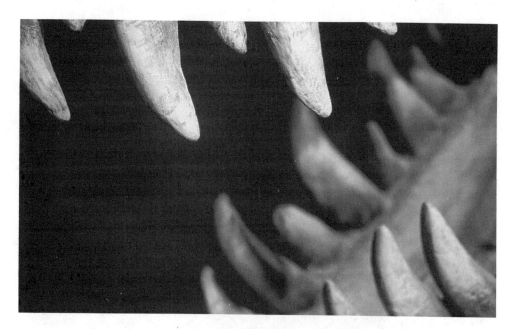

The ferocious teeth of a *Tyrannosaurus rex*. (Photo courtesy of Michael S. Yamashita/Corbis Corporation.)

To what **group** did all the **meat-eating dinosaurs** belong?

All of the carnivorous, or meat-eating dinosaurs, belonged to the theropods, or bipedal carnivores. These dinosaurs, along with the large, herbivorous sauropods, made up the saurischian dinosaurs. This group represents a wide range of dinosaur species—from the large *Tyrannosaurus* to the small *Compsognathus*.

What were some of the **major types** of **theropod** dinosaurs?

The major types of dinosaurs making up the theropods were divided into two lineages: the coelurosaurs and the carnosaurs. This simple classification does not reflect the true relationships of the theropods, and is usually not used by paleontologists to classify the animals. But there is no universally accepted alternative classification of the animals—mainly because there are so many fossils (many of which changed dramatically over the Mesozoic era) and interpretations.

Thus, in general, the theropods were represented by the coelurosaurs and carnosaurs. The smaller, more nimble, meat-eating dinosaurs with

This skull of a *Tyrannosaurus* illustrates the massive jaw and teeth of this carnivore who used its jaw for shearing its meat. (Photo courtesy of University of Michigan Exhibit Museum of Natural History.)

longer grasping arms and long, narrow jaws were known as coelurosaurs, or "hollow-tailed lizards." They developed during the middle Jurassic period and roamed the land until the end of the Cretaceous. They could run very fast and catch insects and small mammals; some were also thought to be cannibals. One of the most well-known coelurosaurs is the *Compsognathus*.

The large, big-headed dinosaurs, with powerful legs and small arms, were known as carnosaurs, or "flesh lizards." These dinosaurs pursued and ate other dinosaurs, using numerous backward-curving teeth and clawed feet—and in many cases, weight—to catch prey. One well-known

Dagger-like teeth

The skull of the allosaur was built to eat meat—large amounts of it. The powerfully muscled jaws were lined with dagger-like teeth, used for tearing and slicing. Allosaurs did not chew their food, but simply gulped down the chunks of meat torn from their hapless prey.

Throughout an allosaur's life, its teeth were continuously shed and replaced by new ones growing from within the jaw bones. This section of jaw shows teeth in several stages of growth, with some recently emerged from the jawbone.

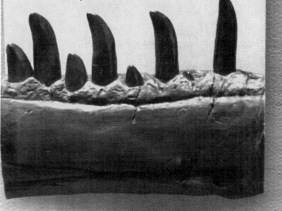

The *Allosaurus* adapted many features t(... become a meat-eater, including these huge sharp teeth. (Photo courtesy of University of Michigan Exhibit Museum of Natura(... History.)

carnosaur is the *Allosaurus*. The popular carnivore *Tyrannosaurus* was once classified under the carnosaurs, but it is now thought that it is more closely related to the smaller coelurosaurs of the Cretaceous period.

What adaptations enabled **carnivorous dinosaurs** to **eat meat**?

All of the carnivorous dinosaurs, known as the theropods, shared many adaptations specific to catching, killing, eating, and digesting meat. These animals had larger, sharper, and more pointed teeth than their herbivorous cousins—and were used to kill the victim and tear the flesh off the

211

What did the carnivorous dinosaurs prefer to eat?

Little is known about the various carnivorous dinosaurs' food preference, but it was probably limited to animals that were sick and ailing (thus easy to kill), or animals that were not as large as the predator—similar to how predators today search for a meal. The carnivores' digestive tracts were probably perfect for breaking down the proteins they needed to survive. And the digestive system was probably not as complex as that of a herbivore, as meat is easier to digest than plants.

The only chance we have had so far to view the carnivorous digestive tract was recently found: One of the few fossils found contains the intestines of a small carnivorous dinosaur, called *Scipionyx samniticus,* and nicknamed "Skippy." This dinosaur is about 113 million years old, and is a distant cousin of both the *Tyrannosaurus rex* and *Velociraptor.* Its intestines shows that the digestive tract was short—at least for this younger carnivore.

body. To power these teeth—and to break down the nutritious bone marrow from their prey—carnivores needed strong jaws and muscles.

The carnivores also had clawed feet for slashing their victims, with the dromaeosaurids possessing the epitome of this adaptation—large, sickle-shaped foot claws. The theropods, being bipedal, had their arms and hands free to grasp their prey; their fingers often had claws used to slash and hold the victim. And being bipedal, they had the relative speed and agility to catch their prey. It is thought by some scientists that for successful hunting, the theropods had good eyesight, a keen sense of smell, and a large brain (in proportion to the body) to calculate hunting strategies.

To what **groups** did the **plant-eating (herbivore) dinosaurs** belong?

All of the ornithischians, or "bird-hipped," dinosaurs were herbivores; as were the sauropods of the saurischians, or "lizard-hipped," dinosaurs

The club tail of the herbivore Ankylosaurus. (Photo courtesy of University of Michigan Exhibit Musuem of Natural History.)

(the other half of the saurischians were the theropods, or meat-eating dinosaurs). The largest dinosaurs found to date have been herbivores—specifically, members of the sauropods, such as the *Brachiosaurus* and *Supersaurus*.

What **adaptations** did the **herbivorous dinosaurs** have that enabled them to **eat plants**?

Some herbivorous dinosaurs did not chew at all, but merely swallowed whole the vegetation they pulled off a tree or bush. They had larger (and probably more rugged) digestive tracts than carnivorous dinosaurs in order to digest the tough, fibrous plants they ate. Some herbivores, such as the *Ankylosaurus,* even had fermentation chambers along their digestive tract, in which tough fibers would be broken down by bacteria. In addition, some herbivores had gastroliths, or "gizzard stones," in their digestive tract, which would grind up the fibrous plants, helping to digest the material. (It is interesting to note that this method is similar to how birds swallow stones to grind up ingested matter in their digestive tracts—and that birds are thought to be directly related to dinosaurs—or are even dinosaurs themselves.) These stones were deliberately swallowed, and are often found with fossils of herbivores. Both of these actions prepared the vegetation for digestion.

Other herbivorous dinosaurs, like the hadrosaurs, also known as the duck-billed dinosaurs, had special teeth that would grind up the food before swallowing. Ceratopsians, like the *Triceratops,* had sharp teeth and powerful jaws that enabled them to cut through tough plants. And still other herbivores had cheek pouches, apparently used to store food for later ingestion.

What **plants** did the **herbivorous dinosaurs** probably **eat** that are still **present today**?

Decendents of the conifers, flowering plants, horsetails, ferns, and cycads continue to grow today, and probably their ancestors served as meals for ancient herbivorous dinosaurs.

What was an **omnivorous dinosaur**?

An omnivorous dinosaur was one that ate both plants and meat. There are only a few known omnivores among the dinosaurs, including *Ornithomimus* and perhaps *Oviraptor,* although new fossil finds may change our opinion about the latter. A diet of an omnivorous dinosaur could include different types of plants, insects, eggs, and small animals. These dinosaurs were probably rare, and only ate that way out of necessity—such as the sudden lack of meat or plants in their surrounding habitat. Other believe these dinosaurs were omnivores by accident—eating insects and small animals as they ate the plants around them.

Have any **fossilized stomach contents** of dinosaurs been found?

Although rare, some dinosaur stomach remains have been found over the years. The best examples are from carnivorous dinosaurs: The fossilized remains of a lizard (*Bavaisaurus*) were found in the gut region of a carnivorous dinosaur called *Compsognathus*—no doubt the dinosaur's last meal. In addition, *Coelophysis* fossils have been found with the fossilized remains of other *Coelophysis* dinosaurs inside the gut region, indicating these dinosaurs probably engaged in cannibalism. Whether this was active predation or scavenging has not been determined.

The stomach contents of herbivorous dinosaurs have not been as definitive, however, due to the organic nature of the material. One case was reported in the early 1900s, where the fossilized remains of an *Edmontosaurus* had been found with conifer seeds, twigs, and needles in the body cavity. However, it could not be determined if these were actual stomach contents, or just debris that had subsequently washed into the carcass.

DINOSAURS IN MOTION

What are **dinosaur trackways**?

Dinosaur trackways are fossil footprints of dinosaurs, and they are found all over the world. These trackways developed as dinosaurs (and other animals) walked in the soft sediment or sand along the shorelines of beaches, rivers, ponds, and lakes. Almost immediately after the animals walked by, the tracks were quickly buried in sediment, eventually becoming fossil footprints (also called ichnotaxia). Because such places were good sources of water and food—including lush plants for the herbivores, and plenty of animals for the carnivores—they became natural pathways for all types of dinosaurs.

So far, the problem with the dinosaur trackways is that it is impossible to tell which dinosaur made the footprints. Scientists can only generally determine what type of dinosaur left the tracks; for example if the tracks belonged to a biped or quadruped dinosaur, and whether it was a sauropod or a theropod.

What are some of the **largest dinosaur trackways**?

Some of the largest dinosaur trackways are called megatrack sites, where footprint-bearing rock can extend for hundreds or even thousands of miles. Several Jurassic and Cretaceous sites in North America

Fossilized dinosaur footprint. (Photo courtesy of Francesa Muntada/Corbis Corporation.)

have such trackways. For example, tracks in the Entrada sandstone beds in eastern Utah (from the middle Jurassic) cover about 116 square miles (300 square kilometers); the density of the prints is estimated to be between one and ten per 10.8 square feet (one square meter).

What do **dinosaur trackways** found in rock tell us about the **behavior** of some dinosaurs?

Dinosaur trackways can tell us a few things about dinosaur behavior: For sauropods, the tracks are usually of more than one creature, and heading in the same direction, indicating a social herding behavior or even a migration. Some trackways include footprints of large theropods—some prints indicating a pack behavior to stalk large sauropods.

What do **dinosaur tracks** tell us about **locomotion** of some dinosaurs?

Dinosaur trackways confirm that certain dinosaurs walked and ran on all four legs (quadrupeds) and others on two legs (bipeds). The tracks also show that some dinosaurs walked in an erect fashion, and walked by putting one foot almost directly in front on the other. In addition, some dinosaurs quickly ran or walked slowly—probably depending on whether the animals were browsing, wading, trotting, running after prey, or running from predators. One interesting observation: So far, no tail marks—indicating the dinosaurs dragged their tails along behind them—have been found along trackways. Because of this, scientists believe dinosaurs probably held their tails erect.

Where and what is the **Dinosaur Freeway**?

The Dinosaur Freeway is a large trackway of dinosaur footprints extending along the Front Range of the Rocky Mountains—from around Boulder, Colorado, to eastern New Mexico. In the middle Cretaceous period, this area was a coastal plain with a wide shoreline, a good source of water and food.

Where did a **dinosaur stampede** take place?

There is such a special place in Australia, discovered in 1960. There, in the Lark Quarry Environment Park, south of Wilton, on the eroded edge of the Tully Range, are hundreds of dinosaur footprints preserved in rock. The footprints were made as dinosaurs walked in mud around a prehistoric lake.

Typical for animal life, most of the tracks were made as large carnivores hunted for prey along the edge of the lake. In particular, large carnosaurs trapped groups of coelurosaurs and ornithopods; in one instance, a carnosaur attacked an unfortunate animal, pursuing its victim along the muddy shore—and causing the rest of the surrounding dinosaurs to stampede in panic.

Although there is no longer a large lake with carnivorous dinosaurs, the area still holds a bit of danger: It isn't easy to get to. The drive to Lark Quarry takes one and a half to two hours by car—and the roads are dangerous, sometimes impassable, in wet weather.

How do paleontologists determine **speeds of dinosaurs** using the **trackways**?

Although it is difficult to tell the type of dinosaur that made a track, scientists can tell the relative speed of the animals as they moved along the trackways. By measuring the distance between the footprints, and the size of the tracks, they can tell that some dinosaurs ran much faster than first assumed. In other words, these tracks prove that the old idea—that dinosaurs were slow and sluggish—wasn't always true!

Did **dinosaurs** travel in **herds**?

Yes, dinosaurs did apparently live and travel in herds—and it was probably because of the old expression, "safety in numbers." Scientists have deduced this behavior based on dinosaur trackways, and huge collections of dinosaur bones that indicate massive kills (places in which large amounts of dinosaurs bones are found in one place).

In particular, many herbivores apparently traveled in herds, based on the multiple tracks left along the dinosaur trackways. The tracks also show that many herbivores held the young in the center of the herd—similar to elephant herds—probably to protect the young.

Some dinosaur fossils have been found in massive collections—indicating many dozens of animals were killed in one spot. Some scientists believe such collections of animal bones show the creatures exhibited a herding behavior. In many cases, while in the herd, these animals were swiftly killed off, perhaps from a major flood, volcanic action, or a huge sandstorm. For example, the bonebeds of about one hundred *Styracosaurus* dinosaurs, an herbivore, have been discovered, as have dinosaur bones that represent dozens of *Protoceratops* and *Triceratops*.

What was the fastest dinosaur?

It is difficult to name the fastest dinosaur based on the few trackways found, but some information has been gathered by analyzing the tracks. The speediest dinosaurs were probably the small, bipedal carnivores, especially those with long, slim hind limbs and light bodies. These swift dinosaurs probably didn't run any faster than the fastest modern land animals. One carnivorous dinosaur called an *Ornithomimus* is thought to have run about 43 miles (70 kilometers) per hour—about the speed of a modern African ostrich.

One particular herbivore called a *Maiasaura* (a hadrosaur) is also thought to have lived in herds—and probably returned to the same nesting grounds every year. Fossil bones of these animals were found in a huge group of about ten thousand animals in Montana. The animals all died suddenly, apparently when a volcano erupted—smothering the animals with volcanic gases and covering the creatures with a thick layer of ash.

Did **dinosaurs migrate**?

Yes, certain dinosaurs apparently migrated, similar to certain animals today. They probably migrated for the same reasons, too: Seeking new food sources as the seasons changed, and migrating for purposes of mating and nesting. Similar to determining the herding behavior of dinosaurs, scientists have deduced dinosaur migrating behavior based on trackways, and huge collections of bones that indicate massive kills.

Did **dinosaurs hunt in packs**?

Yes, paleontologists speculate that certain carnivorous dinosaurs exhibited a social behavior called pack hunting. The large theropods, like *Tyrannosaurus* and *Giganotosaurus,* show some evidence of hunting in packs, similar to modern-day lions.

In a recent discovery in Argentina, scientists have found a huge collection of dinosaur bones of *Giganotosaurus*—a carnivorous dinosaur that grew to 45 feet (13.7 meter) long and weighed about 8 tons. The bones of four or five *Giganotosaurus* indicate that they died together on the Patagonian plains, swept away by a fast-flowing river. The bones show that two of the animals were very big, but the others were smaller. Scientists believe that this shows that there was some kind of social behavior—probably that the animals hunted in packs. In particular, each animal within the group would have different characteristics, giving the pack a great range of capabilities—such as going after smaller and larger animals.

Other evidence shows that at least some of the dromaeosaurids, or "raptors," engaged in pack hunting. When the first fossils of a dinosaur called *Deinonychus* were found—a six-foot (1.8-meter) tall, nine-foot (2.8-meter) long Cretaceous period predator of western North America—the remains of many of these carnivores were clustered near the body of a large herbivore, *Tenontosaurus*. Paleontologists theorized that these predators perished during the struggle with the larger dinosaur—indicating that the hunt was being conducted by a group.

Did any **dinosaurs live** in the **cold polar regions**?

Yes, paleontologists believe that while most flourished in tropical or temperate climates, some dinosaurs actually lived in the cold weather regions of the ancient world. Fossils of these polar dinosaurs have been uncovered on the North Slope of Alaska. Others have been found at Dinosaur Cove, at the southeastern tip of Australia, and dated at 105 to 110 million years ago. Although this part of Australia is presently at approximately 39 degrees south latitude, at the time of the polar dinosaurs, it was much farther south, and lay within the Antarctic Circle. For three months during the winter, the night lasted 24 hours a day, and temperatures fell well below zero. The dinosaur fossils uncovered in this area show that the animals were well adapted to these harsh conditions—and that they apparently had keen night vision and may have been warm-blooded. They were generally small animals, ranging in size from about that of chicken to that of a human, with the largest carnivore about nine feet (three meters) high.

Did any **dinosaurs** climb or live in **trees**?

No known dinosaurs climbed or lived in trees. At one time, the foot bones of the *Hypsilophodon,* a small herbivorous ornithopod, were thought to have the big toe facing opposite to the other toes, similar to a bird's foot. Scientists speculated, based on this erroneous assumption, that this dinosaur lived in trees, perching on branches, similar to today's Australian tree kangaroo. When the true foot bone structure was discovered, it was realized that *Hypsilophodon* was a swift land runner, using its speed and agility to escape predators—not to live in trees.

Did any **dinosaurs fly**?

No known non-avian (avian means bird), flying dinosaur has ever been discovered—but there were creatures that flew at the time of the dinosaurs. The first and most prolific were the pterosaurs. These contemporaries of the dinosaur lived throughout the Mesozoic era and appeared to be close relatives of the dinosaurs, evolving from the archosaurs. The dinosaurs dominated on land; the pterosaurs dominated the air.

The connection of dinosaurs to birds is still highly debated. But if dinosaurs and birds are truly so closely related, then it could be said that avian dinosaurs, or birds, would eventually evolve, take to the air—and would endure until today.

What was the purpose of the giant *Apatosaurus'* tail-tip?

Some scientists believe the *Apatosaurus* (formerly known as the *Brontosaurus*) may have moved its 45-foot (14-meter) tail like a bullwhip—with its 6-foot (1.8-meters) skinny tip creating a loud crack. Recent computer models have compared the movement of a model *Apatosaurus* tail with the motion of a bullwhip. These studies show it is not only feasible the tail moved in this way, but that the relatively slow motion at the base of the tail would translate into supersonic speeds at the tip. This would have created a loud sonic boom of about 200 decibels—much louder than the 140 decibels of a jet taking off!

In the past, paleontologists thought the tail of sauropods like *Apatosaurus* were mainly used for balance or to swat rivals. But the tip of the

Dinosaur egg casts illustrating the massive size of these animals' eggs. (Photo courtesy of University of Michigan Exhibit Museum of Natural History.)

tail contained tiny, fragile bones that could have easily broken in a fight. Now, some scientists think the loud crack from the tail tip could have been used to scare away predators, establish dominance in a herd, resolve disputes, and even to attract a mate.

DINOSAUR YOUNG

What do **dinosaur eggs** look like?

Scientists have collected fossil dinosaur eggs, sometimes finding more than a dozen in a nest-like area. The fossilized eggs are usually the color of the rock in which they are found; and similar to fossil dinosaur bones, their structures have been fossilized and replaced by minerals over time.

Although the eggs are fossilized, scientists have discovered that dinosaur eggs probably looked similar to those of modern birds, reptiles, and some primitive mammals. Most of the eggs were rounded or elongated, with hard shells. They contained an amnion, a membrane that kept the egg moist—a kind of "private pond" for the young animal growing in the egg. The eggs appeared to be similar in other ways, too: The surface of the shell allowed for the exchange of gases necessary for the young to survive (many of the fossilized eggs exhibit a mottled surface that indicates the shell had pores); and the young would crack their way out of an egg when it was ready to enter the world.

No one really knows if the majority of eggs laid by the dinosaurs were soft-, flexible-, or hard-shelled eggs. The eggshell would have to be relatively strong to support the weight of the brooding parents, or the overburden of nesting material; and the shell would still have to allow for the exchange of necessary gases. In reality, hard-shelled eggs have the best chance of fossilizing, as they are harder. Thus, most shells that we find today may not truly represent all the eggs that dinosaurs laid—just the hardest ones that survived.

Did all **dinosaurs lay eggs**?

As far as paleontologists can determine, all dinosaurs reproduced by laying eggs. The first fossilized dinosaur eggs were found in France in 1869, but not everyone agreed the eggs were from dinosaurs. Although it may seem somewhat obvious to us now, it took time before scientists agreed that dinosaurs nested, laid, and hatched eggs. The proof was found in the Gobi Desert in the 1920s, where both nests and eggs of a group of *Protoceratops* were found. Since that time, over 200 sites with fossil eggs of various dinosaurs have been found all over the world, including in the United States, France, Mongolia, China, Argentina, and India.

However, it should also be noted that there are some modern lizards—which are reptiles—that do not lay eggs; rather they give birth to live young (called viviparity). Some scientists suggest that this is a result of adapting to colder climates. And although the idea is highly debated (and no real physical evidence has been found), some scientists speculate that polar dinosaurs may have reproduced in this way.

Where was the **first clutch** of **dinosaur eggs** discovered?

The first known clutch (nest) of dinosaur eggs was found by Roy Chapman Andrews in 1922, in the Gobi Desert, south of the Altai Mountains. The eggs

223

Like most reptiles and birds, sauropods laid eggs. This is a cast of an egg, attributed to a sauropod called *Hypselosaurus*, whose fossils are found in southern France and northern Spain.

Cretaceous period
UMEX

The egg of the *Hypselosaurus*. (Photo courtesy of University of Michigan Exhibit Museum of Natural History.)

were found in one of the most prolific fossil beds in the area, a sedimentary layer known as the Nemget Formation, also known for the more than a hundred fossil skeletons of the small horned dinosaur *Protoceratops*.

What is the **largest dinosaur egg** known?

The largest dinosaur egg found to date is about 12 inches (30 centimeters) long and ten inches (25 centimeters) wide; it may have weighed about 15.5 pounds. It is thought to be from a giant, 100-million-year-old herbivore called a *Hypselosaurus*. To compare, the prize for the largest

Zoologist attempts to free and restore a fossilized egg nest. (Photo courtesy of Corbis Corporation.)

bird egg (and largest flightless bird) on Earth belongs to the African ostrich, with eggs up to 6.8 inches (17 centimeters) long by 5.4 inches (14 centimeters) wide, and weighing up to 3.3 pounds.

What did a **dinosaur nest** look like?

Not all dinosaur nests looked alike. Many were simple pits dug into the soil or sand; others were more complicated, including deep, mud-rimmed nests with grasslike linings. Some dinosaurs even had a certain way of laying their eggs. For example, the *Maiasaura,* a herbivore, would

225

arrange the eggs in a spiral, making sure to allow enough space between hatchlings to aid them in escape from predators. *Protoceratops* also apparently laid their eggs in a spiral fashion.

How have the **latest findings** of *Oviraptor* changed our image of this dinosaur?

The dinosaur *Oviraptor,* or egg thief, was previously thought to have been a dinosaur egg consumer, as its fossilized remains were often found near nests. Recently, scientists uncovered an 80-million-year-old fossil that shows this bipedal, carnivorous dinosaur—approximately the size of a modern ostrich—apparently brooding or guarding a nest of 15 large eggs.

The fossil, uncovered in Mongolia's Gobi Desert in the mid-1990s, is the first hard evidence to date showing the behavior of this dinosaur; other theories on the dinosaur's behavior have been inferred from indirect data. The *Oviraptor* was found lying on its clutch of eggs, with its legs tucked tightly against its body, and the arms turned back to encircle the nest. This is similar to the nesting behavior of modern birds—and suggests such behavior may have started long before the advent of wings and feathers.

How did the **dinosaur eggs hatch**?

Similar to modern birds and reptiles, a dinosaur young cracked its way out of an egg when it was ready to enter the world. Also similar to these modern species, certain dinosaur species were apparently too small and weak to leave the nest after hatching. In most cases, the baby dinosaurs probably remained nest-bound for many weeks after they hatched, and had to be fed and tended by the adults. Scientists have deduced this from several nest sites that show the fragments of trampled egg shells, and remains that look like regurgitated leaves and berries. And similar to the young of most species, dinosaur hatchlings were no doubt especially susceptible and vulnerable to attacks from predators that hunted around the nesting sites.

OLDER DINOSAURS

How **long** did **dinosaurs live**?

Scientists do not know the exact lifespan of the dinosaurs, but they estimate that dinosaurs lived about 75 to 300 years. This educated guess is based on examining the microstructure of dinosaur bones, which indicate that the dinosaurs matured slowly. This is similar to ancestors of the dinosaur, including crocodiles, whose eggs take about 90 days to hatch, and whose lifespans can extend from 70 to 100 years.

Did **dinosaurs sleep** standing up?

No one really knows the sleeping habits of the dinosaurs. It is not easy to infer such activities based on just the fossil record, as sleeping leaves no definitive physical trace. After all, no one knew sharks slept until recently—and sharks are common in today's oceans!

227

Did dinosaurs see in color or black and white?

Because eyes are soft parts of an animal, they do not survive the fossilization process. Thus, we have no idea what a dinosaur eye looked like, much less if the animals could see in color or black and white. And it's hard to guess: Just look at the diversity of modern animals—and the diversity of eyes, and how and what the various animals see.

Still, scientists have inferred the sleeping habits of some of the dinosaurs. For example, most of the smaller animals probably slept like modern reptiles, just flopping down on the ground like a crocodile. Others, such as the huge *Tyrannosaurus,* probably had a much harder time sleeping lying down. Once it had lain down, it would have been difficult for it to get up using its small arms. Other larger dinosaurs would probably find their enormous weight would get in the way—thus, the only way larger dinosaurs could sleep was standing up. It is interesting to note that modern birds (close relatives to the dinosaurs, or maybe even dinosaurs themselves) sleep standing up.

Did **dinosaurs** have **binocular vision** similar to humans?

The majority of dinosaurs had monocular vision, with eyes set into the sides of their heads, and little overlap between the right and left fields of view. Thus, they had good peripheral vision, but the binocular vision was modest—similar to the modern reptile, the alligator. (One of the animals with the best pairs of eyes is the modern house cat: They have binocular vision that takes in 130 degrees in front of them, and have peripheral vision that stretches back farther than any other animal.)

But some scientists believe there were exceptions, and that some dinosaurs may have had binocular vision similar to a human's depth perception. In particular, predators such as the *Tyrannosaurus* may have been able to see depth, suggesting that the animals were hunters, not scavengers as some paleontologists believe. In addition, over time, some carnivores may have evolved facial traits that actually enhanced the animals' ability to see depth. And some dinosaurs may have developed sight similar to a hawk: The raptor can see its prey from far away, but its binocular vision does not kick in until it swoops down from the sky to take down its prey. More work is being done to determine how dinosaurs saw the world. Scientists are using model dinosaur heads and laser beams to ascertain sight position.

How large was a **dinosaur's brain**?

No one really knows the true size of dinosaur brains because as with all soft parts of the dinosaur, brains did not survive the fossilization process. Therefore, scientists can only infer the size of the animals' brains by examining the brain case—or, the part of the skull housing the brain. They found that different dinosaurs had different sized brains, based on the volume of the brain case. For example, sauropods' brains were small in comparison with their body weight; whereas, some dinosaurs, such as the *Velociraptor,* had very large brains in comparison with their body weight.

Were the **dinosaurs intelligent**?

Since there are no dinosaurs around, there is no way we can determine a dinosaur's intelligence quotient—or IQ.

However, we can judge how relatively intelligent dinosaurs were by taking a ratio of brain weight (based on the skull volume) to body weight, then comparing these ratios for various dinosaurs. This ratio is called the encephalization quotient (EQ). Based on this idea, the smartest dinosaurs had the larger brain to body weight ratios than the less intelligent ones.

The following table lists some types of dinosaurs and their EQs. Note that the dromaeosaurids and troodontids are thought to be some of the smartest dinosaurs. The troodontids included the *Troodon,* a carnivore; the dromaeosaurid dinosaurs included the *Velociraptor,* a six-foot (1.8-meter) carnivore with clawed feet, sharp, pointed teeth—and an animal that probably roamed in packs.

Dinosaur	EQ (approximate)
dromaeosaurids	5.8
troodontids	5.8
carnosaurs	1.0 to 1.9
ornithopods	0.9 to 1.5
ceratopsians	0.7 to 0.9
stegosaurs	0.6
ankylosaurs	0.55
sauropods	0.2
sauropodomorphas	0.1

What are the **encephalization quotients (EQs)** for some **typical mammals**?

The encephalization quotient (EQs) for some typical mammals are based on the same formula as for the dinosaurs: The ratio of the brain to body weight. The following table lists the EQs of some well-known mammals.

Mammal	Animal Type	EQ
human	primate	7.4
bottlenose dolphin	cetacean	5.6
bluenose dolphin	cetacean	5.31
chimpanzee	primate	2.5
rhesus monkey	primate	2.09
cat	carnivore	1.71
langur	primate	1.29
squirrel	rodent	1.10
rat	rodent	0.40

WHAT HAPPENED?

THE CRETACEOUS EXTINCTION

What is an **extinction**?

An extinction is the sudden or gradual dying out of a species. There are a multitude of reasons for extinction, ranging from disease, human intervention, climate changes, volcanic eruptions, or colliding space bodies. Each one can cause the extinction of one or many species of animals, depending on the severity.

When did the idea of **extinction** become accepted?

During the seventeenth and eighteenth centuries, scientists knew that fossils were the ancient remains of plants and animals. However, most still felt that these fossils represented known, living species—species that would shortly be discovered living in some remote, unexplored part of the globe.

This changed radically in the 1750s. Explorers in North America found the remains of what they thought were elephants—but in reality, the animals were mastodons and mammoths, animals now known to have lived more than 10,000 years ago toward the end of the Great Ice Age. As these and other fossils from the New World were examined, scientists realized the fossils were actually the remains of recently extinct species.

In 1796, Baron Georges Cuvier (1769–1832) of the Museum of Natural History in Paris (the first comparative anatomist) published a series of papers proving these "fossil elephants" and giant mammal bones from other parts of the world did indeed represent extinct species.

What were the major **extinctions** during the **Earth's** long history?

About five major extinctions have occurred over the Earth's long history. Some of the extinctions greatly affected the animals and plants on land, while other extinctions mainly occurred in the oceans. Most of the major extinctions are based on the fossil record, and usually indicate a time when a large percent of the plants and animals living on the Earth went extinct, usually for unknown reasons. The following table lists some major extinctions and the time periods between which each extinction happened.

Time Period	Date (millions of years ago)	Percent of Species Extinct (approximate)
Cambrian-Ordovician	438	85
Devonian-Carboniferous	360	82
Permian-Triassic	250	97
Triassic-Jurassic	208	76
Cretaceous-Tertiary	65	76

How many species of **dinosaurs** were living at the end of the **Cretaceous period**?

No one knows the exact number of dinosaur species living at the end of the Cretaceous period, as we do not have a complete dinosaur fossil record. This is not anyone's fault, but the nature of fossilization: Not all animals were in the right place at the right time in order to become a fossil; plus, erosion wipes away much of the evidence over time. Although we know there were probably many more dinosaurs, only a few species were still alive toward the end of the Cretaceous period—and most of them lived on the North American continent.

How many **other organisms** became **extinct** at the end of the **Cretaceous period**?

No one knows the exact number of other organisms—land animals, marine animals, and plants—that became extinct at the end of the Cretaceous period. But based on the fossil record, scientists believe that about 76 percent of all species on the Earth went extinct at the end of the Cretaceous period.

Why did certain **plants and animals survive** through the end of the **Cretaceous period**?

Until a definite reason for the extinction is determined, it is difficult to answer such a question. Apparently, some species were not affected by the occurrence. In fact, nocturnal mammals—probably through luck or inborn tolerance to harsh environmental conditions—survived. They quickly exploited all the new nooks and crannies available to them, and soon dominated the planet. Eventually, over millions of years, humans evolved from those species.

Why aren't **huge amounts** of **dinosaur bones** found in late Cretaceous period rock layers?

This is another mystery surrounding the whole question of dinosaur extinction at the end of the Cretaceous period: If indeed the dinosaurs were suddenly killed off by a catastrophe, there should be a thick layer of bones—or a "bone spike"—in the fossil record. However, no such bone spike has been found to date at the boundary between the Cretaceous and Tertiary periods. Equally puzzling, few dinosaur bones have been found within a foot or so below this boundary.

One possible theory to explain these "missing" dinosaur bones (if they truly are missing) involves acid rain. Models have shown that one consequence of a large asteroid impact would be highly acidic rainfall over the planet. This acidic water could have dissolved most of the dinosaur bones lying on the surface, and would have also penetrated below the surface into the upper soil zones. Combined with bacteria, the water would become even more acidic—dissolving any bones found there. Only already fossilized bones would resist the acidic water. And since the fossilization process takes a very long time, none of the more recent dinosaur bones would have been spared.

This theory—and it is only a theory at present—neatly explains why there are so few dinosaur bones found in rock below the boundary, and none at the boundary itself. Supporting evidence comes from the boundary layer itself: In many places around the world, a relatively thin layer of clay exists that could have formed from the erosion of rocks due to acid rain.

THEORIES ON EXTINCTION

How long ago did the **dinosaurs** disappear?

Based on the dinosaur fossil record, larger and smaller dinosaurs died out about 65 million years ago. More recently, many scientists point out that not all dinosaurs disappeared—citing birds as direct descendants of the dinosaur.

What are the **two general theories** as to how fast the dinosaurs went **extinct**?

The two general theories are catastrophism and gradualism. Catastrophism is the rapid change in conditions found on the Earth, such as changes in the atmosphere, that led to the death of most species of dinosaurs. Gradualism says that the dinosaurs died out slowly, over a period of many hundreds of thousands or millions of years. This may be due to, for example, changes of climate caused by continental drift. Some scientists feel both theories are correct, with slow and rapid changes coming together at the end of the Cretaceous period—and leading to the extinction of the dinosaurs.

What is the "climate" theory of dinosaur extinction?

The "climate" theory of dinosaur extinction is one that many scientists believe is more feasible than most other theories. One of the theories of gradualism is that the movement of continents over millions of years brought about changes in the Earth's climate, including the changing of oceanic currents; spreading of deserts; drying up of inland seas; shifts in the Earth's axis, orbit, or magnetic field; spreading of polar ice caps; and the increase in volcanic eruptions. The slow climate changes (produced by either one or all of the above events) resulted in the gradual decline of the dinosaurs, as they could not evolve quickly enough to compensate for or adapt to the changes.

Were the **dinosaurs inferior** because they became extinct?

The fact that dinosaurs became extinct has been used as proof of their inferiority and that they were evolutionary failures. But it is unlikely that anyone can claim the inferiority or superiority of a species: Some species, such as the *Lingula* clams, have been around for 500 million years; the dinosaurs lived for about 150 million years; and the earliest hominids appeared only about three million years ago, with modern humans (*Homo sapiens sapiens*) appearing only about 90,000 years ago. If, as many paleontologists believe, birds are really proven to be dinosaurs, then we may one day say that dinosaurs have existed for almost 200 million years.

What is the **"disease"** theory of **dinosaur extinction**?

The "disease" theory of dinosaur extinction (which falls under the umbrella theory of gradualism) states that dinosaurs eventually died out because of disease. Some say biological changes, brought about by changes in their evolution, made the animals less competitive with other organisms—including mammals that had just started appearing. Others say a major disease, from rickets to constipation, wiped out the dinosaurs, with

237

some dinosaur bones definitely showing signs of these diseases over time. Another idea is that overpopulation led to the spread of major diseases among certain species of dinosaurs—and eventually to them all.

What is the "mammal" theory of dinosaur extinction?

The "mammal" theory of dinosaur extinction (which falls under the umbrella theory of gradualism) states that dinosaurs were slowly wiped out by mammals, animals that only appeared about the end of the Mesosoic era (the end of the Cretaceous period). The mammals could have eaten many of the dinosaurs eggs (thus, the dinosaurs had difficulty reproducing) or the mammals could have taken over territories from the dinosaurs. On a smaller scale, such events happen today, especially when an introduced species takes over another species by eating the native organism's young or by taking over the territory and eating the available food supply.

What is the "poison plant" theory of dinosaur extinction?

The "poison plant" theory of dinosaur extinction involves the development of angiosperms (flowering plants), a new type of plant that flourished during the Cretaceous period. Some of the plants were no doubt poisonous to dinosaurs, as the plants probably developed protective toxins (poisons) in order not to be eaten by animals. The more prolific plant-eating dinosaurs may have died out as the plants became more toxic to them; and in turn, the carnivores had fewer plant-eating dinosaurs to eat.

But this theory is too simplistic. There were many plants in the world, including varieties that were non-poisonous. In addition, the idea does not explain the mass extinction of marine organisms at the end of the Cretaceous period—animals that had nothing to do with flowering plants on land.

Did dinosaurs get blown away by hurricanes?

No one really knows, but several researchers think this may have been possible. These scientists studied huge hurricanes called hypercanes, monster storms that grew much larger than modern hurricanes, especially if the ocean water was greatly warmed. They believe a large impacting meteorite struck or a major volcanic erupted in shallow ocean waters, causing the ocean water temperatures to rise—doubling the temperatures we currently find in the tropics. This increase in water temperature could have created hypercanes that grew to immense sizes. In turn, the storms could have carried water vapor, ice crystals, and dust high into the atmosphere—blocking sunlight and destroying the protective ozone layer that shields animals from the ultraviolet radiation from the Sun. The effect could have devastated the dinosaurs. Scientists admit the idea is a little far-fetched—but it is not impossible.

What is the "human" theory of dinosaur extinction?

There is no such thing! The idea of humans living at the same time as dinosaurs (at least non-avian ones) seems to have been propagated by the B-movies of the 1950s and 1960s, in which dinosaurs attacked humans. In reality, mammals did evolve about the same time as the dinosaurs, but the mammals were not human-like. The dinosaurs died out about 65 million years ago; the first hominids appeared about three to four million years ago; and finally *Homo sapiens sapiens* (or modern humans) appeared about 90,000 years ago.

THE LATEST THEORIES ON DINOSAUR EXTINCTION

What is the "impact" theory of dinosaur extinction?

The impact theory is one of the newest ideas in the catastrophic camp of dinosaur extinction. This theory states that a large object (or objects), such as an asteroid or comet, collided with the Earth, resulting in a large impact crater, giant waves in the oceans that smashed onto land at heights of two to three miles (3.2 to 4.8 kilometers), and radical, rapid changes in the Earth's weather, temperature, amount of sunshine, and climate.

239

An asteroid. (Photo courtesy of National Aeronautics and Space Administration/Corbis Corporation.)

What is an **asteroid**?

An asteroid is a large rocky body found in outer space. They range from about the size of a boulder to about 6 miles (one kilometer), and generally are classified as carbonaceous, stony, or metal. The majority of asteroids are found along the plane of the solar system, called the ecliptic. They are often also called minor planets because of their large size and propensity to orbit along the same plane as the major planets. Most of the asteroids revolve around the Sun in a tight band between the orbits of Mars and Jupiter, called the asteroid belt. Italian astronomer Giuseppe Piazzi (1746–1826) discovered the first asteroid, Ceres, in 1801.

Where did the **asteroids come from**?

The majority of these space objects are thought to have formed at the beginning of the solar system, about 4.6 billion years ago. There are several theories as to asteroid origin. Scientists once believed that the asteroids were leftovers from a shattered planet, but further analysis showed there are few, if any, sources—internal or external—that would have enough

Where do comets originate?

Short-period comets, or those that complete their orbits every few to 200 years, are thought to have originated in the Kuiper Belt, a fat disk of comet-like objects that probably exists beyond the orbit of Neptune and Pluto. Long-term comets, or those that travel into the solar system every thousands of years (or may never return at all), are thought to originate in the Oort Cloud, a theoretical cloud of comets proposed by Dutch astronomer Jan Oort (1909–1992). The cloud surrounds the solar system about 100,000 astronomical units from the Sun. (One astronomical unit is equal to about 93 million miles [149,637,000 kilometers], the average distance between the Earth and Sun.)

energy to crack a planet. A more accepted theory is that the asteroids formed at the same time as the other planets, but the gravitational pull of Jupiter did not allow huge chunks of rock called planetesimals to create a planet. Instead, the rocks settled between the orbits of Mars and Jupiter, colliding and creating the smaller asteroids we see today.

Where are **asteroids found** in our **solar system**?

The majority of the asteroids stay within the asteroid belt, a band of chunks of rock between the orbits of Mars and Jupiter. Over hundreds of thousands of years, because of the gravitational pull of the planets or other space objects, an asteroid may stray from the belt. Such asteroids that come close to the Earth or cross the Earth's orbit are called near-Earth asteroids (the ones that cross the Earth's path are also called Earth-crossing asteroids). It is known that in the past, some near-Earth asteroids struck the Earth, creating impact craters on the planet's surface. Meteor Crater in Arizona is a good example of an impact crater formed by an asteroid. There also seems to be an association between some of the larger Earth impact craters and the extinction of a large number of species during the planet's long history.

A comet descending to Earth during the night. (Photo courtesy of National Aeronautics and Space Administration.)

What is a **comet**?

Comets are a collection of dust, gases, and ice that orbits the Sun. Once described as "dirty snowballs," many comets are now thought to be more like "mudballs," most carrying more dust than ice. In general, comets are composed of carbon dioxide, frozen water, methane, ammonia, and materials such as silicates and organic compounds.

Have there been any **recent comets**?

Comets are relatively common in the solar system, so the chances of seeing one are good. Two comets that were recently readily visible to the naked eye added to our knowledge of comets: Comet Hyakutake in 1996 was merely a ball of ice, measuring only about one to 1.8 miles (2 to 3 kilometers) in diameter. Comet Hale-Bopp, about ten times as big as Hyakutake, entered our sky in 1997. In addition, the discovery of Shoemaker-Levy 9, now thought to have been a fragmented comet, made scientists aware of the impact of space objects on other planets: The comet broke up into about 22 fragments, with each piece plunging into the

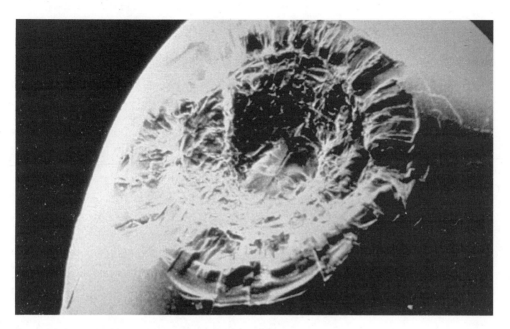

Crater on a planet caused by a meteorite. (Photo courtesy of JLM Visuals.)

atmosphere of Jupiter in July 1994. It was the first time humans had ever witnessed the impact of a space object on another planet.

Who **first formulated** the **impact scenario**?

In 1980, the American physicist Luis Alvarez (1911–1988) proposed that a large asteroid or comet hit the Earth about 65 million years ago. His son, geologist Water Alvarez (b. 1940), discovered a high concentration of iridium at the Cretaceous-Tertiary (nicknamed "K/T") boundary in Italy. Iridium is an element associated with extraterrestrial impacts. Because of this find, and the realization that the dinosaurs and many other species died out at the end of the Cretaceous, Luis and Walter Alvarez, along with colleagues Frank Asaro and Helen Michel, proposed that the extinctions at the K/T boundary were caused by the impact of a large space object. The iridium anomaly has since been found in over 50 K/T boundary sites around the world.

What is an **impact crater**?

An impact crater is a large impression on the surface of a planet, most often caused by a collision with a large space object, such as a comet or

243

an asteroid. All planets and most satellites have impact craters—and even asteroids have impact craters. The Moon is our most obvious example of impacts on a planetary body, as the surface is dotted with hundreds of craters.

How many **impact craters** are on the **Earth**?

To date, scientists have identified about 150 impact craters on our planet. The majority have been found on the surface; less than a dozen or so are buried or are deep in the oceans. There were probably many more craters, but erosion—from wind, water, or the movement of the continental plates—has erased any evidence of their existence. In addition, there may be many more craters under the thick, vegetative growth of the jungles, in high mountains, or buried deep under sediment on land or in the oceans. The largest crater, the Vredefort crater in South Africa, is also one of the oldest, with an age of over two billion years; another large impact crater, the Sudbury in Canada, is also a major source of certain metals. Craters on the planet Mars dwarf the Earth's craters. The largest impact crater (also called a basin) on Mars is Hellas Planitia, measuring 1,243 miles (2,000 kilometers) in diameter.

The following table lists craters discovered around the world and their diameter.

Name	Location	Diameter (miles/kilometers)
Vredefort	South Africa	186/300
Sudbury	Ontario, Canada	155/250
Chicxulub *	Yucatan, Mexico	105/170
Manicouagan	Quebec, Canada	62/100
Popigai	Russia	62/100
Acraman	South Australia, Australia	56/90
Chesapeake Bay	Virginia, USA	53/85
Puchezh-Katunki	Russia	50/80
Morokweng	South Africa	44/70
Kara	Russia	40/65
Beaverhead	Montana, USA	37/60

*Crater thought to be associated, or at least partially associated, with the extinction of the dinosaurs.

What **evidence** supports the **impact theory**?

The most compelling evidence for this theory is the Chicxulub crater in Yucatan Peninsula, Mexico, an impact crater that was discovered by geologists in 1992. This 150-mile-wide (241-kilometer) crater—although recent measurements of the underground crater reveal it may be as large as 186 miles (300 kilometers) in diameter—is thought to be the result of a collision with an asteroid six to 12 miles (10 to 20 kilometers) in diameter. The crater was created approximately 64.98 million years ago, in the right time frame for the extinction of the dinosaurs; it may be totally or partially associated with the extinction of the dinosaurs. The crater is buried, and was actually found in the 1960s during a subsurface survey taken by an oil company. It took years before a geologist looking at the data noticed the circularity of the feature—and brought the impact crater to the attention of the scientific community.

How many **impact craters** are associated with **dinosaur extinction**?

Currently, there is only one Earth impact crater associated with dinosaur extinction—the Chicxulub crater in Mexico. In addition, tiny glass fragments from the impact ejecta (the rock and soil that sprayed from the crater when it formed) were found in 1990 in the Caribbean Ocean, on the island of Haiti. The ejecta debris appears to fall in line with the Chicxulub crater. Another crater, the Manson structure in Iowa, was once thought to have been made at the end of the Cretaceous, but subsequent studies show it is not the correct age.

What would happen if an **asteroid** or **comet impacted** the **Earth** today?

The effects of an asteroid or comet impact on our modern planet would depend on a number of variables, including the size, speed, and composition of the object, and the location of the impact.

Recent advanced computer simulations show that the impact of an asteroid three miles (five kilometers) in diameter in the Mid-Atlantic Ocean would produce huge tsunamis (similar to seismic sea waves caused by earthquakes, and which are usually called tidal waves) that

245

If dinosaurs did become extinct from impacts, how did they die?

After the impact, scientists theorize that several events occurred. Right after the impact, huge amounts of dust and debris from the impact would have been thrown high into the atmosphere. The dust would have been carried by the upper winds all around the world, filtering or blocking out the sunlight. Heat from the blast may have created firestorms—huge forest fires that added smoke, ash, and particles to the already dust-filled atmosphere. If the dust-filled winds did not kill the animals, the lack of sunlight would kill off plants, creating a serious crisis: The animals feeding off of the vegetation would die, and in a domino-like effect, the rest of the other organisms in the food chain would die off, including the dinosaurs.

would spread out in all directions. These waves would be large and powerful enough to completely inundate the upper East Coast of the United States, extending inward to the Appalachian Mountains; a similar scenario would play out in Western Europe. A smaller asteroid of approximately 1,300 feet (400 meters) in diameter, striking in the same place, would still generate tsunami waves up to 300 feet (90 meters) high on all the surrounding coastlines, leading to considerable destruction and loss of life.

If an asteroid measuring more than a mile (1.6 kilometers) in diameter struck the Earth's land surface or a shallow water area, the impact would throw large amounts of dust into the atmosphere, blocking the rays of the Sun. The result would be darkness, a mini ice age, disrupted weather and climate, and the cessation of plant growth for a year, if not longer. This would be a catastrophe without precedent in the history of the human race. Scientists feel the impact of a large asteroid or comet more than three miles (five kilometers) in diameter would eliminate most flora and fauna from the planet, certainly destroying life as we know it.

Which **asteroids** have **come close** to the Earth in recent time?

On June 30, 1908, a small asteroid of about one hundred to two hundred feet (30 to 60 meters) in diameter, with a mass between ten thousand and one hundred thousand tons, exploded about three miles (five kilometers) above the ground near Tunguska, Siberia, destroying hundreds of square miles of remote forest lands. Fortunately, this object had a grazing trajectory instead of coming straight down, and was composed of mostly volatiles, rather than iron-nickel metal. Even so, it released the energy equivalent to a nuclear bomb, with the effects felt hundreds of miles away.

In 1972, a small, one-thousand-ton asteroid skimmed our outer atmosphere, but few knew about it. Other asteroids have just passed by: On March 23, 1989, asteroid 1989 FC, with the kinetic energy of over 1,000 one-megaton hydrogen bombs, passed close by the Earth; in the 1991–1994 time frame, four asteroids came closer to the Earth than half the distance to the Moon. Geographos, a very massive, cigar-shaped asteroid 3.2 miles by 1.2 miles (5.1 by 1.9 kilometers) in length, passed near the Earth in 1969 and 1994.

The larger objects are the most devastating, and get the most attention. But the smaller asteroids, approximately 328 feet (100 meters) in diameter, are more of a present danger, since they strike the Earth approximately once every hundred years.

Are there any **asteroids** heading for the **Earth** in the future?

We have only in fairly recent times become aware of the dangers posed by the potential impact of asteroids and comets. As such, we are just beginning to search the skies for objects that might, sooner or later, impact the planet on which we live.

The estimates for the number of near-Earth objects (NEOs) are high. These objects revolve around the Sun with orbits that occasionally cross or closely approach the Earth's orbit. Scientists believe there could be 1,600 to 2,000 objects that are larger than just over a half mile (one kilometer) in diameter; 300,000 NEOs over 328 feet (100 meters); and probably about 100,000 smaller ones that we are unable to detect. To date, only 7 percent of the NEOs larger than just over a half mile (one kilometer) have been discovered.

Recently, scientists found an asteroid, named 1997 XF11, and calculated its orbit. It appeared that a collision in the near future was imminent. After further study, however, it was concluded that this asteroid, though making several close passes by Earth, posed no danger for at least the next century.

The following table lists just a few of the asteroids that will come within 0.2 astronomical units (18,600,000 miles or 29,927,400 kilometers) of our planet during the next 33 years. One astronomical unit is equivalent to 93,000,000 miles (149,637,000 kilometers); for comparison, the mean distance to the Moon is 238,866 miles (384,400 kilometers).

Object Name	Date of Encounter	Distance from Earth, in astronomical units (AU)
1863 Antinous	April 1, 1999	0.1894
6489 Golevka*	June 2, 1999	0.0500
4486 Mithra*	August 14, 2000	0.0465
2100 Ra-Shalom	September 6, 2000	0.1896
4179 Toutatis	October 31, 2000	0.0739
3362 Khufu	December 29, 2001	0.1597
3362 Khufu	December 25, 2002	0.1498
2100 Ra-Shalom	August 17, 2003	0.1745
3362 Khufu	December 20, 2003	0.1946
4179 Toutatis *	September 29, 2004	0.0104
1862 Apollo	November 6, 2005	0.0752
4450 Pan*	February 19, 2008	0.0408
1620 Geographos	March 17, 2008	0.1251

* listed by some scientists as potentially hazardous

What **other theory** involves a large **catastrophe** that may have led to the **extinction** of the dinosaurs?

Some scientists feel that an incredibly large volcanic eruption occurred in the right time frame. The lava flows of this eruption, called the Deccan Traps, formed the highlands of India. The volcanic event could have produced enough ash to block out much of the sunlight, leading to changes in temperature and climate. Some "catastrophists" feel there were two impacts in this time frame: One in the Yucatan, Mexico; and the other in India that triggered the volcanic eruption.

What newly discovered phenomena may be **heading our way** in about **50,000 years**?

The newly discovered phenomena are killer cosmic clouds, found in localized areas of outer space. Theoretical physicist Gary P. Zank believes the clouds would be bad for life on Earth—and may have been the reason dinosaurs died out approximately 65 million years ago. Smaller and less dense clouds, called Local Fluff, could hit our area at any time. The next large, dense cloud we might encounter will be 50,000 years from now, when we meet up with the Aquila Rift, an area of new star formation.

What are **killer cosmic clouds**?

Killer cosmic clouds are large areas in outer space, probably bigger than our entire solar system, that have much higher concentrations of hydrogen than normal. For the past five million years, our planet has been traveling in a relatively empty, typical region of space—with a density of less than one particle (mostly hydrogen) per cubic inch. Killer clouds are found where new stars are being formed and have much higher densities, on the order of hundreds of particles of hydrogen per cubic inch.

Could a **killer cosmic cloud** have caused the **extinction** of the **dinosaurs**?

If supercomputer models are correct, then higher concentrations of hydrogen could have formed a wall and caused the heliosphere around the Earth to collapse. This could have allowed more cosmic radiation to penetrate to the Earth's surface, resulting in changes to the flora and fauna. If this did occur, such an increase in cosmic rays, with elevated levels of radiation, could have directly killed the dinosaurs. Another scenario is that the rays negatively affected the vegetation eaten by the herbivorous dinosaurs and other animals. These animals would have then

What effect could killer clouds have on Earth and its life forms?

Some scientists believe that a killer cloud could collapse the solar system's heliosphere—a bubble of space produced by the solar wind that partially protects our planet (and the other planets and satellites in our solar system) from cosmic rays. Cosmic rays are high-speed particles from outer space that constantly hit the heliosphere, but most are deflected by this shield. And that's good, because exposure to the powerful radiation from these rays could fry a human being. If the heliosphere around our planet collapsed from the introduction of a cosmic cloud, much higher levels of cosmic radiation would strike the Earth, dramatically altering life—although scientists are not sure how much or in what ways.

died off, leaving no prey for the carnivorous dinosaurs, which also then died off.

Is there any **proof** that the Earth has encountered a **cosmic cloud** in the past?

No, we do not know what happened 65 million years ago—or any other time in the past. But we don't have to wait 50,000 years until we reach Aquila Rift to obtain proof of cosmic clouds. Some scientists believe that, from time to time, our planet could have encountered smaller, less dense clouds of hydrogen, known as the Local Fluff. These less devastating encounters, predict the models, would have only weakened the heliosphere, resulting in slight increases in cosmic rays hitting the Earth.

One of the known side effects of cosmic rays striking the Earth is the production of the rare metal beryllium. An increase of this metal could be proof that we had encountered one of these relatively benign clouds in the past. Ice cores taken from the South Pole do indeed show an increase in beryllium levels at approximately 35,000 and 60,000 years ago, leading scientists to speculate that contacts were made with Local Fluff. What were the effects of these minor encounters? Scientists speculate the effect of the Earth coming into contact with Local Fluff might have produced anything from an ice age to an increased greenhouse effect.

What is the **true story** of **dinosaur extinction**?

Many scientists believe that dinosaurs became extinct not due to one reason—but a combination of reasons, most of which have been covered in these pages. In addition, some scientists believe that dinosaurs were already gradually declining when the catastrophe occurred. There is a chance that they would have become extinct anyway—with or without a catastrophic occurrence.

AFTER THE DINOSAURS

WHAT SURVIVED AFTER THE DINOSAURS WENT EXTINCT

What groups **survived** the **extinction** at the end of the Cretaceous period?

The survivors include most land plants and land animals—insects, snails, frogs, salamanders, lizards, snakes, turtles, and placental mammals. Most marine invertebrates also survived, including starfishes, sea urchins, mollusks, arthropods, and most fishes.

What groups **did not survive** the **extinction** at the end of the Cretaceous period?

The groups that did not survive the massive extinction include the dinosaurs, pterosaurs, and some families of birds and marsupial mammals on land. In the oceans, mosasaurs, plesiosaurs, some families of teleost fishes, ammonites, belemnites, rudist, trigoniid, and inoceramid bivalves became extinct; as well as over half the ocean's various plankton groups. Some groups appear to have vanished rather suddenly and completely at the end of the Cretaceous period, like the switching out of a light; whereas others were already gradually diminishing in diversity in the last ten million years of the Cretaceous period.

255

Marsupial animals, distant relatives of this opossum, remained after the dinosaurs' extinction. (Photo courtesy of D. Robert Franz/Corbis Corporation.)

Why did **certain animals survive** and other animals did not?

No one is really sure why certain animals died out and others did not. In some ways, the animal extinctions at the end of the Cretaceous period were very selective.

What **mammals** lived at the **end of the Cretaceous** period?

Mammals had been around for millions of years before the end of the Cretaceous period; in fact, the first group of true mammals, the morganucodontids, evolved in the late Triassic period. And they were a successful group of animals for about 150 million years before the dinosaurs became extinct.

By the end of the Cretaceous period, some mammals had developed many innovations vital to their survival: Many stopped laying eggs and were able to deliver live young. Various mammal species eventually grew specialized teeth for a variety of tasks—such as cutting, gnawing, and grinding—for the better processing of food. They developed better ways to compete for food, such as having more energy in proportion to their

When did modern reptiles evolve?

The earliest turtles evolved during the Triassic period, but they probably could not withdraw into their shells like modern turtles. Lizards and snakes have poor fossil records. This is probably due to the animals' tendencies to live in dry uplands, far from the areas that are most likely to produce fossils (most animal bones survive if they are quickly buried with sediment, such as along riverbanks). It is thought that lizards appeared in the late Triassic; the earliest remains of snakes are found in the late Cretaceous (in North America and Patagonia, South America).

size, or adapting to changing diets by becoming omnivores (plant- and meat-eating animals).

The therian mammals—marsupials and placentals—became the apparent heirs to the land the dinosaurs (and other organisms) left behind. Some mammal subgroups had already disappeared before the demise of the dinosaurs; others made it through the end of the Cretaceous period; and some even survive to this day.

Are **mammals** the most abundant animals on **modern Earth**?

No, mammals are not the most abundant animals—in terms of species or individuals—on our planet. There are many more kinds of fish, reptiles, and birds, and there are even more invertebrate species on Earth, including insects and mollusks.

What is a **reptile**?

Modern reptiles include the alligators and crocodiles, turtles, lizards, and snakes. They all have several typical characteristics: They have a protective covering of scales or plates, five clawed toes on each foot (with exceptions, of course, such as snakes), and lungs instead of gills.

An alligator lizard, one of the 6,000 reptile species alive today. (Photo courtesy of Field Mark Publications.)

Most lay eggs (although most poisonous snakes in the United States, except coral snakes, produce live young) and eat animals (the land tortoise is one exception).

How did **reptiles** fare at the end of the **Cretaceous period**?

After the Cretaceous period, most reptiles were wiped out. About 6,000 reptiles species exist today, fewer in number and much smaller in size than their ancestors—but greater in diversity.

What reptile **species survived** past the end of the **Cretaceous** period?

One remarkable group of reptiles—also close relatives of the dinosaurs—are the crocodiles. They appear to have evolved from archosaurian ancestors during the late Triassic; but unlike most of their contemporaries, they survived to the present day. They are also remarkable: These moderate- to large-sized semi-aquatic predators have remained relatively unchanged since the Triassic period.

A modern crocodile, relatively unchanged since the Triassic. (Photo courtesy of Danny Lehman/Corbis Corporation.)

What are the types of **modern crocodiles**?

There are two types of modern crocodiles found in tropical and subtropical environments: The gavialids are found in India; they eat fish and have slender snouts. The crocodylids are found almost worldwide, and consist of crocodiles and alligators. They have long bodies, and powerful tails used for swimming or defense. Their limbs allow the animals to maneuver and steer in the water; on land, they use their limbs to walk with a slow gait, with their bellies held high off the ground. These animals choose from a wide variety of food, including fish, large vertebrates, and carrion.

What is the difference between an **alligator** and a **crocodile**?

Although there are some overlapping habitats of alligators and crocodiles, it is rare to see these reptiles together. The best way to tell the difference between the two animals is by checking the size and head: Crocodiles are slightly smaller and less bulky than alligators. In addition, the crocodile has a narrower snout, with a pair of enlarged teeth in the lower jaw that fit into a "notch" on each side of the snout. The alligator has a broader snout, and all the teeth in its upper jaw overlap with those in the lower jaw.

Florida alligator near a swamp. (Photo courtesy of Field Mark Publications.)

How would **dinosaurs** have **evolved** if they had **not gone extinct** 65 million years ago?

One theory comes from Dale Russell, curator of fossil vertebrates at the Canadian Museum of Nature, Ottawa, Canada, who believes that dinosaurs were evolving toward more humanlike features at the end of the Cretaceous period. These features included a larger brain, forward focused eyes, and bipedalism. Extrapolating from these tendencies, Russell "evolved" a dinosaur. He called the bipedal creature he came up with a Dinosauroid, which, though reptilian in many ways—including its extremities and somewhat scaly skin—also looked very humanoid.

Are there any descendants of the **dinosaurs** living **today**?

Some scientists believe that modern birds are actually the descendants of dinosaurs—or may actually *be* dinosaurs.

Feathers of this peacock certainly distinguish this creature from any other. (Photo courtesy of Field Mark Publications.)

MODERN BIRDS

What are **birds**?

Birds are members of the animal kingdom; they have their own class, known as Aves. (A possible origin of the word "bird" is thought to be the Old English *brid,* which originally referred to the young of animals.) Birds are vertebrate animals, warm-blooded, and reproduce by laying eggs. They have four limbs, with the front two limbs modified into wings.

Why are **birds unique**?

The feature unique to birds, and what makes them so adaptable and fascinating, is a body covered with feathers. These light-weight structures provide insulation from the changing temperatures; are used as ornamentation and coloration for establishing dominance and attracting mates; and most importantly, they give the animals the ability to fly freely through the air. There are exceptions: Although certain birds possess feathers, they cannot fly, such as penguins.

Which birds lay the **largest** and **smallest eggs**?

Ostriches lay the largest eggs, averaging approximately 6.8 by 5.4 inches (17.3 by 13.7 centimeters) in diameter. These eggs are small compared to those of the extinct elephant bird of Madagascar whose eggs averaged approximately 13 inches (33 centimeters) long, with a diameter of 9.5 inches (24 centimeters) at the widest part. These eggs weighed approximately 18 pounds each and had a capacity of two gallons—which means each egg could hold six ostrich eggs inside its shell.

The smallest eggs known are laid by the hummingbirds. The smallest of the hummingbirds, the vervain hummingbird *Mellisuga minima,* lays eggs less than 1/2 inch (1.3 centimeters) long.

Do all **birds fly**?

The vast majority of birds fly. They are only incapable of flight during relatively short periods while they molt (the shedding of old feathers and the growing of new ones).

True flightless birds are very unusual. There are some familiar examples of flightless birds throughout the world: the African ostrich; the South American rhea; and the emu, kiwi, and cassowary of Australia are all land, but flightless, birds. The penguins of the Southern Hemisphere also are incapable of air flight. They have feathers for insulation and breeding purposes, but use a different means of locomotion—their sleek bodies "flying" through the oceans using flipper-like wings.

All of these flightless birds have wings, but over millions of years of evolution, have lost the ability to fly—even though they probably descended from flying birds. These species may have lost their ability to fly through the gradual disuse of their wings. Perhaps they became isolated on oceanic islands and had no predators, thus, they had no need to fly and escape danger. Another possibility is that food became abundant, eliminating the necessity to fly long distances to search for food.

Ostriches lay the largest eggs of any bird. (Photo courtesy of Field Mark Publications.)

What do **birds eat**?

The answer is simple: Taken as a group, birds eat just about everything. Over millions of years, birds have evolved certain features that allow them to obtain food from many animal and plant sources. Wherever there was an ecological niche with abundant food sources, birds adapted to exploit those resources.

Some birds eat mostly insects; others, like penguins, prefer to dine on seafood. Some birds, such as ducks or geese, float on the water, dipping or diving to extract plants from oceans, lakes, and rivers; while still others, such as raptors, swoop out of the sky, killing and devouring small land-dwelling mammals. Individual bird species not only exploit specific chosen food sources—but also have developed physical (and sometimes internal) characteristics to maximize their ability to harvest the food.

Overall, the list of what certain birds eat is enormous. A sampling of this menu includes: One-celled protozoans, jellyfishes, sea urchins, starfishes, marine and earthworms, crabs, shrimps, barnacles, all types of insects (including centipedes, millipedes, flies, butterflies, spiders, ticks, and scorpions), slugs, snails, squids, mussels, fishes, salamanders, frogs,

263

What is bird migration?

The word migration comes from the Latin *migrare,* meaning "to go from one place to another." When discussing birds, migration is the regular, periodic movements of bird species from one area to another.

Year after year, many species of birds mate and nest in specific areas of the world. Most of these areas are only hospitable during the warmer months of the year; when the cold weather arrives, the birds migrate to warmer climates. These trips can be as long as thousands of miles. For example, the American golden plover breeds north of Canada and Alaska during the Northern Hemisphere's spring and summer. In the Northern Hemisphere's fall, the plovers journey to southeastern South America to spend the "winter"—which is the summer season in the Southern Hemisphere—allowing the birds to find plenty of food. When spring arrives again in the Northern Hemisphere, the trip is reversed, and the plovers migrate back to the northern nesting grounds to breed.

In addition to the obvious reasons for migration, such as warmth and the availability of food and water, scientists believe breeding in areas with longer daylight hours presents more opportunity to gather food for nestlings. All of these factors help ensure the survival of the brood—and with it, the continuation of the species.

toads, lizards, snakes; small mammals such as shrews, mice, rats, ground and tree squirrels, rabbits, and skunks; and larger mammals such as marmots, foxes, porcupines, young deer, and antelope. It seems that for every animal around, there is a bird species that will eat it!

Some birds also prey on each other, such as various large predatory birds (eagles, hawks, and owls) that kill and eat smaller birds. Many birds, like crows, jays, and magpies, eat the eggs and young of other birds.

Worms are a favorite delicacy of birds. (Photo courtesy of Field Mark Publications.)

Plants are not immune from being eaten, either. Specific birds have adapted to feasting on algae, sea lettuce, lichens, grasses, herbs, flower nectar, leaves and buds of trees, mosses, ferns, berries, fruits, tree sap, acorns, nuts, seeds of all kinds, and corn and rice. Again, it seems for almost every plant, there is a bird eating some part of it.

Where are **birds** found around the **world**?

Birds can be found in almost every part of the world: High mountain regions; ocean shores; arid grasslands; the middle of large oceans; warm climates; and even frigid, ice-locked areas. Over millions of years, birds evolved characteristics that allowed them to adapt to their chosen habitats.

Most living species (approximately 85 percent) of birds live in the tropical regions of the world, and two-thirds of those are found in the humid tropical climates. The remaining 15 percent of birds live in the temperate or cold climates.

The factors influencing the distribution of birds over the world include the amount and distribution of landmasses and oceans over geologic time; physical barriers to movement, such as mountain ranges and deserts; a region's climate and environmental conditions; and the ability (or inability) of individual bird species to travel distances.

THE LINK BETWEEN
BIRDS AND DINOSAURS

Did some **early scientists** believe **birds** were **related to dinosaurs**?

Yes, some early scientists believed there were similarities between birds and reptiles. It was noted as far back as 400 years ago. But the idea did not come to the forefront of science until the mid-nineteenth century—especially after the 1855 discovery of an unusual fossilized skeleton in a German rock quarry: the remains (subsequently called *Archaeopteryx lithographica*) exhibited a mixture of dinosaur- and bird-like features.

Who first published papers noting the **resemblance** of **birds to dinosaurs**?

In 1867, American paleontologists Edward Drinker Cope (1840–1897) and Othniel Charles Marsh (1831–1899) were the first to publish papers noting the resemblance of birds to dinosaurs.

Who first proposed that **birds** were **descendants of dinosaurs**?

English naturalist Thomas Henry Huxley (1825–1895)—an authority on bird evolution and a champion of Charles Darwin's theory of evolution—first noted characteristics shared by dinosaurs and birds. Huxley observed that a particular species of chicken (called a Dorking fowl) raised in his area had leg bones similar to those of theropod dinosaurs; he also cited as evidence the fossil of a bird-like dinosaur, *Archaeopteryx lithographica,* discovered in 1855 in Germany. Between 1868 and 1869, using a method of anatomical comparison resembling modern cladistic

Thomas Henry Huxley. (Photo courtesy of Gale Research.)

analysis (which is a way of determining an organism's family tree), Huxley decided birds had descended from dinosaurs.

What is *Archaeopteryx lithographica*?

Archaeopteryx lithographica is one of the world's most famous fossils. The first fossil of an *Archaeopteryx lithographica*—thought by many modern paleontologists to represent the oldest bird yet discovered—was found in 1855, in the Solnhofen quarries in southern Germany. The fossil would not be recognized as a bird until 1970. The fossil remains—a small bird about the size of a crow—were found in sedimentary rock from the upper Jurassic period, and six more fossil skeletons have been uncovered over the years.

Archaeopteryx lithographica, literally "ancient wing from lithographic limestone," fossils are dated at 125 to 147 million years old (most scientists use 150 million years as the date). The fossils, though not recognized as birds, were used by some paleontologists (such as Thomas Henry Huxley) to confirm Darwin's theory of evolution; later, for other scientists, the *Archaeopteryx lithographica* represented the transition between dinosaurs and birds—and provided proof for the argument that birds descended from dinosaurs.

Did some scientists believe *Archaeopteryx lithographica* was a **transition** between dinosaurs and modern birds?

Yes, some scientists did believe *Archaeopteryx* was the transition between dinosaurs and modern birds—mainly because the fossilized skeletons exhibited a mixture of dinosaur- and bird-like features. The dinosaur (or reptilian) characteristics include such features as bony tails, teeth, and claws on the fingers; the bird-like characteristics include such features as feathers, wishbones, and beaks. Today, many scientists believe *Archaeopteryx lithographica* may have just been a link in dinosaur progression, eventually evolving into modern birds.

Have other skeletons of *Archaeopteryx lithographica* been found?

Yes, other *Archaeopteryx lithographica* fossils have been discovered. An almost complete skeleton was found in 1861. It was referred to as the "London specimen" and was the basis for a continuing debate between supporters and detractors of Charles Darwin's newly published theory of evolution. A third skeleton was discovered in 1877, and is referred to as the "Berlin specimen." Subsequent finds over the years bring the current total to seven—the latest found in 1992.

Do all scientists believe *Archaeopteryx lithographica* is a link between birds and dinosaurs?

No, not everyone believes *Archaeopteryx lithographica* was a direct link to the dinosaurs. Some scientists believe birds and dinosaurs evolved separately from a common reptilian ancestor—but so far, no one has yet found acceptable fossil evidence to support or disprove this idea.

Has there been a recent revival of the idea that **birds** are the **descendants of dinosaurs**?

Yes, the idea that birds descended from dinosaurs was revived in 1969, by paleontologist John Ostrom. He suggested that dinosaurs may have been warm-blooded—thus, more active and similar to birds; and Robert Bakker's article in *Scientific American* the next year pursued the same theory. At this time, scientists also began to delve deeply into dinosaur physiology (cells and tissues), noticing the physiological similarities and differences between dinosaurs and other species such as birds. And it is these studies, in combination with skeletal evidence, that scientists hope will lead to the correct answer about bird lineage.

DINOSAURS AROUND US?

What are the major camps in the **dinosaur-bird evolution debate**?

There are several camps of paleontologists in the dinosaur-bird evolution debate. One group believes birds descended from certain dinosaurs about 70 million years ago. Another camp believes birds evolved separately from dinosaurs about 200 million years ago. And there is another group that has emerged: Scientists who believe that birds are actually dinosaurs. Right now, there are not enough fossils to come to a definite conclusion—and all sides have good arguments.

What **characteristics** are seemingly shared by **dinosaurs** and **birds**?

Not all dinosaur characteristics are similar to those of modern birds—but there are many similarities. For example, some dinosaurs had features such as bony tails, claws on the fingers, beaks, and on some, feathers.

Feathers are only one major characteristic that links dinosaurs to birds. Scientists have found feathered dinosaur fossils of the *Archaeopteryx lithographica,* and more recently, another specimen was found in northeast China, the *Sinosauropteryx prima.* These fossils exhibit feather-like impressions in the sedimentary rock in which they were found.

Other links between dinosaurs and birds involve certain skeletal similarities. For example, fossils of the dinosaur *Deinonychus* have many bird-like characteristics: The large head was balanced on a slender, almost bird-like neck; and the chest was short, with the arms folding inward in a resting position, similar to the wings of a bird at rest. The creature's foot was the most extraordinary of any dinosaur: It had a huge claw on the second toe. In many ways, the feet of the *Deinonychus* appear to be enlarged representations of a bird's feet.

Which **dinosaurs** are thought to have evolved into **birds**?

Paleontologists who believe birds evolved from dinosaurs think that the most likely bird ancestors were the small, carnivorous theropods. At least one fossil finding seems to indicate that dromaeosaurs, a subgroup of the theropods, eventually branched into many lines, including birds. This subgroup line also included such dinosaur species as *Velociraptor, Deinonychus,* and *Utahraptor.*

What is **cladistic analysis**?

Cladistic analysis is a relatively new method used to determine an organism's family tree. The older system of classification, developed by Swedish botanist Carl von Linne (1707–1778; also known as Carolus Linnaeus) in the eighteenth century, categorizes plants and animals by organisms' overall similar characteristics. A cladistic analysis uses specific characteristics, such as wrist bones, and relates them to previous and following generations, thus tracing the evolution of these structures. The more characteristics previous and following generations share, the more likely they are related. (A cladogram represents a diagram of all the clades, or groups of organisms.)

What does **cladistic analysis** tell us about **birds and dinosaurs**?

According to cladistic analysis, birds share some 132 characteristics with dinosaurs. Some scientists believe this hard evidence indicates that birds are, indeed, a kind of dinosaur. But many scientists still disagree.

What is the **latest theory** stating **birds** are truly **dinosaurs**?

One recent theory goes one step further than "birds are descendants of dinosaurs"—some paleontologists now feel modern birds are *truly* dinosaurs. This theory states that dinosaurs eventually evolved certain bird-like characteristics, such as light weight, agility, wings, feathers, and beaks. These specialized characteristics enabled the animals to somehow survive the extinction at the end of the Mesozoic era—and to continue evolving into modern birds.

Do all paleontologists believe that **birds and dinosaurs** are related?

No, not all paleontologists believe that birds are dinosaurs—or even that birds evolved directly from dinosaurs. Many feel birds and dinosaurs descended from a common, older ancestor, and developed many superficial similarities over millions of years due to what is called convergent evolution: because both dinosaurs and birds developed body designs for bipedal motion, they eventually started to resemble each other.

There are four major reasons why some scientists feel there is not a direct dinosaur-bird link: The timing problem, body size differences, skeletal variations, and the mismatch in finger evolution. First, in regard to timing, there is some fossil evidence that bird-like dinosaurs evolved 30 to 80 million years after the *Archaeopteryx lithographica,* which seems to put the cart before the horse—or the bird before the bird-like dinosaur, if you will. This is the opposite of what you would expect if birds descended from dinosaurs.

Second, some scientists feel it was nearly impossible for theropods to give rise to birds because of differences in body size. They point out that these carnivorous dinosaurs were relatively large, ground-dwelling animals, with heavy, balancing tails and short forelimbs—not the sort of body that could evolve into a lightweight, flying creature.

Third, although birds and dinosaurs have skeletons that appear, in some ways, to be similar, there are many variations as well: The teeth of theropods were curved and serrated, but early birds had straight, unserrated, peg-like teeth; dinosaurs had a major lower jaw joint that early birds did not; the bone girdle of each animal was very different; and birds have a reversed rear toe for perching, while no dinosaur had a reversed toe.

Fourth, there is a discrepancy between the fingers of dinosaurs and birds: Dinosaurs developed hands with three digits, or fingers, labeled one, two, and three—corresponding to the thumb, index, and middle fingers of humans. The fourth and fifth digits, corresponding to the ring and little fingers of humans, remained as tiny bumps, which have been found on early dinosaur skeletons. However, as recent studies of embryos have shown, birds developed hands with fingers two, three, and four, corresponding to the index, middle, and ring fingers of humans. Fingers one and five, corresponding to our thumb and little finger, were lost. Some paleontologists wonder how a bird hand with fingers two, three, and four, could have evolved from a dinosaur hand with fingers one, two, and three. These scientists assert that such an evolution is impossible.

THE SEARCH FOR THE MISSING LINK

Is there any fossil evidence that **not all dinosaurs became extinct**?

Several recent fossil discoveries are used by some scientists as proof that not all dinosaurs become extinct—but rather are the animals we call birds. The latest fossil findings of *Caudipteryx zoui* and *Protarchaeopteryx robust* from China are seen by some paleontologists as proof that birds not only descended from dinosaurs, but are dinosaurs. The remains of these two 120 million-year-old species were found in Liaoning Province in northeast China; two fossils were that of *Protarchaeopteryx robust,* while a third fossil was that of a *Caudipteryx zoui.*

The *Protarchaeopteryx robust* fossils indicate this animal was a relative of *Archaeopteryx lithographica:* it was turkey-sized, and covered with down- and quill-like feathers. The *Caudipteryx zoui* fossil remains show features of a theropod dinosaur, but it was also covered with down- and quill-like feathers. The wing feathers were not swept back (as needed for flight), but were symmetrical in shape.

Both animals had the shape of swift, long-legged runners and, based on their skeletal characteristics, were more closely related to dinosaurs than birds; and even though they had feathers, neither appeared capable of flight. This seems to indicate that certain dinosaurs developed feathers for reasons other than flight. These feathered dinosaurs did not go extinct at the end of the Cretaceous period—and some scientists believe they continued to evolve into modern birds.

Another fossil that may link birds and dinosaurs is named *Rahona ostromi,* or "Ostrom's menace from the clouds," in honor of American paleontologist John Ostrom (now professor emeritus of geology at Yale University). This fossil was found in 1995 off the eastern coast of Africa, on the island of Madagascar. Dating of the fossil indicates that the animal lived about 65 to 70 million years ago, or during the late Cretaceous period of the Mesozoic era. The fossil remains show a primitive bird about the size of a modern raven, with a two-foot (0.6-meter) wing span; it also has tiny bumps along the wing bones indicating where the flight feathers were attached.

273

Many paleontologists are convinced that *Rahona ostromi* had feathers and could fly. The first toe of each foot points backward, indicating the animal had a perching foot, similar to modern birds. But it also retained many dinosaur-like features—the most interesting of which is on the second toe of each foot: *Rahona ostromi* had a sickle-shaped killing claw on each of its second toes, a feature found in the subgroup of theropod dinosaurs known as dromaeosaurids. Apparently, *Rahona ostromi* was an animal with both bird- and dinosaur-like characteristics.

What is the bird-like animal named *Shuvuuia deserti*?

The 70 million-year-old fossil remains of *Shuvuuia deserti*—derived from the Mongolian word for "bird" and the Latin word for "desert"—were recently found in the Gobi Desert of Mongolia. This was the first skull found from an animal belonging to a group called the *Alvarezsauridae,* which some scientists believe represents an advanced stage in the transition from dinosaurs to birds. *Shuvuuia deserti* was flightless, turkey-sized, walked on two legs, had a long tail and neck, and short forearms ending in a single, blunt claw.

Although it was more advanced than the earlier *Archaeopteryx lithographica, Shuvuuia deserti* did not look like a stereotypical modern bird—leading paleontologists to conclude that birds in the late Cretaceous period were as diverse as they are today. Although many of these primitive species during the Cretaceous period were quite different, they did have some unique characteristics that are also found in modern birds. In the case of *Shuvuuia deserti,* the similarity was prokinesis—the up and down, independent movement of the snout that allowed the mouth to open wide.

What is the bird-like animal named *Sinosauropteryx prima*?

Fossils of a *Sinosauropteryx prima,* found in China, are of a theropod dinosaur with what appears to be feathers. Some scientists believe the dinosaur had feather-like structures that were used for movement; other scientists believe the structures were probably protofeathers, an early step toward the evolution of bird feathers.

What is the bird-like animal named *Unenlagia comaheunsis*?

Unenlagia comaheunsis, or the "half-bird from northwest Patagonia," was a dinosaur living approximately 90 million years ago. The animal had a bird-like pelvis and arms that could flap like wings. Similar to many other recent reptile discoveries, scientists are taking a close look at the animal's bird-like characteristics. In fact, some scientists believe that *Unenlagia comaheunsis* is the actual missing link between birds and dinosaurs.

What was the **original purpose** of **feathers** on dinosaurs?

Based on the recent fossil discoveries of feathered, flightless dinosaurs, some paleontologists now think feathers were originally developed for insulation or ornamentation purposes.

What **baby bird fossil** seems to link dinosaurs and birds?

A 135-million-year-old baby bird was found in the Pyrenees mountains of northern Spain. It had wings, feathers, and tiny holes in its immature bones just like modern birds, but also had a head and neck similar to carnivorous dinosaurs, with sharp teeth and powerful neck muscles for chewing.

Have any carnivorous **dinosaur** fossils shown traces of a **beak**?

In the Red Deer River Badlands of western Canada, the remains of a carnivorous ornithomimid dinosaur were found that included traces of keratin around the front of the animal's skull. Keratin, the material found in hair and fingernails, is also found in the beaks of birds. This was also the first carnivorous dinosaur with evidence of a beak—and it showed that dinosaurs could make the transition from teeth to a beak-like structure.

U.S. DINOSAUR DISCOVERIES

EARLY DINOSAUR HISTORY IN THE UNITED STATES

Where and when were dinosaur **fossils first discovered** in the United States?

The first dinosaur fossils found in the United States were discovered in 1787 in New Jersey, by Caspar and Matelock Wistar of Philadelphia. They read a description of their findings before the American Philosophical Society that year, but the report of their discovery would not be published for 75 years.

Where were the bones of an *Anchisaurus* first found in the United States?

The Connecticut Valley of the northeastern United States was the scene of the first *Anchisaurus* discovery. Solomon Ellsworth Jr. and Nathan Smith found the bones in 1818—but mistook the remains for human bones.

Where were the first **dinosaur footprints** found in the United States?

The first dinosaur footprints in the United States were found in 1800, by Pliny Moody (a student at Williams College) on his farm in Connecticut.

Even though each footprint was about one-foot (0.3-meter) long, scientists from Yale and Harvard universities theorized that the dinosaur prints were the "footprints of Noah's Raven," in reference to the great flood from the Bible.

What creatures did **Edward Hitchcock** think made the Connecticut **dinosaur tracks**?

In the mid-1800s, American geologist Edward Hitchcock (1793–1864) was a clergyman and president of Amherst College, Massachusetts. In 1836, six years before the term "dinosaur" was coined, Hitchcock presented a paper describing the footprints in stone found in the Connecticut Valley. He collected over twenty thousand of these fossil footprints over his life-time, and organized the world's largest collection at Amherst College. He believed giant birds made the tracks—not lizards or reptiles.

When were the **first fossils** found in the Western Hemisphere accurately identified as belonging to a **dinosaur**?

In 1856, American paleontologist Joseph Leidy (1823–1891), professor of anatomy at the University of Pennsylvania, accurately identified several fossil bones as being those of dinosaurs. These fossil remains were among the first to be collected in the American west, by an official geological survey team in 1855; the bones were found in the area now known as Montana. The remains were mostly fossil teeth—subsequently shown to be from *Trachodon* and *Deinodon* dinosaurs.

Who first suggested that some **dinosaurs** were **bipedal**?

Originally, dinosaurs were thought of as either giant, sprawling lizards, or bulky, quadrupedal reptiles with some mammal-like features. But, in 1858, American paleontologist Joseph Leidy described an almost complete skeleton discovered by W. P. Foulke at Haddonfield, New Jersey. The fossil skeleton, named a *Hadrosaurus,* was more complete than any yet discovered. It also indicated that the dinosaur was bipedal—a radical notion for the time.

What was the first mounted dinosaur cast in the U.S. to reflect a bipedal stance?

In the 1860s, at the Philadelphia Academy of Sciences, a mounted cast skeleton of a *Hadrosaurus* was the first to reflect a bipedal stance. Named and described by Joseph Leidy in 1858, this *Hadrosaurus* was the first cast skeleton in North America to be free-mounted. Working with Leidy on this project were Edward Drinker Cope (American paleontologist) and Benjamin Waterhouse Hawkins, sculptor of the Crystal Palace (England) dinosaurs.

What was the **first mounted dinosaur skeleton** in the Western Hemisphere?

In the Western Hemisphere, the first skeleton composed of real dinosaur bones was mounted in 1901 at Yale's Peabody Museum of Natural History, Connecticut. A skeleton of an *Edmontosaurus* was mounted in an erect, bipedal, running stance.

What were the great North American **"Bone Wars"** of the late 1800s?

The "Bone Wars" was the name given to the great rush to find, collect, name, and describe dinosaur fossils discovered from the American west. The impetus to this fervor was the intense, bitter, personal rivalry between two American paleontologists, Othniel Charles Marsh and Edward Drinker Cope.

Starting in the 1870s, both men—who were once friends—funded and led competing expeditions to sites in the American West; each was trying to discover and name more dinosaurs than the other. Their objectives were the remains of late Jurassic dinosaurs in the Morrison formation located in numerous sites in Colorado and in Como Bluff, Wyoming. Among the new dinosaurs they discovered were several well-

281

Othniel Charles Marsh. (Photo courtesy of Archive Photos, Inc.)

known ones, such as *Allosaurus, Apatosaurus* (formerly known as *Brontosaurus*), *Diplodocus, Camarasaurus, Triceratops, Camptosaurus, Ceratosaurus,* and *Stegosaurus.* By the 1890s, the two men uncovered and described a total of some 136 species of dinosaurs—although later analysis of the fossils reduced this number somewhat.

Who was **Othniel Charles Marsh**?

Othniel Charles Marsh (1831–1899) was an American paleontologist who made numerous contributions to the field. In addition to his contributions to the evolutionary history of the horse, he discovered and named numerous dinosaurs during the "Bone Wars" of the late 1800s. In 1866, he helped establish, with the financial backing of his uncle, George Peabody, the Peabody Museum of Natural History at Yale University, Connecticut; he was also a professor at Yale.

In 1882, Marsh published the first dinosaur classification, which formed the foundation for the modern dinosaur classification. In the same year, Marsh was appointed as an official vertebrate paleontologist of the United States Geological Survey.

Who was **Edward Drinker Cope**?

Edward Drinker Cope (1840–1897) was an American paleontologist who spent eight years with the U.S. Geological Survey and who was the most prolific namer of reptiles, both extinct and living. He named over 1,000 new species, including many fish and mammal species; and in his lifetime he was considered one of the top experts on amphibians. For a time, Cope worked as a freelance scholar associated with the Philadelphia Academy of Science. He was also a professor—at Haverford College (1860) and the University of Pennsylvania (1889–1897). Cope was owner and editor of *American Naturalist* from 1878 until his death.

What is the **Morrison formation** in the United States?

The world-famous Morrison formation is a specific layer of sedimentary rock made up of deposits of sand, mud, and volcanic ash. It formed over the period of approximately eight million years, from roughly 156 to 141 million years ago, during the late Jurassic period. This rock is one of the richest dinosaur fossil spots in the United States, usually yielding excellent specimens. It was first discovered near Morrison, Colorado, in the late 1800s—hence its name.

What **Colorado sites** have been historically fruitful in terms dinosaurs finds?

Colorado contains four major historically significant dinosaur sites, especially in terms of the nature and number of finds. These sites are Dinosaur Ridge, Garden Park, the Grand Junction area, and Dinosaur

What is the significance of the Hogback Ridge on the Colorado and Utah border?

From 1909 to 1922, the Hogback Ridge at Split Mountain was worked by American paleontologist Earl Douglass for the Carnegie Museum. On October 4, 1915, President Woodrow Wilson would designate the spot as Dinosaur National Monument—because of its importance to paleontology, and to stop any future development of the area.

In 1909, Douglass found the dorsal bones of *Apatosaurus* at this site; it took six more years to remove the skeleton from the rock and mount it at the Carnegie Museum. After 1922, Douglass worked the quarry for two more years (for the University of Utah and the Smithsonian Institution) finding a *Diplodocus* that is currently mounted at the Smithsonian Institution. Today, tourists at the visitors center at Hogback Ridge can view the quarry face that acts as the north wall of the building—the bones left in place after the overlying rocks were removed.

National Monument. The reason there have been numerous good finds in these areas is the presence of exposed rocks from the Morrison formation of the Jurassic period.

Where and what is **Como Bluff**?

Como Bluff is a long east-west oriented ridge located in southern Wyoming—and it is also the site of a famous Jurassic dinosaur fossil bed excavated during the great "Bone Wars" of the late 1800s. It was discovered by two employees of the Union Pacific Railway, W. E. Carlin and Bill Reed, as a new rail line was being built through the general area. They secretly contacted American paleontologist Othniel Charles Marsh, trying to sell him some gigantic bones. Marsh subsequently sent his assistant, S. W. Williston to investigate the situation. Williston informed Marsh that the bones "extend for seven miles and are by the ton. . . . The bones are very thick, well preserved, and easy to get out." Because of Williston's words, Marsh hired Carlin and Reed to work the beds exclusively for him, and to send the fossil bones back to Yale University. From samples of bones uncovered at Como Bluff, Marsh named the dinosaurs *Stegosaurus, Allosaurus, Nanosaurus, Camptosaurus,* and *Brontosaurus* (now known to be the same animal as *Apatosaurus*). Excavations at Como Bluff were discontinued after 1889.

What is **Dinosaur Ridge**?

Dinosaur Ridge is composed of mostly rock of the Morrison formation, and is located north of the town of Morrison and just west of Denver, Colorado. This site was first discovered in 1877 by Arthur Lakes—and was subsequently excavated during the great "Bone Wars"; the fossil site was worked by American paleontologist Othniel Marsh and his crew.

When was the **first complete fossil** skeleton of a *Stegosaurus* found in the United States?

In 1886, near Canyon City, Colorado, the fossilized remains of *Stegosaurus* were found by Othniel Charles Marsh's crew. The animal's dorsal armor plates were arranged in two rows along the back, with the plates alternating position. This skeleton was subsequently displayed in the Smithsonian Institute as it was found in the field.

When was the first *Tyrannosaurus rex* fossil discovered in the United States?

The first *Tyrannosaurus rex* skeleton discovered in the United States was in 1902 by Barnum Brown—perhaps the greatest collector of dinosaurs. Brown, working for the American Museum of Natural History, discovered the remains in the area of Hell Creek, Montana.

When was the first *Triceratops* fossil discovered in the United States?

A fossilized skull of a three-horned, Cretaceous period, herbivorous dinosaur was discovered by John Bell Hatcher and Othniel Charles Marsh in 1888, in the Judith River beds of Montana. This dinosaur would subsequently be named *Triceratops*.

Where is the **largest known accumulation** of **theropod skeletons** found in the United States—or in the world?

The largest mass accumulation of theropod skeletons in the United States (and the world) was found at the Ghost Ranch quarry, in northwestern New Mexico. In 1947, George Whitaker and E. H. Colbert, members of an expedition from the American Museum of Natural History, found over one hundred skeletons of the late Triassic period dinosaur *Coelophysis*. They found the dinosaur skeletons in Arroyo Seco (dry canyon) on the lands of the Ghost Ranch.

The skulls in this bone bed show considerable variations in size, ranging from three to ten inches (8 to 26 centimeters) in length, indicating the presence of juveniles and adults. In 1948, during further excavations, George Whitaker and Carl Sorenson discovered two skeletons of *Coelophysis* with juveniles inside the stomach areas—thought to indicate that this species was cannibalistic.

It is still a mystery why so many of these animals ended up in such a small area. Some paleontologists suggest that a herd of *Coelophysis* was overwhelmed by a flood, perhaps while crossing a river. If this was true, then this discovery was the first evidence for herding behavior among a dinosaur species.

Where was the **first** known fossilized **dinosaur skin** found in the United States?

In 1908, the fossil impression of a duck-billed dinosaur's skin was discovered in Wyoming, by paleontologist Charles H. Sternberg and his sons, Charles M., George, and Levi Sternberg.

Where was an **almost complete skeleton** of an *Apatosaurus* found in the United States?

In 1909, American paleontologist Earl Douglass discovered an *Apatosaurus* (formerly known as a *Brontosaurus*) skeleton in the Carnegie Quarry (now Dinosaur National Monument) on the border between Utah and Colorado. Through 1923, further excavations in this area uncovered the largest known concentration of Jurassic period dinosaurs in the United States.

Where and when was the **first** skeleton of a *Brachiosaurus* found in the United States?

In 1900, the first *Brachiosaurus,* or "arm reptile," was discovered in the area of Grand Junction, Colorado. The dinosaur earned this name since its front legs were longer than its hind legs; it was regarded as the largest known dinosaur at that time. The *Brachiosaurus* was discovered by Elmer Riggs, assistant curator of paleontology at the Field Columbian Museum (now the Field Museum of Natural History) in Chicago, and H. W. Menke.

The area where the bones were discovered and quarried is now known as Riggs Hill. Riggs broke with the conventional thought of his day, and suggested that the sauropod was not amphibious (living on land and in water)—but a land-dwelling animal with habits similar to those of the modern elephant.

RECENT DINOSAUR FINDS

What was the **significance** of the dinosaur *Maiasaura* discovery in the United States?

In 1978, American paleontologists John R. Horner and Bob Makela discovered the fossilized remains of what would subsequently be called

287

> ## Where was the first skeleton of *Supersaurus* found in the United States?
>
> The "home" of the *Supersaurus*—believed to be one of the world's largest dinosaurs—is the Dry Mesa Quarry, on the Uncompahgre Plateau in western Colorado. This site was first explored in 1971, by Ed and Vivian Jones, amateur paleontologists from Delta, Colorado. It is also home of another large dinosaur, the *Ultrasaurus*.

Maiasaura, or "good mother lizard," in Montana. This was the first known nest of baby dinosaurs, and indicated the young had been cared for by adult dinosaurs. Starting in 1979, and working into the 1980s, Horner uncovered evidence of herding behavior in the dinosaurs—providing new insights into the social behavior of these dinosaurs. The herd was estimated to have been almost ten thousand dinosaurs strong.

Where is one of the **largest sets** of **dinosaur tracks** in the United States?

In 1989, paleontologists found approximately one thousand well-preserved dinosaur footprints in a quarry in Culpeper, Virginia. These tracks were dated to about 210 million years ago.

Where was the **first** skeleton of a *Utahraptor* found in the United States?

In 1991, paleontologist Jim Kirkland found the first skeleton of *Utahraptor,* a large dromaeosaurid with long foot claws, in the Gaston Quarry, Utah. The quarry itself had been discovered in 1989 by Robert Gaston.

What famous dinosaur is nicknamed **"Sue"**?

"Sue" is the nickname given to the most complete *Tyrannosaurus rex* skeleton yet discovered. "Sue" represents almost 90 percent of the total skeleton, compared to other T. rex skeletons, which are usually only 40 to 50 percent complete. This alone makes it an important specimen.

But the legal controversy surrounding the ownership of the bones made "Sue" a household name. The remains were found in 1990 by Sue Hendrickson, for whom it is named. Hendrickson came upon the fossilized bones while walking on a Cheyenne River Reservation ranch in South Dakota owned by Maurice Williams. The complete remains, eventually totaling 130 crates and boxes, were excavated by Peter Larson and associates of the Black Hills Institute. In 1992, a subsequent legal dispute over ownership of the bones led to an FBI raid on Larson's museum to seize the remains, followed by a lengthy court battle. The case ended in Larson's incarceration and the ownership of the bones was given to Williams, who in turn decided to sell them at a public auction. In October 1997, the remains were auctioned by Sotheby's, with the winning bid of $8.36 million submitted by the Chicago Field Museum of Natural History.

The museum plans to restore the dinosaur bones, and exhibit "Sue" in her own gallery, a task that should be finished around the turn of the century. Until then, visitors can watch the restoration process through a glass wall at the Fossil Preparation Laboratory. And for those who cannot make it to Chicago, two replicas are being made—one will tour the United States, while the other will go on display at Walt Disney World in Florida.

What discovery in the United States led to new theories about dinosaur **behavior and physiology**?

The discovery and description of *Deinonychus,* "terrible claw," by John Ostrom of the Yale Peabody Museum—turned out to be the catalyst that changed our perceptions about dinosaurs. In 1964, *Deinonychus* bones were excavated from the Cloverly Formation rocks of the lower Cretaceous period in Montana; Ostrom presented his findings in 1969. The information from these fossils, and other fossil finds related to *Deinonychus,* increased our knowledge of dromaeosaurids—which may have been the most aggressive and maybe the most intelligent of the theropods.

Based on fossil evidence found during the excavation, Ostrom concluded that these animals may have hunted in packs, indicating a social structure. Also, the animals' skeletons were light and slender, with a stiffened tail for balance, long clawed arms for grasping, sharp backward-curving teeth for tearing flesh, and a huge sickle-shaped claw on the second toe of the foot for slashing. The animal was built for speed and agility, quite unlike the perception of dinosaurs up until that time. From these findings, Ostrom theorized that *Deinonychus* may have been warm-blooded. This radical notion opened up new thinking about dinosaur physiology—and led to the modern ideas of dinosaurs as active, social animals.

Where has the world's **largest *Tyrannosaurus rex*** been found?

The current size champion was found in the summer of 1997, in a late Cretaceous period bone bed near the Fort Peck reservoir in Montana. This area is in the badlands of eastern Montana; the remains were found in the Hell Creek rock layer, a geological formation well-known for its dinosaur bones. The site appears to have been a river channel; the bones of dead dinosaurs were washed into the channel and collected in one place.

This skeleton, though only partially excavated, appears to be nearly complete, and is the largest specimen of a *Tyrannosaurus rex* yet found. Its pubis bone is at least 52 inches (133 centimeters) long; the previous largest known *Tyrannosaurus rex* skeleton had a pubis bone approximately 48 inches (122 centimeters) long. The skull of this animal measures approximately 6.6 feet (two meters) long. In fact, this is the largest carnivorous animal found to date on the planet—eclipsing the claim of the *Giganotosaurus.*

Which states have the **most dinosaur fossil sites**?

Although many states have dinosaur sites, so far, the states that seem to be the most prolific are Colorado, Utah, Wyoming, and Montana.

INTERNATIONAL DINOSAUR DISCOVERIES

EARLY DINOSAUR HISTORY OUTSIDE THE UNITED STATES

Who wrote the earliest **description** of **dinosaur bones**?

The author's name was Chang Qu; around 300 B.C., he wrote about "dragon bones" found in Wucheng, China (now Sichuan Province). These bones were often ground up by the Chinese, and used as medicine or for magical potions. More than 1,500 years later, these "dragon bones" would be recognized as dinosaur fossils.

When was *Scrotum humanum* discovered?

Around 1676, the Reverend Plot of England reported a fossil bone find: A "human thigh bone of one of the giants mentioned in the Bible." In 1763, R. Brooke named the bone based on its shape. He referred to it as *Scrotum humanum*—the genitals of a giant man. Today, the bone is thought to be from a megalosaurid dinosaur, from the distal end of a femur. The name, *Scrotum humanum*—though unofficially the first assigned name given to dinosaur bones—has never been used, since it was an erroneous designation.

Where were **dinosaur** bones **first scientifically studied**?

Dinosaur bones were first scientifically studied in Europe—specifically in England, where many dinosaur fossils are found. This occurred fairly recently, during the 1800s. In fact, three Englishmen, William Buckland, Gideon Mantell, and Richard Owen, are now recognized as the "discoverers" of dinosaurs.

Who first published a **scientific name** for fossil **dinosaur** bones?

In 1822, English surgeon and paleontologist James Parkinson (1755–1824) published the name *Megalosaurus,* based on fossil findings in England; unfortunately, he did not provide a description.

Who **first** published information on fossils **classified as a dinosaur**?

Although James Parkinson published the name *Megalosaurus* in 1822, the first officially recognized scientific naming and description of a dinosaur was by William Buckland (1784–1856), a professor at Oxford University in England. In 1824, Buckland published his studies of a Cretaceous period carnivore whose fossils had been found in Stonesfield, England, describing the animal based on fossilized jaws and teeth. He also used the name *Megalosaurus,* and presented his data at a meeting of the Geological Society of London. This was subsequently accepted as the first dinosaur to be described.

Who **first proposed extinctions** had occurred during the Earth's history?

Baron Georges Cuvier (1769–1832), a French scientist at the National Museum of Natural History in Paris, was the first to propose the idea of extinctions. Around 1800, his work with mammoth and mastodon bones (although they were not labeled such until later) which had recently been found in North America led to his theory of extinction. He was able to show that these creatures recently went extinct—refuting claims that all creatures that ever existed were still alive and living on unexplored areas of the Earth.

What town features the dinosaur *Iguanodon* on their civic coat of arms?

The town of Maidstone, Kent, England, has the *Iguanodon* embedded on its coat of arms. In 1834, Gideon Mantell made an identification of a partial skeleton as being an *Iguanodon;* the fossil remains had been dug up by W. H. Bensted in his own quarry. Though Mantell purchased the skeleton for his own collection, the town still felt a sense of ownership and, in 1949, petitioned the Royal College of Arms to add the dinosaur to part of their civic shield. Their request was approved.

He is considered to be the father of modern paleontology and comparative anatomy. His confirmation of the extinction process opened the door for the study of more ancient animals—the dinosaurs.

Who **first recognized** certain fossils as **giant reptiles**?

Gideon Mantell (1784–1856), an English country doctor and fossil collector, was the first to recognize certain fossils as giant reptiles. The well-known story—but perhaps not completely true—is that Mantell's wife, Mary Ann, found some fossilized teeth in rocks along the roadside while accompanying her husband on a house call. (Some people believe that Mantell actually found the fossils.) The rocks had come from the Bestede Quarry, Cuckfield, Sussex, England. In 1822, Mantell's examination of these teeth—and of subsequent remains from the same area— led him to the first reconstruction of what is now known as a dinosaur. In 1825, a year after William Buckland's published description of *Megalosaurus,* Mantell published a description of this ancient reptile. He named it *Iguanodon,* or "iguana tooth," as the teeth, though much larger, matched those of the modern lizard.

This was the second published description of a creature that became known as a dinosaur. Mantell subsequently used a pictorial representation of the *Iguanodon* on the coat of arms for his residence, Maidstone, Kent, England.

What **other discovery** can be attributed to **Gideon Mantell**?

Gideon Mantell also scientifically described the first known dinosaur skin in 1852. This was from the forelimb of a *Pelorosaurus becklesii* dinosaur.

Who **coined** the word **palaeontology**?

In 1830, Sir Charles Lyell (1797–1875), a Scottish geologist, coined the word *palaeontology,* or "discourse on ancient things." Between 1829 and 1833, Lyell recognized that this was a separate field of science. In general, "paleontology" is the U.S. spelling.

Who **coined** the term **dinosaur**?

The first person to realize the bones of the ancient giant reptiles belonged to their own unique group was Sir Richard Owen (1804–1892), an English anatomist and paleontologist. In 1841, based on several partial fossil remains of *Iguanodon, Megalosaurus,* and *Hylaeosaurus,* he coined the term *dinosaur* ("terrible lizard") to describe them.

Where were the first **life-sized dinosaur models** publicly displayed?

The first life-sized dinosaur models were publicly displayed at Sydenham Park, site of the relocated Crystal Palace in southeast London, England. The year was 1854, and the sculpting of these figures by Benjamin Waterhouse Hawkins had been supervised by paleontologist Sir Richard Owen. The figures were placed in the park, later renamed the Crystal Palace Park; the dinosaurs were all portrayed as giant, elephantine lizards. These figures were enormously popular with the public. And although the Crystal Palace itself burned down years ago, the sculptured dinosaurs can still be viewed on the grounds.

Who was first to reconstruct the way dinosaurs behaved?

Louis Dollo (1857–1931), a French mining engineer, was the first to interpret the remains of dinosaurs. Dollo did this with an eye toward reconstructing their lifestyles. In 1878, the remains of approximately 40 *Iguanodon* were discovered in the Fosse Sainte-Barbe coal mine near the town Bernissart in southwestern Belgium. Their excavation took three years. Dollo spent the rest of his life assembling, studying, and interpreting the fossil remains.

In 1882, he started as an assistant naturalist at the Royal Natural History Museum in Brussels, Belgium; in 1904, he became director of the museum, based on the strength of his scientific discoveries associated with the *Iguanodon*. Not only did he assemble the bones for exhibit and write papers concerning his findings— but he attempted to portray the behavior of these animals.

Who **first classified dinosaurs** based on the structure of the pelvic area?

In 1887, English paleontologist Harry Govier Seeley realized there were two distinct groups of dinosaurs. He classified them as *Ornithischia* (bird-hipped) and *Saurischia* (lizard-hipped), basing this primarily on the bone structure of the pelvic area. This system of classification was widely adopted and is still in use today. Seeley also grouped the dinosaurs with crocodiles, birds, and extinct reptiles known as thecodonts; this common ancestral group is now known as the archosaurs.

Why are the **Solnhofen quarries** of Germany so **important** to paleontology?

The Solnhofen quarries of Bavaria, Germany, are important not just because they are home to the oldest known bird fossils, the

297

Archaeopteryx lithographica; this area is also what paleontologists call a *Lagerstatten*—German for "fossil lode" or "storehouse." Because of their unique prehistoric conditions, these sites have preserved numerous animals, giving us a virtual snap-shot of ancient fauna. There are only approximately one hundred fossil sites around the world designated as *Lagerstatten*—each representing different time periods, and all rich in fossil varieties.

What were the **conditions** that formed the rock in the **Solnhofen quarries**?

The Solnhofen quarries were the site of a quiet, warm-water, anoxic (lacking oxygen) lagoon. It lay behind reefs on the northern shores of the Tethys Ocean approximately 150 million years ago. The tropical climate at this time was perfect for the animals and plants living along its shores. And the ocean itself teemed with life beyond the stagnant lagoon.

Storms would sweep in dead or dying animals from the ocean; dying land creatures either fell into the lagoon, or drifted into it from the shore. Their bodies fell to the bottom of the lagoon and were covered by soft lime mud; little oxygen was present to decompose the organisms. The ensuing fine limestone rock preserved, in exquisite detail, the remains of over 600 species, including the smallest dinosaur, *Compsognathus;* pterosaurs by the hundreds; numerous insects; and, of course, the remains of *Archaeopteryx lithographica.*

When was the most spectacular **dinosaur fossil expedition** mounted?

The most spectacular dinosaur fossil expedition ever mounted began in 1909 and lasted through 1912. The expedition took place in German East Africa—now known as Tanzania—around the village of Tendaguru.

In 1907, W. B. Sattler found gigantic fossil bones weathering out of the surface rock as he explored the area around Tendaguru for mineral resources. After reporting his findings, the area was subsequently visited by noted paleontologist Professor Eberhard Fraas, who took samples back to Germany. There, Dr. W. Branca, the director of the Berlin Muse-

What dinosaur remains were excavated during the Tendaguru expedition?

The Tendaguru expedition was itself spectacular—and so were the dinosaur fossils discovered at the site. Among the findings were three types of theropods—the small, agile *Elaphrosaurus,* and the larger *Ceratosaurus* and *Allosaurus.* Six herbivorous dinosaurs were also found: the tiny ornithopod *Dryosaurus; Kentrosaurus,* a stegosaur; and four sauropods, *Dicraeosaurus, Barosaurus, Tornieria,* and the largest one of the time, *Brachiosaurus.* The reconstructed skeleton of a Tendaguru *Brachiosaurus* at the Berlin Museum is the largest complete dinosaur skeleton in the world.

In addition to these spectacular dinosaur finds, the expedition also uncovered remains of pterosaurs, fishes, and a tiny mammal jaw bone. All of the animals were similar to those found earlier in the Morrison formation in the western United States, indicating that migration between North America and Africa was relatively easy during the time of these animals.

um, realized the importance and scope of the findings—and started raising funds for an expedition.

The expedition began in 1909—a search larger in scope than anything to date. In the first year, 170 native laborers were employed by the expedition; in the second year 400 were used. The third and fourth years saw 500 natives at work on the dig sites, which were located in an area extending almost two miles (three kilometers) between Tendaguru Village and Tendaguru Hill. The laborers were accompanied by their families; thus, the expedition had to accommodate upward of 700 to 900 people. As if that wasn't enough, after the fossils were mapped, measured, excavated, and encased in plaster, they had to be hand carried from Tendaguru, in the interior, to Lindi, on the coast—a trek that took four days. There, the enormous number of bones, eventually totaling 250 tons, were shipped to Germany for preparation, study, and reconstruction.

Where were the **first *Albertosaurus*** fossil remains found?

The first fossil remains of the late Cretaceous dinosaur *Albertosaurus* were found in the badlands of the Red Deer River Valley of Alberta, Canada. Geologist Joseph Burr Tyrrell found the fossil remains in the spring of 1884, as he led an expedition near present-day Drumheller for the Geological Survey of Canada.

In the early 1900s, the discovery of these and other remains brought numerous paleontologists to the area, including Barnum Brown of the American Museum of Natural History, and Charles H. Sternberg and sons for the Canadian Geological Survey. The friendly rivalry between Brown and the Sternbergs was dubbed the "Great Canadian Dinosaur Rush."

Today, the badlands of the Red Deer River Valley in Alberta, Canada, are recognized as one of the world's leading fossil collecting areas, with some 25 species of dinosaurs so far uncovered. The significance of this area led to the establishment of the Royal Tyrrell Museum, established in June 1990, in Drumheller.

How did the **"badlands"** of the Red Deer River Valley **form**?

The badlands of the Red Deer River Valley, in Alberta, Canada, were carved by melt-water torrents when the ice sheets retreated approximately 10,000 to 15,000 years ago. There is some evidence that flash floods, rather than rivers, were the agents that created the present badland topography. These landscapes include narrow, winding gullies and channels; heavy erosion; steep slopes; and little or no vegetation.

During the time of the dinosaurs, this area included numerous deltas and river flood plains that extended out into a shallow, inland sea. The late Cretaceous deposits of sand and mud often included the bodies of dinosaurs. Over millions of years, as material was laid down layer upon layer, the deposits turned into rock—fossilizing the dinosaur bones.

The advance and retreat of four glacial ice sheets over millions of years—along with other natural erosional processes by wind and water—caused significant wearing away of the area. The material on top was removed, and the exposed Cretaceous period sedimentary rocks were carved into the badlands of today. The Cretaceous layer is known as the Horseshoe Canyon Formation—and is continually eroding, exposing fresh dinosaur fossils.

RECENT FINDS

Where were the remains of the **oldest known dinosaur** discovered?

The fossil remains of *Eoraptor* ("dawn hunter") were discovered in the Ischigualasto formation rock layer in Argentina, South America—the same area where the second oldest dinosaur, the *Herrerasaurus,* was found. In 1991, Ricardo Martinez made the first find of a *Eoraptor;* this was followed by the discovery of another skeleton in the 1990s, by Fernando Novas and Paul Sereno. In 1993, the analysis of these remains led Sereno to name *Eoraptor* the "first," or most primitive known, form of dinosaur.

Eoraptor was smaller than *Herrerasaurus,* being about three feet (one meter) long. It had all the dinosaur characteristics found in *Herrerasaurus,* but its skull was a basic design. It also had a few specializations that would allow it to be placed in any of the major dinosaur groups. The primitive dinosaurs probably represented 5 percent of the total animal population in the beginning of the late Triassic period. But they would soon spread throughout the world—and dominate the land in the Jurassic and Cretaceous periods.

Where was the **second oldest dinosaur** found?

In 1959, the remains of a *Herrerasaurus*—thought by some paleontologists to be the second oldest known dinosaur—were discovered in Argentina, South America. The remains were found in a layer of rock known as the Ischigualasto formation; the area is located in the Ischigualasto Valley, or the "valley of the moon."

The discoverers were Victorino Herrera, a goat-herder, and Osvaldo Reig, a paleontologist. In 1988, a complete skull and skeleton of *Herrerasaurus* was found in the same area by Paul Sereno and Fernando Novas. This 10-to-20 foot (three-to-six meter) reptile had numerous characteristics enabling it to succeed at its carnivorous lifestyle:

> ## Where were the first duck-billed dinosaur fossils found outside the Americas?
>
> The first duck-billed dinosaur (plant-eating hadrosaurs) fossils found outside the Americas were discovered on Vega Island, off the eastern side of the Antarctic Peninsula. A tooth found there was dated at approximately 66 to 67 million years old; this finding gives more credence to theories about a land bridge connecting South America and Antarctica during this time. It also indicates that this cold climate and ecosystem were once lush and robust enough to support large plant-eaters.

recurved teeth, powerful hind limbs, a bipedal stance, and strong arms. It was excavated from rock laid down during the beginning of the late Triassic period, approximately 230 million years ago.

What **dinosaur** species had **unusually long hind legs**?

The fossil remains of a 12-foot (3.7-meter) carnivorous dinosaur was recently discovered on an island off the southern coast of England. This new species of dinosaur had unusually long hind legs on which it ran at high speed; and it was equipped with claws and razor-sharp teeth. Though not yet named, this is the first small, meat-eating dinosaur found in Britain. It is unusual because it appears to be from the early Cretaceous period—and remains from this time are not often found in this area.

Where are the **oldest fossilized dinosaur embryos** found?

The oldest fossil embryos were discovered among approximately 100 dinosaur eggs recently found in the area around Lourinha, a small town about 37 miles (60 kilometers) north of Lisbon, Portugal.

The embryos—identified as those of theropods—were dated at approximately 140 million years old. They are the oldest embryos to date, and the only ones currently known from the Jurassic period. Until this finding, all other fossilized dinosaur embryos came from the Cretaceous period, with the oldest of those being approximately 80 million years old.

What great **Jurassic** and early **Cretaceous** period **discovery** was made in **Asia**?

The site of spectacular fossils, including many dinosaur remains, was found in Liaoning Province, northeast China, near the village of Beipiao. Included in the finds were the first fossilized internal organs of dinosaurs—and the first fossil of a dinosaur containing the remains of a mammal it might have eaten.

This site has so far yielded the remains of *Confuciusornis,* the oldest beaked bird; the possibly feathered dinosaur *Sinosauropteryx prima;* the oldest modern bird *Liaoningornis; Protarchaeopteryx,* perhaps a primitive bird older than *Archaeopteryx lithographica;* and many other species of dinosaurs, mammals, insects, and plants.

The fossils found at the site were preserved in great detail. This was because the prolific rock layer is from a lacustrine (lake) deposit and covered with a fine volcanic ash. Paleontologists speculate that a brief catastrophe, such as a volcanic eruption, killed and quickly buried everything in the area. Thus, even impressions of soft body parts, such as feathers and organs, were preserved.

In what northern locale were **dinosaur footprints** found in 1960?

The Arctic island of West Spitzbergen (in the Svalbard island group) in the Northern Hemisphere is where an international team of geologists discovered dinosaur footprints. These tracks were thought to have been made by *Iguanodon,* an early Cretaceous period dinosaur.

What great **fossil find** was made in **Argentina** that further **linked dinosaurs to birds**?

In the Patagonia region of Argentina, paleontologists have uncovered fossil remains of a dinosaur creature that embodies many physical char-

The Gobi Desert has been the site of many remarkable fossil finds. (Photo courtesy of Dean Conger/Corbis Corporation.)

acteristics that strengthen the argument that birds are descendants of dinosaurs. Named *Unenlagia comahuensis,* this meat-eating creature stood nearly four feet tall and was nearly seven feet long. Even though it could not fly and did not have wings, its bone structure was similar to that of ancient birds, allowing the dinosaur to tuck its upper arm bones close to its body, similar to the way modern birds fold their wings.

What **Cretaceous dinosaur fossils** were recently found in **Mongolia**?

At Ukhaa Tolgod, in the Gobi Desert of Mongolia, lies what is billed as one of the greatest Cretaceous fossil finds in history. Starting in 1993, the discoveries include the remains of more than 13 troodontid skeletons; over 100 uncollected dinosaur specimens; numerous mammals; and a nest-brooding adult *Oviraptor.*

The reason for the huge number and extraordinary states of preservation is thought to be due to a series of catastrophic occurrences. These events swiftly buried the animals, precluding any damage by the elements or scavengers. Scientists believe normally stable sand dunes became drenched with rain water, triggering sudden debris flows that trapped—and preserved—the animals.

What is one of the most **famous dinosaur sites** in the world today?

Flaming Cliffs, located in the Gobi Desert, Mongolia, is one of the most famous dinosaur sites in the world today. In the 1920s, an expedition from the American Museum of Natural History, led by Roy Chapman Andrews, found the first dinosaur eggs at this site. It was closed for many years; and in the late 1980s, the site was reopened to scientific study and dinosaur fossil gathering. Since that time, numerous findings have continued to occur in this dinosaur-rich area.

Where is the **world's largest paleontological institute** located?

The world's largest institute is located in Moscow, Russia, and is known as the Paleontological Institute of the Russian Academy of Sciences. No other institute in the world has more paleontologists under one roof, with research interests ranging from the dinosaurs of Mongolia and mammals from Georgia (near Russia), to the origins of life itself. There are extensive collections of fossils from all over the former Soviet Union and the world, along with a Museum of Paleontology and great public exhibits. The exhibits include Mongolian dinosaurs, synapsids from the Perm region (of Russia), and Pre-Cambrian fossils from Siberia.

Unfortunately, with all of these wonderful resources and exhibits, the institute and museum are largely underfunded and remain relatively unknown to those outside the paleontological world, unlike more popular museums such as the American Museum of Natural History (in New York City).

Have there ever been **thefts** in the field of dinosaur **fossil collecting**?

Yes, for example, in 1996, fossil collectors stole a set of dinosaur footprints from a site in northwest Australia, approximately 1,800 miles (3,000 kilometers) from Sydney. These were the world's only known fossil footprints made by a *Stegosaurus,* and represent a loss not only to science, but to the aborigines of Australia, who regarded the location of the footprints as one of their sacred sites. The thieves apparently used power tools to remove the rock containing these trace fossils. Under aboriginal law, this offense is punishable by death.

Also in 1996, the remains of five dinosaurs disappeared from the fossil repository of the Paleontological Institute of the Russian Academy of Sciences, Moscow, and are believed to have been stolen. They included a lower jaw and maxilla with teeth from the large carnivore *Tarbosaurus efremovi;* a skull of *Breviceratops kozlowskii,* a late Cretaceous herbivore; and two skulls of *Protoceratops.*

DIGGING FOR DINOS

FINDING DINOSAUR FOSSILS

What is **the first precaution** one should take before searching for dinosaur fossils?

The first and most important precaution to take before searching for dinosaur fossils—or any other fossils—is to make sure you have permission to search the area. In addition, verify that you can collect and keep any specimens you find on the land. Without permission, you may be arrested and charged with trespassing, destruction of property, or even theft. It is much easier to ask permission beforehand than to deal with legal proceedings, arrest, or jail-time afterward. Always find out what person, organization, or government agency owns the property—and always ask permission first!

How do paleontologists or amateur collectors **find dinosaur fossils**?

The key to finding dinosaur fossils (or fossils of any kind) is to search in the right types of rocks. This generally means searching in sedimentary rock—or rocks composed of materials such as sand or mud that were deposited in a lake, river, or ocean. However, not all sedimentary rock contains fossils, much less dinosaur fossils. The right combination of factors must have existed for a dinosaur to have been transformed into a fossil in sedimentary rock.

A dinosaur dig site. (Photo courtesy of James L. Amos/Corbis Corporation.)

To find dinosaur fossils, paleontologists must locate sedimentary rocks laid down during the right time—in this case, periods within the Mesozoic era. For example, if the paleontologist is interested in Jurassic period dinosaurs, then he or she should be looking for rocks deposited during that time. Once the fossil hunter knows which age of rocks he or she is looking for, the location of such rocks can be determined from a geologic map of the area. These maps pinpoint the locations of the various rock types exposed at the surface, and show an area's topography (height of the land).

Once a location with the right type of rock is determined, the paleontologist explores the area on foot, checking for exposed rock, and features that may have led to exposed rock, such as folds and faults. The paleontologist also looks for areas where erosion—due to action by water, wind, or even humans—continually wears away the sedimentary rock. This ensures a continuing exposure of the rock and of any fossils within the rock.

The last step is to continually search the area, which often leads to spotting an exposed bone or other fossil part. This may all sound very simple, but it is not: Patience and perseverance are the key ingredients at this stage of the search. Once the paleontologist makes a dinosaur or other fossil find, then the excavation, transportation, and restoration processes begin.

What is a **dig site**?

A dig site is a localized area where numerous fossil remains are found and excavated by paleontologists. For example, if a herd of dinosaurs drowned while crossing a flood-swollen river, their bodies could have been deposited in a bend of the river. There, their bodies would be quickly covered over with mud, and fossilization would take place. Millions of years later, if a fossil collector discovered a few exposed fossils—and subsequent exploratory digging uncovered a large amount of fossils—then the area would become an active dig site.

A site where excavation is currently ongoing (or was worked in the past) is generally referred to as a quarry—after all, fossil hunters are digging into the rock! Many times these quarries are named after the collectors who found the first fossil remains there. Others are named after nearby towns.

Where are **dinosaur dig sites** usually **located**?

Dinosaur remains can be found worldwide—from the barren deserts of Mongolia to the cold slopes of the Antarctic. This is because, at the time dinosaurs roamed the land, all of today's landmasses were connected or closeby—allowing dinosaurs to freely move about.

Still, all dinosaur dig sites have something in common: The action of natural—or sometimes even human—agents have eroded the land, exposing the buried, fossil-bearing rock to the light of day. In many cases, the best place to discover the first bones that signal a major find is where this erosional action continues today. In the Gobi Desert, the passing of another sandstorm means a fresh batch of bones will be waiting on the surface. Bases of sea cliffs, where the water batters the rock during high tides or storms, will have new fossils exposed. Areas of heavy downpours, flash flooding, and excavation in a commercial quarry are all good places to find the bones that will trigger the start of the formal dig process.

How do paleontologists use ground-penetrating radar?

Ground-penetrating radar is a technique in which radio waves are transmitted deep into the ground from a lawnmower-sized mobile unit. Some of these waves are reflected and travel back to the surface, where they are detected, recorded, and printed out. There are various reasons why the radio waves are reflected, including changes in the types of rock, cracks in the ground, changes in the amount of water in the rock, or a boundary between rock and a dinosaur bone. It takes considerable talent and intuition to figure out which reflections are due to the presence of dinosaur bones, and which reflections are not. And there are no positive images of bones produced by this technique—just indications of possible sites.

What **methods** do paleontologists use to find **buried dinosaur bones**?

Predicting where dinosaur bones lie beneath the surface of the ground is a very difficult task, and for many years this process has depended on the experience and intuition of the field worker. If a paleontologist knew where dinosaur bones and skeletons were precisely located underground, this would eliminate many of the current hit-and-miss searches for new discoveries. And it would make excavations of known locations much more efficient.

There are currently no methods specifically developed to find dinosaur bones beneath the ground. But there are a few instruments paleontologists have adapted from diverse fields such as hydrology and archaeology to search rock layers for clues. Some of the most promising ones include ground-penetrating radar; acoustic diffraction tomography; proton free precession magnetometry; and radiation detection using scintillation counters.

Unfortunately, all of these techniques have limitations: None of them can give the paleontologist an "X-ray of the ground" to reveal the location of buried bones. And an experienced engineer is needed to operate the equipment, understand the theory behind the instrument's design, and interpret the generated data.

What is **acoustic diffraction tomography**?

Acoustic diffraction tomography is also known as seismic tomography. And it is a technique that cannot, by any stretch of the imagination, be called subtle—at least not in its execution. An instrument known as a "betsy" (essentially a high-powered 8-gauge Magnum shotgun mounted on wheels) is used to fire a lead slug into the ground at a predetermined point. This generates a seismic shock wave in all directions. The wave is detected by hydrophones suspended in vertical, pipe-lined, water-filled holes dug deep into the ground—preferably twice as deep as the suspected location of any bones.

The exact arrival time of the shock wave is recorded by the hydrophones. Any discrepancy in arrival time, whether too slow or too fast, can indicate the presence of something buried between the hydrophones and the site where the "betsy" was fired. If slugs are fired into the ground at different places, the results, along with geometric calculations, can give the paleontologist an idea of where and how deep to dig, and the approximate size of the object. But again, short of digging, there is no real way of knowing whether or not the object is a dinosaur bone.

What is **proton-free precession magnetometry**?

This technique measures the differences in the intensity of the Earth's magnetic field along a predetermined grid. The instrument is very precise, and has the advantage of being portable; it is mounted on a pole and can be carried in the field. Because the magnetic properties of buried dinosaur bones can be different from the surrounding rock (due to their chemical composition), differences in the magnetic field intensity may mean there are bones beneath the surface. However, materials other than dinosaur bones may also produce these differences—leading paleontologists to fall back on the tried-and-true method of excavation to determine the cause of the anomalous readings.

What is **radiation detection with scintillation counters**?

Scintillation counters are instruments sensitive enough to detect the radiation coming from objects below the surface. Some dinosaur bones, because of the location in which they were buried, may contain radioactive isotopes of uranium. These isotopes decay over time, producing radiation levels above the normal background level for that area. These slight increases can be detected by the scintillation counters. However, this technique is only useful for bones that are buried at very shallow depths below the surface.

How is **modern technology** helping map and study **dinosaur fossil** finds?

At a dig site, the exact location of fossil discoveries can now be determined using the Global Positioning System (GPS)—an instrument that uses satellite technology to pinpoint a location on Earth. This technique eliminates errors due to poor maps, shifting landmarks, and inaccurate compass readings. The orientation and distribution of the fossil bones in all three dimensions can also be obtained using Electronic Distance Measurement (EDM) and other survey devices. These instruments minimize the human errors inherent to using compasses and tape measures.

There is another advantage to using these techniques: The data can be fed directly into a computer. With the help of such programs as Geographic Information Systems (GIS) and Computer-Aided Design (CAD), a three-dimensional map of a quarry site, showing the location and orientation of all the bones, can be generated. The paleontologist can then study the site from different orientations, attempting to answer questions such as: What social structure did these dinosaurs have? Or what caused dinosaur bones to be concentrated in this location?

How do paleontologists **dig for dinosaurs**?

Once an initial bone find has been made, evaluated, and the decision made to dig further, the process of excavating the rest of the bones commences. This is, contrary to the perception given in the media, a long, hard, labor-intensive practice, especially if the dinosaur was large, and a complete skeleton is present. The overlying rock must first be removed, using appropriate tools. These tools can range from dynamite, bulldozers and jackhammers, to picks and shovels. Once this overlying layer has been removed, finer tools, such as dental picks and toothbrushes, are used to expose the upper bone surfaces. To prevent these exposed bones from drying out, cracking, or oxidizing, they are stabilized by applying appropriate chemical hardeners.

The exposed bone surfaces are then completely mapped, and a plan for the excavation of the entire skeleton is made. The first step is to isolate each bone, or group of bones, by digging vertical trenches around each, leaving a substantial thickness of rock in place for protection. Any bones exposed on the sides by this trenching should be stabilized, and each bone must be numbered with permanent ink and recorded on the map records.

The exposed bones on the top and sides are covered with layers of damp newspapers, tissues, or paper towels; then, top and sides are covered with a jacket of plaster-soaked burlap strips. When dry, this jacket locks the bones into the rock, preventing any cracking or damage. Next, the rock on the underside of this block is carefully removed, a little bit at a time. Any exposed bones are again stabilized, and the newly exposed areas are jacketed. Pieces of wood or metal are used to prop up the jacketed block as the amount of rock on the underside is slowly reduced.

Once this rock is small enough, and all of the rest of the block has been jacketed, the block can be turned over. But before that, labels are placed on the jacket using permanent ink, indicating the mapping number for each bone inside, an orientation arrow, the date, the site name and number, and any other information needed by the museum for restoration. After the block has been turned over, any remaining exposed area of rock is jacketed—and this bone or group of bones is ready for transportation to the museum.

What is **grid mapping**?

Grid mapping is a standardized method for recording the positions of bones found at a dinosaur dig. Long pegs are notched at equal intervals along their length, usually at every four inches (ten centimeters); they are pounded into the ground around the outside of the fossil discovery. **315**

These pegs are placed at one-yard (one-meter) intervals, forming a square or rectangle around the fossil of interest. The pegs must be pounded into the ground to the same heights so they are level. String then connects all the pegs; the string is attached to the first, or highest, notches on each peg. This forms a large grid with many squares measuring a yard (one meter) on each side.

A survey grid consists of a wood frame one yard (one meter) square that holds a wire mesh with four-inch (ten-centimeter) squares. It is placed in one of the larger string grids on top of the fossil remains. Then the paleontologist uses graph paper to draw (to scale) what he or she sees beneath each of the smaller wire mesh squares. This process is repeated for each large square by moving the survey grid frame. When all of the grid squares have been mapped, the string is removed, and the excavation continues down to the next notch on each peg. The mapping process is repeated for this layer—and any subsequent layers—until the fossil is removed. This gives a "three dimensional map" of the excavated fossils and the site.

What types of **tools** are used at **dinosaur digs**?

There are a large variety of tools used at dig sites. But the excavation of any one fossil is a unique process—and may only require a few of them. Also, different stages of the excavation process may require different tools. With that in mind, the following table is a general list of the major tools that might come in handy at dig sites. (Also note: Some dig sites may be miles from roads, with tools carried in—so light weight and multi-usefulness are important considerations.)

Tool	Comments
shovel or spade	A lightweight model is used for digging out loose material
geologic hammer	These hammers have a square at one end and a chisel or pick at the other end. They are indispensable, general-purpose tools.
club hammer	This tool is used for hitting heavy chisels. Geologic hammers are often substituted for this tool.
rock saw and stonemason's chisels	These are chisels with an assortment of blade widths. They are used for removing rock from around fossil.
trowel or old knife	Trowels or old knives are used to scrape away soft rock.

Why is grid mapping important?

The grid mapping process may be long and tedious, but the recorded information is crucial to the paleontologist. The position in which the dinosaur was found may give information about its morphology, and how it lived. The relative positions of the bones often form the basis for reconstruction of the skeleton. Any other fossils around the bones are also helpful: Shells, plant material, or other bones may give clues as to what this dinosaur ate, and what other creatures existed at the same time. If there are enough clues, paleontologists can reconstruct how the animal died and became fossilized. Unless this important data is recorded during the excavation, such details will be lost.

Tool	Comments
brushes	All types of brushes, from tooth- to paint-brushes, are used on a dig. They are good for removing loose rock.
strainer or sieve	Strainers or sieves are useful for separating small fossil pieces from loose rock or washing samples.

What kind of **clothing and equipment** is taken into the field?

The best clothing and equipment would be similar to those you take hiking or rockhunting. Of course, the clothing and equipment must be suitable for the local environment. For example, clothing for a dinosaur dig in the Gobi Desert would be much different than for one in Antarctica. And equipment needed for a day dig at a local quarry would be different than the equipment needed for a months-long expedition in a remote part of the world.

The following is just a general guide to clothing and equipment. It is by no means complete. If you are inexperienced in hiking or working in the outdoors, seek more specific advice from those who are—such as geologists, backpackers, paleontologists, and mountain-climbers. There are numerous books on preparing yourself for the outdoors, and outdoor stores can be gold mines of advice. Also, many organizations sponsoring dinosaurs digs have lists of required clothing and equipment to use as guidelines.

The following is a list of the proper clothing need to engage in any type of digging situation.

Clothing and Equipment	Comments
appropriate clothing for weather and local conditions	For example: Long-sleeved shirts, T-shirts, shorts, long pants, sweaters, jackets, underwear. Control your temperature through the shedding or adding of multiple layers of clothing. Take enough for the length of the expedition.
backpack	Used to carry tools, food, water and extra clothing.
sturdy boots	For hiking to the dig site and for protection from falling rocks and hard surfaces.
gloves	For hand protection during digs. Also to keep hands warm in colder climates.
safety helmet	Protection from falling rocks if working in an area with cliffs, or collecting in a working quarry.
rain gear	Protection from getting wet; can also be used to stay warm.
flashlight	For illumination at night or under dark overhangs.
hat	Protection from sun or rain. Use when there is no danger from falling rocks
sunglasses/sunblock	Protection from the sun's ultraviolet rays.
goggles	Eye protection from flying rock chips.
canteens	For carrying water in remote areas.
camera/video camera	To record excavation of fossils.
compass/map	For finding directions in remote locations.
first aid kit	In case of injury or other medical emergencies.
tent/sleeping bag/cooking gear	For shelter, rest, and cooking food at remote site.

How are **dinosaur fossils distinguishable** from other fossils?

There are a number of ways to find out if a fossil is from a dinosaur. There are numerous fossil guides and books to help determine the identity of a fossil. It's helpful to have some knowledge of taxonomy (the classification of plants and animals) as well as a general knowledge of biology and geology.

If you find a fossil that you cannot identify yourself, you may try consulting a fossil club in your area. Also, a local university or nearby natural history museum usually has someone who will help identify the fossil for you, although sometimes a fee may be charged for this service. And if they cannot identify the fossil, they may be able to suggest someone who can help.

If your fossil does not correspond to anything known, it might be a new dinosaur species. In this case, your finding is very important to scientific knowledge, and you may be asked to donate the specimen to the museum or university for their collection—not only for the collection but for additional scientific study. Your name might even be used as the basis for the scientific name of the new species! Also, you might be asked to assist with further excavation at the dig site.

Can **amateurs find dinosaur fossils** of new or important species?

With the right tools and knowledge of where to look, amateurs are just as competent at finding dinosaur fossils as professional paleontologists. In fact, most dinosaur finds are made by amateur collectors. This is mainly because there are far more amateurs who have time to devote to searches. There are numerous examples from around the world of discoveries made by amateurs that have led to profound leaps in our knowledge of dinosaurs.

What are some examples in which **amateurs found dinosaur sites**?

One good example is the site of what is now the Mygatt-Moore Quarry near Fruita, Colorado: It was discovered on a late March hike in 1981, by Grand Junction, Colorado, residents Pete and Marilyn Mygatt, and J. D. and Vanetta Moore. They were amateur rock and fossil hunters who had "cabin fever" that day—and decided to go for a hike near the Utah border. During a lunch break, Pete Mygatt noticed a rock and picked it up. It split apart, revealing a partial tail vertebra of what was later identified as an *Apatosaurus*. This site is now named the Mygatt-Moore Quarry, and has yielded eight species of dinosaurs, including *Mymoorapelta,* a small armored dinosaur, and the first ankylosaur from the Jurassic period to be found in North America.

Another example is Rob Gaston, a local Fruita, Colorado artist who found some of the earliest dinosaur tracks in western Colorado. His discoveries led to the discovery of the Gaston Quarry, where the *Utahraptor* was subsequently found.

PUTTING DINOSAURS TOGETHER

What happens to **excavated dinosaur bones** after they reach a museum?

It depends on whether or not the museum or institute plans to exhibit the find in the near future. If there are no immediate plans for the bones, they will be placed in safe storage until time and funds are available for their preparation. However, if the skeleton is to be put on display relatively quickly—as in the case of a new, spectacular species—then the bones will go through a fairly standard preparation process.

Simply put, the bones must be removed from the encasing rock during the preparation process. Next, any missing parts must be identified and substitutes found. Lastly, the bones are attached together and the entire skeleton is mounted for display. This process is tedious and time-consuming. For example, it took seven years of work until the *Apatosaurus* at the American Museum of Natural History was exhibited to the public.

How are **dinosaur bones prepared** for study and display?

The process of preparing dinosaur bones excavated from the field is generally done in a laboratory, where a wide variety of tools and chemicals are available. The first step in preparation is to remove the rock from around the bones, using hand tools, dental picks, needles, microscopes, small pneumatic tools—or anything else that does the job. This technique is laborious and exacting, and can only be mastered through hours of hands-on experience.

Once the bones are exposed, they must be repaired, if needed, and stabilized to prevent further degradation. There are a wide variety of glues and

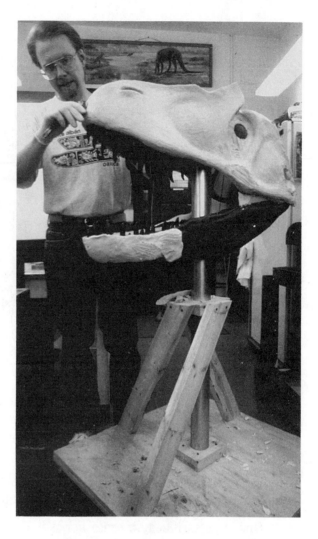

Museum worker prepares an Allosaurus mount. (Photo courtesy of University of Michigan Exhibit Museum of Natural History.)

adhesives that serve this purpose. Weak or cracked bones may require the addition of structural supports, such as fiberglass or steel bands.

How are **missing** dinosaur **bones restored** to a skeleton?

When a dinosaur skeleton that is to be exhibited has missing bones (which is the case for the vast majority of fossil finds), these bones must be restored. This is accomplished in a variety of ways: Some missing bones can be replaced with fossil bones or casts from another individual of the same dinosaur species. Often times, two or more partial skeletons

321

A paleontologist works at cleaning and preparing this dinosaur mount for display. (Photo courtesy of Corbis Corporation.)

can be combined to produce one complete skeleton. If these methods cannot be used, the missing bones can be sculpted from a variety of materials such as wood, epoxy, or ceramic.

How are **dinosaur bones mounted** for display?

Once the fossilized dinosaur bones have been prepared and stabilized—and any missing pieces obtained or substituted—the skeleton is ready to be free-mounted. The purpose of the mounted dinosaur is to display the skeleton as it might have looked in real life.

The first step, as in any large-scale project, is planning. Sketches and scale models are made, showing what the display will look like. Any variations to the posture—perhaps to reflect new information or to make the display more life-like—can be made at this stage, avoiding costly changes during actual assembly. The sketches and models will also show whether the skeleton will fit into its designated exhibition space. It would be very costly, time-consuming—not to mention embarrassing—to find out during assembly that the skeleton does not "fit." A good, final

The initial stages of preparing a *Pterosaur* mount. (Photo courtesy of University of Michigan Exhibit Museum of Natural History.)

sketch can also be used as a guide during the actual assembly, as well as showing where extra support is needed.

Next, a strong steel armature is constructed and the individual dinosaur bones attached to it—in their proper places, of course. The armature is custom-made to provide enough support, but shaped to be unobtrusive. Because dinosaur bones are very brittle, no stress can be placed on them; the armature is designed to support the weight of all the bones. Attachment of the bones to the armature is made using pins, bolts, or steel straps. Sometimes, it becomes necessary to hang cables from above to provide more support for parts of the skeleton.

Once the entire skeleton is mounted, there are still a few more details: The base on which the skeleton rests must be made visually appealing; barriers must be placed around the mount to protect it from the curious; and labels and display information created and positioned. At last, the dinosaur skeleton, which has remained hidden for millions of years, is ready to be viewed by the public.

How will **modern technology** help paleontologists **prepare, reproduce,** and **study** dinosaur fossil finds in the near future?

New technologies are rapidly changing the way paleontologists prepare, reproduce, and study dinosaur fossils. For example, Computed Tomography (CT) uses X-rays to generate a three-dimensional image of an internal structure of an object. In fact, it has already been used to determine if fossilized eggs contain baby dinosaur remains. Only those rocks containing fossils, or those eggs that contain baby dinosaurs, will be prepared, eliminating much of the destructive guess-work. In the near future, lab workers will also have a three-dimensional image of a specimen to help them in the preparation process.

Once fossil remains have been prepared, precise measurements will be made using new instruments such as electronic calipers, or two- and three-dimensional digitizers. This data will be sent directly to a computer, which guide machinery to automatically generate reproductions of the remains in materials such as metal or plastic. This will make highly accurate casts available to more scientists—and the public—at lower costs. Another exciting possibility: Three-dimensional data might be obtained from such non-destructive techniques as CT, allowing paleontologists to make highly accurate reproductions of dinosaur fossils— without ever removing the fragile bones from the encasing rock!

The research into dinosaur behavior and physiology will be greatly enhanced by the combined use of three-dimensional imaging, modeling, and virtual reality. Scientists will be able to study individual specimens, or even complete skeletons, from any angle or view— perhaps even from the inside looking out. And with data stored on computers, paleontologists will have much quicker access to rare specimens. Such systems as the World Wide Web will allow scientists to study a rare specimen on the computer—without having to travel to the few museums and institutions that house the actual fossils.

GETTING EDUCATED

Where can I obtain more **education** in **dinosaur paleontology**?

If you desire more education and experience in dinosaur paleontology, there are numerous opportunities available—at all levels. Your local college or university might offer courses in this specific subject, or the field of paleontology in general. Most colleges will allow a person to audit a course or take courses for credit even if you are not working toward a degree. If you are really ambitious, you might want to take courses that could lead to a degree in paleontology, with an emphasis on dinosaurs. Some organizations offer formal instruction in conjunction with dinosaur digs—and often for college credit.

Because of the interest in fossil collecting in general—and dinosaurs in particular—some museums and colleges are starting programs geared toward "professionalizing" the amateur fossil collector. These programs are intended to give the amateur the same level of practical field knowledge as the professional paleontologist. They can be certification programs—or can even lead to an Associate's degree.

What **formal studies** are required to become a **professional paleontologist**?

The field of paleontology is an interdisciplinary field, requiring knowledge from many other fields of science; for example, biology, geology, physics, and chemistry. Because the field requires a broad range of knowledge, there are relatively few educational institutions that offer degrees in paleontology, or in the more specialized field of dinosaur paleontology. But, this does not mean there is no way to become a dinosaur paleontologist.

In high school, the best strategy would be to take as many science and math courses as possible, such as physics, chemistry, biology, geology, computers, calculus, and algebra. A foreign language would also be helpful. The student should also read as much as possible on fossils and dinosaurs; visit museums with dinosaur displays; talk to dinosaur paleontologists for information; and perhaps volunteer to participate in dinosaur digs.

325

In college, the more science courses you take, the better. Most paleontologists have degrees in zoology or geology, and some have degrees in both. Zoology is useful for understanding the biology and taxonomy (classification) of animals, in this case dinosaurs; geology is needed to understand the fossil environment, as well as interpreting the natural processes that occurred when the animal lived. A double major in zoology and geology would be ideal; but if that is not possible, a major in one and minor in the other would suffice. Any other course to broaden the student's knowledge would be useful, such as statistical analysis and ecology. Conversing with professional paleontologists would help give the student a working knowledge about the field of paleontology, how it works, and what is required to succeed in the field.

Most professional paleontologists have advanced degrees; a Master's or Ph.D. in paleontology can be obtained at a few universities. The student should carefully research the particular emphasis at their chosen school and check out the academic interests of the faculty, making sure there is a match with the student's own interests.

What does a **professional paleontologist** do?

The work of a professional paleontologist varies, depending on where he or she works. Most paleontologists in the United States are college or university professors; some also work in museums, as independent consultants, or for government surveys.

In general, a professional paleontologist can conduct research, and write and publish academic research papers. They also curate, catalogue, and inventory fossils in a museum or university. They can run a research program, teach, or engage in a combination of these activities. Most of this work requires an advanced degree, although there are notable exceptions.

For people with undergraduate degrees, paleontology work can include preparing fossils, excavating and collecting fossils, mounting specimens for display, and casting specimens.

Where can I get information about **participating in dinosaur digs**?

As a novice, you will need education, training, and experience. The best way to obtain this is to participate in an organized dig. Depending on the program, there are opportunities ranging from one-day digs in pleasant surroundings, to week or longer expeditions in far-flung places like Mongolia. Some programs include formal instruction for college credit—so check the details of the program in which you are interested.

Dinosaur Digs and Programs

Name	Comments	Contact
Exposaur Excursions	Opportunities to dig in the Drumheller area	Box 7500, Drumheller, Alberta, Canada T0J 0Y0; (888) 440-4240; FAX: (403) 823-7131
Dinosaur Research Expeditions	six-day expeditions to recover fossil eggs and embryos from the Badlands of Montana with Vickie Clouse of Montana State University—Northern	(800) 662-6132 ext. 3716
Judith River Dinosaur Institute	five days of dig site instruction at an established dinosaur site in the Judith River formation of Montana	Box Y, Mata, Montana 59583; (406) 654-2323
Museum of the Rockies	A variety of programs at Egg Mountain	Montana State University, 600 W. Kasy Blvd., Bozeman, Montana 59717-2730; (406) 994-2251
Timescale Adventures	Hands-on programs at active research sites near the Rocky Mountains	P.O. Box 356, Choteau, Montana 59422
Dinamation International Society Expeditions	Paleontological expeditions to sites around the world	Director of Expeditions, 550 Crossroads Court, Fruita, Colorado 81521; (800) DIG-DINO
Wyoming Dinosaur Center	Day-long informational dig with scientists from the center	P.O. Box 868, Thermopolis, Wyoming 82443; (800) 455-DINO or (307) 864-2997
Western Paleo Safaris	Week-long educational outings in search of fossils in the American West	P.O. Box 1042, Laramie, Wyoming 82073; (888) 875-2233 (PIN 7737)
Grand River Museum	Two week-long sessions at the Hell Creek formation in South Dakota	Grand River Museum, Lemmon, South Dakota 57638

The choices of dinosaur digs are limitless and can sometimes seem overwhelming. The programs listed in the previous table represent only a sampling of the programs offered by museums, education institutions, and private concerns. Information about other opportunities can be found on the Internet, or in the classified ad sections of magazines dealing with paleontology, science, or nature. (Note: Some institutions charge fees for participating in the dinosaur digs.)

What are **certification programs** in the field of dinosaur paleontology?

In response to the growing number of fossil collectors interested in dinosaur paleontology and field work, a number of museums and institutions are running programs designed to turn amateurs into "parapaleontologists." Students are trained to collect and prepare dinosaur fossils. With this training, some people may make the transition into a full-time paleontological career.

What are some **examples of certification programs**?

There are several certifications programs. For example, if you are lucky enough to live around the Denver, Colorado, area, the Denver Museum of Natural History has a Paleontology Certification Program for adults (17 years of age and older). It is offered to people who want to learn more about paleontology and develop skills in the collection and preservation of fossils. Established in 1990, the core certification program includes a series of required courses. These courses provide an introduction to the history of life revealed through the fossil record, and knowledge of the theories and techniques of paleontology. After obtaining the basic Certificate of Competency—which requires completing the mandatory classes, passing a final exam, and receiving approval of a Museum committee—the student can continue studies in fossil preparation or field work. After courses in hands-on laboratory methods and a final exam, the student obtains a Lab Specialization Certificate; or, after additional related classwork, six days of actual field work, and a final exam, the student can obtain a Field Specialization Certificate. Some students may want to pursue both areas of interest. Classes are usually held in the evenings, with field trips on the weekends.

Another program is offered by Montana State University—Northern, located in Havre, Montana. The university is starting a program in paleontology technology, with options to earn an associate of science degree in this field, or to have paleontology technology as a minor. These programs will combine an emphasis on scientific research with practical training in this field. Contact the university at (800) 662-6132 for more information about this proposed program.

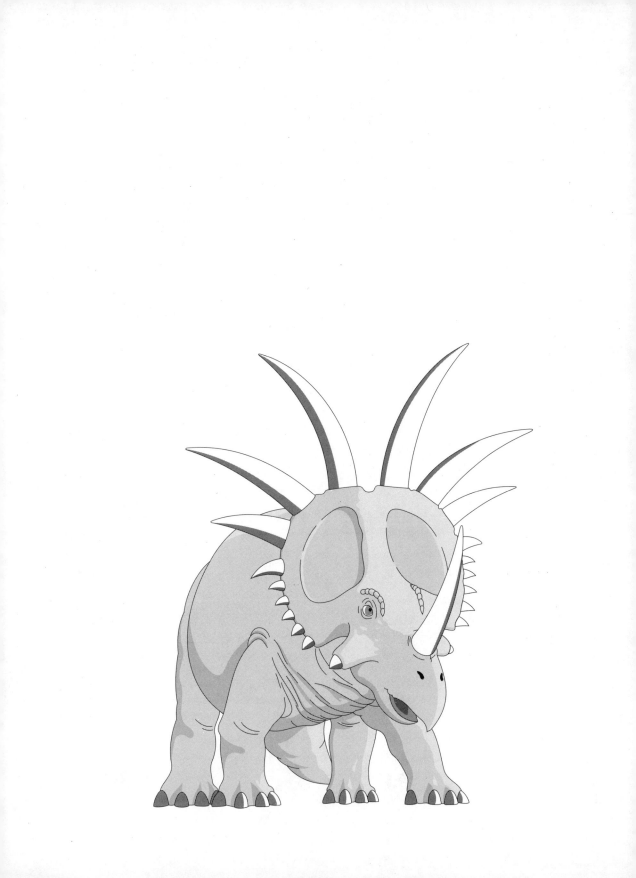

LEARNING MORE

DINOSAUR-MANIA

I'm hooked! How can I **learn more about dinosaurs**?

There are numerous resources available on dinosaurs. (Check the resource section in this book for more listings.) Your local library and bookstore probably have good selections of the latest dinosaur books. There are museums located around the world with permanent exhibits of dinosaur fossils, skeletons, and reconstructions—and most are extremely informative. Sometimes there are television specials, or movies dealing with dinosaurs; many of these can also be obtained in VCR format (often from your local library) for home viewing. In addition, there are traveling exhibits of animated dinosaurs; and there are parks and trails around the world where you can travel in the footsteps of early dinosaur explorers—and maybe observe digs still in process. In addition, if you can connect to the Internet (either at home or in a local library), there are innumerable sites dealing with dinosaurs and related subjects.

Where can I find **books about dinosaurs** at my local library?

Your local library has a wealth of information about dinosaurs—you just have to know where to look. A card catalog or computer search system is a good place to start. Look under the subject: dinosaurs. Most of the adult non-fiction books on dinosaurs will be in the science section, with

Dewey Decimal numbers ranging from 567.91 to 568.19. Ask your information librarian for directions to this section if you need help.

And do not forget the juvenile section of the library—whether you are a juvenile or an adult. Many juvenile sections of libraries seem to have more books on dinosaurs, albeit on a less technical level. The same Dewey Decimal numbers apply here: With a prefix J (for juvenile), look in the range 567.91 to 568.19.

Where can I find **books about dinosaurs** at my local **bookstore**?

Books about dinosaurs are usually found in the science and/or nature section of your local bookstore. There may also be books of a less technical nature (and often more pictorial) found in a separate children's section.

What **magazines** carry articles relating to **dinosaurs**?

Sometimes, it seems as though articles about dinosaurs are everywhere, especially when there is a major discovery or change in an existing theory. Usually, magazines that cover the natural sciences, such as *National Geographic, Nature, Natural History, New Scientist, The Sciences,* and *Scientific American* (just to name a few), are good bets for dinosaur articles on a continuing basis. There are even some specialized magazines dealing only with the subject, such as *Prehistoric Times.*

Why **visit a museum** that has dinosaurs exhibits?

There are many reasons to visit a museum that deals with dinosaurs. Maybe you have always wanted to participate in a dinosaur dig. Maybe you have seen specials on television, or read about digs in a book—and you find you are interested in learning more about the animals. Perhaps you want to encourage a budding paleontologist in your family. Or perhaps you want to experience the thrill of seeing a fossil that was buried for 65 million years—or you want to hold a bone in your hand that is *very* old. Perhaps you are a teacher who wants to show your students all about how to collect, or help them understand dinosaurs a little more.

Many museums have dinosaur exhibits open to the public. (Photo courtesy of Gail Mooney/Corbis Corporation.)

Or you want to lean how paleontologists really explore, dig, collect, and excavate dinosaur bones. There are many reasons to seek out information about dinosaurs in museums—and plenty of museums to visit.

What are some of the top **U.S. museums** with **dinosaur collections** and **exhibits**?

There are numerous museums with dinosaur collections and exhibits in the United States. Some are small museums, often associated with a university or college that offers courses or majors in paleontology; others are small museums started by amateurs or professionals with a special interest in dinosaur collection and education. It would be impossible to list all the museums with dinosaur collections in the United States. The following table lists some of the more well-known museums with dinosaur collections (skeletons, casts, or fossil remains) in the 48 contiguous states. (Also check the Resources section in the back of this book for more information.)

Location (alphabetical by state)	Museum Name	Comments
Flagstaff, Arizona	Museum of Northern Arizona	Displays of *Coelophysis* and *Scutellosaurus*
Los Angeles, California	Los Angeles County Museum	Displays of *Camptosaurus, Dilophosaurus, Edmontosaurus,* and *Tyrannosaurus*
Boulder, Colorado	University of Colorado Museum	
Denver, Colorado	Denver Museum of Natural History	
Grand Junction, Colorado	Dinosaur Valley, Museum of Western Colorado	
New Haven, Connecticut	Peabody Museum, Yale University	
Chicago, Illinois	*Field Museum of Natural History*	
Ann Arbor, Michigan	University of Michigan Exhibit Museum of Natural History	
Bozeman, Montana	Museum of the Rockies	Exhibit of the *Maiasaura*
New York City, New York	American Museum of Natural History	
Cleveland, Ohio	Cleveland Museum of Natural History	
Philadelphia, Pennsylvania	Academy of Natural Sciences	
Houston, Texas	Houston Museum of Natural Science	
Provo, Utah	Earth Science Museum	Displays of a *Supersaurus* and *Ultrasaurus.*
Salt Lake City, Utah	Utah Museum of Natural History	Displays of *Allosaurus, Barosaurus, Camptosaurus,* and *Stegosaurus*
Washington, D.C.	National Museum of Natural History (at the Smithsonian Institution)	
Laramie, Wyoming	University of Wyoming Geological Museum	Displays of *Anatosaurus, Apatosaurus, Anchiceratops,* and *Tyrannosaurus.*

A child on an educational journey at a museum. (Photo courtesy of Michael S. Yamashita/Corbis.)

What are some of the top **Canadian museums** with **dinosaur collections** and **exhibits**?

Canada has numerous museums with dinosaur collections and exhibits, including skeletons, casts, and fossil remains. The following list represents some of the more well-known Canadian museums.

Location	Museum Name	Comments
Alberta	Dinosaur Provincial Park	The park is an excavation in progress.
Ottawa, Ontario	National Museum of Natural Sciences	
Alberta	Provincial Museum of Alberta	
Quebec	Redpath Museum	Displays of *Majungatholus, Saurornithoides,* and *Zephyrosaurus*
Toronto, Ontario	Royal Ontario Museum	
Drumheller, Alberta	Tyrrell Museum of Paleontology	

What are some of the top **museums outside North America** with **dinosaur collections** and **exhibits**?

Dinosaur museums are not only restricted to the United States and Canada. Many famous collections of dinosaur bones are found in such places as Europe, Africa, and Asia. Some of the more well-known overseas museums are listed in the table on page 339.

Have any **museums re-posed** their **dinosaur skeletons**?

A number of museums around the world have changed their dinosaur exhibits to reflect revised thinking about the animals. One of them is the American Museum of Natural History in New York City. Here, the "new" *Tyrannosaurus rex* is portrayed as a ferocious, stalking carnivore whose tail waves in the air. The original version of the *Tyrannosaurus rex* stood straight up—but scientists now think this posture would have dislocated many of his vertebrae! The dinosaur's tail is now horizontal for balance, and his head is held lower, as though he is hunting.

Also at the American Museum of Natural History—in an exhibit sure to generate a lot of controversy—a *Barosaurus* is posed rearing up on its hind legs to protect its young from an attacking *Allosaurus*. This is certainly not the traditional view of this extremely large, plant-eating sauropod.

Another example of a skeleton that has been reconstructed based on more up-to-date research is at the Carnegie Museum of Natural History in Pittsburgh. The museum has a *Tyrannosaurus rex* posed in a more life-like posture—as if it is confronting prey or another *Tyrannosaurus rex*.

How can I make a **fashion statement** that includes **dinosaurs**?

If you find yourself reading about dinosaurs, digging for dinosaur fossils, collecting dinosaur stamps, and even dreaming about dinosaurs, then you're ready for the next step! After exploring the great dinosaur exhibits at the American Museum of Natural History (Central Park West at 79th Street, New York, New York 10012), stop by their gift shop. There, you can purchase a *Tyrannosaurus rex* T-shirt featuring the finest specimen of *T. rex* skull ever described. Or if you do not want to

Location	Museum Name	Comments
Cape Town, South Africa	South African Museum	Displays of *Anchisaurus, Heterodontosaurus, Massospondylus,* and *Melanorosaurus.*
Buenos Aires, Argentina	Museo Argentino de Ciencias Naturales	Displays of *Antarctosaurus, Mussaurus, Noasaurus, Saltasaurus,* and *Titanosaurus*
Birmingham, England	Birmingham Museum	
London, England	British Museum of Natural History	
London, England	Crystal Palace Park	Displays of Waterhouse Hawkins' 19th-century dinosaur models
Dorchester, England	The Dinosaur Museum	
Cambridge, England	Sedgwick Museum	
Oxford, England	University Museum	
Paris, France	National Museum of Natural History	Displays of *Compsognathus, Diplodocus, Iguanodon, Protoceratops, Tarbosaurus,* and *Triceraptops.*
Berlin, Germany	Natural History Museum, Humboldt University	Displays of *Archaeopteryx, Brachiosaurus, Dicraeosaurus, Dryosaurus, Elapbrosaurus,* and *Kentrosaurus.*
Chorzow, Poland	Dinosaur Park	Displays of *Saichania, Saurolophus,* and *Tarbosaurus.*
Warsaw, Poland	Institute of Palaeobiology	Displays of *Deinocheirus, Gallimimus, Homalocephale, Nemegtosaurus, Pinacosaurus, Proceratops, Opishthoceolicaudia, Saichania, Tarbosaurus,* and *Velociraptor*
Edinburgh, Scotland	Royal Scottish Museum	

limit yourself to just one species, buy a cladistics T-shirt, featuring the evolution of different dinosaur species. Don't forget the baby—Dino Babywear includes colorful renditions of *Triceratops* and *Stegosaurus*. For more formal wear, there is the *Tyrannosaurus rex* 100-percent silk tie that features everyone's favorite theropod in a stalking posture.

Now that your attire is properly "dino," what about your desk? The gift shop has something for that, too. There is the *Tyrannosaurus rex* mousepad, in various colors. Also available are mousepads depicting early Jurassic or Cretaceous period scenes, reproduced from the mural in the Hall of Vertebrate Origins. Of course, there are matching mugs for those who want to reflect on prehistory during coffee breaks or long meetings.

Where can **animated, life-like dinosaurs** be seen?

A tremendous exhibit of animated, robotic *life-sized* dinosaurs can be found at the Devil's Canyon Science and Learning Center, the permanent home of the Dinamation International Society. The center is located just south of Interstate 70, in Fruita, Colorado, a short distance west of Grand Junction. The highlights of the animated dinosaurs include a *Utahraptor* eating its prey—and a *Dilophosaurus* spitting a stream of water at unwary visitors (to simulate the animal's poison it would spray to keep away predators or to catch prey). There are also numerous static and hands-on exhibits, a gift shop, and a preparation laboratory. The center is located in the middle of dinosaur country, with numerous interpretive trails and working quarries within a short driving distance. Don't miss this one!

MEDIA SOURCES

Where can **television** or **video specials** on **dinosaurs** be found?

Most of the television specials on dinosaurs are found on stations with a predilection toward science and nature. For example, the Public Broadcasting System (PBS) and the Discovery Channel offer nature shows. Check your local guide for times and dates of any upcoming dinosaur programs. Also, consult their websites for archival information on past programming. (See the Resources section in the back of this book.)

A scene from the B-movie *Carnosaur* that came close to realistically portraying dinosaurs. (Photo courtesy of the Kobal Collection.)

Both PBS and the Discovery Channel often offer videos of their shows on dinosaurs. These tapes can be ordered directly, or sometimes can be found in your local library's video section. They may also make their way to your local video rental store; look for them in the documentary or nature sections.

How accurate was the movie *Jurassic Park*?

In the movie *Jurassic Park* scientists took blood (DNA) from an ancient mosquito—an insect that had fed on a dinosaur just before being

341

A scene from the film *Jurassic Park*. (Photo courtesy of the Kobal Collection.)

trapped in tree resin that eventually became hardened amber. The first mistake the movie made was to use amber from the Dominican Republic: Such amber is only 20 to 40 million years old—and dinosaurs died out about 65 million years ago! Amber from Switzerland, Kuji, Japan, or even Israel could have worked, as the amber that formed in these areas is from the Cretaceous period.

Another problem was the ecosystem: Not only was the island too small for all those creatures to flourish, but there is nowhere known on Earth where herbivores and carnivores live separately—except maybe in a zoo. Still another problem is the actual use of the "dinosaur DNA" to clone the dinosaurs. Just the total process, based on what we know now, would take years: Scientists would have to get the correct DNA sequence, and using a frog to fill in the DNA sequences would not result in a perfect dinosaur. There is a long list of why dinosaur DNA cloning would not work (right now).

If you really want to find out more about the "reality" of the movie, try picking up the book *The Science of Jurassic Park: The Lost World; or, How to Build a Dinosaur* by Rob Desalle and David Lindley. And just

King Kong's vision of dinosaurs involved the cinematic technique of claymation. (Photo courtesy of the Kobal Collection.)

remember, in spite of the problems—you have to take this movie (and those like it) as what it truly is—entertainment.

What were the first **dinosaur bones** in **outer space**?

The first, and so far, only dinosaur to make the journey into outer space was a *Coelophysis*. But it was not a living dinosaur—and the journey did not happen millions of years ago. On January 22, 1998, the Space Shuttle *Endeavor* lifted off from the Kennedy Space Center at Cape Canaveral, Florida, bound for a rendezvous with Russia's *MIR* space station. Aboard the shuttle was the fossilized skull of a *Coelophysis,* a small carnivorous dinosaur that lived in North America about 220 million years ago. The skull had been found—along with numerous other fossilized bones and skulls—at the famous Ghost Ranch, New Mexico, quarry. The *Coelophysis* skull was one of a group of lightweight items that a shuttle normally carries on each trip. These items are not onboard for research purposes, but to give them the uniqueness of having been in space.

343

What movies depict dinosaurs in realistic ways?

Most movies have a pretty miserable track record of portraying dinosaurs as real animals—and even show the dinosaurs as contemporaries of humans! In addition, the special effects tend to be poor, ranging from an obvious stuntman in a rubber suit, to the stiff, jerky, stop-motion action of small models.

For the best, most realistic portrayal of dinosaurs, rent *Jurassic Park* and *Jurassic Park: The Lost World.* The combination of state-of-the-art special effects, such as computer graphics imagery (CGI), and input on behavior and motion of dinosaurs from paleontologists such as Robert Bakker, brings these creatures to awe-inspiring—and sometimes terrifying—life.

Are any **models** of **dinosaurs** available?

Models of dinosaurs seem to be everywhere, from discount department stores to museum gift shops. Unfortunately, many of the inexpensive models are not accurate, reflecting the attitude that the models are "only for kids."

The first dinosaur models were marketed to the public during the mid-1800s, through the Ward's catalog of scientific supplies; they were plaster-cast miniature replicas of the life-size models sculpted by Benjamin Waterhouse Hawkins for the exhibit at the Crystal Palace grounds in London, England. During the 1940s, the SRG company produced the metal-cast figures, which were usually sold in museum shops; they were among the few small replicas available to the general public at that time.

Today, numerous companies are making dinosaur models available for sale in toy stores, museum shops, and department stores. Many of the replicas trade off accuracy for price, being viewed as toys or media tie-ins. Some, however, are quite accurate, and are backed by large museums—such as the hard-rubber figures found at the Carnegie Museum of Natural History (in Pittsburgh). These models can also be found in stores specializing in nature or museum gifts.

344

There are also smaller, private firms dealing in accurate dinosaur models. These companies can usually be found in magazines that specialize in nature and science; a good place to find these sources is *Prehistoric Times,* a magazine devoted to the dinosaur collector and enthusiast. A few of these companies are the Dinosaur Studio, Battat Dinosaur Resin Replicas, and Link & Pin Hobbies.

Are there any **stamps** depicting **dinosaurs**?

There are many stamps issued by different countries depicting all types of dinosaurs. Although the images of dinosaurs have been seen on stamps as early as 1935, dinosaurs on postage stamps appeared in 1958 in China. Since then, many countries have followed suit.

Stamps (postage or otherwise) depicting dinosaurs have generated enough interest to have their own advertisements in numerous stamp magazines. In addition, there are several international stamp-collecting houses that, for a fee, will automatically send you new dinosaur stamps when they are issued by most countries.

For information about dinosaur stamps, the books *Dinosaur Stamps of the World* by Baldwin and Halstead (1991) and *Dinosaurs Resurrected* by Hasegawa and Shiraki (1994) are recommended, as is the periodical *Biophilately.*

What did the most **recent dinosaur stamps** depict?

The U.S. stamps are part of two separate scenes on a large stamp sheet—the entire page called "The World of Dinosaurs." The scenes represent Colorado 150 million years ago, toward the end of the Jurassic period, and Montana 75 million years ago, during the Cretaceous period. In the Colorado scene, dinosaurs represented are *Ceratosaurus, Camptosaurus, Camarasaurus, Goniopholis, Brachiosaurus, Stegosaurus, Allosaurus,* and *Opisthias,* with cycads, pterosaurs, and sundry other organisms of that time. The Montana scene includes *Edmontonia, Einiosaurus, Daspletosaurus, Palaeosaniwa, Corythosaurus, Ornithomimus,* and *Parasaurolophus,* with dinosaur hatchlings, birds, frogs, mammals, and other organisms of that time.

Are there any **traveling exhibits** of **dinosaurs**?

There are indeed exhibits of dinosaurs, both static and animated, that make their appearance at fairs, convention centers, malls, and schools. The schedule and location of each varies, so be sure to call for the latest information. The following table lists some traveling dinosaur exhibits and their contact information.

Name	Address	Phone Number
Dinamation International	189A Technology Drive Irvine, CA 92718	(714) 753-9630
The Dinosaurs of Jurassic Park	The Dinosaur Society 200 Carleton Avenue East Islip, NY 11730	(516) 277-7855
Mr. Buddy Davis	1040 Henpeck Road Utica, OH 43080	(614) 668-3321
Kokoro Dinosaurs	6005 Yolanda Avenue Tarzana, CA 91356	(818) 996-8303
Jurassic Journey/Dino Discovery	1024 County Rd. #365 Taylor, Missouri 63471	800-723-9571

Are there any **dinosaur meetings** I can attend?

Many meetings dealing with dinosaurs may be too technical for the average person. But, if you can, by all means attend the Dinofest®, which bills itself as the "World's Fair of Dinosaurs." This event has something for everyone—for every age and interest level. There are exhibits, animated dinosaurs, technical symposia, and everything related to dinosaur paleontology. A Dinofest® will be held in St. Louis, in the year 2000. You can keep up-to-date on the scheduled happenings by calling 800-736-1420; or accessing the Internet site: http://www.dinofest.org.

Are there any **outdoor sites** devoted to **dinosaur education** and **discovery**?

There are numerous sites for the dinosaur enthusiast that have an outdoor, "hands-on" component. The following are just a few examples:

Cleveland-Lloyd Dinosaur Quarry, Price, Utah: This quarry was discovered in 1928, and has so far yielded over 10,000 dinosaur bones. It is still being worked today; most of the bones collected are from the dinosaur *Allosaurus.* There are tours to the quarry site from a visitors center.

Dinosaur National Monument, Vernal, Utah: The Dinosaur National Monument is located on the border of northeast Utah and northwest Colorado. It covers about 211,272 acres (85,500 hectares) and has the largest concentration of fossilized dinosaur bones in the United States. The visitors center is built around one of the quarry faces, and visitors can observe paleontologists removing dinosaur bones from the rock.

Dinosaur Provincial Park, Patricia, Alberta, Canada: This is one of the richest dig sites in the world, and it is the source of many of the fossils in the Royal Tyrrell Museum. Some areas are open to the public to explore and hike through.

Dinosaur Ridge, Morrison, Colorado: This tour takes a drive up the Alameda Parkway as it climbs the ridge through the rocks of the Morrison formation; this is also where famed American paleontologist Othniel Charles Marsh and his crew uncovered numerous types of dinosaur fossils. There are dinosaur tracks and fossilized remains of *Apatosaurus* still present.

Rabbit Valley Research Nature Area/Trail Through Time, Grand Junction, Colorado: An approximately two-mile (3.2-kilometer) hike along a historic trail, complete with interpretive trailside markers. Highlights include *Camarasaurus* bones still in the rock, and the active Mygatt-Moore Quarry, where the remains of more than a dozen dinosaur species have been found.

Riggs Hill Trail/Dinosaur Hill Trail, Grand Junction, Colorado: These short (approximately 1-mile [0.62-kilometer]) trails take the hiker through areas of historical paleontological dig sites. Complete with interpretive trailside markers, Riggs Hill is the site of the world's first *Brachiosaurus* discovery in 1900. It also contains the Holt quarry, where partial skeletons of *Stegosaurus, Allosaurus,* and *Brachiosaurus* were excavated in 1937. Dinosaur Hill contains the quarry where an *Apatosaurus (Brontosaurus)* was excavated in 1901.

Wyoming Dinosaur Center, Thermopolis, Wyoming: The Center has a working fossil lab, and exhibits of numerous dinosaur skeletons. But the

347

real centerpiece is the trip to the actual bone beds of the Morrison and Cloverly formations. There, excavations of camarasaurs, stegosaurs, an allosaur, and Wyoming's first *Brachiosaurus* are being carried out; visitors can ask questions of the paleontologists as they work.

Are there any **travel guides** to **museums** and **public dinosaur sites**?

One of the best travel guides that encompasses museums and public sites in the United States and Canada is *Dino-Trekking: The Ultimate Dinosaur Lover's Travel Guide,* by Kelly Milner Halls (John Wiley & Sons, February 1996). Though ostensibly written for children, this book is suitable for anyone with an interest in seeing dinosaurs—whether indoors or outside. It contains descriptions of museums and public dinosaur sites, and lists places carrying dinosaur products.

DINOSAURS ON THE INTERNET

How can I find information about **dinosaurs** on the **Internet**?

If you have access to the Internet—whether through your local library, education institution, or even better, at home—then you're in luck! There are so many resources dealing with dinosaurs on the Internet that it would take a complete book to list them all. The easiest way to get started on your journey is to access one of the many search engines on the World Wide Web. Just type "dinosaur" in the appropriate box, click on "go" (or "search"), and stand back. You will end up with a list of thousands of sites mentioning the word "dinosaur." Some reliable search engines are listed in the following table.

Search Engine	Internet Address
AltaVista	http://www.altavista.digital.com/
Excite	http://www.excite.com/
HotBot	http://www.hotbot.com/
Lycos	http://www.lycos.com/
Northern Light Search	http://www.northernlight.com/

Where can I find information on the **Internet** about **museums** exhibiting **dinosaurs fossils**?

Many museums have their own web sites, with details and pictures. Typing in the name of a particular museum in a search engine listed above will get you to that particular institution's web page.

A quick reference guide to museums in the United States can be found at The Cyberspace Museum of Natural History and Exploration Technology—The Paleontology Museum Database Page (http://www.cyberspace museum.com/paleodbase.htm). This site lists the museums found in each of the states. Clicking on the name of any museum takes you to a page that gives its location, telephone number, hours, fees, and a list of the dinosaurs currently on exhibit.

Another site that lists selected museums around the world is Dinosaur Dreaming—Other Dinosaur and Palaeo Websites (http:// www.earth. monash.edu.au/dinodream/resource/dinosite.htm). Simply click on the museum of interest to access a particular institution. Also, selected museums (those offering substantial information about dinosaurs or even virtual exhibits on their sites) are listed in the Resources section of this book.

What **dinosaur research societies** or **organizations** can I join?

There are numerous dinosaur-oriented societies and organizations in existence worldwide. Some are local in scope, and sponsored by local universities; while others are larger, non-profit or for-profit groups sponsoring digs, buying land for preservation purposes, and educating the public. Internet addresses for some of these associations are listed below. Also, check the Resources section in the back of the book for more information on dinosaur-related organizations.

Organization Name	Internet Address
The Dinosaur Society	http://www.dinosociety.org/
Dinamation International Society	http://www.dinamation.org/
Denver Dinosaur Trackers Research Group	http://carbon.cudenver.edu/public/trackers/

Organization Name	Internet Address
Dinosaur Dreaming	http://www.earth.monash.edu.au/dinodream/
The Paleobiological Fund	http://members.aol.com/cpaleo/
The Society of Vertebrate	http://eteweb.lscf.ucsb.edu/svp/Paleontology

Where can I buy actual **dinosaur fossils** or **reproductions**?

There are numerous companies that specialize in the production and sale of dinosaur fossils and reproductions. Advertisements for these companies can be found in many nature and science magazines; the following list is of selected companies that have websites on the Internet.

Company Name	Web Site Address
Black Hills Institute of Geological Research	http://www.global-expos.com/BHIGR/
Extinctions	http://www.extinctions.com/
The Fossil Company	http://www.fossil-company.com/
Skullduggery, Inc.	http://skullduggery.com
Western Paleontological Laboratories, Inc.	http://www.itsnet.com/~western/wplhome.html

Where can I find **dinosaur posters and prints** on the Internet?

One Internet source that carries dinosaur poster and prints, along with videos, models, books, and toys can be found at Monstrosities: http://www.monstrosities.com/Products/

DINOSAUR
RESOURCES

Books

General/Reference

Alexander, R. McNeill. *The Dynamics of Dinosaurs and Other Extinct Giants.* Reprint. New York: Columbia University Press, 1989. Applies simple physics and engineering principles to understand the mechanics of animals—living and extinct.

Colbert, Edwin H. *Men and Dinosaurs.* New York: Dutton, 1968. Outlines the history of dinosaur collecting. Considered a seminal work by paleontologists and students of paleontology.

Creagh, Carson, Angela C. Milner, and Simone End. *Dinosaurs (The Nature Company Discoveries Library).* Alexandria, Virginia: Time Life Books, 1995. Covers diet, possible causes of extinction, coloration, and dinosaurs' relation to birds. Illustrations and diagrams, glossary, index.

Currie, Philip J., and Kevin Padian, editors. *Encyclopedia of Dinosaurs.* San Diego: Academic Press, 1997. Illustrations include color plates; also a chronology of dinosaur history; index.

Dodson, Peter. *The Horned Dinosaurs: A Natural History.* Princeton, New Jersey: Princeton University Press, 1996. Comprehensive study of horned dinosaurs, the rhinoceros-like creatures that were among the last dinosaurs to walk the earth.

Farlow, James O., and M. K. Brett-Surman. *The Complete Dinosaur.* Bloomington: Indiana University Press, 1997. Comprehensive, easy-to-use reference. Illustrations; chronology; glossary. Also, a list of science fiction and fantasy books about dinosaurs.

Glut, Donald F. *The Dinosaur Dictionary.* Introductions by Alfred Sherwood Romer and David Techter. New York: Bonanza Books, 1972. General-use dictionary of dinosaur and paleontology terms. Available at some public libraries.

Glut, Donald F. *The Dinosaur Scrapbook.* Introduction by Ray Harryhausen and Robert A. Long. Secaucus, New Jersey: Citadel Press, 1980. Dinosaurs in the mass media.

Glut, Donald F. *Dinosaurs: The Encyclopedia.* Foreword by M. K. Brett-Surman. Jefferson, North Carolina: McFarland & Co., 1997. Heavily illustrated general reference book. 1,000 pages in hardcover. Glossary; index.

351

The Great Dinosaur Fact File. Cherry Hill, New Jersey: Dinosaurs To Go!, semiannual. Directory covers all recognized dinosaurs from around the world, including more than 625 dinosaur genera and museums where they are displayed.

Harper, David. *Basic Paleontology.* London: Addison-Wesley Longman, 1997. Thirteen subject chapters cover the basics. Geological time scale; glossary; index.

Horner, John R., and Don Lessem. *The Complete T. rex: How Stunning New Discoveries Are Changing Our Understanding of the World's Most Famous Dinosaur.* New York: Simon & Schuster, 1993. Dinosaur experts cover recent findings and their impact on the science of paleontology.

Horner, John R., and Edwin Dobb. *Dinosaur Lives: Unearthing an Evolutionary Saga.* New York: HarperCollins, 1997. Celebrated paleontologist Horner recounts his discoveries of dinosaur eggs, babies, nests; also examines the impact dinosaurs have on our lives—from blockbuster films like *Jurassic Park* and *The Lost World* to cutting-edge research on how dinosaurs evolved.

Lambert, David. *Dinosaur Data Book: The Definitive Illustrated Encyclopedia of Dinosaurs and Other Prehistoric Reptiles.* Revised and updated edition. New York: Grammercy, 1998. Illustrated factbook; updated to account for recent dinosaur discoveries. Also, information on dinosaurs in popular media.

Lockley, Martin. *Tracking Dinosaurs: A New Look at an Ancient World.* New York: Cambridge University Press, 1991. Nontechnical study of the prehistoric reptiles' footprints. Reviews and dispels popular myths and misconceptions.

Norman, David. *Dinosaur! The Definitive Account of the "Terrible Lizards"—from Their First Days on Earth to Their Disappearance 65 Million Years Ago.* Reprint. New York: MacMillan General Reference, 1995. World-renowned paleontologist takes readers on a tour of the Mesozoic era. Covers the latest theories of how dinosaurs lived and theories on their extinction. Full-color illustrations.

Russell, Dale A. *An Odyssey in Time: The Dinosaurs of North America.* Reprint. Toronto: University of Toronto Press, 1992. The curator of the National Museum of Natural Sciences (Ottawa, Ontario) gives a readable, intelligent account of prehistoric North America and its dinosaurs. Color illustrations; maps; bibliography.

Spinar, Zdenek V. *Life Before Man.* Revised edition. With Michael J. Benton, consulting editor. New York: Thames and Hudson, 1995. Sequence of more than 200 illustrations (most of them color) reconstructs in detail the conditions on earth from its beginnings more than three million years ago to the arrival of Homo sapiens.

Weishampel, David B., Peter Dodson, and Halszka Osmolska. *The Dinosauria (Centennial Book).* Berkeley: University of California Press, 1992. Comprehensive reference book for paleontologists, geologists, students, and serious amateurs. Illustrations; extensive bibliography.

Weishampel, David B., and Luther Young. *Dinosaurs of the East Coast.* Baltimore, Maryland: Johns Hopkins University Press, 1996. Survey of East Coast dinosaur findings and their importance in recreating the fossil records of dinosaurs in the region. More than 130 illustrations.

Evolution and Extinction

Archibald, J. David. *Dinosaur Extinction and the End of an Era: What the Fossils Say.* New York: Columbia University Press, 1996. Addresses problems with the theory that an asteroid impact caused the extinction of the dinosaurs.

Asimov, Isaac. *Did Comets Kill the Dinosaurs?* Milwaukee, Wisconsin: Gareth Stevens Media, 1988. The renowned scientist Asimov addresses the theory.

Bakker, R. T. *Dinosaur Heresies: New Theories Unlocking the Mystery of the Dinosaurs and Their Extinction.* Reprint. Kensington Publishing, 1996. Dispels common misconceptions about dinosaurs, presenting new evidence that the creatures were warm-blooded, agile, and intelligent.

Chatterjee, Sankar. *The Rise of the Birds: 225 Million Years of Evolution.* Baltimore, Maryland: Johns Hopkins University Press, 1997. In 1983 in fossil beds in west Texas, Chatterjee discovered the Protoavis, a primordial bird. The book examines the origins of birds and the dinosaur link.

Dingus, Lowell, and Timothy Rowe. *The Mistaken Extinction: Dinosaur Evolution and the Origin of Birds.* New York: W. H. Freeman, 1997. Examines the theory that dinosaurs didn't disappear; they merely took flight. Illustrations.

Fastovsky, David E., and David B. Weishampel. *The Evolution and Extinction of the Dinosaurs.* Illustrated by Brian Regal. New York: Cambridge University Press, 1996. Highly readable reference presents "dinosaurs as professionals understand them." Illustrations; subject index.

Officer, Charles B., and Jake Page. *The Great Dinosaur Extinction Controversy.* Perseus Press: 1996. Debunks popular theory that a catastrophic collision between earth and a giant meteor caused the extinction of dinosaurs; discusses how the hypothesis became widespread and offers alternative explanation for the mass extinctions at the end of the Cretaceous period.

Powell, James Lawrence. *Night Comes to the Cretaceous: Dinosaur Extinction and the Transformation of Modern Geology.* New York: W. H. Freeman, 1998. Describes the debate over the impact theory.

Shipman, Pat. *Taking Wing: Archaeopteryx and the Evolution of Bird Flight.* New York: Simon & Schuster, 1998. Story of how the 1861 discovery of the fossil skeleton of a transitional bird-reptile changed theories of evolution. Illustrations.

Sutcliffe, Antony J. *On the Track of Ice Age Mammals.* Cambridge, Massachusetts: Harvard University Press, 1985. Unravels the puzzle of worldwide animal extinction; examines causes and consequences of drastic fluctuations in the earth's climate.

Ward, Peter D. *The Call of Distant Mammoths: Why the Ice Age Mammals Disappeared.* New York: Springer-Verlag, 1997. Addresses the question of why the great mammals that once walked the earth are now largely extinct outside of Africa; builds a case for human hunting of these mammals (versus climate change) as the culprit for their extinction.

Wicander, Reed, and James Monroe. *Historical Geology: Evolution of Earth and Life through Time.* West Publishing, 1993. Includes several chapters devoted to prehistoric life.

Fossils

The Audubon Society Field Guide to North American Fossils. New York: Alfred A. Knopf, 1982. An all-color, illustrated guide to fossils. Includes more than 470 identification pictures and 15 maps.

Fenton, Carroll Lane, and Mildred Adams Fenton. *The Fossil Book.* Revised and expanded edition by Patricia Vickers Rich, Thomas Hewitt Rich, and Mildred Adams Fenton. New York: Doubleday, 1958, 1989. Called "the classic work for fossil collectors and enthusiasts." Guide to the earth's life forms—including flying and gliding reptiles and hairy reptiles. More than 1,500 illustrations.

Lauber, Patricia. *Dinosaurs Walked Here and Other Stories Fossils Tell.* New York: Simon & Schuster, 1987. Through dozens of photos, explains how to identify fossils and tells what they reveal about the prehistoric world.

Webby, B. D., editor. *Fossil Collections of the World: An International Guide.* Lawrence, Kansas: International Palaeontological Association of the Paleontological Institute, n.d. Directory covering institutions and organizations holding fossil collections; includes description of holdings. Index. Published irregularly.

Wolberg, Donald, and Patsy Reinard. *Collecting the Natural World: Legal Requirements and Personal Liability for Collecting Plants, Animals, Rocks, Minerals, and Fossils.* Geoscience, 1995. Discusses all applicable federal and state laws; a reference for the amateur collector.

Guidebooks

Costa, Vincenzo. *Dinosaur Safari Guide: Tracking North America's Prehistoric Past.* Stillwater, Minnesota: Voyageur Press, 1994. Complete descriptions of and directions to more than 170 dinosaur and other prehistoric creature sites, museums, fossil exhibits, track sites, and parks in the United States and Canada.

Gaffney, Eugene S. *Dinosaurs.* Illustrated by John Dawson. New York: Golden Books Adult Publishing Company, 1990. A field guide to dinosaurs most likely to be found in museums. For all ages.

Halls, Kelly Milner. *Dino-Trekking: The Ultimate Dinosaur Lover's Travel Guide.* Illustrated by R. C. Spears. New York: John Wiley & Sons, 1996. Guidebook to more than 300 paleontological exhibits in the United States and Canada. Covers museums, science centers, parks and monuments, track sites, roadside attractions, and amusement parks.

Morell, Mark A., and Eugene Gaffney. *Discovering Dinosaurs in the American Museum of Natural History.* New York: Alfred A. Knopf, 1997. Written by curators at the American Natural History Museum exhibits. Guidebook also provides summaries of the museum's dig sites, recounts stories of the paleontologists who discovered the bones, and presents information on 40 specimens. More than 150 illustrations, charts, and maps (in color and black & white).

Wallace, Joseph E. *Dinosaurs: Audubon Society Pocket Guides.* New York: Alfred A. Knopf, 1993. Guide explains the lives and behavior of the world's prehistoric animals; also discusses their extinction. Full-color paintings and skeletal line drawings are from museum specimens around the world. Also includes maps.

Will, Richard, and Margery Read. *Dinosaur Digs: Places Where You Can Discover Prehistoric Creatures.* Castine, Maine: Country Roads Press, 1992. A directory of museums and parks; photos.

Paleontologists and Expeditions

Colbert, Edwin H. *The Great Dinosaur Hunters and Their Discoveries.* Reprint. New York: Dover Publications, 1984. Includes chapters on first discoveries, skeletons in the earth, two evolutionary streams, the oldest dinosaurs, Jurassic giants of the western world, Canadian dinosaurs, and Asiatic dinosaurs.

Doescher, Rex A., editor. *Directory of Paleontologists of the World, 5th edition.* Lawrence, Kansas: International Palaeontological Association, 1989. Lists more than 7,000 paleontologists (name, office address, area of specialization or interest, and affiliation).

Horner, John R., and James Gorman. *Digging Dinosaurs: The Search That Unraveled the Mystery of Baby Dinosaurs.* Reprint. Illustrated by Donna Braginetz and Kris Ellingsen. New York: HarperPerennial, 1996. One of the world's leading paleontologists chronicles the search that unraveled the mystery of baby dinosaurs. The book is credited with revolutionizing the way people think about dinosaurs; considered a classic.

Jacobs, Louis L. *Quest for the African Dinosaurs: Ancient Roots of the Modern World.* New York: Villard Books, 1993. After discovering a major fossil site in Malawi (Africa), Jacobs and his team went on to identify thirteen kinds of vertebrate animals that "give a window into the world of this part of Africa one hundred million years ago."

Lessem, Don. *Kings of Creation: How a New Breed of Scientists Is Revolutionizing Our Understanding of Dinosaurs.* Illustrated by John Sibbick. New York: Simon & Schuster, 1992. Dinosaur expert Lessem takes readers on a journey through dinosaur time.

Novacek, Michael. *Dinosaurs of the Flaming Cliffs.* Illustrated by Ed Heck. New York: Anchor Books/Doubleday, 1996. Chronicles the groundbreaking discoveries made by of one of the largest dinosaur expeditions of the late twentieth century.

Psihoyos, Louie, and John Knoebber. *Hunting Dinosaurs.* New York: Random House, 1994. Recounts the experiences of paleontologists who have scoured remote lands in search of evidence of dinosaurs. Full-color photos; charts and maps.

Simpson, George Gaylord. *Concession to the Improbable: An Unconventional Autobiography.* New Haven, Connecticut: Yale University Press, 1978. The life of one of the world's great paleontologists.

Simpson, George Gaylord. *Discoverers of the Lost World.* New Haven, Connecticut: Yale University Press, 1984. An account of some of those who unearthed long-buried mammals of South America, which was cut off from other land masses during most of the Age of Mammals. Covers the careers of more than 20 researchers.

Wilford, John Noble. *The Riddle of the Dinosaur.* Illustrated by Doug Henderson. New York: Alfred A. Knopf, 1985. The life and behavior of the giant beasts in the days of their dominion. Chronicles the adventures and achievements of paleontologists.

Books for Children and Families

Aliki. *Digging Up Dinosaurs.* New York: Thomas Y. Crowell, 1988. Introduces various types of dinosaurs, explaining how scientists find, preserve, and reassemble dinosaur skeletons.

Aliki. *Dinosaurs Are Different.* DemcoMedia, 1986. Explains how scientists categorize dinosaurs (including orders and suborders).

Arnold, Caroline. *Dinosaurs All Around: An Artist's View of the Prehistoric World.* Photos by Richard Hewett. New York: Clarion Books, 1993. Through illustrations, the reader is taken on a visit to a workshop where a life-size dinosaur model is being constructed. Information about dinosaurs and how conclusions are made from the study of fossils.

Benton, Michael J. *Dinosaur and Other Prehistoric Animals Factfinder.* New York: Kingfisher Books, 1992. Alphabetical guide to 200 dinosaurs and other prehistoric creatures.

Benton, Michael J. *The Penguin Historical Atlas of the Dinosaurs.* London: Penguin Books, 1996. Plots the development of dinosaurs from their emergence from the ocean, their dispersal across the shifting continents, and their gradual evolution, to their sudden and mysterious extinction 64 million years ago. More than 60 full-color maps; more than 70 illustrations (color and black & white); index.

Clark, Neil, and William Lindsay. *Dinosaurs.* New York: DK Publishing, 1995. A guide for the dinosaur enthusiast as well as teachers; compendium of all dinosaur groups and detailed information on their lifestyles and environment. Author Clark is a curator at the Hunterian Museum in Glasgow, Scotland.

Cooper, John A.. *Dinosaurs* (CD-ROM). Illustrated by Chris Leishman. New York: Smithmark Publishers, 1997. Interactive multimedia product.

Dixon, Dougal. *Dinosaur: An Interactive Guide to the Dinosaur World.* New York: DK Publishing, 1994. Action Pack includes book, press-out scale model, 3-D diorama, wall chart, and game for ages 9–12; hands-on learning.

Eldredge, Niles, Douglas Eldredge, and Gregory Eldredge. *The Fossil Factory: A Kid's Guide to Digging Up Dinosaurs, Exploring Evolution and Finding Fossils.* Reading, Massachusetts: Addison-Wesley Longman, 1989. Covers facts about the Earth's life forms; includes activities and a guide to more than fifty sites where children can look for fossils.

Gabriel, Diane L., and Judith Love Cohen. *You Can Be a Woman Paleontologist.* Illustrated by David A. Katz. Cascade, 1994. Good information for aspiring paleontologists—regardless of gender. Discusses career options, encourages reading and study. Also available in a Spanish-language edition, *Tu puedes ser una paleontologa.*

Kitamura, Satoshi. *Paper Dinosaurs: A Cut-Out Book.* New York: Farrar, Straus & Giroux, 1995. Kids ages 8–11 can create their own world of dinosaurs.

Kricher, John C. *Peterson First Guides: Dinosaurs.* Illustrated by Gordon Morrison. New York: Houghton Mifflin, 1990. Gives the names and characteristics of dinosaurs and covers theories about how they lived. Field guide format useful for museum visits.

Lambert, David, and Ralph E. Molnar. *The Visual Dictionary of Dinosaurs.* New York: DK Publishing, 1993. Part of the Eyewitness series, dictionary provides readers of all ages. More than 200 color illustrations; charts; index.

Lambert, David, and John H. Ostrom. *The Ultimate Dinosaur Book.* New York: DK Publishing, 1993. A-to-Z dinosaur dictionary covers all known species of dinosaurs; full-color photos, diagrams, and illustrations.

Lauber, Patricia. *Living with Dinosaurs.* Illustrated by Douglas Henderson. New York: Bradbury Press; Toronto: Collier Macmillan Canada, 1991. Recreates life among the dinosaurs of North America 75 million years ago.

Lindsay, William. *On the Trail of Incredible Dinosaurs.* New York: DK Publishing, 1998. Published in association with the American Museum of Natural History. Covers four dinosaurs. Photographs of realistic scale-models bring creatures to life. Full color.

Lindsay, William. *Prehistoric Life.* New York: DK Publishing, 1994. Part of the Eyewitness series. Illustrations tell the story of evolution on earth.

Lindsay, William. *Tyrannosaurus.* New York: DK Publishing, 1993. Published in association with the American Museum of Natural History, Lindsay describes the discovery and excavation of fossil evidence for the Tyrannosaurus.

Norman, David, and Angela Milner. *Dinosaur.* New York: Dorling Kindersley, 1989. Part of the Eyewitness series. Introduction to dinosaurs covers fossils, skeleton reconstruction. Heavily illustrated.

Norman, David. *The Humongous Book of Dinosaurs.* New York: Stewart, Tabori and Chang, 1997. Describes all known dinosaurs, their world, and the scientists who study them. Includes special glasses for viewing the 3-D illustrations.

Norman, David. *The Illustrated Encyclopedia of Dinosaurs.* New York: Random House Value Publishing, 1995. Heavily illustrated book covers 68 dinosaurs. Glossary.

Parker, Steve. *Dinosaurs and How They Lived.* Illustrated by Guiliano Fornari Sergio. New York: DK Publishing, 1991. Parker traces discoveries of recent years, describing breakthroughs and changes in our understanding of these creatures. Full color. For young readers.

Parker, Steve. *Inside Dinosaurs and Other Prehistoric Creatures.* Illustrated by Ted Dewan. New York: Delacorte Press, 1994. Cutaway color illustrations take kids on a guided tour of the anatomy of dinosaurs.

Pearce, Q. L. *How to Talk Dinosaur with Your Child.* Los Angeles: Lowell House, 1991. Explains how parents can share dinosaur facts with their children and foster a love of science.

Preston, Douglas. *Dinosaurs in the Attic: An Excursion into the American Museum of Natural History.* New York: St. Martin's Press, 1993. Readers can "travel" to the ends of the earth in this chronicle of the expeditions, discoveries, and scientists behind the greatest natural history collection ever assembled. 16 pages of photos.

Walker, Cyril, and David Ward. *Fossils.* New York: DK Publishing, 1992. Eyewitness Handbook covers 500 vertebrate, invertebrate, and plant fossils, including descriptions, informal names, range, distribution, and occurrence.

Whitfield, Philip. *Macmillan Children's Guide to Dinosaurs and Other Prehistoric Animals.* New York: Simon & Schuster Children's, 1992. For ages 7–10. Describes the prehistoric animals that lived in different parts of the world during each geological period, from the Triassic through the Cretaceous.

Museums

The following museums (listed by state/province) offer paleontological displays as part of their permanent exhibits. Many museums also maintain their own Websites, which often include information about exhibits, schedules, and even virtual tours. For a selected listing, check the Websites information (in this Resources section).

Alaska

University of Alaska Museum
907 Yukon Dr.
Fairbanks, AK 99775
(907) 474-7505
Fossils from dinosaurs and prehistoric mammals.

Arizona

Museum of Northern Arizona
Fort Valley Rd.
Flagstaff, AZ 86001
(602) 774-5211
Exhibits include a 3-D skeleton reproduction.

Mesa Southwest Museum
53 North Macdonald St.
Mesa, AZ 85201
(602) 644-2230
(602) 644-2169
Features displays on dinosaurs in Arizona.

Arizona Museum of Science and Technology
80 North St.
Phoenix, AZ 85004
(602) 256-9388
Displays include dinosaur fossils and casts of skulls of Tyrannosaurus rex and Triceratops.

Arkansas

Arkansas Museum of Science and History
MacArthur Park
Little Rock, AR 72202

(501) 324-9231
Displays include dinosaur track castings and information on how fossils are formed.

California

Museum of Natural History
University of California
Berkeley, CA 94720
(510) 642-1821

The Page Museum at the La Brea Tar Pits
5801 Wilshire Blvd.
Los Angeles, CA 90036
(323) 936-2230
Thousands of Ice Age mammals and birds died in the infamous asphalt pits, often referred to as the Death Trap of the Ages. According to museum scientists, the sticky tar trapped and preserved in pristine condition some four million fossils, many of which have been recovered and are on display. From time to time, the museum holds public viewings of pit excavations.

Colorado

Denver Museum of Natural History
2001 Colorado Blvd.
Denver, CO 80205
(303) 370-6357
Features fossil displays and dioramas plus the Prehistoric Journey exhibit, which includes several dinosaur skeletons.

Devil's Canyon Science and Learning Center
550 Jurassic Court
Fruita, CO 81521
(303) 858-7282
Robotic dinosaurs are on display, courtesy of a cooperative effort between the museum and Dinamation International Society (*see* entry under Organizations). Working fossil lab.

Museum of Western Colorado and Dinosaur Valley
PO Box 20000-5020
Grand Junction, CO 81502-2020
(303) 242-9210
Exhibits include five animated scale models of dinosaurs and a working fossil lab.

Connecticut

Peabody Museum of Natural History
Yale University
170 Whitney Ave.
New Haven, CT 06511
(203) 432-3775
Features the renowned Great Hall of Dinosaurs. Displays include the Deinonychus, the

small but deadly meat-eater, which was discovered in 1964 by the Peabody's (now-retired) curator, Dr. John H. Ostrom.

Illinois

Chicago Academy of Science
2001 North Clark St.
Chicago, IL 60614
(312) 871-2668
Features include an Ice Age Cave and the Dinosaur Alcove.

Field Museum of Natural History
Roosevelt Rd. and Lake Shore Dr.
Chicago, IL 60605
(312) 922-9410
In 1994 the world-renowned Field moved its extensive dinosaur displays into the museum's new hall (called the Elizabeth Morse Genius Dinosaur Hall) and reassembled the skeletons according to the most up-to-date research.

Indiana

Wayne Geology Museum
2101 Coliseum Blvd. East
Fort Wayne, IN 468050
(219) 481-6100
Indiana University and Purdue University paleontological exhibits are housed here.

Kansas

Dyche Museum of Natural History
University of Kansas
Jayhawk Blvd.
Lawrence, KS 66045
(913) 864-4540
Displays include the fossils of a prehistoric bird with a twenty-five-foot wingspan, marine animals, and prehistoric sea turtles.

Louisiana

Audubon Institute
6500 Magazine St.
New Orleans, LA 70118
(504) 861-2537
Pathways to the Past at the institute's natural history museum explores the dinosaur-bird connection. Includes hands-on learning for all ages.

Massachusetts

Pratt Museum of Natural History
Amherst College
Amherst, MA 033103

(800) 723-1548

Begun as the private collection of a fossil-hunter enthusiast (who was then president of Amherst College), the museum displays fossils of prehistoric bird tracks and dinosaur bones from the area.

Michigan

University of Michigan Museum of Natural History
1109 Geddes Ave.
Ann Arbor, MI 48109
(734) 763-6085
Prehistoric life is on display in the museum's Hall of Evolution.

Minnesota

The Science Museum of Minnesota
30 E. 10th St.
St. Paul, MN 55101
(612) 221-9444
The museum has a Paleontology Hall, featuring impressive displays—including a dinosaur egg.

Missouri

St. Louis Science Center
5050 Oakland Ave.
St. Louis, MO 63110
(314) 289-4444
The science center includes a fossil center, dinosaur models, educational videos, and Dinosaur Park.

Montana

Museum of the Rockies
Montana State University
600 West Kagy Blvd.
Bozeman, MT 59717
(406)-994-DINO
Renowned paleontological display includes locally discovered fossils, including those of the female lizard Maiasaura. Exhibits focus on how the species lived. The museum also runs the Paleo Field School (tel. 406-994-2251), which leads students on explorations of Montana dig sites.

Nevada

Las Vegas Natural History Museum
900 Las Vegas Blvd. North
Las Vegas, NV 89101
Prehistoric room includes an extensive dinosaur collection.

New Jersey

New Jersey State Museum
205 West State St.
Trenton, NJ 08625
(609) 292-6308
The excellent collection of fossils and other paleontological exhibits here bears testimony to New Jersey's rich prehistory. Children's exhibits.

New Mexico

Ruth Hall Museum of Paleontology
Ghost Ranch Conference Center
Abiquiu, NM 87501
(505) 685-4333
More than 100 complete skeletons of the small, carnivorous dinosaur Coelophysis are on display.

New Mexico Museum of Natural History
1801 Mountain Rd., NW
Albuquerque, NM 87104
(505) 841-8837
Excellent paleontological exhibit takes many forms—most notably an elevator (called the Evo-lator) that takes visitors on a ride through evolutionary history. Also, fossils, reconstructions, and sculptures.

New York

American Museum of Natural History
79th St. and Central Park West
New York, NY 10024
(212) 769-5100
A national treasure, this world-renowned museum features three dinosaur halls. Extensive displays are must-sees for any aspiring paleontologist.

North Carolina

Natural Science Center
4301 Lawndal Dr.
Greensboro, NC 27401
(919) 288-3769
Features a Dinosaur Gallery, Tyrannosaurus rex restoration model, and a skeletal mount of a Triceratops.

North Carolina Museum of Natural Science
102 North Salisbury St.
Raleigh, NC 27604
(910) 733-7450
Skull replicas, a prehistoric bird hall, and a hall of mammals.

North Dakota

Dakota Dinosaur Museum
1226 Simms Rd.
Dickinson, ND 58601
(701) 227-0431
Full-scale dinosaur skeletons, models, and fossils. Fossil lab.

Ohio

McKinley Museum of History
800 McKinley Monument Dr. NW
Canton, OH 44708
(216) 455-7043
A robotic model of an Allosaurus greets visitors to the museum's Discovery World, featuring dinosaur reproductions, skulls, and a dig-site reproduction.

The Cleveland Museum of Natural History
University Circle
1 Wade Oval Dr.
Cleveland, OH 44106
(216) 231-4600
Excellent prehistoric displays include an Ice Age mammal exhibit.

Oklahoma

Oklahoma Museum of Natural History
1335 Asp Ave.
Norman, OK 73019
(405) 325-4712
The paleontological offerings include a dinosaur collection as well as a prehistoric mammals exhibit.

Pennsylvania

Academy of Natural Science Museum
1900 Benjamin Franklin Parkway
Philadelphia, PA 19103
(215) 299-1000
International museum of natural history founded in 1812, the Academy of Natural Science boasts a newly renovated dinosaur hall, which includes numerous life-size skeletons, nests, and even a huge footprint. Visitors can explore the dinosaur discovery process from beginning to end.

Wagner Free Institute of Science
17th St. and Montgomery Ave.
Philadelphia, PA 19121
(215) 763-6529
Many of the museum's displays of dinosaur bones and other fossils were first mounted in

363

1865 and are typical of that era, providing visitors a historical perspective on paleontological exhibits.

The Carnegie Museum of Natural History
4400 Forbes Ave.
Pittsburgh, PA 15213
(412) 622-3131
Extensive collection of dinosaur skeletons, prehistoric mammals, and marine reptiles.

South Dakota

Black Hills Institute of Geological Research
217 Main St.
Hill City, SD 57745
(605) 574-4289
The institute offers an impressive fossil lab and museum. One of the institute's volunteers happened to find Sue—the most complete Tyrannosaurus rex ever discovered.

Texas

Shuler Museum of Paleontology
Southern Methodist University
Dallas, TX 75275
(214) 768-2000
The work and discoveries of renowned paleontologist Dr. Louis Jacobs are on display.

Fort Worth Museum of Science and History
1501 Montgomery St.
Fort Worth, TX 76107
(817) 732-1631
Extensive displays include Texas findings as well as the interactive DinoDig exhibit, a reproduction of a famous dig site.

Utah

Dinosaur National Monument
Jensen, UT 84035
(801) 789-2115
This national monument is one of the richest dinosaur beds ever discovered. Excavation work is still underway but the public is welcome to explore the findings at the year-round visitor center.

Utah Museum of Natural History
University of Utah
President's Circle
Salt Lake City, UT 84112
(801) 581-4303
Highlights include skeletal mounts, extensive fossil displays, and reconstructions.

Virginia

Virginia Museum of Natural History
1001 Douglas Ave.
Martinville, VA 24122
(703) 666-8600
Paleontological display includes a computerized Triceratops model.

Washington

Pacific Science Center
200 Second Ave. North
Seattle, WA 98372
(206) 443-2001
Fossils, footprints, cutaway model of a T. rex leg, and hands-on exhibits for children.

Burke Museum
University of Washington
Seattle, WA 98195
(206) 543-5590
Featuring the Life and Times of Washington State—a hands-on exhibit that begins 545 million years ago. Replicas include carnivorous dinosaurs. Fossil exhibit.

Washington, D.C.

The National Museum of Natural History
The Smithsonian Institution
10th St. and Constitution Ave.
Washington, DC 20560
(202) 357-1300
Among the best—and certainly most extensive— paleontological displays anywhere. In addition to numerous displays of dinosaurs, ancient mammals, and ancient marine life-forms, the museum features a working laboratory.

Wisconsin

Milwaukee Public Museum
800 West Wells
Milwaukee, WI 53233
(414) 278-2702
The museum's dinosaurs exhibit includes recreations of a Triceratops and a T. rex in their habitats.

Wyoming

Wyoming Dinosaur Center
Thermopolis, WY 80443
(307) 864-5522
The dinosaurs once roamed here, and the museum is situated to take advantage of that. The center not only offers extensive exhibits, but also gives tours of the bone beds where paleontologists are at work on excavations.

Canada

Royal Tyrrell Museum of Paleontology
Drumheller, Alberta T0J 0Y0
(403) 823-7707
Features numerous skeletal mounts in what is probably Canada's most extensive paleontological collection.

Royal Ontario Museum
100 Queen's Park
Toronto, Ontario, Canada M5S 2C6
(416) 586-5590
The museum's paleontological exhibit showcases more than ten different dinosaurs. Features live-action puppetry and animation and includes interviews with leading paleontologists.

Organizations

Academy of Natural Sciences
1900 Benjamin Franklin Pkwy.
Philadelphia, PA 19103
(215) 299-1000
(215) 299-1028 fax
http://www.acnatsci.org
Founded: 1812. Natural science research institution and museum with extensive historical and scientific collections of shells, insects, fish, birds, fossils, plants, minerals, and microscopic organisms. Conducts research programs and expeditions.

American Federation of Mineralogical Societies
PO Box 26523
Oklahoma City, OK 73126-0523
(405) 682-2151
Founded: 1947. Promotes popular interest and education in the earth sciences, particularly geology, mineralogy, paleontology, lapidary, and related subjects.

American Museum of Natural History
Central Park West at W. 79th St.
New York, NY 10024-5192
(212) 769-5100
http://www.amnh.org
Founded: 1869. Promotes the study of evolutionary biology. Serves as a research, education, and exhibition center for the study of the zoological, anthropological, and mineralogical sciences. Maintains the Naturemax Theater and permanent exhibits on meteorites, minerals and gems, birds, mammals, reptiles and amphibians, dinosaurs (early and late), the biology of invertebrates, ocean life, and more. Also prepares temporary exhibitions of international significance several times a year.

Dinamation International Society
550 Jurassic Court
Fruita, CO 81521
800-DIG-DINO
(303) 858-3532
Email: dis@gj.net
http://www.dinamation.org
Promotes education, research, and preservation in the biological, earth, and physical sciences, with an emphasis on dinosaurs and paleology.

Dinosaur Society
200 Carleton Ave.
East Islip, NY 11730
(516) 277-7855
(516) 277-1479 fax
Email: dsociety@aol.com
http://www.dinosociety.org
Founded: 1991. Promotes research and education in the study of dinosaurs. Assists merchandisers in accurately presenting products portraying dinosaurs to reflect current scientific knowledge. Operates speakers' bureau. Offers children's services and travel programs.

International Society of Cryptozoology
PO Box 43070
Tucson, AZ 85733
(520) 884-8369
(520) 884-8369 fax
Founded: 1982. Members include biological scientists and other individuals interested in animals of unexpected size, form, or occurrence in time or location. Association investigates and discusses reports of animals such as giant octopuses (spanning 150 feet or more); lake monsters in Loch Ness, Scotland, and other lakes; large, long-necked animals in Central African swamps that resemble Mesozoic sauropod dinosaurs, and large, unknown hominoids. Disseminates cryptozoological information among biological scientists, including information on cryptozoological claims, and analyses of evidence such as photographs, sonar tracks, footprint casts, and tissue and hair samples. Serves as a forum for public discussion and education; provides information to authorities and the news media.

National Geographic Society
17th & M St. NW
Washington, DC 20036
(202) 857-7000
(202) 775-6141 fax
http://www.nationalgeographic.com
Founded: 1888. Sponsors expeditions and research in geography, natural history, archaeology, astronomy, ethnology, and oceanography; sends writers and photographers throughout the world; disseminates information through its magazines, maps, books, television documentaries, films, educational media, and information services for media.

Paleontological Research Institution
1259 Trumansburg Rd.
Ithaca, NY 14850
(607) 273-6623
(607) 273-6620 fax
Email: WDA1@cornell.edu
http://www.Englib.cornell.edu/PRI/
Founded: 1932. Professional and amateur paleontologists, geologists, conchologists, and allied scientists or persons interested in the promotion of natural history. Receives, collects, preserves, and makes accessible to students and scientists paleontological and geological type specimens and exhibits; conducts scientific explorations, research, investigations, and experiments; collects and preserves scientific data, reports, graphs, maps, documents, and publications.

Paleontological Society
Box 28200-16
Lakewood, CO 80228-3108
(303) 236-9228
(303) 236-5690 fax
Email: twhenry@usgs.gov
Founded: 1908. Members include professionals and amateurs interested in the study of paleontology.

Society for Sedimentary Geology
1731 E. 71st St.
Tulsa, OK 74136-5108
(918) 493-3361; 800-865-9765
(918) 493-2093 fax
http://www.ngdc.noaa.gov/mgg/sepm/sepm.html
Founded: 1926. Professional society of geologists interested in sedimentary paleontology and related disciplines. Sponsors continuing education courses; K–12 earth science education; conducts technical sessions, geological workshops, research conference, and field trips.

Society for the Preservation of Natural History Collections
National Museum of Natural History
Smithsonian Institution
MRC-176, Div. Fishes
Washington, DC 20560
(202) 786-2426
(202) 357-2986 fax
http://www.uni.edu/museum/spnhc
Founded: 1985. Individuals interested in the development and preservation of natural history collections. Encourages research on the requirements for preserving, storing, and displaying natural history collections; provides and maintains an international association of persons who study and care for natural history collections. Conducts educational programs.

Society for the Study of Evolution
Business Office
PO Box 1897
Lawrence, KS 66044
800-627-0629
(913) 843-1274 fax
Founded: 1946. Professional society of biologists concerned with organic evolution.

Society of Vertebrate Paleontology
W. 436 Nebraska Hall
Lincoln, NE 68588-0542
(402) 472-4604
(402) 472-8949 fax
Founded: 1940. Serves the common interests of people concerned with the history, evolution, comparative anatomy, and taxonomy of vertebrate animals, as well as the field occurrence, collection, and study of fossil vertebrates and the stratigraphy of the beds where they are found.

Regional Organizations

Santa Rosa Mineral and Gem Society
PO Box 7036
Santa Rosa, California 95407-7036
(707) 528-7610

Garden Park Paleontology Society
PO Box 313
Canon City, Colorado 81215-0313
(719) 269-7150
(800)-987-6379
(719) 269-7227 fax
Email: depot@ris.net

Florida Paleontological Society
Florida Museum of Natural History
Gainesville, Florida 32611
(904) 392-1721
(904) 392-8783 fax

Kentucky Paleontological Society
365 Cromwell Way
Lexington, Kentucky 40503
(606) 223-8884

Los Alamos Geological Society
PO Box 762
Los Alamos, New Mexico 87544
(505) 661-6171

(505) 672-3107
Email: hoffmans@ix.netcom.com

North Dakota Paleontological Society
PO Box 1921
Bismarck, North Dakota 58502-1921
(701) 255-3658

Central Texas Paleontological Society
16420 Edgemere
Pflugerville,Texas 78660
(512) 251-2848
(512) 280-0368

Publications

The following publications, many of them general-interest science magazines, cover new findings relevant to paleontology.

American Paleontologist
Paleontological Research Institution
1259 Trumansburg Rd.
Ithaca, NY 14850
(607) 273-6623
(607) 273-6620 fax
Newsletter publishes articles about paleontology and earth science. Quarterly.

Dinosaur Report
Dinosaur Society
200 Carleton Ave.
East Islip, NY 11730
(516) 277-7855
(516) 277-1479 fax
Email: dsociety@aol.com
http://www.dinosociety.org
Reports on paleontological issues and news. Quarterly.

Discover: The World of Science
114 5th Ave.
New York, NY 10011
(212) 633-4817 fax
http://www.discover.com
Covering science, from astronomy to zoology. Monthly.

Explorer
The Cleveland Museum of Natural History
University Circle
1 Wade Oval Dr.

Cleveland, OH 44106-1767
(216) 231-4600
(216) 231-5919 fax
Email: pubs@cmnh.org
http://www.cmnh.org (site under reconstruction as of fall 1998)
Magazine featuring articles on natural history and science. Quarterly.

Journal of Paleontology
Museum of Natural History & Dept. of Geology
Rm. 245 NHB
1301 W. Green St.
Urbana, IL 61801
(217) 333-3833
(217) 244-4996 fax
Email: fossils@hercules.geology.uiuc.edu
Scientific journal. Bimonthly.

National Geographic
National Geographic Society
1145 17th St. NW
Washington, DC 20036-4688
(202) 857-7000
(800)-NGS-LINE
(202) 429-5712 fax
http://www.nationalgeographic.com
Magazine covering history, culture, the environment, and science. Monthly.

Natural History Magazine
American Museum of Natural History
Exhibition Department
Central Park West at 79th St.
New York, NY 10024
(212) 769-5500
(212) 769-5511 fax
http://www.amnh.org/welcome/smp_publications.html
Covering natural science, anthropology, archeology, and zoology. 10/year.

Nature: International Weekly Journal of Science
Nature Publishing Co.
345 Park Ave. S, 10th Fl.
New York, NY 10010-1707
(212) 726-9200
(212) 696-9006 fax
http://www.nature.com (searchable archive; free registration required)

Paleoclimates
The University of Arizona
Gould-Simpson Bldg.

Tucson, AZ 85721
(520) 621-4595
(520) 621-2672 fax
Journal on the interdisciplinary subject of paleoclimatology, the study of past climate change. Includes articles on all aspects of the climate and environment of the Quaternary Period and earlier times. Quarterly.

Paleontological Journal
John Wiley & Sons, Inc.
605 3rd Ave.
New York, NY 10158
(212) 850-6000
(800)-225-5945
English-language translation of a periodical on the paleontology of Eurasia. Quarterly.

Popular Science
Times Mirror Magazines, Inc.
929 Pearl St., Ste. 200
Boulder, CO 80302
http://www.popsci.com (searchable archive)
General interest science magazine. Monthly.

Quaternary Research: An Interdisciplinary Journal
Academic Press
525 B St., Ste. 1900
San Diego, CA 92101-4411
(619) 699-6825
(800)-894-3434
(619) 699-6380 fax
Publishing articles from disciplines contributing to the knowledge of the Quaternary Period; includes studies from geology, paleontology, and oceanography. Bimonthly.

Rocks & Minerals
Heldref Publications
Helen Dwight Reid Educational Foundation
1319 18th St. NW
Washington, DC 20036-1802
(202) 296-6267
(800)-365-9753
(202) 296-5149 fax
http://www.heldref.org/ (subscription information)
Magazine for students of mineralogy, geology, and paleontology. Bimonthly.

Rotunda: The Magazine of the Royal Ontario Museum
Attn: Publications Dept.
100 Queen's Park
Toronto, ON, Canada M5S 2C6
(416) 586-5590

(416) 586-5827 fax
http://rom.on.ca
Covering art, archaeology, natural sciences, astronomy. 3 times/year.

Children's Publications

Dino Times
Dinosaur Society
200 Carleton Ave.
East Islip, NY 11730
(516) 277-7855
(516) 277-1479 fax
Email: dsociety@aol.com
http://www.dinosociety.org
Magazine for children; includes news on current dinosaur studies. Monthly.

National Geographic World
National Geographic Society
1145 17th St. NW
Washington, DC 20036-4688
(202) 857-7000
(800)-NGS-LINE
(202) 429-5712 fax
http://www.nationalgeographic.com
Magazine featuring factual stories on natural history, outdoor adventure, sports, science, and history for children ages 8 through 13. Monthly.

Dinosaurs on Video

The following listing includes fictional films featuring dinosaurs, educational videos, and documentaries focusing on the creation and extinction of dinosaurs.

Adventure at the Center of the Earth (1963). Mexican horror film featuring dinosaurs, cyclops, bat-creatures, and a rat-faced monster. In Spanish without subtitles.

Adventures in Dinosaur City (1992). Cast: Omri Katz, Shawn Hoffman, Tiffanie Poston, Mimi Maynard, Pete Koch, Megan Hughes, Brett Thompson. Directed by Tony Doyle. Modern-day pre-teen siblings are transported back in time to the stone age. There they meet their favorite TV characters (they're dinosaurs) and help them solve prehistoric crimes. Family film may amuse kids, but adults should stick to *Jurassic Park*.

Adventures in Dinosaurland (1983). Animated story of a little dinosaur who takes kids back to the stone age.

Age of Dinosaurs (1988). A series that's perfect for little kids who are curious about dinosaurs.

All About Dinosaurs (1990). Children in grade school can learn all about the prehistoric creatures that fascinate them so.

373

The Asteroid and the Dinosaur (1981). Scientists explain a theory that a giant asteroid collided with the earth millions of years ago, tossing a killing cloud of dust and debris into the atmosphere.

At the Earth's Core (1976). Cast: Doug McClure, Peter Cushing, Caroline Munro, Kevin Connor, Godfrey James, Keith Barron. Directed by Cy Grant. A Victorian scientist invents a giant burrowing machine, which he and his crew use to dig deeply into the Earth. To their surprise, they discover a lost world of subhuman creatures and prehistoric monsters. Based on Edgar Rice Burrough's novels.

Attack of the Super Monsters (1984). Group of prehistoric monsters are developing dastardly plots below the Earth to ruin the human race.

Baby . . . Secret of the Lost Legend (1985). Cast: William Katt, Sean Young, Patrick McGoohan, Julian Fellowes. Directed by Bill W. L. Norton. A sportswriter and his paleontologist wife risk their lives to reunite a hatching brontosaurus with its mother in the African jungle. Although this Disney film is not lewd in any sense, beware of several scenes displaying frontal nudity and some violence.

Bill Nye the Science Guy: Dinosaurs—Those Big Boneheads (1994). Bill Nye takes a look at dinosaurs and what has been discovered about their lifestyles. In another episode, Bill Nye explains how the Earth's surface and its inner mantle differ.

Box Investigates . . . Children visit Box's Science Lab where they discover and investigate the worlds of dinosaurs, animals, and insects. Includes guide.

Cadillacs and Dinosaurs: "Wild Child" and "Pursuit" (1995). In "Wild Child," Jack and Hannah struggle to rescue a kidnapped child from the evil dino-poachers. In "Pursuit," Jack fights to clear his name when he is wrongly accused of stealing a dinosaur-killing weapon. Animated.

Carnosaur (1993). Cast: Diane Ladd, Raphael Sbarge, Jennifer Runyon, Harrison Page, Clint Howard, Ned Bellamy, Adam Simon. Directed by Nigel Holton. Straight from the Corman film factory, this exploitive quickie about dinosaurs harkens back to '50s-style monster epics. Predictable plot with extremely cheap effects. Genetic scientist Dr. Jane Tiptree (Ladd) is hatching diabolic experiments with chickens when things go awry. The experiments result in a bunch of lethal prehistoric creatures wreaking havoc among the community.

Carnosaur 2 (1994). Cast: John Savage, Cliff DeYoung, Arabella Holzbog, Ryan Thomas Johnson. Directed by Louis Morneau. Technicians investigating a power shortage at a secret military mining facility encounter deadly dinos. Entertaining schlock.

Carnosaur 3: Primal Species (1996). Cast: Scott Valentine, Janet Gunn, Rick Dean, Rodger Halstead, Tony Peck, Jonathan Winfrey. Directed by Kevin Kiner. Terrorists get a big surprise when the cargo they hijack turns out to be three very hungry dinos who make snacks of them all. Then it's up to commando Valentine, scientist Gunn, and some soldiers to get rid of the beasts.

Caveman (1981). Cast: Ringo Starr, Barbara Bach, John Matuszak, Dennis Quaid, Jack Gilford, Shelley Long, Cork Hubbert. Written and Directed by Carl Gottlieb. Starr stars in this prehistoric spoof about a group of cavemen banished from different tribes who band together to form a tribe called "The Misfits."

Clifford (1992). Cast: Martin Short, Charles Grodin, Mary Steenburgen, Dabney Coleman, Sonia Jackson. Directed by Paul Flaherty. Short plays a 10-year-old in an effort delayed by movie studio Orion's past financial crisis. Creepy little Clifford's uncle Martin (Grodin) rues the day he volunteered to babysit his nephew to prove to his girlfriend (Steenburgen) how much he likes kids. Clifford terrorizes Grodin in surprisingly nasty ways when their plans for visiting Dinosaurworld fall through, although Grodin sees to well-deserved revenge. Not just bad in the conventional sense, but bad in a bizarre sort of alien fashion that raises questions about who was controlling the bodies of the producers. To create the effect of Short really being short, other actors stood on boxes and sets were built slightly larger than life.

Common Fossils of the United States (1990). A look at the varieties of fossils common to the U.S., including their age and the environments that produced them.

The Crater Lake Monster (1977). Cast: Richard Cardella, Glenn Roberts, Mark Siegel, Bob Hyman. Directed by William R. Stromberg. The dormant egg of a prehistoric creature hatches after a meteor rudely awakens the dozing dino. He's understandably miffed and begins a revenge campaign. Prehistoric yawner.

Digging Dinosaurs (1988). This video provides an informative introduction to paleontology for young children, and an excellent presentation to be shown before or after field trips to natural history museums.

Digging Dinosaurs—2 Pack (1994). Two-part set aimed at teaching younger audiences about dinosaurs. Covers the different types of dinosaurs, as well as how and where dinosaur bones have been found. Includes computer animation, actual footage of dinosaur digs, and visits to museums and paleontology labs.

Digging Dinosaurs: A Search for the Creatures of the Mesozoic Era (1987). Follows the excitement of a paleontological dig in Western Montana.

Digging Up Dinosaurs (1992). Introduction to paleontology in two parts. Part one includes treks led by Martin Lockley to a site in the Dinosaur National Monument in Utah, and by Scott Madsen to a site where microfossils were uncovered. Part two includes a trek to a site where an Allosaurus was uncovered and reveals the process of excavating, and casting and repairing the bones.

Dino Riders: The Adventure Begins (1988). The Dino Riders must save themselves from the evil Vipers.

Dinosaur (1989). Visit the Dinosaur Quarry in Dinosaur National Monument, an archaeologist's oasis where an abundance of dinosaur fossils, bones, and skeletons have been excavated.

Dinosaur (1997). Follows paleontologists as they uncover fossil bones in Dinosaur National Monument.

Dinosaur (1980). Hosted by Christopher Reeve. Directed by Robert Guenette. An introduction to dinosaurs and the prehistoric world they inhabited millions of years ago. An Emmy Award–winning animated film depicting the environment and lives of the dinosaurs.

The Dinosaur Age (1958). This video presents a look at how we have come to learn about dinosaurs through fossils.

Dinosaur Families (1994). Part of the "Digging Dinosaurs" collection. This section covers the family structure of the dinosaurs and how paleontologists and children can dig for dinosaur bones.

Dinosaur Footprints of the Peace River Valley. In northeastern British Columbia, the Peace River Canyon contains one of the largest concentrations of dinosaur footprints in the world. The film observes a team of paleontologists mapping the area and making molds of the prints.

Dinosaur Hunt (1998). Three-part series features aspects of the dinosaur and the hunt for fossils, including the chaos that erupts when a fossil is found, whether dinosaurs and birds are biologically related, and the false mystique of the Tyrannosaurus rex. Three hours on three videocassettes.

The Dinosaur Hunters (1972). An unusual film asking: How did dinosaurs function? What did they eat? How did they reproduce? How did they defend themselves?

Dinosaur Island (1993). Cast: Ross Hagen, Richard Gabai, Tom Shell, Steve Barkett, Toni Naples, Antonia Dorian, Peter Spellos, Griffin Drew. Directed by Jim Wynorski and Fred Olen Ray. Five military men survive a plane crash and discover an island where scantily clad (leather bikinis being the fashion choice) lascivious ladies live. Will the awesome power of testosterone overcome the fierce dinosaurs that stand between the men and their objects of desire?

The Dinosaur Who Wondered Who He Was (1976). A long time ago, a little creature hatched, grew into a big dinosaur, and had a lot to learn about the world and himself.

Dinosaur! With Walter Cronkite (1991). Hosted by Walter Cronkite. A four-part boxed set that traces the discovery of dinosaurs from the first archeological find to the latest breakthroughs. Includes animatronics. Dramatic re-enactments, and visits to archeological sites. A companion book written by paleontologist David Norman is also available.

The Dinosaurs! (1993). Paleontologists reconstruct the existence of these prehistoric reptiles from ancient artifacts in this four-tape series.

Dinosaurs! Features an animated, live action, and claymated look at dinosaurs, featuring Fred Savage.

Dinosaurs (1988). Music and dinosaurs combine to provide kids with an educational experience.

Dinosaurs (1979). An introduction to the study of dinosaurs and the means used by modern science to attempt to answer the many questions afforded by their history.

Dinosaurs: A Closer Look (199?). Five lessons explore perspective, classification, adaptation, and a global view of dinosaurs. Narrative CAV videodisc sequences contribute content information bolstered by student readings, group activities, and class discussions.

Dinosaurs: A First Film (1979). This animated program shows the changes in dinosaurs, the variety of dinosaurs, and the change in climate that led to their downfall.

Dinosaurs: Age of Reptiles (1979). Paleontologists are seen working with other scientists to reconstruct dinosaurs via fossils.

Dinosaurs: Age of the Terrible Lizard (1970). An animated but completely factual account of the Dinosaur Age: major types of dinosaurs, behavior characteristics, evidence of evolutionary development.

Dinosaurs and Other Creature Features (1996). Introduces a host of creatures including dinosaurs, vampire bats, black widow spiders, and more; lessons include music videos.

Dinosaurs Are Very Big (1994). Part of the "Digging Dinosaurs" collection that takes a look at some of the dinosaurs that roamed the earth in the past. Uses computer animation with visits to digs and museums to help explain the differences between the various dinosaurs.

Dinosaurs! Dinosaurs! (1995). Reveals how paleontologists have relied on fossilized remains to determine the appearance of dinosaurs living 70 million years ago. Animated dinosaur models enhance realistic footage.

Dinosaurs! Dinosaurs! (1994). Hosted by Leslie Nielsen. From dig site to museum laboratory, details how scientists study the characteristics and living habits of dinosaurs.

Dinosaurs, Dinosaurs, Dinosaurs (1987). Cast: Gary Owens and Eric Boardman. Owens is slowly turning into a dinosaur and partner Boardman must learn all he can in order to stop the changes. A semi-educational program that re-creates the world of dinosaurs.

Dinosaurs: Fantastic Creatures That Ruled the Earth. Attempts to dispell myths that have surrounded dinosaurs and offers answers to commonly asked questions.

Dinosaurs: Messages in Stone (1994). Graphically explores the making of a mold from extant dinosaur fossils and discusses theories of dinosaur behavior. Animated dinosaur models enhance realistc footage.

Dinosaurs: Piecing It All Together. Combines animation with comments from paleontologists and paleoartists to answer many questions associated with the history, life, and extinction of dinosaurs.

Dinosaurs: Puzzles from the Past (1981). Explains to youngsters that dinosaurs were different from today's reptiles. They were built differently, moved differently, and roamed the earth for millions of years before they gradually and mysteriously disappeared.

Dinosaurs: Terrible Lizards (1976). Discusses a variety of dinosaurs, explores methods used by paleontologists, and shows how a dinosaur skeleton is assembled and reconstructed for museum display.

Dinosaurs: Terrible Lizards (1970). Brings the age of the dinosaur to realistic life. An overview of what they looked like and how they lived and died.

Dinosaurs: The Ageless Quarry. Recounts the events of June 9, 1884, when geologist Joseph B. Tyrell discoved a fossilized dinosaur bone in Drumheller, Alberta, ushering in the Alberta dinosaur rush. Today the site is the toast of paleontologists worldwide for its rich fossil content and fascinating Tyrell Museum of Paleontology.

Dinosaurs: Then and Now (1995). Centers on an animated journey from the birth of the solar system to the recent discovery of the fossil of Utahraptor, the "Super Slasher."

Dinosaurus! (1960). Cast: Ward Ramsey, Kristina Hanson, Irvin S. Yeaworth Jr. Directed by Paul Lukather. Large sadistic dinosaurs appear in the modern world. They eat, burn, and pillage their way through this film. Also includes a romance between a Neanderthal and a modern-age woman.

Donny Deinonychus: The Educational Dinosaur, Vol. 1 (1993). Narrated by Ruth Buzzi and Richard Moll. Two debut episodes of a non-violent educational series for children that shares the story of prehistory while teaching basic morals, values, judgments, and courtesies. In "Donny Deinonychus" Donny the Parrot is the victim of a misdirected scientific experiment and metamorphosizes into his prehistoric ancestor, Donny Deinonychus (Dine-non-i-kus), whose parrot memory is erased and replaced by that of a dinosaur. Donny wants only to get back "home" to prehistory and flees the house with Professor Stevens hot on his trail. In "Stormy, the Long Lost Friend" Donny introduces Stormy the Triceratops and explains that even though someone may be scary looking, they may not necessarily be bad.

EPIC: Days of the Dinosaurs (1987). Narrated by John Huston. Directed by Yoram Gross. An animated fable about two babies born into a pack of dingoes in a prehistoric world. They must fight for superiority over the mystical powers of nature.

Exploring Dinosaurs (1992). Rather than a lemonade stand, Jeff sets up a dinosaur information booth from which he shares with customers the wonders of the dinosaur kingdom, including their form, diet, habitat, and extinction. Models, archaeological findings, and artwork help illustrate Jeff's findings. Comes with teacher's guide and blackline master.

Eyewitness Dinosaur. Investigates paleontology, explaining the process of discovery from digging to reconstruction.

The Eyewitness Video Series (1996). Features the world of living things. Focuses on evolutionary process, habitats, and more.

The Fascinating World of Prehistoric Animals (1993). Two programs introduce the world of prehistoric animals and dinosaurs. Each program is available individually or together on one tape.

Fossils: Clues to the Past (1983). Explains what fossils are, how they are formed, what they can tell us, and how their age can be determined.

Giant Dinosaurs (1993). Features the Torosaurus, Braceosarus, Diplodocus, and other dinosaurs in full-color graphics and computer animation. Accurate information and realistic representation make this an interesting and educational presentation.

The Great Dinosaur Discovery (1976). The discovery of the "world's largest dinosaur" is documented—a gigantic new sauropod estimated to have been over 60 feet tall, 100 feet long, and weighing near 100 tons. Filmed on the site as the actual discoveries were made.

Hollywood Dinosaur Chronicles (1987). Hosted by Doug McClure. As soon as filmmaking was invented, dinosaurs became stars! Here are a few of those very early appearances. From the silents, *Gertie the Dinosaur* and *Lost World,* to recent productions like *Godzilla* and *Baby,* all the best of the extinct critters is represented here.

Hot-Blooded Dinosaurs (1977). Sheds new light on the intriguing puzzle of how dinosaurs lived. From *Nova.*

The Infinite Voyage: The Great Dinosaur Hunt (1989). An episode of "The Infinite Voyage," wherein via new research and computer graphics, revolutionary discoveries about dinosaurs are being plumbed.

Invasion of the Dinosaurs (1993). A brief overview of the era of the dinosaur as well as descriptions of some of the better-known creatures, with life-size Dinomation replicas used as educational models.

Invasion of the Robot Dinosaurs (1991). Realistically animated dinosaurs live again at the Museum of Natural History. Examine the lives of Tyrannosaurus rex, Triceratops, and others, how they lived and how they may have died. Informative fun for the whole family.

Jurassic Park (1993). Cast: Sam Neill, Laura Dern, Jeff Goldblum, Richard Attenborough, Samuel L. Jackson. Directed by Steven Spielberg. Michael Crichton's spine-tingling thriller translates well (but not faithfully) due to its main attraction: realistic, rampaging dinosaurs. Genetically cloned from prehistoric DNA, all is well until they escape from their pens—smarter and less predictable than expected. Contrived plot and thin characters (except Goldblum), but who cares? The true stars are the dinos, an incredible combination of models and computer animation. Violent, suspenseful, and realistic with gory attack scenes. Not for small kids, though much of the marketing is aimed at them. Spielberg knocked his own *E.T.* out of first place as "JP" became the highest-grossing movie of all time. Also available in a letterbox version.

King Dinosaur (1955). Cast: Bill Bryant, Wanda Curtis, Patti Gallagher, Douglas Henderson. A new planet arrives in the solar system, and a scientific team checks out its giant iguana–ridden terrain.

The Land Before Time (1988). Voices: Pat Hingle, Helen Shaver, Gabriel Damon, Candice Houston, Burke Barnes, Judith Barsi, Will Ryan. Directed by Don Bluth. Lushly animated children's film about five orphaned baby dinosaurs who band together and try to find the Great Valley, a paradise where they might live safely. Works same parental separation theme as Bluth's *American Tail*. Charming, coy, and shamelessly tearjerking; producers included Steven Spielberg and George Lucas.

The Land Before Time 2: The Great Valley Adventure (1994). Sequel to 1988's animated adventure finds dinsosaur pals Littlefoot, Cera, Ducky, Petrie, and Spike happily settled in the Great Valley. But their adventures don't stop as they chase two egg-stealing Struthiomimuses and retrieve an egg of unknown origin from the Mysterious Beyond.

The Land Before Time 3: The Time of the Great Giving (1995). Directed by Roy Allen Smith. Littlefoot and his pals try to find a new source of water when the Great Valley experiences a severe water shortage.

The Land Before Time 4: Journey Through the Mists (1996). The little dinosaurs travel through the land of the mists in search of a rejuvenation flower that can save the life of Littlefoot's sick grandpa.

The Land Before Time 5: The Mysterious Island (1997). Directed by Charles Grosvenor. When a swarm of insects devour all the plants in the Great Valley, the herds are forced to move. But with the adults fighting, Littlefoot and his pals go off on their own. They cross the Big Water to a mysterious island, which just happens to be the home of their old friend, the baby T-rex, Chomper. And it's up to Chomper to protect his plant-eating friends from the island's meat-eaters, who look on the little band as dinner.

Land of the Lost (1992). Cast: Timothy Bottoms. Tom Porter and his children Kevin and Annie are transported back to prehistoric times where they are joined by a mysterious jungle girl and a monkey-boy named Stink. They must fight for survival in a jungle filled with gigantic dinosaurs, evil lizard-men, and other dangers.

The Land That Time Forgot (1975). Cast: Doug McClure, John McEnery, Susan Penhaligon, Kevin Connor. Directed by James Cawthorn. A WWI veteran, a beautiful woman, and their German enemies are stranded in a land outside time filled with prehistoric creatures. Based on the 1918 novel by Edgar Rice Burroughs. Followed in 1977 by *The People That Time Forgot.*

The Land Unknown (1957). Cast: Jock Mahoney, Shawn Smith, William Reynolds, Henry (Kleinbach) Brandon, Douglas Kennedy. Directed by Virgil W. Vogel. A Naval helicopter is forced down in a tropical land of prehistoric terror, complete with ferocious creatures from the Mesozoic Era. While trying to make repairs, the crew discovers the sole survivor of a previous expedition who was driven to madness by life in the primordial jungle. Good performances from cast, although monsters aren't that believable. Based on a story by Charles Palmer.

Legend of the Dinosaurs (1983). Slavering, teeth-gnashing dinosaurs are discovered on Mt. Fuji.

Life During the Mesozoic Era. Takes a look at the different forms of life that existed during the Mesozoic Era (70 million to 220 million years ago). Comes with teacher's manual.

The Lost Continent (1951). Cast: Cesar Romero, Hillary Brooke, Chick Chandler, John Hoyt, Acquanetta, Sid Melton, Whit Bissell, Hugh Beaumont. Directed by Sam Newfield. An expedition searching for a lost rocket on a jungle island discovers dinosaurs and other extinct creatures.

Lost in Dinosaur World (1993). A ten-year-old boy and his seven-year-old sister have the experience of a lifetime when they get lost in a dinosaur park. Tension mounts as their parents are warned that it's almost feeding time for the dinosaurs. Fun and informative, offering a fair amount of scientific facts about dinosaurs and the world in which they lived.

The Lost World: Jurassic Park 2 (1997). Cast: Jeff Goldblum, Julianne Moore, Vince Vaughn, Arliss Howard, Pete Postlethwaite, Peter Stormare, Vanessa Lee Chester, Directed by Steven Spielberg. Sequel to *Jurassic Park,* proves only that Spielberg has tapped this well one too many times. It's four years after the first adventure and the surviving dinos have peacefully set up house on a deserted island near Costa Rica. Mathematician Ian Malcolm (Goldblum, reprising his role) reluctantly becomes part of an expedition to monitor the beasts, only because his paleontologist girlfriend (Moore) is so gung-ho. Other characters exist, but are reduced to the role of entrees. More dinos (two T-rexes, a clan of Raptors, and bite-sized newcomers Compsognathus), thrilling special effects, and more gore make up for thin subplots involving a rich businessman who wants to use the dinosaurs for a new zoo and another who hunts them for sport. Ironically, Spielberg's predictablity owes much to better films such as *King Kong,*

Aliens, and *Godzilla.* Still, T-rex and buddies, the true stars, rise to the occasion to entertain in an otherwise lackluster sequel. Based on Michael Crichton's book.

Lost Worlds, Vanished Lives (1991). Naturalist David Attenborough looks at the world of paleontology. He examines the Earth's fossil records, as well as computer-enhanced studies of dinosaurs, to offer new insights into humankind's earliest ancestors. On four cassettes.

A Magical Field Trip to the Dinosaur Museum (1991). Cast: Rosie O'Flanigan. Chris takes a trip to a dinosaur museum with his friend Nicole and Rosie O'Flanigan, which provides him with knowledge about dinosaurs and a great story to tell at school. Available at a special series price.

Maia: A Dinosaur Grows Up (1990). Learn what life was like 80 million years ago through the eyes and experiences of Maia, a duck-billed dinosaur.

Massacre in Dinosaur Valley (1985). Cast: Michael Sopkiw, Suzanne Carvall. A dashing young paleontologist and his fellow explorers go on a perilous journey down the Amazon in search of the Valley of the Dinosaur.

Message from a Dinosaur (1965). Shows how life of the past is reconstructed from fossil remains and how new forms of life evolved from adaptations to environmental changes.

More about Dinosaurs (1993). Part of the 14-part First Time Science Series that uses animation to outline factors leading to the extinction of the dinosaurs.

More Dinosaurs (1985). Hosted by Gary Owens and Eric Boardman. Owens and Boardman go on an African safari to investigate the legend of the living dinosaur and tour Dinosaur National Monument and the Smithsonian to learn more.

My Science Project (1985). Cast: John Stockwell, Danielle von Zerneck, Fisher Stevens, Raphael Sbarge, Richard Masur, Barry Corbin, Ann Wedgeworth, Dennis Hopper. Directed by Jonathan Betuel. Teenager Stockwell stumbles across a crystal sphere with a funky light. Unaware that it is an alien time-travel device, he takes it to school to use as a science project in a last-ditch effort to avoid failing his class. Chaos follows and Stockwell and his chums find themselves battling gladiators, mutants, and dinosaurs. Plenty of special effects and a likeable enough teenage movie.

Nature Connection: Badlands. Dr. Suzuki brings a group of children to Dinosaur Provincial Park where they learn about the creatures from the prehistoric era.

Nova: The Case of the Flying Dinosaur (1992). Discusses whether or not birds are the direct descendents of dinosaurs.

One Million B.C. (1940). Cast: Victor Mature, Carole Landis, Lon Chaney Jr. Directed by Hal Roach and Hal Roach Jr. The strange saga of the struggle of primitive cavemen and their battle against dinosaurs and other monsters. Curiously told in flashbacks, this film provided stock footage for countless dinosaur movies that followed. Portions of film rumored to be directed by cinematic pioneer D. W. Griffith.

One Million Years B.C. (1966). Cast: Raquel Welch, John Richardson, Percy Herbert, Robert Brown, Martine Beswick. Directed by Don Chaffey. It's Welch in a fur bikini and special effects expert Ray Harryhausen doing dinosaurs so who cares about a plot (which involves Welch and her boyfriend, who's from a rival clan). Remake of the 1940 film *One Million B.C.*

One of Our Dinosaurs Is Missing (1975). Cast: Peter Ustinov, Helen Hayes, Derek Nimmo, Clive Revill, Joan Sims. Directed by Robert Stevenson. An English nanny and her cohorts help British Intelligence retrieve a microfilm-concealing dinosaur fossil from the bad guys that have stolen it. Disney film was shot on location in England.

The Outer Planets/Shooting Stars (1993). Part 6 of the 12-part Galactic Encyclopedia series. Focuses on the planets furthest from the sun—Uranus, Neptune, and Pluto—and speculates on whether a collision with a comet or asteroid is the possible cause of the extinction of dinosaurs.

Paleo World (1994). Three-volume series looks at the Jurassic era of pre-history, examining predators, early mammals, and ideas on evolution. Available as a boxed set or individually.

The People That Time Forgot (1977). Cast: Doug McClure, Patrick Wayne, Sarah Douglas, Dana Gillespie, Thorley Walters, Shane Rimmer. Directed by Kevin Connor. Sequel to *The Land That Time Forgot,* based on the Edgar Rice Burroughs novel. A rescue team returns to a world of prehistoric monsters to rescue a man left there after the first film.

Planet of Dinosaurs (1980). Cast: James Whitworth. Directed by James K. Shea. Survivors from a ruined spaceship combat huge savage dinosaurs on a swampy uncharted planet.

Prehistoric World (1988). Hosted by Gary Owens and Eric Boardman. A companion to *More Dinosaurs* and *Dinosaurs, Dinosaurs, Dinosaurs,* examines prehistoric mammals. Kids can see recreations of the saber tooth tiger, woolly mammoth and other animals, as well as a trip to the La Brea Tar Pits.

Prehysteria (1993). Cast: Brett Cullen, Austin O'Brien. Directed by Albert Band. Fantasy/adventure about a widower, his 11-year-old son and teenage daughter, and what happens when some mysterious eggs from South America accidentally wind up at their farm. Imagine their surprise when the eggs hatch and out pop a brood of pygmy dinosaurs. The dinosaurs are cute (as is the family).

Prehysteria 2 (1994). Cast: Dean Scofield, Kevin R. Connors, Jennifer Harte, Bettye Ackerman, Larry Hankin, Greg Lewis, Alan Palo, Michael Hagiwara, Owen Bush. Directed by Albert Band. While their adoptive family is on vacation the pygmy dinosaurs get loose and aid a lonely rich boy whose governess is plotting to send him to military boarding school.

Prehysteria 3 (1995). Cast: Fred Willard, Bruce Weitz, Whitney Anderson. Directed by Julian Breen. The mini-dinos take up miniature golf. Seems Thomas MacGregor's (Willard) putt-putt business is about to sink when his daughter Ella (Anderson) finds the pygmy dinosaurs and a promotional bonanza is born. But Thomas's evil brother Hal (Weitz) hatches a plot to take over the now-successful enterprise.

Pterodactyl Woman from Beverly Hills (1997). Cast: Beverly D'Angelo, Moon Zappa, Brion James, Brad Wilson, Aron Eisenberg. Written and directed by Philippe Mora. California housewife Pixie Chandler (D'Angelo) is the victim of an eccentric witch doctor (James) when her paleontologist husband Dick (Wilson) disturbs an ancient burial site and the doc curses Pixie by turning her into a dinosaur. This is the first so-called family release from those madcap Troma people who brought you the *Toxic Avenger.*

Reading Rainbow: Digging Up Dinosaurs (1983). Voice(s) by Jerry Stiller, hosted by LeVar Burton. Burton takes viewers back in time to do some dinosaur watching.

Return of the Dinosaurs (1983). A comet is about to collide with the Earth. Never fear! The dinosaur patrol will interfere (and ultimately save the planet).

The Return of Dinosaurs. Hosted by Gary Owens and Eric Boardman. Hosts Owens and Boardman join a group of kids at the Natural History Museum in Los Angeles for a dinosaur bone hunt and lots of dino-info. At the Canadian Museum of Paleontology the viewer will see how fossils are dug up and reconstructed for museum display.

Return to the Lost World (1993). Cast: John Rhys-Davies, David Warner, Darren Peter Mercer, Geza Kovacs. Directed by Timothy Bond. Rival scientists Challenger and Summerlee set out for the Lost World and find it threatened by oil prospectors. With a volcano about to explode the scientists set out to save their prehistoric paradise and its dinosaur inhabitants. Based on a story by Sir Arthur Conan Doyle. Sequel to *The Lost World.*

Sir Arthur Conan Doyle's The Lost World (1998). Cast: Patrick Bergin. Zoologist George Challenger (Bergin) recruits a team of scientists to help him find a mythic land where dinosaurs and other prehistoric creatures exist. Lots of cliches although the special effects aren't bad.

64,000,000 Years Ago (1987). Chronicles the days when magnificent, majestic dinosaurs ruled the earth.

Son of Dinosaurs (1990). Cast: Gary Owens, Eric Boardman, Kenneth Mars, Alex Rodine, James Stewart. Owens and Boardman are back as those intrepid dinosaur hunters, this time as sworn "Protectors" of the discovery of a lifetime—a dinosaur egg containing a live embryo. But watch out . . . there's a man who'll stop at nothing to steal the precious egg.

Sound of Horror (1964). Cast: James Philbrook, Arturo Fernandez, Soledad Miranda, Ingrid Pitt. Directed by Jose Antonio Nieves-Conde. Efforts to keep budgets down backfire on this Spanish production. A dinosaur egg hatches, and out lashes an invisible predator. Yes, you'll have to use your imagination as archaeologists are slashed to bits by the no-show terror.

Sound of Thunder. A man goes on safari 60 million years into the past to hunt Tyrannosaurus rex.

Story of Dinosaurs (1993). Part of the 14-part First Time Science Series that uses animation to summarize the life and habits of dinosaurs.

Super Mario Bros. (1993). Cast: Bob Hoskins, John Leguizamo, Dennis Hopper, Annabel Jankel, Samantha Mathis, Lance Henriksen, Fisher Stevens, Fiona Shaw, Richard Edson. Directed by Rocky Morton. This $42 million adventure fantasy is based on the popular Nintendo video game. The brothers are in hot pursuit of the Princess Daisy who's been kidnapped by evil slimebucket Hopper and taken to Dinohattan, a fungi-infested, garbage-strewn, rat-hole version of Manhattan. Hopper will amuse the adults, doing a gleeful reptilian version of Frank Booth from *Blue Velvet.* Hoskins and

Leguizamo act gamely in broad Nintendo style, enthusiastically partaking in high-tech wizardry and the many gags. Hits bullseye of target audience—elementary and junior high kids—with frenetic pace, gaudy special effects, oversized sets, and animatronic monsters.

T. Rex Exposed (1991). Presents facts and myths surrounding the Tyrannosaurus rex, and includes footage of the 1990 Montana excavation of one of the largest and most complete T. rex skeletons to date.

Tammy and the T-Rex (1994). Cast: Terry Kiser, John Franklin, Paul Walker, Denise Richards. Directed by Stewart Raffill. All Michael (Walker) wanted was a date with the lovely Denise (Richards)—he didn't expect to almost die for her. Nor did he expect a mad scientist to transplant his brain into a mechanical three-ton dinosaur. Part teen angst—part camp horror—all good-natured hooey.

Teenage Caveman (1958). Cast: Robert Vaughn, Darrah Marshall, Leslie Bradley, Frank De Kova. Directed by Roger Corman. A teenage boy living in a post-apocalypse yet prehistoric world journeys across the river, even though he was warned against it, and finds an old man who owns a book about past civilizations in the 20th century. Schlocky, and one of the better bad films around. The dinosaur shots were picked up from the film *One Million B.C.*

Teenage Mutant Ninja Turtles: Turtles at the Earth's Core (1991). The Turtles have a fantastic adventure in a land populated by dinosaurs.

Theodore Rex (1995). Cast: Whoopi Goldberg, Armin Mueller-Stahl, Richard Roundtree, Juliet Landau. Written and directed by Jonathan Betuel. Futuristic comedy finds cynical, seasoned cop Katie Coltrane (Goldberg) furious at being teamed with Teddy, who just happens to be an eight-foot-tall, three-ton, returned-from-extinction Tyrannosaurus rex (who has a taste for cookies). And Teddy's not exactly the brightest dinosaur on the block, which makes Katie's job all the harder when they stumble across a major crime caper.

Two Lost Worlds (1950). Cast: James Arness, Laura Elliott, Bill Kennedy. Directed by Norman Dawn. A young hero battles monstrous dinosaurs, pirates, and more in this cheapy when he and his shipmates are shipwrecked on an uncharted island. Don't miss the footage from *Captain Fury, One Billion B.C.,* and *Captain Caution.*

Unknown Island (1948). Cast: Virginia Grey, Philip Reed, Richard Denning, Barton MacLane. Directed by Jack Bernhard. Scientists travel to a legendary island where dinosaurs supposedly still exist. Bogus dinosaurs and cliche script.

The Valley of Gwangi (1969). Cast: James Franciscus, Gila Golan, Richard Carlson, Laurence Naismith, Freda Jackson. Directed by James O'Connolly. One of the best prehistoric-monster westerns out there. Cowboys discover a lost valley of dinosaurs and try to capture a vicious, carnivorous allosaurus. Bad move, kemosabe! The creatures move via the stop-motion model animation by special effects maestro Ray Harryhausen, here at his finest.

VITSIE Video Sitter: Dinosaurs (1990). The Vitsie series designed for young children has received an Award of Excellence from the Film Advisory Board. *Dinosaurs* lets the little ones play and sing while learning about the ancient reptiles.

We're Back! A Dinosaur's Story (1993). Voices: John Goodman, Felicity Kendal, Walter Cronkite, Joey Shea, Jay Leno, Julia Child, Kenneth Mars, Martin Short, Rhea Perlman. Directed by Dick Zondag. Animated adventures of a pack of revived dinosaurs who return to their old stomping grounds—which are now modern-day New York City. Smart-mouth human boy Louie and his girlfriend Cecilia take the dinos under their wing (so to speak), wise them up to modern life, and try to prevent their capture by the evil Professor Screweyes. Slow-moving with some violence. Adapted from the book by Hudson Talbott.

What Ever Happened to the Dinosaurs? (1992). Informative video explores the current theories about dinosaurs with the help of four curious kids.

When Dinosaurs Ruled the Earth (1970). Cast: Victoria Vetri, Robin Hawdon, Patrick Allen, Drewe Henley, Sean Caffrey, Magda Konopka, Imogen Hassall. Directed by Val Guest. When *One Million Years B.C.* ruled the box office the Brits cranked out a few more lively prehistoric fantasies. A sexy cavegirl, exiled because of her blond hair, acquires a cave-beau and a dinosaur guardian. Stop-motion animation from Jim Danforth, story by J. G. Ballard. Under the name Angela Dorian, Vetri was Playmate of the Year in 1968 (A.D.).

Where Did They Go? A Dinosaur Update (1988). The fun and excitement of dinosaurs have been captured for children to enjoy.

A Whopping Small Dinosaur (1988). This documentary follows a team of dedicated paleontologists into the Painted Desert, where the bones of a "whopping small dinosaur" are removed from the ground, shipped to a museum, and then assembled.

Websites

Dinofest: http://www.acnatsci.org/dinofestarchive/index.html. In the spring of 1998, Philadelphia's Academy of Natural Sciences presented Dinofest, called "The World's Fair of Dinosaurs." Visit this award-winning site to see the archives from the exhibit. Also, dinosaur news and kids' art show. The promotional site for the show can still be visited (at http://www3.phillynews.com/packages/dinofest/), where more info on Dinofest is available along with lessons, games, links and resources, as well as video tours.

Dinosaur Eggs: http://www.nationalgeographic.com/dinoeggs/index.html. National Geographic Magazine takes visitors behind the scenes of the Great Dinosaur Egg Hunt. Follow fossil researchers as they "hatch" fossilized dinosaur eggs; tour a museum of hatchlings.

Dinosaurs in the Gobi Desert: http://www.discovery.com/area/specials/gobi/ gobi1.html. During the summer of 1998 the Discovery Channel sent a correspondent along on a 20-day paleontological expedition through the Gobi Desert. Visit this website to read daily dispatches from the paleontologists, learn about their finds, and check out online areas such as the Bone Zone, Paleo-Talk, and an email exchange between visitors to the website and a paleontologist from the American Museum of Natural History.

Dinosaurs in Print: http://www.lhl.lib.mo.us/pubserv/hos/dino/welcome.htm. View the publications that told the world about dinosaurs. The Linda Hall Library (Kansas City, Missouri) hosts this web exhibition, which consists of a hypertext catalog of pictures and text from some eighty works about dinosaur discovery and theory published between 1824 and 1969.

Expedia's Mungo Park: http://www.mungopark.com. Join world-renowned paleontologists Jack Horner and Phil Currie on an expedition to some of North America's richest fossil sites: Read their dispatches, find out what detours they took, and get a dossier and resource information for planning your own (real-world) expedition.

Giganotosaurus: http://www.giganotosaurus.com. "Dino" Don Lessem takes you on a tour of discovery of this remarkable animal—the largest carnivorous dinosaur ever found, even bigger than T. rex. For all ages.

Haddonfield Hadrosaurus: http://www.levins.com/dinosaur.html. Haddonfield, New Jersey, was home to the first dinosaur skeleton ever excavated (in 1858). The Hadrosaurus found there and the site where it was found are celebrated as the beginning of modern paleontology. Visit this website to see photos, graphics, and maps, and to find information for planning a visit to this historic site. (The feature is by Hoag Levins.)

Bill Nye the Science Guy: http://nyelabs.kcts.org/nyeverse/episode/e03.html. Kids' favorite scientist and host of the popular TV show, Nye turns his attention to dishing up the dirt on dinosaurs. Forget about *Jurassic Park* ("Jurassic Shmurassic") and get the facts about dinosaurs. Also follow simple instructions for making you own "fossils."

Sue: The Tyrannosaurus Rex: http://www.sothebys.com/search/index.html. Visit the site of Sotheby's Auction House: A search here (keyword = Sue) pulls up excellent archival articles on how the T. rex was discovered (in August 1990 in South Dakota), the significance of the find, the restoration of the skeleton, and the auction (in October 1997). Also, you can view quick-time videos of Sue's skull, tooth, vertebra, and forelimb.

WaybackMachine: http://www.discovery.com:80/area/wayback/wayback970324/wayback1.html. Travel in Discovery Channel's Wayback Machine to 1902, and be there as renowned paleontologist Barnum Brown finds an almost-complete skeleton of a Tyrannosaurus rex—in a desolate spot in Montana. Dinosaur enthusiasts of all ages will enjoy the trip.

Virtual Tours

American Museum of Natural History: http://www.amnh.org/exhibitions/index.html. Get an online preview of the famed museum's dinosaur hall, which includes the world's tallest free-standing dinosaur skeleton. Includes floor plans to help guide you.

Children's Museum of Indianapolis: http://www.childrensmuseum.org/dino.htm. Online exhibit of dinosaurs is specifically geared toward kids. Also, dinosaur fact sheets and FAQ.

Dinosaur Hall: http://www.acnatsci.org/dinosaurs/dinonew.html. The Dinosaur Hall at Philadelphia's Academy of Natural Sciences features five different guided online tours of exhibits: From the Fossils; The Big Dig; Fossil Prep Lab; Bones, Guts, and Behavior;

and Science through Art. Also, a kids section and links for teachers, as well as academy news, museum info, and newsletter of online events.

Field Museum of Natural History: http://www.fmnh.org/exhibits/web_exhibits.htm. Visit this page to begin an online tour of the Field's Life Over Time exhibit, tracing 3.8 billion years of the evolution of life on earth—from single cells to dinosaurs and humans.

Finland's Museum of Natural History: http://www.fmnh.helsinki.fi/. English-language site of the Finnish Museum of Natural History (part of Helsinki University) offers information about and pictures from its exhibitions and collections. At press time, the museum was showing After the Ice Age, an exhibition about how the Ice Age affected the biology and geology of Finland, and about what happened as the icecap withdrew. Previous exhibitions include Dinosaurs—Rulers of Their Time; Backyard Monsters; and Treasures of the Museum.

Florida Museum of Natural History: http://www.flmnh.ufl.edu/. The Florida Museum of Natural History (Gainesville) offers virtual exhibits and a photo gallery to online visitors as part of their museum outreach program.

Hall of Archosaurs: http://www.ucmp.berkeley.edu/diapsids/archosy.html. Learn about the dinosaur family tree at the University of California Museum of Paleontology. Click on a map to explore the major dinosaur phyla, a grouping that includes all descendants, living or extinct, known and unknown, of an inferred common ancestor. Not geared for young children, but terrific for older students.

Honolulu Community College Dinosaur Exhibit: http://www.hcc.hawaii.edu/dinos. Take a narrated tour (conducted by history instructor Rick Ziegler) of the Honolulu Community College's exhibit of replicas of fossils from the American Museum of Natural History.

La Brea Tar Pits: http://www.lam.mus.ca.us/nhm/dino/kiosk and http://www.lam.mus.ca.us/page. Educational website of the Natural History Museum of Los Angeles County features ten different dinosaurs. Also, the Page Museum at the La Brea Tar Pits, where scientists discovered an unusually diverse assemblage of extinct Ice Age plants and animals, offers a look at fossils, kids' stuff, and a calendar of events at its searchable site.

National Museum of Natural History: http://www.nmnh.si.edu/VirtualTour/Tour/First/Dinosaurs/index.html. Visit the virtual exhibits at the Smithsonian. Dinosaurs are on the first floor of the Museum of Natural History; a floor plan helps you navigate through the halls.

Peabody Museum: http://www.peabody.yale.edu/mural. Visit Yale University's Peabody Museum online to view the famous mural, *The Age of Reptiles,* painted by Rudolph Zallinger between 1942 and 1947. The Peabody's homepage (at http://www.peabody.yale.edu/) offers museum news, events and exhibits info, and historical information (including a "who was who" among paleontologists).

Russian Paleontological Institute: http://www.ucmp.berkeley.edu/pin/pinentrance.html. Visit the Russian Paleontological Institute, hosted by the University of California. Includes sections on Pleistocene mammals, Mongolian dinosaurs, and Tertiary mammals. Graphics and (English-language) text.

Time Traveling: http://www.washington.edu/burkemuseum/ltws.html. The University of Washington offers virtual tours of its Burke Museum of Natural History and Culture, featuring the Life and Times of Washington State exhibit—a hands-on adventure that begins 545 million years ago. Also, info on exhibits, collections, news, and events at the museum.

T. rex at the University of California Museum of Paleontology: http://www.ucmp.berkeley.edu/trex/trexpo.html. Visit the T. rex skeleton at the University of California Museum of Paleontology, and learn more about these huge creatures, the world they lived in, and how scientists excavated the skeleton. Also, read the scientists' write-up on "Building the Perfect Beast," which tells the story of how they reconstructed the forty-foot skeleton.

University of California Museum of Paleontology: http://www.ucmp.berkeley.edu/exhibit/exhibits.html. Browse the extensive online exhibit, Paleontology without Walls. Features illustrations but it's text-heavy, so it's not kid-friendly, but older students will find it highly informative. Online visitors can choose their paradigm for touring the museum: Phylogeny—the Family Tree of Life or Geological Time or Evolutionary Thought.

Virtual Dinosaurs: http://sunsite.anu.edu.au/Questacon/. Virtual tours, 3-D Zone, Kidspace, Hands-On Zone, and Cool Science are among the possibilities for exploration at the interactive site of Questacon, the Natural Science and Technology Centre in Canberra, Australia. Features online dinosaur activities for children as well as quick-time videos of their robotic dinosaurs, including the Muttaburrasaurus, which was discovered in Australia.

Virtual Reality Fossils: http://www.nhm.ac.uk/museum/tempexhib/VRML/index.html. Britain's Natural History Museum (London) lets you explore and manipulate virtual fossils online (provided you have a VRML–capable browser). The site also explains how they made the 3-D exhibits and provides links to the VRML software so you can download it if you don't already have it.

Art

Dinosaur Cartoons by Charley Parker: http://www.zark.com/extra/dinotoons/dinos.html. Charley Parker was the talent behind the Dinofest® website's cartoons, which originally appeared in Isaac Asimov's *Science Fiction*. Visit his site to click through an entertaining gallery of dinosaur cartoons.

Pictures-a-Go-Go: http://web.syr.edu/~dbgoldma/pictures.html. Dinosaur expert David Goldman and Syracuse University offer this vault of dinosaur pictures. A-to-Z index of links to sites where you can view dinosaur and other paleontological art. Updated regularly.

Walters & Kissinger: http://www.dinoart.com. The Curators of the Dinofest® Art Show, Robert F. Walters and Tess Kissinger, give online visitors an inside peak on what they're working on in their complete dinosaur art studio (includes paintings and sculptures).

Information and News

Dinamation: http://www.dinamation.org. The site of the Dinamation International Society, which promotes science education and research, and of the Dinamation International Corporation, which produces a line of scientifically accurate products for all ages. Visit to learn about their work in robotic dinosaurs and find out about where you can see their creatures in person. Also, plenty of online information—including a weekly term, a "Dinosaur of the Month" feature, and details about the Devil's Canyon Science and Learning Center.

"Dino" Don: http://www.dinodon.com. Dinosaur expert and writer "Dino" Don Lessem put together and maintains this excellent site offering "Dinosaurs, dinosaurs, and more dinosaurs!" It's dino-everything: art, dictionary, contest, news, digs, scientists, books, links, and "all manner of cool stuff" for children of all ages.

"Dino" Russ's Lair: http://denr1.igis.uiuc.edu/isgsroot/dinos/vertpaleo.html. Don't be put off by the URL; this site is worth the visit. Sponsored by the Illinois State Geological Survey (as part of its educational extension program) and known as "Dino Russ's Lair" (after its keeper, Russell Jacobson), visitors will find information on art, digs, eggs, exhibits, real-world places to visit, tracks, organizations, links, and software. National Geographic Society Online named it one of best dinosaur sites on the Web.

The Dinosaur Interplanetary Gazette: http://www.dinosaur.org/frontpage.html. Featuring "245 million years of dinosaur news at Dinosaur Central," this mega-site of paleo-info includes news, discoveries, articles about dinosaurs in the media, book reviews, and much more. The National Education Association gave this jam-packed site the nod for its informative content.

Dinosaur News: http://rexfiles.newscientist.com. Visit the online magazine *New Scientist* to find links to several brief but informative articles on the latest dinosaur theories and findings.

The Dinosaur Pages: http://www.gl.umbc.edu/~tkeese1/dinosaur/index.htm. This award-winning site moved recently and is under reconstruction, but is still worth visiting for its rich content. T. Mike Keesey began this project while he was a college student and he's collected loads of information about dinosaurs. Also, a list of links to other paleo-related sites on the Internet.

Dinosauria Online: http://www.dinosauria.com. Read articles by paleontologists and others, and get in on discussions about dinosaurs at this award-winning site. Plenty of content, plus picture gallery, a store, and a searchable vertebrate catalog. For the amateur and serious dinosaur enthusiast alike.

The Dinosaur Society: http://www.dinosociety.org/homepage.html. Founded in 1991, the Dinosaur Society is dedicated to dinosaur research and educating people about dinosaurs. Their honored site is true to that goal: It features a dig visit, society news, dinosaur art, gift shop, links, publications lists, and much more. For enthusiasts of all ages, but especially fun for kids—who will probably find it interesting enough to want to sign up to be a member of the society.

Dinosaurs in New Mexico: http://www.aps.edu/htmlpages/dinosinnm.html. Exhibits, research, collections info, and links, all courtesy of the New Mexico Museum of Natural History and Science.

National Geographic: http://www.nationalgeographic.com/index.html. The renowned magazine has run more than a few articles on dinosaur discoveries of recent years; readers can search the archives electronically to find stories.

Nova's "Life with T. Rex": http://www.pbs.org/wgbh/nova/trex. Information about life during the time of the Tyrannosaurus rex from Public Television's *Nova*. Includes information on the animals, plants, and insects that inhabited the earth during the time of the dinosaurs.

Paleontological Research Institution: http://www.englib.cornell.edu/pri. The site of the Ithaca, NY–based Paleontological Research Institution. Educational resource provides information on PRI's collection of fossils (many of which can be viewed online). Also "What Is It?"—a new feature challenging visitors to look at a fossil and try to identify it (not as easy as it sounds since these are fossils that have stumped the PRI experts).

Strange Science: http://www.turnpike.net/~mscott/. This site "follows the sometimes crazy assumptions of early fossil collectors," tracing the rocky road to modern paleontology and biology. Science isn't always as exact as we think it should be, and before great scientists and scholars arrived at the knowledge we take for granted today, they put forth some interesting (but erroneous) theories. Visit this site to learn about how scientific theory is formulated.

Tomorrow Morning's News: http://www.morning.com/archives/tm241/science.html. The Internet edition of Tomorrow Morning's News Stories for Kids features an archived article on the discovery of fossils in New Mexico; the finds are believed to be the remains of the oldest horned dinosaur ever found. Interesting reading for all ages, but definitely geared toward kids.

Wyoming Dinosaur Center: http://www.trib.com/DINO/facts.html. Fast facts and quick quizzes can be found at this site, sponsored by the Wyoming Dinosaur Center and Big Horn Basin Foundation.

Museum Sites (Informational)

Carnegie Museum of Natural History: http://www.clpgh.org/cmnh/discovery/dinoscience. Mix and match dinosaurs at the Carnegie Museum of Natural History site. DinoScience challenges visitors to match the right dinosaur skull with its skeleton. A fun way to learn, no matter what your age.

American Museum of Natural History: http://www.amnh.org/. A site for all ages; it offers information on the museum's dinosaur hall and newly renovated fossil halls (displaying the largest array of vertebrate fossils in the world). Visitors to the Manhattan museum can follow the story of vertebrate evolution, a story extending back some 500 million years, along a giant "family tree" of vertebrates. Online visitors can read museum news and learn about personalities in paleontology.

Carnegie Museum of Natural History: http://www.clpgh.org/cmnh/exhibits/index.html. Preview exhibits at Pittsburgh's Carnegie Museum of Natural History, featuring (at press time) China's feathered dinosaurs (at http://www.clpgh.org/cmnh/exhibits/feathered/index.html).

Children's Museum of Indianapolis: http://www.a1.com/children/dinoapat.htm. A brontosaurus by any other name . . . . Visit the Children's Museum of Indianapolis to view images and read up on the Apatosaurus, which used to be known as the Brontosaurus.

Field Museum of Natural History: http://www.fmnh.org/exhibits/perm_exhibits_nature.htm. Information on the Field Museum's new Elizabeth Morse Genius Dinosaur Hall and the McDonald's Fossil Preparation Laboratory, where visitors can watch museum staff and volunteers ready fossilized Tyrannosaurus rex bones for study. Also, listing of current exhibitions; museum news.

National Museum of Natural History: http://www.nmnh.si.edu/paleo/faq.html. The Natural History Museum at the Smithsonian Institution clears up the top ten misconceptions about dinosaurs. For information about the museum's exhibits (permanent and temporary), visit their homepage (at http://mnh.si.edu/museum/online.html).

Natural History of Texas: http://www.utexas.edu/depts/tnhc/. Information (mostly text, but some images) about the Texas Memorial Museum's holdings, including the research and collections of its Vertebrate Paleontology Laboratory.

NatureNet: http://www.vmnh.org/. Information, news, drawings, and photos of exhibits at the Virginia Museum of Natural History.

Recreating Dinosaurs?: http://www.nhm.ac.uk/sc. London's Natural History Museum examines the possibility of recreating dinosaurs: In *Jurassic Park* and its sequel, *The Lost World,* dinosaurs are recreated from fragments of their DNA. Scientists in the film extracted the DNA from ancient bloodsucking insects trapped in amber. How possible is this? The museum's scientists find out. The site also offers information on the museum's exhibits.

Sue at the Field Museum: http://www.fmnh.org/new/trex.htm. The Field Museum of Natural History recently acquired the T. rex known as "Sue." Approximately 90% complete by bone count (and more than 90% complete by volume since most of the missing bones are relatively small), this example dwarfs all other known T. rex skeletons and became known as Sue after Susan Hendrickson, the field paleontologist who found it weathering out of the Dakota badlands. Visit the site to learn about the results of the CT scan on Sue's skull, read about the museum's plans for the T. rex, and read a list of Q&As about the famous skeleton.

T. rex and the "Death Star": http://www.mov.vic.gov.au/planetarium/trds.html. The planetarium at Australia's Museum of Victoria (Melbourne, Australia) provides information on the theory that an asteroid colliding into earth wiped out the dinosaur population sixty-five million years ago.

Links Pages

University of California Museum of Paleontology's Dinosaur Links:
http://www.ucmp.berkeley.edu/diapsids/dinolinks.html. A treasure trove of dino-related
information on the Internet.

Paleobook: http://www.paleobook.com. Lists paleontological and archaeological books—
fiction and nonfiction, for all age groups.

T Rex Surfs the Net: http://pioneer.mov.vic.gov.au/dinoExhibit/mainTrex.html. The Museum of Victoria, Australia, provides pages of links to other dinosaur sites on the Internet. Beware of some out-of-date connections; this site was last updated more than two
years ago. Still worth the visit.

University of California Museum of Paleontology's "Subway": http://www.ucmp.berkeley.
edu/subway/subway.html. This site will lead you to many online destinations related to
paleontology. Links include the National Science Foundation and natural history
resources. Site map categorizes the possible destinations. (Beware of some links, since
the site was last updated summer 1997.)

BIBLIOGRAPHY

Bakker, Robert T. *The Dinosaur Heresies.* New York: William Morrow & Company, 1986.

Benton, Michael J. *Historical Atlas of Dinosaurs.* London, England: Penguin Books, 1996.

Bird, Roland T. *Bones for Barnum Brown.* Fort Worth: Texas Christian University Press, 1985.

Dixon, D., B. Cox, R. J. G Savage, and B. Gardiner, *Dinosaurs and Prehistoric Animals.* New York: Macmillian Publishing, 1988.

Farlow, James O., and M. K. Brett-Surman, eds. *The Complete Dinosaur.* Bloomington: Indiana University Press, 1997.

Fraser, Nicholas C., and Hans-Dieter Sues, eds. *In the Shadow of the Dinosaurs.* New York: Cambridge University Press, 1997.

Gardom, Tim, and Angela Milner. *The Book of Dinosaurs.* Rocklin, California: Prima Publishing, 1993.

Halls, Kelly Milner. *Dino-Trekking: The Ultimate Dinosaur Lover's Travel Guide.* New York: John Wiley & Sons, Inc., 1996.

Horner, John R., and Edwin Dobb. *Dinosaur Lives.* New York: HarperCollins, 1997.

Jenkins, John T., and Jannice L. Jenkins. *Colorado's Dinosaurs.* Denver: Colorado Geological Survey, 1993.

Norman, David. *The Illustrated Encyclopedia of Dinosaurs.* New York: Crescent Books, 1985.

Officer, Charles, and Jake Page. *The Great Dinosaur Extinction Controversy.* New York: Addison-Wesley (Helix Books), 1996.

Parker, Steve. *The Practical Paleontologist.* New York: Simon & Schuster, 1990.

Psihoyos, Louis. *Hunting Dinosaurs.* New York: Random House, 1994.

Silbernagel, Bob. *Dinosaur Stalkers.* Fruita, Colorado: Dinamation International Society, 1996.

Wallace, Joseph. *The Complete Book of the Dinosaur.* New York: Gallery Books, 1989.

Wallace, Joseph. *Book of Dinosaurs and Other Ancient Creatures.* New York: Simon & Schuster, 1994.

Index

Page numbers in bold refer to illustrations.

A

accretion, defined 7

acid rain 235-236

acoustic diffraction tomography 313

Acraman crater (Australia) 244

aetosaurs 110

Agassiz, Louis 59

Alamosaurus 148

Alaska, dinosaur fossils in 220

Albertosaurus (Albert lizard) 146, 300

Alfveen, Hannes Olof Goost 7

ALH84001 (meteorite) 26, 27, **27**

alligator lizards **258**

alligators 110, 259-260, **260**

Allosaurus ("other lizard")
bones of 169, **187, 188, 191**
classification of 89
claws of **188**
eating habits of 128, 208, 211
evolution of 119, 127
reconstruction of **321**
recovery of fossils of 299

size of 130
teeth of **187,** 187-188, **211**

Alpha Centari, distance from Earth 9

Alvarez, Luis 243

Alvarez, Walter 243

Alvarezsauridae 274

amateur paleontologists 319-320

American Indians, perception of dinosaur fossils 70

American Museum of Natural History (New York City) 320, 336, 338

amino acids, formation of 28

ammonites
eaten by plesiosaurs 116
extinction of 255
fossils **57**

ammonoids
evolution of 115
extinction of 120, 134-135

amphibians
defined 78, 81
distribution of 78
earliest-known fossils of 78
evolution of 77-78, 109, 132, 154
modern species of 80
problems encountered during shift to land 78-80

Amphicoelias 200

anapsids 84-85, 110

Anchisaurus ("near lizard") 107, 279

Andes Mountains, formation of 144

Andrews, Roy Chapman 223, 305

angiosperms (flowering plants)
evolution of 141, 151-152, 153
and extinction of dinosaurs 238

animals *See also* paleozoology
of Cretaceous period 141, 153
impact of ice ages on 60-61
intelligence of 230
in Jurassic period 132-136
oldest, in oceans **35,** 36
oldest, on land 34
paleobiogeography of 101

Ankylosaurus (ankylosaurs)
classification of 89
eating habits of 148, 213
evolution of 127, 145
intelligence of 230
recovery of fossils of 320
tail of **213**

anomodonts
evolution of 111

395

extinction of 132

Antarctic Search for Meteorites (ANSMET) 27

Antarctica
dinosaur fossils from 50, 302
ozone hole over 25

ants 151

Anura (order) 80

Apatosaurus ("deceptive lizard")
eaten by *Allosaurus* 208
eating habits of 128
evolution of 119, 127
naming of 130-131
reconstruction of 320
recovery of fossils of 284, 287, 319
size of 67, 129
tail of 221-222

Aquila Rift 249, 250

arachnids *See* spiders

arachnoids, on Venus 12

Archaeon epoch 44

Archaeopteryx ("ancient wing")
bones of 172, **173**
evolution of 119, 127, 133, **134**
as possible bird-dinosaur link 266, 268-269, 270

Archaeopteryx lithographioca 266, 268-269, 270, 297-298, 303

Archelon 154

Archosauromorpha 110-111

archosaurs
description of 86, 297
evolution of 86-87, 110, 113
extinction of 107

Arctic Circle
dinosaur footprints in 303
ozone hole over 25

Arctic Ocean, depth of 20

Argentina
fossil assemblages in 220
large fossils discovered in 177-178, 192

oldest-known fossils in 71, 301
Unenlagia comaheunsis discovered in 275, 303-304

Argentinosaurus
discovery of fossils of 177
eating habits of 148
size of 200

Argentinosaurus huinculensis 149

Arizona
dinosaur trackway in 57
impact craters in 19, 241

Armillaria bulbosa (fungus) 65

Arrhenius, Svante 28

arthritis 169-170

arthropods 34, 255

Asian tree frogs 79

aspen trees 65, **66**

Assaro, Frank 243

asteroids
defined 4, 240, **240**
dinosaur extinction due to 239-248
impact of 245-246
origins of 240-241
recent occurrences of 247-248

asymmetrical bone growth 168

Atlantic Ocean
depth of 20
formation of 104, 124, 142, 144

atoms, formation of 6

Australia
dinosaur stampede in 217-218
fossil dinosaurs in 196, 220
oldest fossils in 33
theft of dinosaur footprints from 305

Australopithecus afarensis 56, **57**

Aves (class) See birds

Avimimus ("bird mimic") 146, 148

B

bacteria
fossilized 26
size of 26

Bakker, Robert T. 193, 194, 269, 344

Baptornis 154

Barosaurus ("heavy lizard")
evolution of 127
reconstruction of 338
recovery of fossils of 299
size of 130, 201

Baryonyx ("heavy claw") 146

basalt, on Moon 17

Beagle, HMS 75

Beaverhead crater (Montana) 244

bees 132, 151

beetles 151

belemnites
evolution of 134
extinction of 255

Belgium, dinosaur fossils from 297

Bensted, W. H. 295

beryllium, formation of 250-251

big bang theory 6

binocular vision 228-229

biogeography
defined 100
purpose of 100-101

bipedal motion 87, 106, 126, 164-165, 217, 280, 281

birch trees 153

birds
bones of 172
defined 261
distribution of 265-266
eating habits of 263-265
eggs of 262
evolution of 119, 133, 149, 154, 155, 221, 260
flying by 262-263
migration of 264
relationship to dinosaurs 260, 266-275

unique characteristics of 261-262

Birmingham Museum (England) 339

bivalves, extinction of some 255

Black Hills Institute of Geological Research 350

Bolivia, dinosaur trackway in 208

Boltwood, Bertram 13

"Bone Wars" 281-282

bones, fossilized 51

bony fishes 115, 134, 157

bookstores 334

Brachiosaurus ("arm lizard")
classification of 89
distribution of 122
eating habits of 128
evolution of 127
extinction of 149
recover of fossils of 287, 299
size of 129-130, 149, **198,** 199-200, 201-202, 213

bradymetabolic, defined 192-193

brain, of dinosaurs 228

Branca, W. 298

Brazil, oldest-known fossils in 71

breccia
formation of 31
on Moon 17

Breviceratops kozlowskii 306

British Museum (London) 339

Brontosaurus See Apatosaurus

Brookes, R. 68, 293

Brown, Barnum 57, 285, 300

bubbles 30

Buckland, William 130, 294, 295

buffalo 70

Buffon, Comte de Georges Louis Leclerc 5, 13

Burgess Shale (British Columbia) 51

buried sites, discovery of 312-314

butterflies 151

button (honey) mushrooms 66

C

caecilians 80, 154

caimans 110

Camarasaurus ("chambered lizard") 89, 127

Cambrian period
description of 43
explosion of life during 32, 44-48, **45**

Cambrian-Ordovician extinctions 234

camouflage 181-182

Camptosaurus ("bent lizard") 127, 128

Canada
coprolites discovered in 206-207
dinosaur fossils from 195, 275, 300
earliest-known fossil reptiles from 83
museums in 337

cannibalism 215, 286

carbon dioxide
in atmosphere 20-21
as evidence of life on other planets 10

carbon films 51

Carboniferous period
description of 42
evolution of amphibians during 78
evolution of reptiles during 80, 111
naming of 43

Carcharodontosaurus
eating habits of 148
size of 149-150, 199

Carlin, W. E. 284-285

Carnegie Museum of Natural History (Pittsburgh) 338

carnivorous dinosaurs
adaptations of 211-212
bone structure of 167-168
evolution of 87, 107, 127, 128, 148
preferred diet of 212
teeth of **187,** 187-188
types of 209-211

Carnosaur (movie) **341**

carnosaurs ("flesh lizards")
eating habits of 209-211
intelligence of 230

casts
defined 56
formation of 50

catastrophism 236, 239-250

Caudata (order) 80

Caudipteryx zoui 273

Cenozoic era
description of 42, 48, 92
evolution of dinosaurs during 149
subdivisions of 48

Centrosaurus ("horned lizard") 146

ceratopsians
bones of 169, 175, **177**
eating habits of 148, 214
evolution of 146
intelligence of 230
size of 174-175

Ceratosaurus 89, 299

Ceres (asteroid) 240

certification programs 328-329

chalk deposits 139, 153

Chamberlin, Thomas Chrowder 5

Charon (moon of Pluto) 4, 16

Chasmatosaurus 87

Chasmosaurus ("cleft lizard") 146

Chesapeake Bay 244

Chicxulub crater (Mexico) 244, 245

China
   dinosaur fossils from 69-70, 197, 270, 273, 275, 303
   dinosaurs as dragons in 69-70, 293
   evolution of dinosaurs in 86

chlorofluorocarbons (CFCs) 23, 25

cinder cones 19

cladistic analysis 271

cladograms 271

clams 64, 157, 237

claws, of dinosaurs 188-192

clay 30

Cleveland (OH) Museum of Natural History 336

Cleveland-Lloyd Dinosaur Quarry (Price, Utah) 347

climate change, extinction due to 236, 237

clothing
   for paleontology digs 317-318
   showing dinosaurs 338-340

coccolithophorids (calcareous nanoplankton) 131

cockroaches 63

coelacanths 63-64

Coelophysis ("hollow form")
   eating habits of 107, 214-215, 286
   evolution of 107
   in outer space 343
   recovery of fossils of 286

coelurosaurs ("hollow-tailed lizards") 209-211

Coelurus ("hollow tail") 127

Colbert, E. H. 286

cold-bloodedness 106, 193

Coloradisaurus 201

Colorado, dinosaur fossils from 283-284, 285, 287, 288, 290, 311, 319

comets
   defined 4, 242, **242**
   dinosaur extinction due to 239-248
   impact of 245-246
   origins of 241
   recent occurrences of 242-243

Como Bluff (Wyoming) 284-285

composite cones 19

Compsognathus ("pretty jaw")
   eating habits of 214
   evolution of 127, 210
   size of 198, 200, **200**

Computed Tomography (CT) 324

Computer-Aided Design (CAD) 314

Confuciusornis 303

conifers 113-114, 125, 131, 153

Connecticut, first dinosaur footprints discovered in 279-280

Connecticut Valley, dinosaur bones discovered in 279

continental drift 97-100
   defined 97-98
   evidence of 99
   during Jurassic period 122-126
   rate of 46
   during Triassic period 97-98, 102-103

Cope, Edward Drinker 266, 281, 283

coprolites
   defined 206
   formation of 50
   study of 206-207

corals 115

core 17

Corythosaurus ("helmet lizard")
   bony head projections of 172
   classification of 90
   evolution of 146

cosmic clouds, killer 249-251

crabs 115, 157

Craspedodon ("edge tooth") 146

Cretaceous period
   climate during 141, 143
   description of 42, 48, 139
   description of dinosaurs during 145-150
   description of other living organisms during 151-157
   duration of 141
   Earth's land masses during 141-143
   end of 92, 149
   evolution of dinosaurs during 139-157, 234
   geological events during 144
   mass extinction at end of 80, 91-92, 149, 233-251
   naming of 139
   oceans during 142, 143-144
   subdivisions of 139-140

Cretaceous-Tertiary (K/T) boundary 243

crocodiles
   evolution of 84, 86, 110, 116, 154, 157
   survival of 258-260
   types of 259, **259**

crocodylians 132

crocodylids 259

crocodylomorphs 110

crust 17-18

crustaceans 115

Crystal Palace (London)
   dinosaur display 66, 281, 296, 339, 344

cuttlefishes 134

Cuvier, Baron Georges 234, 294-295

cyanobacteria 33

cycadeoids (bennettitales) 114

cycads 113, 124, 131, 153

cynodonts 112, 132

D

Dacentrurus ("pointed tail") 127

Darwin, Charles 75-76

dating *See also* geologic time scale
of fossils 54-55
of rocks 41, 43-44

Deccan Traps 144, 248

Deimos (moon of Mars) 12

Deinocheirus ("terrible lizard") 146, 150

Deinodon teeth 280

Deinonychus ("terrible claw")
bird-like characteristics of 270-271
body temperature of 194
claws of 189
eating habits of 148
evolution of 146, 271
in fossil assemblages 207
pack hunting by 220, 289-290
size of 190

Deinosuchus 154

Denver (CO) Dinosaur Trackers Research Group 349

Denver (CO) Museum of Natural History 328-329, 336

Devils Canyon Science and Learning Center (Colorado) 340

Devonian period
description of 43
evolution of fish during 77

Devonian-Carboniferous extinctions 234

diapsids
classification of 88
evolution of 84-85, 110-111

diatoms 153

Dicraeosaurus 299

dicynodonts 112

didelphids 63

diet *See* eating habits

diffuse idiopathic skeletal hyperostosis (DISH) 170

dig sites *See also* dinosaur discoveries
defined 311
description of **310**
discovery of 312-314
location of 311
mapping of 314, 315-316, 317
permission to search at 309

digestive system, fossilized 184, 212, 214-215

digs, participation in 326-328

Dilophosaurus 87

Dimetrodon 83

Dinamation International Society
displays 340, 346
expeditions 327
membership 349

"Dino Discovery" (display) 346

Dinofest 346

dinosaur bones
abnormal 168-171
adaptations of 172-178
asymmetrical growth of 168
description of 163-168
development of 161-163
failure to locate large numbers of 235-236
gender identity from 163, **164**
number of 163
trauma to 169-171
types of 161-163

Dinosaur Cove (Australia) 220

dinosaur discoveries See also dig sites; paleontology
outside the United States 293-306
techniques for 309-329
in the United States 279-290

Dinosaur Dreaming (organization) 349

Dinosaur Freeway 217

Dinosaur Museum (Dorchester, England) 339

Dinosaur National Monument (Colorado-Utah border) 283-284, 287, 347

Dinosaur Park (Chorzow, Poland) 339

Dinosaur Provincial Park (Canada) 337, 347

Dinosaur Research Expeditions 327

Dinosaur Ridge (Colorado) 283, 285, 347

dinosaur skin 181-184, **182,** 286, 296

Dinosaur Society 349

dinosaur teeth 184-188, **186, 187**

dinosaur tracks and trackways 57-58, 69, 156, 208, 215-218, **216,** 279-280, 288

Dinosaur Valley, Museum of Western Colorado 336

dinosauria (infraclass), classification of 88

Dinosauroid (hypothetical) 260

dinosaurs
arms of 188-189
bipedal motion of 87, 106, 126, 164-165, 217, 280, 281
body temperature of 106, 193, 194, 195-197
bones of 161-178, 235-236
brain of 229
as buffalo ancestors 71
classification of 88, 283, 296-297
claws of 188-192
defined 66
as dragons 69-70, 293
earliest appearance of 36
eating habits of 87, 107-108, 127, 128, 148, 205-215

eggs of **222,** 222-227
as elephants 70
evolution of 75-92
evolutionary tree of 90
extinction of 80, 91-92, 149, 233-251, 255
first discovered bones of 67-69
flying 109
fossilization of 51-55
as griffins 70
health of 168-171
identification of 318-319
identification of species of 67
impact of theory of evolution on identification of 76
intelligence of 228-229
largest 108, 128-130, 148-150, 197-200, 201-202, 290
last 150, 236
lifespan of 131, 227
longest 202
longest lived 131, 227
longest necked 201-202
metabolism of 192-197
migration of 219
models of 296
most savage 190
naming of 66, 88
number of known species 88-89
in oceans 109
oldest-known fossils of 71
pack hunting by 219-220
in polar regions 220
predator-to-prey ratio of 193-195
reconstruction of 320-324, **321, 322, 323**
relationship to birds 260, 266-275
running speed of 57-58
size of 197-202
skin of 181-184, **182,** 286, 296
sleeping by 227-228
smallest 108, 128, 148, 200-201
sounds made by 173-174
special adaptations of 87

speed of 57-58, 168, 218, 219
stance of 165
teeth of 184-188, **186, 187,** 208
vision of 228-229
"Dinosaurs of Jurassic Park" (display) 346
Dino-Trekking (Halls) 348
Diplodocus ("double beam")
bones of 165
classification of 89
evolution of 127
recovery of fossils of 284
size of 128-129
teeth of 185
Diplurus 115
Discovery Channel 340
diseases
of dinosaurs 168-171
extinction due to 237-238
displays, of dinosaurs 67, 281, 296, 320-324, **321, 322, 323,** 346 @index - 2nd level:*See also* museums
DNA
cloning of 342
testing of 62
docodonts 133
Dollo, Louis 297
Douglass, Earl 284, 287
dragonflies
evolution of 151, **152**
survival of 63
dragons 69-70, 293
drinking water 205
Dromaeosaurus (dromaeosaurids, "running lizard")
bird-like features of 190, 270-271
classification of 89
claws of 189-190, 212
evolution of 147
intelligence of 230
pack hunting by 220
Dry Mesa Quarry (Colorado) 288
Dryosaurus ("oak lizard")

bone structure of 164-165
distribution of 101
evolution of 127
recovery of fossils of 299
Dryptosaurus ("wounding lizard") 147
dwarf dinosaur fossils 201
Dysalotosaurus 101

E

Earth
age of 13, 15
atmosphere of 15, 20-21
beginnings of life on 25-37
conditions for life on 27-28
elements in crust of 18
greenhouse effect on 22-25
largest-known living organism on 65, **66**
layers of 17-18
magnetic fields of 46-47, 313
map of **101**
moon of 4, 16-17
oldest rocks and minerals on **15,** 15-16
oldest-known living organism on 65
radius of 17
in solar system 3
view from space **14**
water on 20
Earth Science Museum (Provo, Utah) 336
earthquakes 17
earthworms 112
eating habits 87, 107, 127, 128, 148, 205-215 *See also* carnivorous dinosaurs; herbivorous dinosaurs; omnivorous dinosaurs
Echinodon 128
ectothermic, defined 192
Edaphosaurus 83-84
Edmontonia ("of Edmonton") 147

Edmontosaurus (Edmonton lizard)
  bipedal stance of 281
  eaten by *Tyrannosaurus* 208
  eating habits of 215
  evolution of 145, 147
  skin of 181
  speed of 168
  teeth of 185-186

education, in paleontology 325-329

eggs
  of birds 262
  of dinosaurs *222,* 222-227, **224**
  largest and smallest 262
  evolution of *82,* 82-83

Elaphrosaurus 299

electron spin resonance dating 54

Electronic Distance Measurement (EDM) 314

elephant bird eggs 262

elephants 70

Ellsworth, Solomon Jr. 279

embryos, fossilized 302-303

encephalization quotient (EQ) 229-230

endothermic, defined 192

England, dinosaur fossils from 294-296, 302

Entrada sandstone beds (Utah) 216

Eoraptor ("dawn hunter")
  description of 86, 301
  eating habits of 107
  evolution of 106
  oldest-known fossils of 71, 301
  size of 108

equipment, of paleontology 317-318

erosion, impact on fossil records 55

erractics (boulders) 59

Esmark, J. 59

Eucentrosaurus 90

Eudimorphodon 112

Euoplocephalus ("well-armoured head") 147

Euparkeria 87

Europa (moon of Jupiter) 26

euryapsids 84-85, 114

evaporites 126

evolution
  defined 75
  development of theory of 75-76
  of dinosaurs 75-92

"evolutionary big bang" 32, 44-48, **45**

Exposaur Excursions 327

extinction
  acceptance of 233-234
  causes of 233, 236-251
  defined 233
  at end of Cretaceous period (Mesozoic era) 80, 91-92, 149, 233-251
  at end of Permian period (Paleozoic era) 91, 96-97, 234
  at end of Triassic period 120-121, 234
  major periods of 234
  theories of 236-251, 294-295

Extinctions (company) 350

F

fauna *See* animals

feathers
  development of 197
  purpose of 275

ferns
  evolution of 124, **125,** 131
  oldest 34

Field Museum of Natural History (Chicago) 289, 336

Fifty-one (51) Pegasi b (star) 9

fishes
  evolution of 77, 115, 133, 157
  survival of 255

Flaming Cliffs (Mongolia), dinosaur fossils from 305

flies 132, 151

flightless birds 262-263

flora *See* plants

flying animals *See* birds; pterosaurs

footprints *See also* dinosaur tracks and trackways
  recovery of 56-57, **216,** 279-280, 288, 303
  theft of 305

fossil assemblages 207, 297-298

Fossil Company 350

fossil fuels, burning of 23

fossils
  chances of forming 51-55, 181
  defined 49-50
  determining age of 54-55
  DNA testing of 62
  formation of 50, 51-54, 298
  gaps in record 55-56
  identification of 318-319
  largest 198-200
  "living" 62-64
  of modern plants and animals 64
  oldest 33
  photos of **54, 57**
  preservation of 50, 51
  sale of reproductions 350
  types of 50, 56-58

Foulke, W. P. 280

Fraas, Eberhard 298

Frail, Dan 8

France, dinosaur eggs from 223

freshwater animals, in Triassic period 116

frogs
  evolution of 80, 109, 132, 154
  survival of 255

G

Galapagos Islands 75

401

galaxies, formation of 6

Gallimimus ("chicken mimic") 147, 150

Garden Park (Colorado) 283

Gaston, Robert ("Rob") 320

Gaston Quarry (Utah) 288, 320

gastroliths (gizzard stones) 213-214

gavialids 259

gavlals 110

gender identity, of dinosaurs 163, **164**

"Genesis rock" 17

genetic mutations 76

Geographic Information Systems (GIS) 314

Geographos (asteroid) 247

geologic time scale
   dates in 43-44
   description of 42-43
   naming of divisions in 43
   origins of 41

Germany, *Archaeopteryx lithographioca* discovered in 266, 268, 297-298

Ghost Ranch quarry (New Mexico) 286, 343

Giganotosaurus
   discovery of fossils of 177
   eating habits of 148
   evolution of 178
   pack hunting by 219-220
   size of 149-150, 199

Gilmoreosaurus (Gilmore's lizard) 147

Gingko biloba 114

ginkos
   evolution of **115,** 114, 124, 131
   survival of 62

glaciation *See* ice ages

gliding reptiles 109, 111-112, 133

Global Positioning System (GPS) 314

global warming 22-25 *See also* greenhouse effect

Gobi Desert (Mongolia) **304**
   dinosaur eggs and nests from 223-224, 226
   dinosaur fossils from 70, 304-305, 311
   fossil assemblages in 207
   fossil birds from 274-275

Gondwanaland (Gondwana) 46, 47, 102, 122, 123, 141, 142

Goosen, Capt. Hendrik 64

Gracilisuchus 87

gradualism
   in evolution 76
   in extinction 236, 237-238

Grand Junction area (Colorado) 283, 287, 347

Grand River Museum (South Dakota) 327

granite
   formation of 31
   oldest **15**

graptolites 51

Great (Late Heavy) Bombardment 19

Great Britain, dinosaur fossils from 294-296, 302

"Great Canadian Dinosaur Rush" 300

Great Ice Age *See* Ice Ages

Greek mythology 70

greenhouse effect
   defined 21, 22
   on Venus 12, 22

Greenland, fossil amphibians in 78

grid mapping 315-316, 317

griffins, dinosaurs as 70

ground-penetrating radar 312

growth ring bone tissue, development of 161, 162-163

guano 207

Guth, Alan 6

Gymnophiona (order) 80

gymnosperms (seed-bearing plants) 113

H

hadrosaurs ("duck-billed")
   boney head projections of 172, **174**
   classification of 90
   evolution of 146
   gender identity in 163, **164**
   recovery of fossils of 69, 302
   skin of 181
   teeth of 214

Hadrosaurus ("big lizard") 147, 280, 281

Hale-Bopp (comet) 242

Halley, Edmond 15

Halley's comet 4, 15

haramyoids 112, 133

Hatcher, John Bell 286

Haversian (secondary) bones, development of 161, 162

Hawaiian Islands 19

Hawkins, Benjamin Waterhouse 281, 296, 344

head projections, boney
   most prominent 172-173
   purpose of 172

health, of dinosaurs 168-171

heliosphere, collapse of 250

helium, formation of 6

Henrickson, Sue 289

herbivorous dinosaurs
   adaptations of 213-214
   bone structure of 165-167
   evolution of 87, 107, 127, 128, 148
   preferred diet of 214
   teeth of 185-187, **186**
   types of 212-213

herding behavior 108, 217, 218-219, 286, 288

Herrera, Victorino 301

Herrerasaurus ("Herrera lizard")
    description of 86, 301-302
    eating habits of 107
    evolution of 106
    oldest-known fossils of 71, 301
    size of 108
Heterodontosaurus 87, 131
hibernation 195
Hitchcock, Edward 280
Hogback Ridge (Colorado-Utah border) 284, 287
hollow crests 173-174
holly 153
Holocene epoch 48
homeothermic, defined 192, 196
Homo See also humans
    sapiens 36-37, 61
    sapiens sapiens 36-37, 237, 239
honey (button) mushrooms 66
Horner, John R. 287-288
Horseshoe Canyon Formation 301
horsetails
    evolution of 113, 124, 131
    oldest 34
    survival of 62
Houston (TX) Museum of Natural Science 336
humans See also Homo
    arthritis in 169-170
    bone diseases of 170-171
    dinosaur extinction due to 239
    earliest appearance of 36-37, 237, 239
    evolution of 235
    footprints of 57
    fossilization of 55
    intelligence of 230
    migration of 61
hummingbird eggs 262
hurricanes, extinction due to 238-239

Hutton, James 59
Huxley, Thomas Henry 266-268, **267**
Hyakutake (comet) 242
hydrogen
    formation of 6
    in killer cosmic clouds 249
hydrothermal vents 28
Hylaeosaurus ("woodland lizard") 143, 147
Hylonomus 83
hymenopterans (sawflies) 151
Hypacrosaurus **53,** 208
hypercanes, extinction due to 238-239
Hypselosaurus eggs **224,** 224-225
Hypsilophodon (hypsilophodontids, "high-ridge tooth")
    body temperature of 196
    bones of 166-167
    evolution of 147
    mobility of 221
    naming of 88

I

Ice Ages
    changes caused by 60-61
    defined 58-59
    description of 58-60
    end of 60
    number of 59-60
ichnotaxia 215 See also footprints
Ichthyostega 78
Icthyosaurus (ichthyosaurs)
    carbon film of 51
    evolution of 84, 85, 114, **135,** 135-136, 157
    extinction of 136
Ida (asteroid) 3
igneous rock 30-31
Iguanodon ("iguana tooth")
    bones of 167, 169, 170
    classification of 88, 90

evolution of 145, 147
first discovered bones of 143, 295
footprints of 303
in Maidstone (England) coat of arms 295
impact craters
    defined **243,** 243-244
    locations of 244
"impact" theory of extinction 239-248
imprints, formation of 50
Indian Ocean, depth of 20
indirect dating, of fossils 54
inflammatory arthritis (gout) 169-170
inflationary theory 6
insects
    evolution of 78, 112, 132, 141, 151, 154
    survival of 64, 255
Institute of Paleobiology (Warsaw) 339
intelligence, of dinosaurs 228-229
Internet 348-350
interplanetary (and interstellar) dust and gases 4
introns 35
iridium anomalies 243
Italy
    dinosaur fossils from 184
    dinosaur tracks in 69

J

Japan, dinosaur fossils in 136
jellyfish **35,** 36, 76, **77**
Johanson, Donald 56, **57**
Jones, Ed and Vivian 288
Judith River Dinosaur Institute (Montana) 327
Jupiter 3
    gravity of 241
    greenhouse effect on 22
    moons of 26
    physical characteristics of 4

Jura Mountains 119

"Jurassic Journey" (display) 346

Jurassic Park (movie) 67, 184, 189, 341-342, **342,** 344

Jurassic period
climate of 124
continental drift during 122-126
description of 42, 48, 119
description of dinosaurs during 126-131
description of other land organisms during 124-125, 131-136
duration of 119
Earth's land masses during 122-124
evolution of dinosaurs during 119-136
extinction at start of 120-121, 234
geological events during 125-126
naming of 43, 119
oceans during 124, 125
rock formation during 120
subdivisions of 120

K

Kannemeyeria 111, **185**

Kant, Immanuel 5, 7

Kara crater (Russia) 244

Kelvin, Lord (William Thomson) 13, 28

Kentrosaurus ("spikey lizard") 127, 299

keratin 275

killer cosmic clouds 249-251

King Kong (movie) **343**

Kirkland, Jim 288

Kokoro Dinosaurs 346

Kritosaurus ("noble lizard") 147

Kuehneosaurus 111, 112

Kuiper Belt (of comets) 241

L

La Brea Tar Pits (Los Angeles) 62

labyrinthodonts 109

Lagerstatten (fossil lodes) 297-298

Lakes, Arthur 285

Lambeosaurus ("Lambe's lizard") 90, 147

Laplace, Marquis Pierre Simon de 4-5, 7

Lark Quarry Environment Park (Australia) 217-218

Larson, Peter 289

Late Heavy (Great) Bombardment 19

Laurasia 102, 122, 141, 142

Leaellynasaurus 88

Leidy, Joseph 280, 281

lepidosaurs 86

Lepidotes maximus **49**

Liaoningornis 302

life
beginnings on Earth 25-37
Cambrian explosion of 32, 44-48, **45**
multiple development of 33
oldest fossils 33
oldest in oceans 33-34, **45**
oldest on land 33
on planets other than Earth 9-10, 26-27
rate of diversification of 45, 47-48
replication of 29-30

life zone 27

ligaments 171

Lingula clams 63, 237

Linnaeus, Carolus 271

Liopleurodon 135

lissamphibians 109

lithium, formation of 6

liverworts 32, 34-35

"living fossils" 63-65

lizards

evolution of 84, 86, 110-111, 132, 154, 257
skin of 183
survival of 255
viviparity of 223

lobe-finned fishes 77, 115

lobsters 115, 157

Local Fluff 249, 250-251

Loch Ness monster 114

locomotor stamina, of dinosaurs 165

Longisquama 111

Los Angeles County Museum 336

Lost World, The: Jurassic Park 2 (movie) 189, 344

"Lucy" (*Australopithecus afarensis*) 56, **56**

lycopods 124

Lyell, Sir Charles 13, 296

Lystrosaurus 111

M

macropredation 187-188

magazines 334

magma 17, 30-31

magnolia 63, 153

Maiasaura ("good mother lizard")
classification of 90
evolution of 145, 147
herding behavior of 219, 288
nesting behavior of 225-226, 288
recovery of fossils of 287-288

Makela, Bob 287

Mamenchisaurus (Mamenchi lizard)
classification of 89
evolution of 127
size of 202

mammals
dinosaur extinction due to 238
evolution of 111-113, 133, 155

intelligence of 230
survival of 255, 256-257

mammoths
description of 61-62, **64**
fossils of 233-234
tusks of 63, **63**

Manicouagan crater (Canada) 244

Mantell, Gideon 143, 294, 295, 296

Mantell, Mary Ann 295

mantle 17

marble, formation of 32

marine life
in Cretaceous period 153, 157
first animals **35,** 36, **45**
first plants 33-34, **45**
in Jurassic period 131, 134-136
in Triassic period 114-116

Mariner 10 (space probe) 10

Mars 3
atmosphere of 13, 21
composition of 13
moons of 12
orbit of 12
rotation of 12
size of 12
stellar view of **9**
surface features of 12-13, 244
surface temperature of 13

Marsh, Othniel Charles 266, 281, **282,** 282-283, 284-285, 286

marsupials
evolution of 63, 155
extinction of some 255
survival of **256,** 257

Martinez, Ricardo 301

Massospondylus ("massive vertebra") 127

mastodons
description of 61-62
fossils of 233-234
tusks of 61

Matlack, Timothy 69, 279

Mauna Loa (Hawaii) 19

Mayor, Michael 9

Mediterranean Sea, formation of 123, 144

Megalosaurus ("big lizard")
eating habits of 128
evolution of 127, 128
first discovered bones of 68, 130, 143, 294, 295

Megaraptor ("giant thief")
discovery of fossils of 177
eating habits of 150
evolution of 178

Megaraptor namunhuaiquii 191-192

megatrack sites 215-216

Menke, H. W. 287

Mercury 3, 21
composition of 10-11
distance from Sun 10
naming of 10
orbit of 10
physical characteristics of 4
size of 10
surface view of **11**
visibility from Earth 10

Mesozoic era
description of 42, 92
evolution of dinosaurs during 80, 91-92
evolution of reptiles during 84, 91
"marine revolution" in 157
mass extinction at end of 80, 91-92, 149, 233-251
mass extinction prior to 91, 96-97
subdivisions of 48

metabolism, of dinosaurs 192-197

metamorphic rock 32

metamorphosis, of amphibians 81, 82

Meteor Crater (Arizona) 241

meteorites
craters made by **243**
evidence of early life on 26-27, 28, 29

methane 23

Michel, Helen 243

Michigan, oldest-known living organism in 65

micropaleontology, defined 49

Mid-Atlantic Ridge 97, 102, 142

migration
of birds 264
of dinosaurs 219
of humans 61

Milky Way, formation of 6

Miller, Stanley 28

mineralization, of fossils 50

models, of dinosaurs 344-345

molds
defined 56
formation of 50

mollusks
evolution of 76, 157
survival of 255

Mongolia *See* Gobi Desert

monocular vision 228

monotremes 155

Monstrosities (company) 350

Montana
dinosaur fossils from 280, 285, 286, 289, 290
fossil assemblages in 207, 219, 226
impact crater in 244

Montana State University-Northern 329

Moody, Pliny 279

Moon 4
composition of 16-17
distance from Earth 16
gravity on 16
oldest rocks on 17
size of 16
surface features of **16,** 19, 244

moons 3-4

Moore, J. D. and Vanetta 319

Morokweng crater (South Africa) 244

Morrison formation 120, 121, 281, 283, 299

mosasaurs (marine lizards)
  evolution of 157
  extinction of 255

mosses, oldest 34, 35

moths 151

motion *See* bipedal motion; speed

Moulton, Forest Ray 5

Mount Fuji (Japan) 19

Mount St. Helens (Washington) 19

mountains, formation of 105

mounting techniques 322-323

movement *See* bipedal motion; speed

multituberculates 133, 155

Muraenosaurus 135

"muscle scars" 171

muscles 171

Museo Argentino de Ciencias Naturales (Buenos Aires) 339

Museum of Northern Arizona 336

Museum of the Rockies (Montana) 327, 336

museums 334-338, 349

Mussaurus ("mouse lizard") 200-201

mutinaite 30

Muttaburrasaurus 88

Mygatt, Pete and Marilyn 319

Mygatt-Moore Dinosaur Quarry (Colorado) 311, 319

Mymoorapelta 319-320

mythical beasts, dinosaurs as 70

N

National Museum of Natural History (Paris) 339

National Museum of Natural History (Washington, DC) 336

National Museum of Natural Sciences (Canada) 337

Native Americans, perception of dinosaur fossils 71

Natural History Museum, Humboldt University (Berlin) 339

natural selection 76, 237

near-Earth objects (NEOs) 247

nebular theory (hypothesis) 5, 7-8

neck frills 175

Nemget Formation 224

Neptune 3
  greenhouse effect on 22
  physical characteristics of 4

nests **225,** 225-226, 288

New Jersey
  dinosaur bones and fossils from 69, 279, 280
  Triassic period rocks in 103

New Mexico, dinosaur fossils from 286, 343

Newark Supergroup
  defined 103-104
  formation of 103

newts 80, 154

1989 FC (asteroid) 247

1997 XF11 (asteroid) 248

nocturnal mammals, survival of 235

North America *See also* Canada; United States
  glaciation of 59
  Native American perception of dinosaur fossils in 71

nothosaurs 114

Novas, Fernando 301

nuclear fusion 22

O

oceans
  absence of dinosaurs in 109

during Cretaceous period 142, 143-144
  depth of 20
  first animals in **35,** 36, **45**
  first plants in 33-34, **45**
  formation of 20
  during Jurassic period 124, 125
  during Triassic period 104

Oldman rock formation (Alberta, Canada) 195

omnivorous dinosaurs 205, 214

On the Origin of Species (Darwin) 75

Oort, Jan 241

Oort Cloud (of comets) 241

opossums 63, **256**

opportunism 126

Ordovician period 43

Oregon, granite in **15**

organic evolution 75

ornithiscians ("bird hipped")
  classification of 88, 105, 296-297
  description of 89-90
  eating habits of 148, 212
  evolution of 127, 145-146

ornithodira 111

Ornitholestes ("bird robber") 127

ornithomimosaurs 150

Ornithomimus
  classification of 89
  eating habits of 214
  speed of 219

ornithopods
  eating habits of 148
  evolution of 127, 133, 145
  intelligence of 230
  skin of 181

Ornithopsis ("bird-like structure") 147

ornithosuchians 111

Ornithosuchus ("bird crocodile") 87

Orodromeus ("mountain
runner") 147

ossification 170

osteoarthritis (degenerative
arthritis) 169-170

ostrich eggs 262

Ostrom, John H. 194, 269,
273, 289-290

Ouranosaurus ("brave monitor lizard") 147

overpopulation 238

Oviraptor ("egg thief")
eating habits of 214
evolution of 147
nesting behavior of 226,
304

Owen, Sir Richard 66, **68,**
294, 296

oxygen, formation of 21

oysters 134

ozone
as evidence of life on
other planets 10
and greenhouse effect
23-25, **24**

ozone hole 25

P

Pachycephalosaurus (pachycephalosaurs, "thick-headed lizard") 146, 147, 148

Pachyrhinosaurus ("thick-
nosed lizard") 147

Pacific Ocean
depth of 20
formation of 144

pack hunting 219-220, 290

Palaeothyris 83

paleobiogeography 101

Paleobiological Fund 349

paleobotany 49 *See also*
plants

Paleontological Institute
(Russian Academy of Sci-
ence) 305, 306

paleontology *See also* dig
sites; dinosaur discoveries;
fossils
by amateurs 319-320
defined 49
development of 296
education in 325-329
techniques for digging
309-320
techniques for recon-
struction 320-324,
321, 322, 323
tools and equipment of
316-318

Paleozoic era
description of 42-43
mass extinction at end of
91, 96-97, 234

paleozoology 49 *See also*
animals

palm trees 153

Pangea (Pangaea)
breaking apart of 102-
103, 105, 122, 123, 141
description of 99, 100,
102
formation of 102-103

panspermia 28-29

Panthalassa Ocean 100, 104,
124, 143-144

Parasaurolophus ("like
Saurolophus")
boney head projections of
172
evolution of 147
hollow crest of 173-174
sounds made by 173-174

Paricutin (Mexico) 19

Parkinson, James 294

Parkosaurus (Park's lizard)
147

Patagopteryx 154

Peabody, George 283

Peabody Museum of Natural
History (Yale University)
281, 283, 336

peacock feathers **261**

Peking Man 69

Pelorosaurus ("monstrous
lizard") 127

Pelorosaurus becklesii 296

pelycosaurs 83-84, 111

Perleidus 115

permafrost, extent of 61

Permian period
climate during 84
description of 42
evolution of dinosaurs
during 86, 91
mass extinction at end of
91, 96-97, 234

permineralization, of fossils
51

Petrified Forest (Arizona)
114

petrified wood
formation of 50, 51
of Triassic period 114

petroleum traps, formation
of 126

Philadelphia Academy of Sciences 281, 336

Phobos (moon of Mars) 12

photosynthesis 21

phytosaurs 110

Piazzi, Giuseppi 240

placental mammals
evolution of 155
survival of 255, 257

placodonts ("plate tooth")
85, 114

planetesimal theory 7, 8,
241

planets
age of 8
defined 3
extrasolar 8-10
formation of 7
life on (other than Earth)
9-10, 26-27
moons of 3-4
physical characteristics of
4

plankton, extinction of some
255

plants *See also* paleobotany
carbon film of 52
of Cretaceous period
141, 151-153

of Jurassic period 124-125, 131
oldest, in oceans 33-34
oldest, on land 32, 34-35
paleobiogeography of 101
of Triassic period 113-114

plasma theory 7

plate tectonics 97-100, **98,** 122
defined 97-98
development of 99
rate of 46

Plateosaurus ("flat lizard")
eating habits of 107
evolution of 106
size of 108, **108**
teeth of **186**

Pleistocene epoch
description of 48
glaciation during 59

plesiosaurs ("near lizards")
description of 116
eating habits of 116
evolution of 85, 114, 135, 157
extinction of 255

pliosaurs 116

Plot, Robert 68, 70, 293

Pluto 3
moon of 4, 16

poikilothermic, defined 192

poison plants, extinction due to 238

polar regions, dinosaurs in 220

Popigai crater (Russia) 244

Port Jackson sharks 115

Portugal, fossil embryos from 302-303

postage stamps, of dinosaurs 345

posters and prints 350

Precambrian period
description of 43, 44
evolution of single-celled organisms during 76
glaciation during 60
subdivisions of 44

predator-to-prey ratio 193-195

Prehistoric Times 334, 345

primary (fibro-lamellar) bones, development of 161

primordial "soup" theory of early life 28, 29

procolophonids 110

proganochelydians 110

prosauropods 71

Proterozoic epoch 44

Protoarchaeopteryx 303

Protoarchaeopteryx robust 273

Protoceratops ("first horned face")
bones of **176**
eggs of 223
evolution of 147
in fossil assemblages 207, 224
herding behavior of 218
nesting behavior of 226
recovery of fossils of 70
size of 175
teeth of 186-187
theft of bones of 306

proton free precession magnetometry 313

protoplanet hypothesis 8

Provincial Museum of Alberta (Canada) 337

Psittacosaurus ("parrot lizard") 147, 174-175

PSR B1257+12 (pulsar) 9

Pterodactylus (pterodactyls) 111, 133

pterosaurs ("flying reptiles")
evolution of 86, 109, 111, 112, 133, 154, 155, 221
extinction of 255
fossilized tracks of 156
mobility of 155-156, **156**

Public Broadcasting System (PBS) 340

public libraries 333-334

Puchezh-Katunki crater (Russia) 244

pyrite (iron sulfate) 30, **31**

Q

Qu, Chang 293

quadrapedal motion 164-165, 217

Quaternary (Anthropogene) period
description of 42, 48
glaciation during 59

Queloz, Didier 9

Quetzalcoatlus 155

R

Rabbit Valley Research Nature Area (Colorado) 347

radar, ground-penetrating 312

radiation detection with scintillation counters 314

radiometric dating
of fossils 54-55
of rocks 41, 44

Rahona ostromi ("Ostrom's menace from the clouds") 273-274

rauischians 110

ray-finned fishes 115

reconstruction, of dinosaurs 320-324, **321, 322, 323**

Red Deer River Valley (Canada), dinosaur fossils from 275, 300

Redpath Museum (Canada) 337

Reed, Bill 284-285

Reig, Osvaldo 301

relative dating, of rocks 41

remodeling, of dinosaur bones 162

reproductive systems, evolution of 79-80, **82,** 82-83, 154, 256 See also eggs

reptiles
defined 81, 257-258
earliest-known species of 83

evolution of 80-86, 109-111, 114, 132, 154, 257
evolution of dinosaurs from 85-86, 91
reproductive systems of 82-83
subdivisions of 84-85
survival of 255, 258-260

Reptilia class 88

research societies and organizations 349

resources, about dinosaurs 333-350

respiratory systems, evolution of 79

Rhabdodon ("rod tooth") 147

Rhamphorhynchus 133

rhynchosaurs
evolution of 110
extinction of 106

Riggs, Elmer 287

Riggs Hill Trail/Dinosaur Hill Trail (Colorado) 347

rocks
of Jurassic period 120
locating dinosaur fossils in 309-311
oldest **15**, 15-16, 17
of Triassic period 103
types of 30-32

Rocky Mountains
Dinosaur Freeway in 217
formation of 126

Roman mythology 70

Romania, dwarf dinosaur fossils from 201

Royal Ontario Museum (Canada) 337

Royal Scottish Museum (Edinburgh) 339

Russell, Dale 260

S

salamanders
evolution of 80, **81,** 132, 154
survival of 255

Saltasaurus 148

saltoposuchians 110

San Andreas Fault 98

sandstone, formation of 32

Sattler, W. B. 298

Saturn 3
greenhouse effect on 22
moons of 3-4, 26
physical characteristics of 4

saurischians ("lizard hipped")
classification of 88, 105, 296-297
description of 89
eating habits of 148, 209, 212-213
evolution of 127, 145

Saurolophus ("ridged lizard") 147, 173

sauropodomorphs 230

sauropods
brain size of 229
classification of 127
eating habits of 212
herding behavior of 216-217
intelligence of 230
length of necks 202

Saurornithoides ("bird-like lizard") 147

Scartopus ("nimble foot") 147

Scelidosaurus ("limb lizard") 127

scintillation counters, radiation detection with 314

Scipionyx samniticus 184, 212

Score, Roberta 27

Scrotum humanum 68, 293

sea urchins 115, 255

Sedgwick Museum (Cambridge, England) 339

sedimentary rock
description of 31-32
fossils in 50, 120, 121, 309-311

and naming of Triassic period 95

sedimentation, of fossils 50

Seeley, Harry Govier 297

segmented worms 36, 76

Segnosaurus ("slow lizard") 147

seismic tomography 313

Seismosaurus
classification of 89
size of 129, 202

Sereno, Paul 301

Shansisuchus 86

sharks 115, 134, 157

Sharovipteryx 111

shield volcanoes 19

Shoemaker-Levy 9 (comet) 242-243

Shuvuuia deserti 274-275

Siberia
asteroids in 247
fish fossils in 50

Siberian Traps 105

Sierra Nevada 121, 126

Silurian period 43

single-celled organisms
earliest 25-26, 34
evolution of 76
fossils of 50

Sinosauropteryx
body temperature of 197
skin of 181

Sinosauropteryx prima 270, 274, 303

skin, of dinosaurs 181-184, **182**

Skullduggery, Inc. 350

sleeping habits, of dinosaurs 227-228

Smith, J. L. B. 64

Smith, Nathan 279

Smith, William 41

snails 157, 255

snakes
evolution of 84, 86, 154, 257
survival of 255

Snider, Antonio 99

Society of Vertebrate 349

solar nebula *See* nebular theory

solar system
age of 8
defined 3-4
diagram of **5**
formation of 4-8, 19
life on planets other than Earth 9-10, 26-27

solar systems other than ours 8-10

Solnhofen quarries (Germany), *Archaeopteryx lithographioca* discovered in 266, 268, 297-298

Sorenson, Carl 286

South African Museum (Cape Town) 339

South America
large fossils discovered in 177-178, 192
oldest-known fossils in 71, 301

South Dakota, dinosaur fossils from 289

speed, of dinosaurs 57-58, 168, 218, 219

Sphenodon 84

spiders 112

Spinosaurus, tooth of **183**

Spinosaurus aegypticus 202

spontaneous reaction 30

squids 134

stampedes 217-218

stance, of dinosaurs 165 *See also* bipedal motion

starfishes 255

stars, formation of 6, 7 *See also* Sun

Staurikosaurus 86

steady-state theory 6-7

Stegosaurus (stegosaurs, "roof lizard")
boney plates of 176-177
classification of 89
distribution of 122

eating habits of 128

evolution of 119, 127, 146

intelligence of 230

recovery of fossils of 69, 285

theft of footprints of 305

Stenopterygius 135

Sternberg, Charles H. 286, 300

Sternberg, Charles M. 286, 300

Sternberg, George 286, 300

Sternberg, Levi 286, 300

stratigraphy 41

stromatolites (algal mats) 33, 47

Struthiosaurus ("ostrich lizard") 147

Styracosaurus ("spiked lizard")
evolution of 147
herding behavior of 218

subduction, defined 121

Sudbury crater (Canada) 244

"Sue" (*Tyrannosaurus rex*) 289

Sun
defined 3
energy production by 22
temperature of 22

Sundance Sea 121, 126

Sunset Crater (Arizona) 19

Supersaurus
recovery of fossils of 288
size of 130, 200, 213

surge tectonics 98

Switzerland, glaciation in 59

sycamore trees 153

symmetrodonts 133, 155

synapsids 84-85, 111-113

T

tachymetabolic, defined 192-193

tanystropheids 110

Tanzania, fossil expedition in 298-299

tar, fossilization in 62

Tarbosaurus 89
efremovi 306

teeth
fossilized 51
function of 184-188, **186, 187**
marks made by 208

teleosts 134, 255

Telmatosaurus 201

tendons 171

Tenontosaurus ("sinew lizard")
evolution of 147
in fossil assemblages 207
hunted by *Deinonychus* 220

termites 151

Tertiary period 42, 48, 92

Tethys Sea (Ocean) 100, 103, 104, 122, 144

tetrapods 77, 110

Texas, dinosaur trackways in 58, 208

Thecodontosaurus 107

thecodonts ("socket tooth") 86-87

therapsids
evolution of 111-112, 132
extinction of 106, 132

thermoluminescence dating 55

therocephalians 112, 132

theropods
eating habits of 148, 209, 211-212
evolution of 127, 128
extinction of 145
recovery of fossils of 286

Thomson, William (later Lord Kelvin) 13, 28

tidal (Chamberlin-Moulton) theory 5

Timescale Adventures 327

Titan (moon of Saturn) 26

titanosaurids 145, 146

toads 80, 109, 154

tools, of paleontology 316-317

Tornieria 299

tortoises 84

trace fossils
  defined 56-57
  of dinosaur tracks 57-58
  formation of 50

Trachodon teeth 280

tracks
  of dinosaurs 57-58, 69, 156, 208, 215-218, **216,** 279-280, 288
  of glaciers 60

trails 58

trauma, to dinosaur bones 169-171

travel guides 348

tree ferns 124, 131

trees, dinosaurs in 221

Triadobatrachus 109

Triassic period
  climate during 104-105, 124
  continental drift during 97-98, 102-103
  description of 42, 48, 95
  description of dinosaurs during 105-108
  description of other land organisms during 109-116
  duration of 95
  Earth's land masses during 100
  evolution of dinosaurs during 91, 95-116, 126
  extinction at end of 120-121, 234
  landscape during 105
  naming of 95
  nature of Earth at start of 100
  oceans during 104
  rock formation during 103
  subdivisions of 95-96
  transitions during 96-97

Triceratops ("three-horned face")
  bones of 169, 171, 176
  classification of 90
  description of **145,** 175
  eaten by *Tyrannosaurus* 208
  eating habits of 214
  evolution of 146, 147
  herding behavior of 218
  longevity of 150
  recovery of fossils of 286
  size of 175
  speed of 168

triconodonts 112, 133, 155

Troodon ("wounding tooth")
  evolution of 147, 260
  intelligence of 229

true polar wander 46-47

Tsintaosaurus 173

tuatara 63

Tuojiangosaurus ("Tuojiang lizard") 127

turtles
  evolution of 84, 110, 132, 154, 257
  skin of 183
  survival of 255

Tyrannosaurus ("tyrant lizard")
  bones of **166,** 167-168, 169, 171
  classification of 89
  eating habits of 148, 150, 208, 211
  evolution of 145, 147
  muscles of 171
  pack hunting by 219
  reconstruction of 338
  size of 149, 199
  teeth of **210**
  vision of 228

Tyrannosaurus imperator 199

Tyrannosaurus rex
  classification of 88
  coprolite of 207
  evolution of 178
  longevity of 150
  naming of 88
  recovery of fossils of 285, 289, 290

teeth of 208, **209**

Tyrrell, Joseph Burr 300

Tyrrell Museum of Paleontology (Canada) 337

U

Ultrasaurus
  recovery of fossils of 288
  size of 130, 200

Unenlagia comaheunsis 275, 303-304

United States *See also* names of specific states
  famous dinosaur discoveries in 279-290
  museums in 335-336

University Museum (Oxford, England) 339

University of Colorado Museum (Boulder) 336

University of Michigan Exhibit Museum (Ann Arbor) 336

University of Wyoming Geological Museum (Laramie) 336

uranium-series dating 55

Uranus 3
  greenhouse effect on 22
  physical characteristics of 4

Urey, Harold 28

urine (urea) 207

Utah
  dinosaur fossils from 288, 290, 320
  dinosaur trackways in 208, 216
  largest-known living organism in 65, **66**

Utah Museum of Natural History (Salt Lake City) 336

Utahraptor
  claws of 189, 191
  eating habits of 148, 150
  evolution of 271
  recovery of fossils of 288, 320

V

vascular plants, development of 34

Velociraptor ("quick plunderer")
  brain size of 229
  claws of 189
  eating habits of 148, 150
  evolution of 145, 147, 271
  in fossil assemblage 207
  intelligence of 229
  size of 184

Vendian epoch 44

Venus 3
  atmosphere of 11-12, 20-21
  composition of 11-12
  greenhouse effect on 12, 22
  surface features of 12
  surface temperature on 12, 22

vertebral fusion 170-171

vertebrates
  defined 77
  evolution of 77

Virginia, dinosaur tracks in 288

viruses, size of 26

vision, of dinosaurs 228-229

viviparity (live births) 223, 256

volcanoes
  in Cretaceous period 144, 248-249
  dinosaur extinction due to 248-249
  hydrothermal vents of 28
  impact on fossil records 55-56
  in Triassic period 105
  types of 18-19
  on Venus 12

Vredefort crater (South Africa) 244

W

Wallowa Mountains (Oregon), granite in **15**

warm-bloodedness 106, 193, 194, 195-197

wasps 151

water, drinking of 205

water vapor
  as evidence of life (on other planets) 10
  as industrial by-product 23

Wealden Basin 143

Wegener, Alfred 99, **99**

Weizsacker, Baron Carl Friedrich von 7

West Spitzbergen (Svalbard), dinosaur footprints on 303

Western Paleo Safaris 327

Western Paleontological Laboratories Inc. 350

Whitaker, George 286

white fern leaf, fossilized **65**

Williams, Maurice 289

Williston, S. W. 284-285

willow trees 153

Wistar, Caspar 69, 279

Wolszczan, Alexander 8-9

World Wide Web (WWW) 324, 348-350

worms **265**

Wyoming, dinosaur fossils from 284-285, 286, 290

Wyoming Dinosaur Center 327, 347-348

Z

Zank, Gary P. 249

zeolites 30

zircon crystals, oldest 16